WYC WORDS OF WISDOM

A monthly reading of
PSALMS, PROVERBS, ECCLESIASTICUS, ECCLESIASTES, *and the* **WISDOM OF SOLOMON**

Translated by
JOHN WYCLIFFE *and* **JOHN PURVEY**

From **WYCLIFFE'S BIBLE WITH APOCRYPHA,**
a modern-spelling edition of their 14TH century Middle English translation, the 1ST complete English vernacular version, edited by

TERENCE P. NOBLE

My thanks to

QUYNH M. DANG,
for her word processing expertise.

the Jewish People, and the Catholic, Orthodox, and
other Christian communities, who, for millennia,
preserved and protected these Holy Scriptures,
and shared them with ALL humanity.

my parents, AL and FRIEDA NOBLE,
and everyone else, including pets,
who showed kindness along the way,

"Holy is holy."
SEAN GREGORY

"Believe in God's Love that is being stored up for us like an Inheritance, and
have Faith that in this Love, there is a Strength and a Blessing so large, that we
can travel as far as we wish, without having to step outside it."
MINHEE KIM, paraphrasing RAINER MARIA RILKE

Thanks be to
GOD
for this opportunity and uncountable other blessings.

Words of Wisdom: a monthly reading of Psalms, Proverbs, Ecclesiasticus,
Ecclesiastes, and the Wisdom of Solomon ©2018
Wycliffe's Bible with Apocrypha ©2018

"From Wycliffe's Bible with Apocrypha, translated by John Wycliffe and John
Purvey, a modern-spelling edition of their 14TH century Middle English
translation, the first complete English vernacular version, edited by Terence P.
Noble".

Issued also in electronic format.

ISBN 978-1727469042

On the cover: "And I saw the Spirit coming down as a dove from Heaven, and
dwelling on Him." *John* 1:32

Photo courtesy of Dtguy@Dreamstime.com. (ID 13075961)

For more information, contact Terence Noble at terry@smartt.com.

Table of Contents

Note to the Reader

Billy Graham

When I was young, Billy Graham preached around the world in stadiums, arenas, and fields at innumerable Crusades for Christ. These gatherings would be televised, and often a book would be offered to viewers to help them in their walk. One such book was **Words of Wisdom**, https://amzn.to/2MtgeD4, a 31-day read-through of *Psalms* and *Proverbs*. I requested this book, read it, and found it of great value. And so I have decided to replicate it using the Wisdom Literature from **Wycliffe's Bible with Apocrypha**, https://amzn.to/2wmR26b, my modern-spelling version of the 14TH century Middle English translation by John Wycliffe and John Purvey. (I regard wisdom here as advice which can help us in our daily life and our daily walk with God.)

Many of you will not be familiar with the books of the **Apocrypha**, books found in many Bibles, which were written in intertestamental times, that is, between the Old and New Testaments. I did not know these books either, until preparing the modern-spelling **Wycliffe's Apocrypha**. I then became acquainted with, and very impressed by, much of the writing, particularly *Ecclesiasticus*, the "crown jewel", (also known as *Sirach*), which I believe presents a good deal of practical wisdom for daily living (as much as, or perhaps even more than, *Proverbs* itself). And so I have included it in these daily readings (but omitting the Israelite history chapters 44-50). The well-known wisdom writing *Ecclesiastes*, and the lesser known, but still compelling, *Wisdom of Solomon*, round out the daily readings for the month. So this book contains all of the major wisdom literature of the Bible (except for the *Song of Songs*, which I regard as a profoundly beautiful love poem). As well, I have included the *Prayer of Manasseh*, the

Prayer of Esther, the Prayer of Mordecai, the Prayer of Azariah and the Song of the Three from the **Apocrypha**, all excellently-written, moving, and indeed inspired Scripture to fill out the days where I omitted the Israelite history chapters from the Wisdom of Solomon (chapters 16-19).

John Wycliffe

In England 2300 years after David and Solomon, and 1300 years after Jesus and Paul, the Word of God was written almost exclusively in Latin, an unknown language to 99% of that society. Indeed, Latin was only understood by some of the clergy, some of the well-off, and the few who were university-educated. This did not trouble the Church princes, who long before had transformed the "Divine Commission" – to preach the Word and to save souls – into the more temporal undertaking of the all-consuming drive to wield authority over every aspect of life, and in the process, to accumulate ever-greater wealth.

John Wycliffe, an Oxford University professor and theologian, was one of those few who had read the **Latin Bible**. Though a scholar living a life of privilege, he nevertheless felt a strong empathy for the poor and the uneducated, those multitudes in feudal servitude whose lives were "nasty, brutish, and short". He challenged the princes of the Church to face their hypocrisy and widespread corruption – and to repent. He railed that the Church was no longer worthy to be The Keeper of the Word of Truth. And he proposed a truly revolutionary idea:

"The Scriptures," Wycliffe stated, "are the property of the people, and one which no party should be allowed to wrest from them. Christ and his apostles converted much people by uncovering of Scripture, and this in the tongue which was most known to them. Why then may not the modern disciples of Christ

Note to the Reader

gather up the fragments of the same bread? The faith of Christ ought therefore to be recounted to the people in both languages, Latin and English."

Indeed, John Wycliffe earnestly believed that all of Scripture should be available to all of the people all of the time, in their native tongue.

He believed that with the Word of God literally in hand, each individual could have a personal relationship with God, and work out his or her own salvation, with no need for any human or institutional intermediary.

And so John Wycliffe and his followers, most notably John Purvey, his secretary and close friend, and for a limited time, Nicholas Hereford, translated Jerome's **Vulgate**, the Latin Bible, including the books of the **Apocrypha**, into the first complete **English Bible**. Their literal, respectful translation was hand-printed around 1382. Historians refer to this as the "Early Version" of the **"Wycliffe Bible"**.

The Church princes, long before having anointed themselves as sole arbitrator (indeed "soul" arbitrator!) between God and man, condemned this monumental achievement as heretical – and worse:

"This pestilent and wretched John Wycliffe, that son of the old serpent ... endeavour(ing) by every means to attack the very faith and sacred doctrine of Holy Church, translated from Latin into English the Gospel, (indeed all of the Scriptures), that Christ gave to the clergy and doctors of the Church. So that by his means it has become vulgar and more open to laymen and women who can read than it usually is to quite learned clergy of good intelligence. And so the pearl of the Gospel, (indeed of the Scriptures *in toto*), is scattered abroad and trodden underfoot by swine."

(Church Chronicle, 1395)

Note to the Reader

The Church princes decreed that Wycliffe be removed from his professorship at Oxford, and it was done. Two years later, his health broken, he died.

In the decade following John Wycliffe's death, his friend John Purvey revised their Bible. The complete text, including Purvey's *Great Prologue*, appeared by 1395. But portions of his revision, in particular the Gospels and other books of the New Testament, were in circulation as early as 1388.

Historians refer to this as the "Later Version" of the "**Wycliffe Bible**". This vernacular version retained most of the theological insight and poetry of language found in the earlier, more literal effort. But it was easier to read and understand, and quickly gained a grateful and loyal following. Each copy had to be hand-printed – Gutenberg's printing press would not be invented for more than seventy years – but this did not deter widespread distribution. The book you now hold in your hands contains the Wisdom Literature from that "**Wycliffe Bible**", *with modern spelling.*

For his efforts, the Church princes ordered John Purvey arrested and delivered to the dungeon. He would not see freedom again until he recanted of his "sin" – writing the **English Bible**. His spirit ultimately broken, he eventually did recant. Upon release, he was watched, hounded at every step, the Church princes determined that he would tow the party line. His life made a living hell, the co-author of the first **English Bible** disappeared into obscurity, and died unknown.

But the fury of the Church princes was unrelenting. Edicts flew. John Wycliffe's bones were dug up – and burned. Wycliffe's writings were gathered up – and burned. All unauthorized Bibles – that is, all those in the English language – were banned. All confiscated copies were burned. Those who copied out these Bibles were imprisoned. Those who distributed these Bibles were imprisoned. Those who owned an English Bible, or, as has been documented, "traded a cart-load of hay for but a few pages of the Gospel", were imprisoned. And those faithful souls who refused to "repent" the "evil" that they had committed, were burned at the stake, the "noxious" books that they had penned, or even had merely owned, hung about their necks to be consumed by the same flames. In all, thousands were imprisoned, and many hundreds executed. Merry olde England was engulfed in a reign of terror. All because of an English Bible. The "**Wycliffe Bible**".

But the spark that John Wycliffe, John Purvey, and their followers had ignited could not, would not, be extinguished. The Word of Truth was copied, again, and again, and again. The Word of Truth was shared, from hand, to hand, to hand. The Word of Truth was spoken, and read, and heard by the common people in their own language for the first time in over 1000 years. At long last, the Word of God had been returned to simple folk who were willing to lose everything to gain all.

And so the pearls of the Scriptures were spread abroad and planted in their hearts by the servants of God....

Middle English

The "**Wycliffe Bible**" was written in Middle English in the last three decades of the 14TH century. "Middle English" is the designation of language spoken and written in England between 1150 and 1450. The year 1300 is used to divide the period into "Early Middle English" and "Late Middle English". During the time of "Late Middle English", there were 5 regional dialects in England (with a sixth dialect eventually developing in London). Examples of at least three dialects are found in the "Later Version" of the "**Wycliffe Bible**".

What does one encounter reading the "**Wycliffe Bible**"? An alphabet with a widely used 27TH letter, "3", and a 28TH letter, "p", that already was frequently being replaced with "th" (even within the same sentence). A myriad of words which today are either obsolete ("anentis": with), archaic ("culver": dove), or at best, strangely-spelled precursors to our modern words ("vpsedoun": upside-down). Spelling and verb forms that are not standardized, in part because they were phonetic to different dialects. For example, the word "saw" is spelled a dozen different ways (even differently within the same sentence), and differently for singular and plural nouns (similarly, the word "say"); "have take" and "have taken" are found in the same sentence, as are "had know" and "had known"; and so forth. Prepositions and pronouns that often seem misplaced and incorrectly used: "at", "for", "in", "of", "on", "there", "to", "what", and "which" again and again seem wrongly situated; "themself" and "themselves" are found in the same sentence, as are "youself" and "yourselves"; and so forth. Capital- ization, punctuation, and other grammatical conventions that are rudimentary by today's standards, and vary greatly from sentence to sentence. For example, the past tense of a verb was made by adding nothing to the present tense, or an "e", "en", "ed", "ede", "id", "ide", or still other suffixes. In short, one encounters formidable obstacles to being able to understand (what will become) a single verse of Scripture.

And so the need for **Wycliffe's Bible with Apocrypha**. **Wycliffe's Bible with Apocrypha** is the "Later Version" of the "Wycliffe Bible", with its irregular spelling deciphered, the verb forms made consistent, and numerous grammatical variations standardized. **Wycliffe's Bible with Apocrypha** is the key that unlocks the amazing secrets found within the "**Wycliffe Bible**". See the *Introduction* to **Wycliffe's Bible with Apocrypha** (or any other of my Wycliffe volumes) for a detailed explanation of the linguistic procedures I used to produce these modern-spelling versions, which the reader is recommended to read. As well, all of these volumes also include a *Glossary*, a *Bibliography*, and *Endnotes*, all of which are also relevant to the present book.

Wycliffe's Words of Wisdom

Bible historians have determined that there are two versions of the "**Wycliffe Bible**", the Early Version and the Later Version (and there are many different versions of each version, as all the copies were hand-written, and changes occurred as many of these copies were transcribed). **Wycliffe's Words of Wisdom** is primarily derived from the Later Version of the "**Wycliffe Bible**", but also utilizes words and phrases from the Early Version which are better sounding or easier to understand in the 14TH century original text. And when an Early Version verse is used for comparison purposes with a Later Version verse, it is placed in square brackets [ ]. My suggestions to aid reader comprehension and passage flow are in parentheses ( ), often following the word "or". As well, minor additions were made (an "s", an "a", a "the") to help reader comprehension; none significantly changes the original text.

A number of the words that you will recognize, such as lose, enhance, virtue, and comfort, have changed meaning in the intervening six centuries. In many instances I have added the modern meaning or equivalent to the text in parentheses ( ), following the word in question.

But remember, even with these helps to aid in comprehension, the text you are reading is more than 600 years old. I haven't modernized it in order to preserve the sound and rhythm and colour of the 14TH century original text. The authenticity has been retained and so it can be a challenging read. My other Wycliffe volumes (**Wycliffe's New Testament, Wycliffe's Old Testament**

Note to the Reader

vols. 1 & 2, **Wycliffe's Bible**, and **Wycliffe's Apocrypha**) include literally tens of thousands of rewritten verses and phrases (ALL contained within parentheses to clearly distinguish them from the original text) to aid comprehension.

All of these books, including the Billy Graham edition of **Words of Wisdom**, are available at Amazon.com. You can also find my Author's Page there at https://www.amazon.com/Terence-Noble/e/B00IYJLFEE

Below is an example of the original text and the modern-spelling version side-by-side to give you a flavour of the writing from six centuries ago and its modern equivalent:

"WYCLIFFE BIBLE", 1395	WYCLIFFE'S BIBLE WITH APOCRYPHA, 2018
Al wisdom is of the Lord God, and was euere with hym, and is before the world.	All wisdom is from the Lord God, and was forever with him, and is before the world.
Who noumbride the grauel of the see, and the dropis of reyn, and the daies of the world?	Who numbered the sand of the sea, and the drops of rain, and the days of the world?
Who mesuride the hiȝnesse [or the heiȝte] of heuene, and [the] breed of [the] erthe, and the depthe of the see?	Who measured the highness or the height of Heaven, and the breadth of the earth, and the depth of the sea?
Who enserchide the wisdom of God, that goith before alle thingis?	Who searched for or into the wisdom of God, that goeth before all things?
Wisdom was formed firste of alle thingis, and the vndurstonding of prudence, fro the world, that is, fro without bigynnyng.	Wisdom was formed first of all things, and the understanding of prudence, from the world, that is, from without beginning.
"Later Version", *Ecclesiasticus,* Chapter 1	*Ecclesiasticus* 1:1-4

Wycliffe's Words of Wisdom

DAY 1

PSALM 1

1   Blessed *is* the man, that goeth not in the counsel of wicked men; and stood not in the way of sinners, and sat not in the chair of pestilence.

2   But his will (or his delight) *is* in the law of the Lord; and he shall bethink in (or on) the law of him day and night.

3   And he shall be as a tree, which is planted beside the runnings of waters; that shall give his (or its) fruit in his (or its) time. And his (or its) leaf shall not fall down; and all things, whatever he shall do, shall have prosperity.

4   Not so wicked men, not so; but *they be* as dust, which the wind casteth away from the face of the earth.

5   Therefore wicked men rise not again in the doom (or the judgement); neither sinners in the council (or the assembly) of the rightwise.

6   For the Lord knoweth the way of the rightwise; and the way of wicked men shall perish.

PSALM 2

1   Why gnashed with (their) teeth the heathen men; and the peoples thought vain (or empty) things?

2   The kings of the earth stood together; and the princes came together against the Lord, and against his Christ (or his anointed one).

3   Break we the bonds of them; and cast we away the yoke of them from us.

4   He that dwelleth in the heavens (or in heaven) shall scorn them; and the Lord shall bemock them.

5   Then he shall speak to them in his wrath; and he shall trouble them in his strong vengeance (or with his fury).

6   Soothly I am ordained of (or by) him a king upon Zion, his holy hill;

7   preaching his commandment. The Lord said to me, Thou art my son; I have begotten thee today.

8   Ask thou of me, and I shall give to thee the heathen men (for) thine heritage (or thy inheritance); and (for) thy possession the terms of the earth.

9   Thou shalt govern them in (or with) an iron rod; and thou shalt break them altogether as the vessel of a potter.

10   And now, ye kings, understand; ye that deem (or judge) the earth, be ye learned.

11   Serve ye the Lord with dread (or fear, or reverence); and make ye full out joy to him with trembling.

12   Take ye lore *of chastising* or discipline; lest the Lord be wroth sometime, and ye perish from the just or rightwise way. When his wrath shall burn out in a short time; blessed *be* all they, that trust in him.

PSALM 3

1   *The psalm of David, when he fled from the face of Absalom, his son.* Lord, why be they multiplied that trouble me? many men rise up against me.

2   Many men say of my soul, There is not health to him (or There is no salvation or deliverance for him) in his God.

3   But thou, Lord, art mine up-taker; my glory, and enhancing mine head (or the raiser-up of mine head).

4   With my voice I cried to the Lord; and he heard me from his holy hill.

5   I slept, and rested, and I rose up; for the Lord received (or protected) me.

6   I shall not dread (or fear) thousands of people encompassing me;

7   Lord, arise thou; my God, make me safe (or save me). For thou hast smitten all men being adversaries to me without cause; thou hast all-broken the teeth of the sinners.

8   Health is of the Lord (or Salvation is from the Lord); and thy blessing *is* upon thy people.

PSALM 4

1   *To the victory, in organs (or on instruments), the psalm of David.* When I inwardly called, God of my rightwiseness heard me; in tribulation thou hast alarged to me (or hast set me at large, or set me free). Have thou mercy on me; and hear thou my prayer.

2   Sons of men, how long *be ye* of heavy heart? why love ye vanity (or emptiness and futility), and seek leasing (or go after lies)?

3   And know ye, that the Lord hath made marvellous (or hath chosen) his holy man (for himself); the Lord shall hear me, when I shall cry to him.

4   Be ye wroth, and do not ye sin; and *for those evils to* which ye say in your hearts and in your beds, be ye compunct.

5   Offer ye an offering of rightwiseness, and hope ye (or trust) in the Lord;

6   many say, Who showed good things to us? Lord, the light of thy cheer (or thy face) is marked upon us;

7   thou hast given gladness in mine heart. They be multiplied of (or more than by) the fruit of wheat, *and* of wine; and of their oil.

8   In peace in the same thing; I shall sleep, and take rest. For thou, Lord; hast set me singularly or only in hope.

DAY 1

PSALM 5

1   *To the overcomer, on the heritages (or the inheritances), the psalm of David.* Lord, perceive thou my words with ears; understand thou my cry.

2   My King, and my God; give thou attention to the voice of my prayer. For, Lord, I shall pray to thee;

3   hear thou early my voice. Early I shall stand nigh to thee, and I shall see;

4   for thou art God not desiring wickedness. Neither an evil-willed man shall dwell (or stand) beside thee;

5   neither unjust men shall dwell (or stand) before thine eyes. Thou hatest all *them* that work wickedness;

6   thou shalt lose (or destroy) *them* that speak leasing (or lies). The Lord shall hold abominable a man-queller (or a murderer), and a guileful man (or a deceiver).

7   But *Lord*, in the multitude of thy mercy, I shall enter into thine house; I shall worship toward thine holy temple in thy dread (or with reverence).

8   Lord, lead thou forth me in thy rightwiseness for mine enemies; address (or direct) thou my way in thy sight (or before thee).

9   For truth is not in their mouth; their heart is vain. Their throat is an open sepulchre, they did guilefully (or deceitfully) with their tongues;

10   God, deem thou (or judge) them. Fall they down from their thoughts; after the multitude of their wickednesses, cast thou them down; for, Lord, they have stirred thee to wrath.

11   And all that hope in (or trust) thee, be they glad; they shall make full out joy without end, and thou shalt dwell in (or among) them. And all that love thy name shall have glory in thee;

12   for thou shalt bless the rightwise. Lord, thou hast crowned us, as with a shield of thy good will (or with thy favour).

PSALM 6

1   *To the overcomer in psalms, the psalm of David, on the eighth.* Lord, reprove thou (or rebuke) not me in thy strong vengeance (or thy anger); neither chastise thou me in thy wrath.

2   Lord, have thou mercy on me, for I am sick (or weak); Lord, make thou me whole, for all my bones be troubled.

3   And my soul is troubled greatly; but thou, Lord, for how long?

4   Lord, be thou converted or turned again, and deliver my soul; make thou me safe (or save me), for thy mercy (or because of thy love).

5   For none there is in death, that is mindful of (or remembereth) thee; but in hell (or the grave) who shall acknowledge to (or praise) thee?

6   I travailed in (or I am wearied from) my wailing, I shall wash my bed by each night; I shall moisten, *either make wet,* my bedstraw with my tears.

7   Mine eye is troubled of (or by) strong vengeance; I wax (or grow) old among (or because of) all mine enemies.

8   All ye that work wickedness, depart (or go away) from me; for the Lord hath heard the voice of my weeping.

9   The Lord hath heard my beseeching; the Lord hath received my prayer.

10   (Let) all mine enemies be ashamed, and be troubled greatly; be they turned altogether (away), and be they ashamed full swiftly.

PSALM 7

1   *For the ignorance of David, which he sang to the Lord, on the*

words of the Ethiopian, the son of Benjamin. My Lord God, I have
hoped (or trusted) in thee; make thou me safe (or save me) from all
that pursue me, and deliver thou me.

2   Lest any time he as a lion ravish (or tear apart) my soul; while
none there is that again-buyeth (or redeemeth, or rescueth me),
neither that maketh safe (or saveth me).

3   My Lord God, if I did this thing, if wickedness is in mine
hands or works;

4   if I yielded (or did evil) to men yielding to me evils, fall I by
deserving void from (or before) mine enemies;

5   (let) mine enemy pursue he my soul, and take he, and defoul
my life in the earth (or down to the ground); and bring my glory
into the dust.

6   Lord, rise thou up in thy wrath; and be thou raised (up) in the
coasts of mine enemies. And, my Lord God, rise thou up in the
commandment (or the judgement), which thou hast commanded,

7   and the synagogue (or the congregation, or the assembly) of
the peoples shall encompass thee. And for this (or them), go thou
again on high;

8   the Lord deemeth (or judgeth) the peoples. Lord, deem thou
me by my rightwiseness; and by mine innocence upon (or in) me.

9   The wickedness of sinners be ended; and thou, God, seeking
the hearts, *that is, thoughts,* and reins, *that is, delightings,* shall
address (or direct) the rightwise.

10   My just or rightwise help *is* of (or from) the Lord; that maketh
safe (or saveth) rightful men (and women) in heart.

11   The Lord *is* a rightwise judge, strong and patient; whether he
is (or shall be) wroth by all days?

12   If ye be not converted (or turned from evil), he shall flourish
his sword; he hath bent his bow, and made it ready.

13   And therein he hath made ready the vessels of death; he hath

fully made his arrows with burning things (or with fire).

14   Lo! *the wicked* hath conceived (many ways to bring) sorrow; he painfully hath brought forth unrightfulness, and he hath childed wickedness.

15   He opened a pit, and digged it out; and he fell into the ditch which he (himself) made.

16   His sorrow shall be returned into (or onto) his head; and his wickedness shall come down into (or onto) his neck.

17   I shall acknowledge to (or praise) the Lord by (or for) his rightwiseness; and I shall sing to the name of the highest Lord.

PSALM 8

1   *To the overcomer, for the (wine)presses, the psalm of David.* Lord, *thou art* our Lord; thy name is full wonderful in all the earth. For thy great doing is raised up, above the heavens.

2   Out of the mouth of young children, not speaking and sucking milk, thou hast made perfect praising, for (or because of) thine enemies; (so) that thou destroy the enemy and the avenger.

3   For I shall see thine heavens, the works of thy fingers; the moon and the stars, which thou hast founded.

4   What is a man, *that is mankind,* that thou art mindful of him; either the son of a virgin, or the son of man, for thou visitest (or carest about) him?

5   Thou hast made him a little less than the angels; (but) thou hast crowned him with glory and honour,

6   and thou hast ordained him above the works of thine hands. Thou hast made subject all things under his feet;

7   all sheep and oxen, furthermore and the beasts of the field;

8   the birds of the air, and the fishes of the sea, (and all the other creatures) that pass by (or go along) the paths of the sea.

9   Lord, our Lord; how wonderful is thy name in all the earth.

PROVERBS CHAPTER 1

1   The parables of Solomon, the son of David, king of Israel;

2   to know wisdom and knowing (or knowledge); to understand the words of prudence;

3   and to take (or to receive) the learning of teaching; *to take* (*or to gain*) rightwiseness, and doom (or judgement, or justice), and equity (or fairness);

4   that fellness, *or wariness*, be given to little children, and knowing and understanding to a young waxing (or growing) man.

5   A wise man hearing shall be the wiser; and a man (of) understanding shall hold governance (or gain skills).

6   He shall perceive a parable, and the expounding (or the interpretation); the words of wise men, and the dark figurative speeches of them (or riddles).

7   The dread (or fear) of (or reverence for) the Lord *is* the beginning of wisdom; fools despise wisdom and teaching.

8   My son, hear thou the teaching of thy father, and forsake thou not the law of thy mother (or her principles);

9   that grace be added, *either increased*, to thine head, and a band to thy neck. (so that favour be added unto thee, and a band *of honour be put* about thy neck.)

10   My son, if sinners flatter thee, assent thou not to them.

11   If they say, Come thou with us, set we ambush to *shed* (*out*) blood, hide we snares of deceits against an innocent (person) without cause;

12   swallow we him (up), as hell *swalloweth* a man living; and all-whole, as (those) going down into a pit;

13   we shall find all precious chattel or substance (or possessions),

we shall fill our houses with spoils;

14   put thou (thy) lot with us, one purse be there of (or for) us all;

15   my son, go thou not with them; forbid thy foot from the paths of them.

16   For the feet of them run to evil; and they hasten to shed out blood.

17   But a net is laid in vain before the eyes of birds, that have wings.

18   Also they set ambush against their own blood; and make ready frauds, *or guiles*, against their (own) souls.

19   So the paths of each avaricious man ravish, *or take away*, the souls of them that wield *that wisdom*.

20   Wisdom preacheth withoutforth; in the streets it giveth his voice (or raiseth up its voice).

21   It crieth oft in the head of companies (or from the tops of the streets); in the leaves of the gates of the city it bringeth forth his (or its) words, and saith,

22   How long, little men *in wit*, love young childhood, and fools shall covet those things, that be harmful to themselves, and unprudent men shall hate knowing (or knowledge)?

23   Be ye converted at my reproving (or Be ye changed by my rebukes); lo, I shall bring forth to you my spirit, and I shall show (you) my words.

24   For I called, and ye forsook (me); I held forth mine hand, and none there was that beheld (or paid any attention to it).

25   Ye have despised all my counsel; and charged not my blamings, (or would not accept my rebukes or correction).

26   And I shall laugh in (or at) your perishing; and I shall scorn you, when that, that ye dread (or fear), cometh to you.

27   When sudden wretchedness falleth in, and perishing befalleth as a tempest; when tribulation and anguish cometh upon you.

28   Then they shall call me, and I shall not hear (or listen, or answer); they shall rise (up) early, and they shall not find me.

29   For they hated teaching, and they took (or received) not the dread (or fear) of the Lord (or did not have reverence for the Lord),

30   neither they assented to my counsel, and they depraved all mine amending (or they spurned all my correction).

31   Therefore they shall eat the fruits of their (own) way; and they shall be filled with their (own) counsels.

32   The turning away of little men *in wit* shall slay them; and the prosperity of fools shall lose (or destroy) them.

33   But he that heareth (or listeneth to) me, shall rest without dread (or fear); and he shall use (or enjoy his) abundance, when the dread of evils is taken away.

ECCLESIASTICUS   CHAPTER 1

1   All wisdom is of (or from) the Lord God, and was ever with him, and is before the world (or before time or the Creation).

2   Who numbered the gravel (or the sand) of the sea, and the drops of rain, and the days of the world?

3   Who measured the highness or the height of heaven, and the breadth of the earth, and the depth of the sea? Who ensearched (or searched for) the wisdom of God, that goeth before all things?

4   Wisdom was formed first of all things, and the understanding of prudence, from the world, *that is, from without beginning.*

5   The well of wisdom is the Son of God, or the Word of God, in high things (or high places); and the entering of (or into) that *wisdom* is the everlasting commandments.

6   To whom was the root of wisdom showed? and who knew the subtleties thereof?

7   To whom was the lore or the discipline of wisdom showed,

and made open? and who understood the multiplying of the entering thereof, *that is, of the work thereof?*

8   One is the highest Creator or the Maker of nought (or out of nothing) of all things, Almighty, and a mighty King, and worthy to be dreaded (or feared, or revered) full much, sitting on the throne of that *wisdom*, and God having lordship (or ruling).

9   He formed it in the Holy Ghost, and he saw, and numbered, and he measured (it). And he poured out it upon all his works,

10   and upon all flesh by his gift; he giveth it to them that love him.

11   The dread (or fear) of the Lord (or reverence for the Lord) *is* glory, and glorying or joying, and gladness, and a crown of full out joying.

12   The dread of the Lord shall delight the heart; and shall give gladness and joy into the length of days.

13   To him that dreadeth God, it shall be well in the last days; and he shall be blessed in the day of his death. Forsooth they to whom *wisdom* appeareth in sight, *that is, by the revelation of prophecy*, love it in sight, and in the knowing (or knowledge) of his great things. The love of God *is* honourable wisdom.

14   The beginning of wisdom *is* the dread (or fear) of (or reverence for) the Lord; and it is formed together in the womb with faithful men, and it goeth with chosen women, and it is known with just or rightwise men and faithful.

15   The dread (or fear) of the Lord *is* the religiosity of knowing. Religiosity shall keep, and shall justify the heart; and shall give mirth and joy. It shall be well to him that dreadeth God; and he shall be blessed in the days of his comfort, or at the ending of him.

16   The fullness of wisdom *is* for to dread (or to fear, or to revere) God; and fullness *is* of the fruits thereof.

17   It shall fill each gift or each house of him of (or for)

generations, and the receptacles of (or with) the treasures thereof.

18   The crown of wisdom *is* the dread (or fear) of the Lord (or reverence for the Lord), and filleth peace, and the fruit of health. And he saw, and numbered it; forsooth ever either be the gifts of God.

19   Wisdom shall part the knowing and understanding of prudence; and it enhanceth (or exalteth) the glory of them, that hold it.

20   The root of wisdom is for to dread God; forsooth the branches thereof *be* long enduring or long living. Understanding and the religiosity of knowing *be* in the treasures of wisdom; but wisdom *is* an abomination to sinners.

21   The dread (or fear) of the Lord putteth away sin, for he that is without the dread *of God*, shall not be able to be justified;

22   for why the wrathfulness of his pride or willfulness is the destroying of him.

23   A patient man shall suffer *the dis-eases of a proud man* till into a time; and afterward there shall be yielding of mirth.

24   Good wit shall hide the words of him unto a time; and the lips of many men shall tell out the wit (or understanding) of him.

25   In the treasures of wisdom is signifying of knowing; but the worshipping of God is an abomination to a sinner.

26   O son, coveting wisdom, keep thou rightfulness or rightwiseness, and God shall give it to thee.

27   For why the dread (or fear) of the Lord (or reverence for the Lord) *is* wisdom, and knowing (or knowledge), or discipline, and that that is well pleasant (or well-pleasing) to him *is* faith and mildness (or meekness); and *God* or it shall full-fill the treasures of him.

28   Be thou not rebellious, and unbelieveful to the dread of the Lord; and nigh (or approach) thou not to him with a double heart.

29   Be thou not an hypocrite in the sight of (or before) men; and

be thou not slandered in (or caused to stumble by) thy lips.

30   Take thou keep (or care) to those things, lest thou fall, and bring dishonor to thy soul; and lest God show thy privates (or thy secrets) or hid things, and hurtle thee down in the midst of the synagogue, *that is, of the gathering together of faithful men (and women)*; for thou nighedest wickedly or maliciously to the Lord, and thine heart was full of guile (or deceit) and of falseness.

ECCLESIASTICUS   CHAPTER 2

1   Son, nighing to the service of God, stand thou in rightfulness or rightwiseness, and dread (or fear, or reverence); and make ready or prepare thy soul to (or for) temptation.

2   Bear down thine heart, and suffer, and bow down thine ear, and take (in, or receive) the words of understanding, and haste thou not into the time of death or oppressing.

3   Suffer thou the sustainings of God; be thou joined to God, and abide thou, (so) that thy life wax (or grow, or increase) in the last time.

4   Take thou all thing that is set (or put) to thee, and suffer thou in sorrow, and have thou patience in thy lowness or meekness.

5   For why gold and silver is proved in fire; forsooth men worthy to be received *be proved* in the chimney of lowness or meekness.

6   Believe thou to God, and he shall recover thee; and address (or direct) thou thy way, and hope thou into (or trust) him. Keep thou his dread (or fear, or reverence), and wax thou (or grow) old in him.

7   Ye that dread (or fear, or revere) the Lord, abide his mercy, and bow ye not away from him, lest ye fall.

8   Ye that dread the Lord, believe to (or in) him, and your meed (or your reward) shall not be voided away.

9   Ye that dread the Lord, hope into (or trust) him, and mercy shall come to you into delighting.

10   Ye that dread the Lord, love him, and your hearts shall be lightened or enlightened. Sons, behold ye the nations of men, and know ye, that no man hoped (or trusted) in the Lord, and was shamed (or confounded); *none* dwelled or abode still in his behests (or his commandments), and was forsaken; either who inwardly called him, and he despised him?

11   For why God is piteous (or compassionate), and merciful, and he shall forgive sins in the day of tribulation; and he is the defender to (or of) all men (and women), that seek him in truth.

12   Woe *to the* double in heart, and with cursed lips, and mis-doing or evil-doing hands; and to a sinner entering into the land by two ways.

13   Woe to them that be dissolute of heart, or unstable in heart, that believe not to God; and therefore they shall not be defended of (or by) him.

14   Woe to them that have lost patience, and that have forsaken rightful or right ways, and have turned away or aside into shrewd (or depraved) ways. And what shall they do, when the Lord shall begin to behold (upon them)?

15   They that dread (or fear, or revere) the Lord, shall not be unbelieveful to his word; and they that love him, shall keep his ways.

16   They that dread the Lord, shall inquire (of) or inwardly seek those things, that be well pleasant (or well-pleasing) to him; and they that love him, shall be filled with his law.

17   They that dread the Lord, shall make ready or prepare their hearts, and shall hallow their souls in his sight. They that dread the Lord, shall keep his commandments, and they shall have patience unto the beholding or inwardly looking of him;

18   and shall say, If we do not penance (or repent), we shall fall into the hands of the Lord, and not into the hands of men. For by the greatness of him, so and his mercy is with him. The sons of wisdom *be* the church (or the congregation, or assembly) of just or rightwise men, and the nation of them *is* obedience and love.

ECCLESIASTES CHAPTER 1

1   The words of Ecclesiastes, the son of David, king of Jerusalem, *that is, of Solomon, for 'Ecclesiastes' is said 'a speaker to the people'* (*or a preacher*).
2   Vanity of vanities (or Emptiness and futility), said Ecclesiastes; vanity of vanities, and all things *be* vanity (or empty and futile).
3   What hath a man moreover of (or from) all his travail (or all his labour), by which he travaileth (or laboureth) under the sun?
4   A generation passeth away, and an(other) generation cometh; but the earth standeth without end (or remaineth forever).
5   The sun riseth up, and goeth down, and returneth again to his (or its) place; and there it riseth again,
6   and compasseth by the south, and (then) returneth again to the north. The spirit (or The wind) compassing all things goeth about, and returneth again into his (or its) circles.
7   All the floods (or All the rivers) enter into the sea, and the sea floweth not over *the marks* (*or the boundaries*) *set of* (*or by*) *God*; the floods (or the rivers) return again to the place from whence they come forth, (so) that they (can) flow out again.
8   All things *be* hard; a man may not declare those things by words (alone); the eye is not (ful)filled by sight, neither the ear is filled by hearing.
9   What is that thing that was, (but) that that shall come? What is that thing that is made, (but) that that shall be made? Nothing under

the sun *is* new,

10   neither any man may say, Lo! this thing is new; for now it went before in worlds (or times), that were before us.

11   Mind of (or Remembering) the former things is not (done), but soothly neither thinking of those things, that shall come afterward, shall be at (or with) them that shall come in the last time.

12   I Ecclesiastes was king of Israel in Jerusalem;

13   and I purposed in my soul to seek and ensearch wisely of (or into) all the things, that be made under the sun. God gave this evil occupation (or this difficult task) to the sons of men, (so) that they should be occupied in it.

14   I saw all things that be made under the sun, and lo! all things *be* vanity (or empty and futile) and a torment of (or for) the spirit.

15   Wayward men (can only) be amended of hard (or can only be corrected with great difficulty); and the number of fools is great without end.

16   I spake in mine heart, and I said, Lo! I am made great, and I (have) surpassed in wisdom all men, that were before me in Jerusalem; and my soul saw many things wisely, and I (have) learned (much).

17   And I gave mine heart (or I applied my mind), (so) that I should know prudence and doctrine, and errors and folly. And I knew that in these things also was travail (or suffering) and a torment of (or for) the spirit;

18   for in much wisdom is much indignation, and he that increaseth knowing (or knowledge), increaseth also travail (or also increaseth his own suffering). Δ

DAY 2

PSALM 9

1   *Into the end, for the privates (or the secrets) of the son, the psalm of David.* Lord, I shall acknowledge to (or praise) thee in (or with) all mine heart; I shall tell all thy marvels.

2   Thou Highest, I shall be glad, and I shall be fully joyful in thee; I shall sing to thy name.

3   For thou turnest mine enemy aback; they shall be made feeble, and shall perish from (before) thy face.

4   For thou hast made my doom (or justice), and my cause; thou, that deemest rightfulness or rightwiseness, hast set upon the throne.

5   Thou hast blamed (or rebuked) the heathen men, and the wicked perished; thou hast done away the name of them into the world (or forever), and into the world of world (or forever and ever).

6   The swords of the enemy have failed into the end; and thou hast destroyed the cities of them. The mind of them (or Their memory) hath perished with sound;

7   and the Lord dwelleth without end. He hath made ready his throne in doom (or for judgement);

8   and he shall deem the world in equity (or with fairness), he shall deem (or judge) the peoples in (or with) rightwiseness.

9   And the Lord is made the refuge, *either a help,* to the poor; an helper in covenable (or opportune) times in tribulation (or trouble).

10   And they, that know thy name, have hope (or trust) in thee; for thou, Lord, hast not forsaken them that seek thee.

11   Sing ye psalms to the Lord, that *dwelleth* in Zion; tell ye his studies (or his deeds) among the heathen men.

12   God forgetteth not the cry of poor men; for he hath mind *of* (or remembereth) *them,* and he seeketh the blood of (or for) them.

13   Lord, have thou mercy on me; see thou my meekness of (or before) mine enemies. Which enhancest me (or liftest me up) from the gates of death;

14   (so) that I tell (out) all thy praisings in the gates of the daughter of Zion. I shall be fully joyful in thine health (or in thy deliverance of me);

15   the heathen men be fast-set in the perishing, which they (themselves have) made. In this snare, which they hid, the foot of them is caught.

16   The Lord making dooms (or judgements) shall be known; the sinner is taken in the works of his (own) hands.

17   The sinners be turned altogether into hell; all the folks (or the nations), that forget (about) God.

18   For the forgetting of the poor shall not be into the end; the patience of poor men shall not perish into the end.

19   Lord, rise thou up, a man be not comforted (or strengthened); the folks be deemed in thy sight (or the nations be judged before thee).

20   Lord, ordain thou a law-maker upon them; know the folks (or the nations), that they (only) be men.

PSALM 10

1   Lord, why hast thou gone far away? thou despisest us in covenable times in tribulation (or in our time of trouble)?

2   While the wicked man waxeth (or groweth) proud, the poor man is burnt; they be taken (or caught) in the *wicked* counsels (or plans), which they thinked.

3   For why the sinner is praised (or glorieth) in the desires of his soul; and the wicked is blessed. The sinner (who) hath stirred the Lord to wrath;

4   after the multitude of his wrath, he shall not seek (after God). God is not in his sight (or in any of his thoughts);

5   his ways be defouled (or defiled) in all time. Thy dooms (or judgements) be taken away from his face; he shall be lord of all his enemies.

6   For he said in his heart, I shall not be moved (or shaken), from generation into generation without evil (or without any trouble).

7   Whose mouth is full of cursing, and of bitterness, and of guile (or deceit); travail and sorrow *is* under his tongue.

8   He sitteth in ambushes with rich men in privates (or in villages); to slay the innocent. His eyes behold *cruelly* (up)on the poor;

9   he setteth ambushes in a hid place, as a lion in his den. He setteth ambushes, for to ravish (or to catch) the poor; for to ravish (or catch) the poor, while he draweth (in) the poor man. In his snare he shall make meek (or low) the poor man;

10   he shall bow himself down, and he shall fall, when he hath been (or hath become) the lord of poor men.

11   For he said in his heart, God hath forgotten (them); he hath turned away his face, (so) that he see not into the end.

12   Lord God, rise thou up, and thine hand be enhanced (or be lifted up); forget thou not the poor.

13   For what thing stirred the wicked man God to wrath? for he said in his heart, *God* shall not seek (me out).

14   (But) thou (do) seest, for thou beholdest travail (or trouble, or suffering) and sorrow; (so) that thou take them into thine hands. The poor man is left to thee; thou shalt be an helper to the fatherless and the motherless.

15   All-break thou the arm (or the power) of the sinner, and the evil-willed; his sin shall be sought, and it shall not be found.

16   The Lord shall reign without end, and into the world of world (or forever and ever); folks (or nations), ye shall perish from the

land of him.

17   The Lord hath heard the desire of poor men; thine ear hath heard the making ready (or the desires) of their hearts.

18   To deem (or To judge) for the motherless and the meek; (so) that a man presume no more to make himself great upon the earth.

PSALM 11

1   *To the victory, the psalm of David.* I trust in the Lord; how say ye to my soul, Pass thou (or Fly) over into the hill, as a sparrow *doeth*?

2   For lo! The sinners have bent a bow; they have made ready their arrows in an arrow case; (so) that they shoot in darkness the rightful (or upright) men in heart.

3   For they have destroyed, whom thou hast made perfect (or good); but what did (or can) the rightwise man (do)?

4   The Lord *is* in his holy temple; *he is* Lord, his seat (or his throne) *is* in heaven. His eyes behold (up)on the poor; his eyelids ask (or assay) the sons of men.

5   The Lord asketh (or assayeth) the rightwise man, and the unfaithful man; but he, that loveth wickedness, hateth his soul.

6   He shall rain snares upon the sinners; fire, and brimstone, and the spirit (or the wind) of tempests *be* the part of (or the portion in) the cup of them.

7   For the Lord *is* just or rightwise, and loveth rightwiseness; his cheer (or his face) hath seen evenness, *or equity* (or fairness).

PSALM 12

1   *To the victory, on the eighth, the song of David.* Lord, make

thou me safe (or save me), for the holy (man) failed; for truths be made little from the sons of men.

2   They spake vain things, each man to his neighbour; *and they having* guileful (or deceitful) lips, spake in their heart, and with their heart (or with a double heart).

3   The Lord destroy all guileful (or deceitful) lips; and the great speaking (or proud) tongue.

4   Which said, We shall magnify (with) our tongue, our lips be of us-selves (or our own); who (else) is our lord?

5   For the wretchedness of the needy, and for the wailing of the poor; now I shall rise up, saith the Lord. I shall set or put (him) in health (or in safety); I shall do trustily in (or with) him.

6   The speeches of the Lord be chaste speeches; (as) silver assayed by fire, proved from the earth, purged sevenfold.

7   Thou, Lord, shalt keep us (safe); and thou shalt keep us (safe) from this generation without end (or evermore).

8   Wicked men go in compass (or be all around); by thine highness thou hast multiplied the sons of men.

PSALM 13

1   *To the victory, the psalm of David.* Lord, how long forgettest thou me, into the end (or forever)? how long turnest thou away thy face from me?

2   How long shall I put counsel in my soul; sorrow in my heart by (each) day? How long shall mine enemy be raised (or exalted) upon me?

3   My Lord God, behold thou, and hear thou me. Lighten thou mine eyes, lest any time I sleep in death;

4   lest any time mine enemy say, I had the mastery against him. They, that trouble me, shall have joy, if I shall be stirred (or shaken);

5   but I hoped in thy mercy (or I trusted in thy love). Mine heart shall fully have joy in thine health (or salvation);

6   I shall sing to the Lord, that giveth goods (or good things) to me, and I shall say a psalm to the name of the highest Lord.

PSALM 14

1   *To the victory, the psalm of David.* The unwise man said in his heart, God is not. They be corrupt, and they be made abominable in their studies (or in their deeds); none is that doeth good, none is till to one.

2   The Lord beheld from heaven upon the sons of men; (so) that he see, if any is understanding, either seeking God.

3   (But) all (be) bowed away, altogether they be made unprofitable; none is that doeth good, none is till to one. The throat of them is an open sepulchre, they did guilefully (or deceitfully, or deceptively) with their tongues; the venom of snakes *is* under their lips. Whose mouth is full of cursing and bitterness; their feet *be* swift to shed out blood. Sorrow and cursedness *is* in the ways of them, and they knew not the way of peace; the dread (or fear) of God is not before their eyes.

4   Whether all men that work wickedness shall not know; that devour my people, as the meat (or food) of bread? They called not (on) the Lord;

5   they trembled there for dread (or fear), where was no dread; for the Lord is in (or with) a rightwise generation.

6   Thou hast shamed the counsel (or plans) of the needy or the poor; for the Lord is his hope.

7   Who shall give from Zion health (or salvation) to Israel? When the Lord hath turned away the captivity (or restored the fortunes) of his people; Jacob shall fully be joyful, and Israel shall be glad.

DAY 2

PSALM 15

1   *The psalm of David.* Lord, who shall dwell in thy tabernacle (or Temple); either who shall rest in (or on) thine holy hill?

2   He that entereth without wem (or blemish); and worketh rightwiseness. He that speaketh truth in (or from) his heart;

3   which did not guile (or deceit) in (or with) his tongue. Nor did evil to his neighbour; and took not reproof (or reproach) against his neighbour.

4   A wicked man is brought to nought (or nothing) in his sight; but he glorifieth them that dread (or fear, or revere) the Lord. He that sweareth (a pledge) to his neighbour, and deceiveth *him* not;

5   which gave not his money to usury; and took not gifts upon (or against) the innocent. He, that doeth these things, shall not be moved (or shaken) without end (or evermore).

PSALM 16

1   *Of the meek (or humble) and simple (or honest), the psalm of David.* Lord, keep thou me (safe), for I have hoped (or trusted) in thee;

2   I said to the Lord, Thou art my God; for thou hast no need of my goods (or all the good things that I have come from thee).

3   To the saints (or God's people) that be in the land of him; he made wonderful all my wills in them (or they be the wonderful ones in whom be all my delight).

4   The sicknesses of them be multiplied; afterward they hastened (or of those who hastened to other gods). I shall not gather together the conventicles, *or small covents*, of them of bloods; and I shall not be mindful of (or remember) their names by (or on) my lips.

5   The Lord *is* the part of mine heritage (or the portion of my

23

inheritance), and of my passion; thou art, that shall restore mine heritage to me.

6   The cords (or boundary lines) felled to me in full clear things; for mine heritage (or my inheritance) is full clear (or beautiful) to me.

7   I shall bless the Lord, that hath given understanding to me; furthermore and my reins have blamed (or warned, or instructed) me unto the night.

8   I saw before (me) evermore the Lord in my sight; for he is at the right half (or hand) to me, (so) that I be not moved (or shaken).

9   For this thing mine heart was glad, and my tongue joyed fully (or rejoiced); furthermore and my flesh shall rest in hope.

10   For thou shalt not leave my soul in hell (or the grave); neither thou shalt give thine holy (man) to see corruption (or decay).

11   Thou hast made known to me the ways of life; thou shalt full-fill me with gladness with thy cheer (or thy face, or in thy presence); delightings *be* in thy right half (or at thy right hand) unto the end (or forever).

PROVERBS CHAPTER 2

1   My son, if thou receivest my words, and hidest my behests (or my commands) with thee;

2   (so) that thine ear hear wisdom, bow (down) thine heart to know prudence.

3   For if thou inwardly callest (to) wisdom, and bowest thine heart toward prudence;

4   if thou seekest it as money, and diggest it out as treasures;

5   then thou shalt understand the dread (or fear) of (or reverence for) the Lord, and shalt find the knowing (or knowledge) of God.

6   For the Lord giveth wisdom; and prudence and knowing (or

knowledge) *is* of his mouth (or *cometh* from his mouth).

7   He shall keep (safe) the health (or salvation) of rightful men, and he shall defend them that go simply (or honestly).

8   And he shall keep (safe) the paths of rightwiseness, and he shall keep (safe) the ways of holy men.

9   Then thou shalt understand rightfulness or rightwiseness, and doom (or judgement), and equity (or fairness), and each good path (or each good way).

10   If wisdom entereth into thine heart, and knowing (or knowledge) pleaseth thy soul,

11   good counsel shall keep thee (safe), and prudence shall keep thee (safe);

12   (so) that thou be delivered from an evil way, and from a man that speaketh wayward (or wicked) things.

13   Which forsake a rightful or right way, and go by dark ways;

14   which be glad, when they have done evil, and make full out joy (or rejoice) in the worst things;

15   whose ways *be* wayward, and their goings *be* of evil fame (or shameful).

16   (So) that thou be delivered from an alien (or foreign) woman, and from a strange *woman*, that maketh soft her words;

17   and (who) forsaketh the duke, *or the leader*, of her time of marriage, and hath forgotten the covenant of (or with) her God.

18   For the house of her is bowed to (or on the way to) death, and her paths (lead down) to hell.

19   All that enter to her, shall not return again, neither they shall catch (or walk again upon) the paths of life.

20   (See) that thou go in (or on) a good way, and keep (to) the paths of rightwise men.

21   Forsooth they that be rightful, shall dwell in the land; and simple (or honest) men shall perfectly dwell therein.

22   But unfaithful men shall be lost (or cut off) from the land; and they that do wickedly, shall be taken away from it.

ECCLESIASTICUS   CHAPTER 3

1   Dearworthy sons, hear ye the doom (or judgement) of the father; and do ye so, that ye be safe (or so that ye be saved).

2   For why God honoured the father in (or over) the sons, and he seeketh, and hath made steadfast the doom (or confirmed the judgement or authority) of the mother into (or over) the sons.

3   He that loveth God, shall pray for (his own) sins, and he shall abstain himself from them, and (then) he shall be heard in the prayer of days.

4   And as he that treasureth, so he that honoureth his mother.

5   He that honoureth his father, shall be made merry in sons, and he shall be heard in the day of his prayer.

6   He that honoureth his father, shall live by or with longer life; and he that obeyeth to the father, shall refresh the mother, *that is, shall comfort her.*

7   He that dreadeth (or feareth, or revereth) the Lord, honoureth (his) father and mother; and he shall serve in work, and word, and in all patience to them that engendered or begat him, as to lords.

8   Honour thy father, *so* that the blessing of God come to thee; and his blessing dwelleth into (or unto) the last (breath).

9   The blessing of the father maketh steadfast the houses of the sons; but the cursing of the mother draweth out the foundaments (or the foundations) by the root.

10   Have thou not glory in the despising of thy father; for it is not glory to thee, but confusion or shame.

11   For why the glory of a man *is* of (or from) the honour of his father; and the shame of the son *is* a father without honour.

12   Son, receive (or accept) the last age of thy father, and make thou not him sorry or have sorrow in his life;

13   and if he faileth in wit (or understanding), give thou forgiveness, and despise thou not him in thy virtue (or thine own strength);

14   for why the alms-deeds of (or for) the father shall not be in forgetting (or forgotten). For why good shall be restored to thee for the sin of the mother, and building up shall be made to (or for) thee in rightfulness or rightwiseness;

15   and it shall be remembered of thee in the day of tribulation (or trouble), and thy sins shall be released or loosened, as ice in the clearness, *either heat*, of the sun.

16   He is of full evil fame, that forsaketh the father; and he that wratheth the mother, is cursed of (or by) God.

17   Son, perform thy works in mildness (or in meekness, or humility), and thou shalt be loved over (or above) the glory of men.

18   In as much as thou art great, make thee meek in all things, and thou shalt find grace before God;

19   (This verse is omitted in the original text.)

20   for why the power of God alone is great, and he is honoured of (or by) meek (or humble) men.

21   Seek thou not (out) higher things than thou or thyself, and inquire or search thou not (about) stronger things than thou;

22   but evermore think thou (upon) those things, which God commanded to thee; and be thou not curious in (or about) the full many works of him. For it is not needful to (or for) thee to see with thine eyes those things, that be hid.

23   In superfluous things do not thou seek or ensearch manyfold; and be thou not curious in the many works of him; for why full many things above the wit (or understanding) of men be showed to thee.

24   For the suspicion of many men hath deceived themselves,

and withheld their wits (or held back their reason) in vanity.

25 (This verse is omitted in the original text.)

26 An hard heart shall have evil in the last time; and he that loveth peril shall perish in it. An heart that entereth by two ways, *that is, that hath the knowing of good in understanding, and malice in will*, shall not have prosperities, *either rest*; and a man of shrewd (or depraved) heart, shall be slandered in them (or be caused to stumble by them).

27 A wicked heart shall be grieved in (or with) sorrows; and a sinner shall heap or add to, to do sin.

28 Health (or Deliverance) shall not be to (or for) the synagogue of proud men; for why the thick wood or bush of sin shall be drawn out or taken up by the root in them, and it shall not be understood *of (or by) the sinners who will not think on God's dooms (or judgements)*.

29 The heart of a wise man is understood in wisdom, and a good ear shall hear wisdom with all covetousness. A wise heart and able to understand shall abstain itself from sins, and shall have prosperities in the works of rightfulness or rightwiseness.

30 Water quencheth a burning fire, and alms-deeds against-standeth sins.

31 And God, the beholder of him that yieldeth grace, *that is, that doeth alms-deeds*, hath mind (or is remembered) afterward; and he shall find steadfastness in (or at) the time of his fall.

ECCLESIASTES CHAPTER 2

1 Therefore I said in mine heart, I shall go, and I shall flow in (or enjoy all) delights, and I shall use goods (or enjoy all good things); and I saw also that this was vanity (or empty and futile).

2 And laughing I areckoned (as but) error, and I said to joy,

What art thou, deceived in vain? (or Of what value art thou?)

3   I thought in mine heart to withdraw my flesh from wine, (so) that I should lead over my soul to wisdom, and (so) that I would eschew folly (or shun foolishness), till I should see, what were profitable to the sons of men; in which deed the number of days of their life under the sun is needful, (or which deeds or works be useful or meaningful, all the days of their lives under the sun).

4   I magnified, *either made great*, my works, I builded houses to me (or for myself), and I planted vines (or vineyards);

5   I made gardens and orchards, and I planted them with trees of all kinds;

6   and I made cisterns of (or for) waters, for to water the wood of the burgeoning or growing trees.

7   I had in possession servants and handmaids; and I had much household (or many slaves born in my house), and droves (or herds) of great beasts, and great flocks of sheep, over (or more than) all men that were before me in Jerusalem.

8   I gathered together to me (or for myself) silver and gold, and (or from) the castles of the kings and (out) of the provinces; I made to me (or I got for myself) singers and singeresses, and (enjoyed all) the delights of the sons of men, and cups and vessels in service, (for) to pour out wines (into them);

9   and I surpassed in riches all men that were before me in Jerusalem. Also wisdom dwelled stably with me,

10   and all things which mine eyes desired, I denied not to them; neither I refrained mine heart, (so) that not it used all lust (or desire), and delighted itself in these things which I had made ready (or prepared for it); and I deemed (or judged) this my part (or my portion), if I used my travail (or for all my labour).

11   And when I had turned me to (look upon) all the works which mine hands had made, and to the travails in (or upon the labour)

which I had sweated (over) in vain, I saw in all things vanity (or emptiness and futility) and a torment of (or for) the soul, and that nothing under the sun dwelleth stably.

12   I passed forth to behold wisdom, and errors, and folly; *I said*, What is a man, that he may follow the king, his maker? (or What new thing can he who followeth the king do?)

13   And I saw, that wisdom went so much before folly, as much as light is diverse from darknesses.

14   The eyes of a wise man *be* in his head, (and) a fool goeth in darknesses; and I learned, that one perishing was of ever either (or that the same death would come to both of them).

15   And I said in mine heart, If one death shall be both of (or for) the fool and of (or for) me, what profiteth it to me, that I gave more busyness (or more effort and study) to wisdom? And I spake with my soul, and perceived, that this also was vanity (or empty and futile).

16   For the mind of a wise man shall not be (or a wise person shall not be remembered), (and) in like manner as neither (that) of a fool, without end (or evermore), and the times to come shall cover all things altogether with forgetting; (for) a learned man dieth in like manner as an unlearned man.

17   And therefore it annoyed me of my life (or it vexed me to live), seeing that all things under the sun be evil (or troublesome), and that all things *be* vanity and a torment of (or for) the spirit.

18   Again I cursed all my busyness, by which I travailed most studiously under the sun; and I shall have an heir after me,

19   whom I know not, whether he shall be wise either a fool; and he shall be the lord in my travails (or of all my works), for which I sweated greatly (over), and was (so) busy; and is there anything so vain (or so empty and futile)?

20   Wherefore I ceased, and mine heart forsook for to travail further (or to labour any more) under the sun.

21 For why when another man travaileth in wisdom, and teaching, and busyness, he leaveth things gotten to an idle man; and therefore this *is* vanity (or empty and futile), and great evil.

22 For why what shall it profit to a man of all his travail, and torment of spirit (or for all his labour, and trials and tribulations), with which he was tormented under the sun?

23 All his days be full of sorrows and mischiefs, and by (or at) night he resteth not in soul (or his soul resteth not); and whether this is not vanity (or emptiness and futility)?

24 Whether it is not better to eat and drink, and to show to his soul the goods of his travails (or to enjoy the good things from his labour)? and this *thing is* of (or from) the hand of God.

25 Who shall devour so (or such food), and shall flow in (or shall enjoy such) delights, as I *have*?

26 God gave wisdom, and knowing (or knowledge), and gladness to a good man in his sight; but he gave torment, and superfluous busyness to a sinner, (so) that (first) he increase, and gather together, and (or but then must) give to him that pleaseth God; but also this *is* vanity (or empty and futile), and vain busyness of the soul. Δ

D A Y 3

P S A L M 1 7

1   *The prayer of David*. Lord, hear thou my rightfulness or rightwiseness; behold thou my prayer. Perceive thou with ears (or listen to) my prayer; not *made* in (or with) guileful (or deceiving) lips.

2   My doom (or judgement) come forth of thy cheer (or from thy presence); thine eyes see they equity (or what is right).

3   Thou hast proved mine heart, and hast visited (me) in the night; thou hast examined or assayed me by fire, and wickedness is not found in me.

4   (So) that my mouth speak not (of) the works of men; for (or through) the words of thy lips I have kept (myself from) hard ways.

5   Make thou perfect my goings in thy paths; (so) that my steps be not moved (or waver, or stumble).

6   I cried, for thou, God, heardest me; bow down thy ear to me, and hear thou my words.

7   Make wonderful thy mercies; that makest safe (or savest) them that hope (or trust) in thee.

8   Keep thou me as the apple of thine eye; *and* from them that against-stand thy right hand. Cover thou (or Hide) me under the shadow of thy wings;

9   from the face of unpious men, that have tormented me. Mine enemies have encompassed my soul;

10   they have enclosed altogether (themselves in) their (own) fatness; the mouth of them spake pride.

11   They casted me forth, and have encompassed me now; they ordained to bow down their eyes into the earth (or to the ground).

12   They, as a lion made ready to *his* prey, have taken me; and as

the whelp of a lion dwelling in hid places.

13   Lord, rise thou up, before come thou him, and overturn thou him; deliver thou my life from the unpious (or the wicked), *deliver thou* (me with) thy sword;

14   from the enemies of thine hand. Lord, part thou them from a few men of the land in the life of them; their womb is full-filled of (or with) thine hid things. They be full-filled with sons; and they left their remnants, *either residue*, to their little children.

15   But I in rightwiseness shall appear to thy sight; I shall be fulfilled, when thy glory shall appear.

PSALM 18

1   *To victory, the word of the Lord to David, which spake the words of this song, in the day in which the Lord delivered him from the hand of all his enemies, and from the hand of Saul; and he said*: Lord, my strength, I shall love thee;

2   the Lord *is* my steadfastness, and my refuge, and my deliverer. My God *is* mine helper; and I shall hope in him. My defender, and the horn of mine health (or my salvation); and mine up-taker.

3   I shall praise, and inwardly call the Lord; and I shall be safe (or be saved) from mine enemies.

4   The sorrows of death encompassed me; and the streams of wickedness have troubled me.

5   The sorrows of hell (or the grave) encompassed me; the snares of death before-occupied me (or were set for me).

6   In my tribulation I inwardly called the Lord; and I cried to my God. And he heard my voice from his holy temple; and my cry in his sight (or before him) entered into his ears.

7   The earth was moved altogether, and trembled greatly; the foundaments (or foundations) of the hills were troubled altogether,

and moved altogether, for he was wroth to them.

8   Smoke went up in the wrath of the Lord, and fire burnt out
from his face; coals were kindled of him (or by it).

9   He bowed down the heavens, and came down; and darkness
was under his feet.

10   And he ascended or went upon cherubim, and flew; he flew
over the pens (or on the wings) of the winds.

11   And he setted or put darknesses as his hiding place, his
tabernacle in his compass; and dark water *was* in the clouds of the
air.

12   Full clear clouds passed (by) in his sight (or before him); hail
and the coals of fire.

13   And the Lord thundered from heaven or in the heavens; and
the Highest gave his voice, hail and coals of fire.

14   And he sent his arrows, and destroyed those men; he
multiplied lightnings, and troubled those men.

15   And the wells of waters appeared; and the foundaments (or
foundations) of the earth were showed. Lord, of thy blaming (or
from thy rebuke); of the breathing of the spirit (or from the blast) of
thy wrath.

16   He sent (or reached down) from the highest place, and took
(hold of) me; and he took me (out) from many waters.

17   He delivered me from my strongest enemies; and from them
that hated me, for they were comforted on me (or too strong for me).

18   They came before me in the day of my torment; and the Lord
was made my defender.

19   And he led out me into the breadth; he made me safe, for he
would (or he delighted in) me.

20   And the Lord shall yield to me by my rightwiseness; and he
shall yield to me by the cleanness of mine hands.

21   For I (have) kept the ways of the Lord; and I did not (go away)

unfaithfully from my God.

22   For all his dooms (or judgements) *be* in my sight; and I putted not away from me his rightfulnesses (or decrees).

23   And I shall be unwemmed (or without blemish) with him; and I shall keep me from my (own) wickedness.

24   And the Lord shall yield to me by my rightwiseness; and by the cleanness of mine hands in the sight of his eyes (or before him).

25   With the holy, thou shalt be holy; and with an innocent man, thou shalt be innocent.

26   And with a chosen man, thou shalt be chosen; and with (or to) a wayward man, thou shalt be wayward.

27   For thou shalt make safe (or save) a meek (or humble) people; and thou shalt make meek the eyes of proud men.

28   For thou, Lord, lightenest my lantern; my God, lighten thou my darknesses.

29   For by thee I shall be delivered from temptation; and in (or with) my God('s) (help) I shall go over the wall.

30   My God, his way *is* undefouled (or undefiled); the speeches (or words) of the Lord *be* examined (or assayed) by fire; he is the defender of all men hoping (or trusting) in him.

31   For why, who *is* God, except the Lord? either who *is* God, except our God?

32   God that hath girded me with virtue (or strength); and hath set my way unwemmed (or without blemish).

33   Which made perfect my feet as *the feet* of harts; and ordaining me upon the high things (or high places).

34   Which teacheth mine hands to (or in) battle; and thou hast set mine arms as a brazen (or a bronze) bow.

35   And thou hast given to me the covering of thine health (or thy salvation); and thy right hand hath up-taken me (or hath taken me up). And thy chastising or discipline amended me into the end;

and that chastising or discipline of thee shall teach me.

36   Thou alargedest or madest large my paces under me; and my steps be not made unsteadfast.

37   I shall pursue mine enemies, and I shall take (hold of) them; and I shall not return (again) till they fail (or fall).

38   I shall all-break them, and they shall not be able to stand; they shall fall under my feet.

39   And thou hast girded me with virtue to (or strength for) the battle; and thou hast overturned under me men rising against me.

40   And thou hast given (or turned) mine enemies' backs to me (or they have retreated); and thou hast destroyed them that hated me.

41   They cried, and none there was that made them safe (or saved them); *they cried* to the Lord, and he heard not them.

42   And I shall all-break them, as dust before the face of the wind; I shall do them away, as the clay of the streets.

43   Thou shalt deliver me from the against-sayings of the people; thou shalt set me into the head of the folks (or the nations). The people, which I knew not, hath served me;

44   in the hearing of the ear it (or they) obeyed to me. Alien (or Foreign) sons lied (down) to (or before) me,

45   alien sons waxed (or grew) old; and (went) crooked from thy paths.

46   The Lord liveth, and my God *be* blessed; and (let) the God of mine health (or my salvation) be enhanced (or exalted).

47   God, that givest vengeances to me, and makest subject the peoples under me;

48   *thou art* my deliverer from my wrathful enemies. And thou shalt enhance (or exalt) me from them, that rise against me; thou shalt deliver (or rescue) me from a wicked man.

49   Therefore, Lord, I shall acknowledge to (or praise) thee among the nations; and I shall say a psalm to thy name.

50   Magnifying the healths (or the victories) of his king; and doing mercy to his christ (or his anointed one) David, and to his seed till into the world (or forever).

PSALM 19

1   *To victory, the psalm of David.* The heavens tell out the glory of God; and the firmament telleth (about) the works of his hands.

2   The day telleth out to the day a word; and the night showeth knowing (or knowledge) to the (next) night.

3   No languages be, neither words; of which the voices of them be not heard.

4   The sound of them went out into all the earth; and the words of them into the ends of the world. In the sun he hath set his tabernacle (or In the sky he hath pitched a tent for the sun);

5   and he, (the sun), as a spouse coming forth of (or from) his chamber. He fully joyed, as a giant, to run his way;

6   his (or its) going out was from the highest heaven. And his (or its) going again was to the highest thereof; and none there is that hideth himself from his (or its) heat.

7   The law of the Lord is without wem (or fault), and converteth souls; the witnessing (or the testimony) of the Lord is faithful, and giveth wisdom to little, *either meek,* children.

8   The rightfulnesses (or decrees) of the Lord *be* rightful, gladdening hearts; the commandment of the Lord *is* clear, enlightening eyes.

9   The holy dread (or the fear) of (or reverence for) the Lord dwelleth into the world of world (or forever and ever); the dooms (or judgements) of the Lord be true, justified unto themselves.

10   Desirable more than gold, and a stone much precious; and sweeter than honey and honeycomb.

11   For why thy servant keepeth them; much yielding, *or reward,*

is in those *dooms (or judgements)* to be kept.

12   Who understandeth trespasses? make thou me clean from my privy (or secret) *sins;*

13   and of alien (or presumptuous) *sins* spare thy servant. If they have not lordship of (or over) me, then I shall be undefouled *of alien sins, or without wem (or blemish);* and I shall be cleansed of the most (or the greatest) sins.

14   And the speeches of my mouth shall be *such,* that they please (thee); and the thinking of mine heart *is* evermore in thy sight. Lord, mine helper; and mine again-buyer (or my redeemer).

PROVERBS   CHAPTER 3

1   My son, forget thou not my law; and thine heart keep my commandments.

2   For they shall set to thee the length of days, and the years of life, and peace.

3   Mercy and truth forsake thee not; bind thou or encompass them to thy throat (or about thy neck), and write *them* in the tables (or on the tablets) of thy heart.

4   And thou shalt find grace (or receive favour), and good teaching before God and men.

5   Have thou trust in the Lord, of (or with) all thine heart; and lean thou not to thy prudence (or thine own understanding).

6   In all thy ways think (up)on him, and he shall address (or direct) thy goings.

7   Be thou not wise with thyself; dread thou (or fear, or revere) God, and go away from evil.

8   For why health shall be in thy navel (or thy whole body), and moistening of thy bones.

9   Honour thou the Lord of (or with) thy chattel or substance,

and of the best of all thy fruits give thou to poor men;

10   and (then) thy barns shall be filled with abundance, and thy (wine)presses shall flow with wine.

11   My son, cast thou not away the teaching of the Lord; and fail thou not, when thou art chastised of (or by) him.

12   For the Lord chastiseth him, whom he loveth; and as a father in (or with) the son he pleaseth him (or who pleaseth him).

13   Blessed *is* the man that findeth wisdom, and that floweth with prudence.

14   The getting thereof is better than the merchandise of gold and of silver; the fruits thereof *be* the first and the cleanest.

15   It is more precious than all riches; and all things that be desired, may not (or cannot) be comparisoned to it.

16   The length of days *is* in the right half thereof (or its right hand), and riches and glory *be* in the left half of it (or its left hand).

17   The ways thereof *be* fair ways, and all the paths thereof *be* peaceable.

18   It is a tree of life to them that take it; and he that holdeth it, is blessed.

19   The Lord founded the earth by (his) wisdom; he stablished the heavens by (his) prudence.

20   The depths of the waters brake out by his wisdom; and the clouds waxed (or grew) altogether with dew.

21   My son, these things float or flow not away from thine eyes; keep thou my law (or instructions), and my counsel;

22   and life shall be to thy soul, and grace to thy cheeks (or and thou shalt gain favour).

23   Then thou shalt go trustily in (or on) thy way; and thy foot shall not stumble.

24   If (or when) thou shalt sleep, thou shalt not dread (or fear); thou shalt rest, and thy sleep shall be soft or (be) sweet.

25   Dread thou not of sudden fear, and the powers of wicked men falling in (up)on thee.

26   For the Lord shall be at thy side; and he shall keep thy foot (safe), (so) that thou be not taken (or caught).

27   Do not thou forbid to do well (or good) him that may (or who can do good); if thou mayest, also do thou well (or good).

28   Say thou not to thy friend, Go (away), and return again, and tomorrow I shall give to thee; when thou mayest give anon (or at once) to him.

29   Imagine thou not evil to (or against) thy friend, when he hath trust in thee.

30   Strive thou not against a man without cause, when he doeth none evil (or hath done nothing wrong) to thee.

31   Pursue (or Follow) thou not an unjust man (or a law-breaker), follow thou not his ways.

32   For each deceiver is an abomination to the Lord; and his speaking *is* with simple (or honest) men.

33   Neediness *is sent* of (or by) the Lord in(to) the house of a wicked man; but the dwelling places of rightwise men shall be blessed.

34   He shall scorn the scorners; and he shall give grace to mild (or humble) men.

35   Wise men shall have glory (or honour); the enhancing (or exalting) of fools *is* a shame.

ECCLESIASTICUS CHAPTER 4

1   Son, defraud thou not the alms-deeds of a poor man, and turn not over (or away) thine eyes from the poor.

2   Despise thou not an hungry man, and stir thou not out to wrath a poor man in his neediness or mis-ease.

3   Torment thou not the heart of a needy man or the helpless, and tarry thou not the gift to a man *that is* set in anguish, or draw thou not along a gift to the man put in straits.

4   Cast thou not away the praying of a man set in tribulation or of the troubled, and turn not away thy face from the needy.

5   Turn not away thine eyes from a poor man for wrath, and give not *occasion or cause*, to men asking to curse thee (from) behind.

6   For the prayer of him that curseth thee in the bitterness of (his) soul, shall be heard; forsooth he that made him, shall hear him.

7   Make thee easy to speak to the congregation of poor men, and make meek thy soul to a priest, *that is, do thou due reverence to an old man*, and make meek thine head to a great man.

8   Bow down without sorrow thine ear to the poor, and yield thy debt, and answer thou peaceably in mildness (or with meekness).

9   Deliver thou him that suffereth wrong from the hand of a proud man, and bear thou not heavily in thy soul (when deeming).

10   In deeming (or judging) be thou merciful as a father to father-less children, and *be thou* for an husband to the mother of them; and thou shalt be as an obedient son of the Highest, and he shall have mercy on thee more than a mother *hath mercy on her child*.

11   Wisdom inspireth or inbreathed life to his (or to its) sons, and receiveth men seeking him (or it), and shall go before (them) in the way of rightfulness or rightwiseness;

12   and he that loveth that *wisdom*, loveth life, and they that wake to it, shall embrace the peaceableness, or the gladness, *either sweetness*, of it.

13   They that hold it, shall inherit life; and whither it shall enter, God shall bless.

14   They that serve it, shall be obeying to the Holy (One); and God loveth them, that love it.

15   He that heareth it, deemeth folks (or judgeth the nations); and

he that beholdeth it, shall dwell trustily.

16 If a man believeth to it or give faith to it, he shall dwell, and inherit it; and the creatures of them shall be in confirming, *that is, the works of them shall be confirmed in good.*

17 For in temptation it goeth with him, and among the first it chooseth him. It shall bring in upon him dread, and fear, and proving, and it shall torment him in the tribulation of his doctrine or his teaching, till it tempt him in his thoughts, and (it) believe to (or in) his soul.

18 And it shall make him steadfast, and shall bring the right way to him, and it shall make him glad; and shall make naked his privates to him (or shall make open his secrets to him), and shall treasure on him knowing (or knowledge), and understanding of rightfulness or rightwiseness.

19 Forsooth if he erreth, *God* or it shall forsake him, and shall betake him into the hands of his enemy.

20 Son, keep thou or wait (on) the time, and eschew thou or shun away from evil. Be thou not ashamed (even) for thy life to say the truth;

21 for why there is shame that bringeth sin, and there is shame that bringeth glory and grace.

22 Take thou not a face against thy face, *that is, against thy soul,* neither a leasing (or a lie) against thy soul.

23 Shame thou not thy neighbour in his falling, neither withhold thou a word in the time of health.

24 Hide not thy wisdom in the fairness thereof; for why wisdom is known in the tongue, and wit (or understanding), and knowing (or knowledge), and teaching in the word of a wise man; and steadfastness *is* in the works of rightfulness or rightwiseness.

25 Against-say thou not (or Say thou not against) the word of truth in any manner; and be thou ashamed of the leasing (or lies) of

thy mis-learning.

26   Be thou not ashamed to acknowledge thy sins; and make thee not subject to each man for sin.

27   Do not thou stand against or withstand the face of the mighty, neither endeavor thou against the stroke of the flood (or the river).

28   For rightfulness or rightwiseness fight thou for *the health of* thy soul, and unto the death strive thou for rightfulness or rightwiseness; and God shall overcome thine enemies for thee.

29   Do not thou be swift in (or with) thy tongue, and unprofitable and slack, or sloth(ful), in (or with) thy works.

30   Do not thou be as a lion in thine house, turning upside down thy menials, and oppressing them that be subject/s to thee.

31   Thine hand be not ready to take (or to receive), and closed altogether to give.

ECCLESIASTICUS CHAPTER 5

1   Do not thou take heed to wicked possessions, and say thou not, There is to (or for) me sufficient life, *that is, long is to coming to me, therefore I must get many things*; for it shall nothing profit in the time of vengeance, and of failing or oppressing, *either death*.

2   Pursue thou not or Not follow thou the covetousness of thine heart in (or with all) thy strength,

3   and say thou not, As I might, either, who shall make me subject for my deeds? For why God avenging shall avenge.

4   Say thou not, I have sinned, and what sorrowful thing befell to me? For the Highest is a patient yielder.

5   Of the forgiveness of sins, do not thou be without dread (or fear), neither heap thou, or lay thou, sin upon sin.

6   And say thou not, The mercy of God is great; he shall have mercy on the multitude of my sins. For why mercy and wrath

nigheth soon from him, and his wrath beholdeth (up)on sinners.

7   Tarry thou not to be converted to the Lord, and delay thou not or put thou it off from day into day. For why his wrath shall come suddenly, and he shall lose (or destroy) thee in the time of vengeance.

8   Do not thou be anguished in (or with) unjust or unright riches; for they shall not profit in the day of failing, *either of death*, and of vengeance.

9   Winnow thee not into each wind, and go thou not into each way; for so a sinner is proved in (or with) a double tongue.

10   Be thou steadfast in the way of the Lord, and in truth and the knowing (or the knowledge) of thy wit (or understanding); and the word of peace and of rightfulness or rightwiseness pursue thee perfectly.

11   Be thou mild (or meek) to hear the word of God, (so) that thou understand, and with wisdom bring thou forth a true answer.

12   If thou hast understanding, answer thy neighbor; else thine hand be upon thy mouth, lest thou be taken (or caught) in a word unwisely taught, and be ashamed.

13   Honour and glory *is* in the word of a wise man; but the tongue of an unprudent man is his destroying.

14   Be thou not called a privy evil speaker in thy life, and be thou not taken in (or with) thy tongue, and be ashamed. Shame and penance is upon a thief, and worst shame, *either cursing, is* upon a man of (or with) a double tongue. Forsooth hatred and enmity and despising *is* to a privy backbiter.

15   Justify thou the little and the great in like manner.

ECCLESIASTES CHAPTER 3

1   All things have a time, and all things under the sun pass

(forth) by (or in) their spaces.

2   Time of birth, and time of dying; time to plant, and time to draw up that that is planted.

3   Time to slay, and time to make whole (or to heal); time to destroy, and time to build.

4   Time to weep, and time to laugh; time to bewail, and time to dance.

5   Time to scatter stones, and time to gather (them) together; time to embrace, and time to be far from embracings (or embraces).

6   Time to get, and time to lose (or to set free); time to keep, and time to cast away.

7   Time to cut, and time to sew together; time to be still (or to be silent), and time to speak.

8   Time to love, and time of hatred (or to hate); time of battle, and time of peace (or to make peace).

9   What hath a man more of his travail (or for all his labour)?

10   I saw the torment, which God gave to the sons of men, (so) that they be occupied therein (or by it).

11   God made all things good in their time, and gave the world to disputing of (or over) them, (so) that a man find not (out, or shall not understand) the work that God hath wrought from the beginning unto the end.

12   And (so) I knew that nothing was better *to (or for) a man*, but to be glad, and to do good *works* in his life.

13   For why each man that eateth and drinketh, and seeth the good of his travail (or the good that cometh from all his labour); (yea), this is the gift of God.

14   I have learned that all the works, that God made, last steadfastly unto without end; we may not (or cannot) add anything to those *works*, neither take away from those *things*, which God made, (so) that he be dreaded (or revered).

15 That thing that is made, dwelleth perfectly; those things that shall come, were before; and God restoreth that, that is gone.

16 I saw under the sun unfaithfulness in the place of doom (or judgement); and wickedness in the place of rightfulness or rightwiseness.

17 And I said in mine heart, The Lord shall deem (or judge) a rightwise man, and an unfaithful man; and the (proper) time of (or for) each thing shall be then.

18 I said in mine heart of (or about) the sons of men, that God should prove them, and show (them) that they be like beasts.

19 Therefore one (and the same) is the perishing of man and of beasts, and even (or equal) condition *is* of ever either; (for) as a man dieth, so and those *beasts* die; all (of) *those* breathe in like manner, and a man hath nothing more than a beast. All things be subject to vanity (or Everything is empty and futile),

20 and all things go to one place; they be made of the earth, and they return again altogether into the earth.

21 Who knoweth, if the spirits of the sons of Adam (or of mankind) goeth upward (to heaven), and if the spirits of beasts goeth downward (into the ground)?

22 And I perceived that nothing is better, than that a man be glad in his work, and that this be his part (or portion); for who shall bring (to) him (the knowledge), (so) that he know the things that shall come after him? Δ

DAY 4

PSALM 20

1   *To victory, the psalm of David.* The Lord hear thee in the day of tribulation; the name of God of Jacob defend thee.

2   Send he help to thee from the holy *place*; and from Zion defend he thee.

3   Be he mindful of (or remember) all thy sacrifice; and thy burnt sacrifice be made fat.

4   Give he to thee after thine heart; and confirm he all thy counsel.

5   We shall be glad in thine health (or thy salvation); and we shall be magnified in the name of our God. The Lord fulfill all thine askings (or requests);

6   now I have known, that the Lord hath made safe his christ (or hath saved his anointed one). He shall hear him from his holy heaven; the health (or the deliverance) of his right hand *is* in (or through his) powers.

7   These, *that is, the adversaries, trust* in chariots, and these in horses; but we shall inwardly call in (or upon) the name of our Lord God.

8   They be bound, and felled down; but we have risen, and be raised (up, or victorious).

9   Lord, make thou safe (or save) the king; and hear thou us in the day in which we inwardly call thee.

PSALM 21

1   *To victory, the psalm of David.* Lord, the king shall be glad in thy virtue (or strength); and he shall full out have joy greatly on

thine health (or in thy victory, or salvation).

2   Thou hast given to him the desire of his heart; and thou hast not defrauded him of the will (or the request) of his lips.

3   For thou hast before-come him or wentest before him in the blessings of sweetness; thou hast set or puttest on his head a crown of precious stone.

4   He asked of (or from) thee life, and thou gavest *it* to him; the length of days into the world (or forever), and into the world of world (or forever and ever).

5   His glory is great in thine health (or through thy salvation); thou shalt put glory, and great fairness, upon him.

6   For thou shalt give him into blessing into the world of world (or forever and ever); thou shalt make him glad in joy with thy cheer (or before thy face, or in thy presence).

7   For the king hopeth (or trusteth) in the Lord; and in the mercy of the Highest he shall not be moved (or shaken).

8   (Let) thine hand be found to all thine enemies; (let) thy right hand find all them that hate thee.

9   Thou shalt put them as (in) a furnace of fire in the time of thy cheer (or thy coming); the Lord shall trouble them in his wrath, and fire shall devour them.

10   Thou shalt lose (or destroy) the fruit of them from the earth; and the seed of them from the sons of men.

11   For they bowed (or brought in) evil against thee; they thought (out) counsels (or plans), which they might not stablish.

12   For thou shalt put (or turn) them aback (or make them retreat); in thy remnants thou shalt make ready the cheer of them, (or when thou shalt aim thy arrows at them).

13   Lord, be thou enhanced (or exalted) in thy virtue (or thy strength); we shall sing, and say openly (of) thy virtues (or power).

DAY 4

PSALM 22

1 *To the overcomer, for the morrowtide hind, the psalm of David.*
God, my God, behold thou on me, why hast thou forsaken me?
the words of my trespasses *be* far from mine health (or salvation).

2 My God, I shall cry by day, and thou shalt not hear; and by
night, and not to unwisdom to me (or and I shall not have rest).

3 Forsooth thou, the praising of Israel, dwellest in holiness;

4 our (fore)fathers hoped (or trusted) in thee; they hoped (or
trusted), and thou deliveredest them.

5 They cried to thee, and they were made safe (or saved); they
hoped (or trusted) in thee, and they were not shamed.

6 But I am a worm, and not a man; the shame of men (or
despised), and the out-casting of the people.

7 All men seeing me scorned me; they spake with (their) lips,
and wagged the(ir) heads, *and said,*

8 He hoped (or trusted) in the Lord, deliver he him; make he
him safe (or save him), for he will (or delights in) him.

9 For thou it art that drewest me out of the womb, *that art* mine
hope from the teats (or the breasts) of my mother;

10 into thee I am cast forth from the womb. From the womb of
my mother thou art my God;

11 depart thou not from me. For tribulation is next (or near); for
none there is that helpeth (me).

12 Many calves encompassed me; fat bulls besieged me.

13 They opened their mouth upon me; as (or like) a lion
ravishing (or catching) and roaring.

14 I am poured out as water; and all my bones be scattered. Mine
heart is made, as wax melting; in the midst of my womb.

15 My virtue (or strength) dried (up) as a tilestone, and my

tongue cleaved to my cheeks; and thou hast brought forth me into the dust of death.

16   For many dogs encompassed me; the council of wicked men besieged me. They delved (or pierced) mine hands and my feet;

17   they numbered all my bones. Soothly they looked, and beheld me;

18   they parted my clothes to (or for) themselves, and they sent lot upon my cloth (or my cloak).

19   But thou, Lord, delay not thine help from me; behold thou to my defence.

20   God, deliver thou my life from the sword; and deliver thou mine one alone from the hand, *or the power*, of the dog.

21   Make thou me safe (or save me) from the mouth of a lion; and my meekness from the horns of unicorns (or of these bulls).

22   I shall tell thy name to my brethren (or my kinsmen); I shall praise thee in the midst of the church (or the congregation).

23   Ye that dread (or fear, or revere) the Lord, praise him; all the seed of Jacob, glorify him. All the seed of Israel, dread him;

24   for he forsook not, neither despised the prayer of a poor man or the poor. Neither he turned away his face from me; and when I cried to him, he heard me.

25   My praising is with thee in a great church (or congregation); I shall yield my vows in the sight of men dreading (or fearing) him.

26   Poor men shall eat, and shall be fulfilled, and they shall praise the Lord, that seek him; the hearts of them shall live into the world of world (or forever and ever).

27   All the ends of the earth shall bethink (upon him); and shall be converted to the Lord. And all the families of heathen men, shall worship in his sight (or before him).

28   For the realm (or the kingdom) is the Lord's; and he shall be Lord of the heathen men.

29   All the fat men of the earth ate and worshipped; all men, that go down into the earth, shall fall down in his sight (or before him). And my soul shall live to (or for) him;

30   and my seed shall serve him. The generation to come shall be told to (or about) the Lord;

31   and the heavens shall tell (about) his rightwiseness to the people that shall be born, whom the Lord made (or what the Lord hath done).

PSALM 23

1   *The psalm of David.* The Lord governeth me, and nothing shall fail to me (or there is nothing that I shall lack);

2   in the place of pasture there he hath set me. He nourished me on (or by) the waters of refreshing;

3   he converted (or transformed) my soul. He led me forth on the paths of rightfulness or rightwiseness; for his name.

4   For why though I shall go in the midst of the shadow of death; I shall not dread (or fear) evils, for thou art with me. Thy rod and thy staff; those (or they) have comforted me.

5   Thou hast made ready a board (or a table) in my sight (or before me); against (or before) them that trouble me. Thou hast made fat (or covered) mine head with oil; and my cup, that filleth greatly, is full clear, (or and my cup, which *thou* greatly filleth, is full, and runneth over).

6   And thy mercy (or love) shall pursue or follow me; in all the days of my life. And that I dwell in the house of the Lord; into the length of days (or forever).

PSALM 24

1   *The psalm of David.* The earth and the fullness thereof is the

Lord's; the world, and all that dwell therein.

2   For he founded it upon the seas; and made it ready upon the floods (or rivers).

3   Who shall ascend or go up into (or onto) the hill of the Lord; either who shall stand in the holy place of him?

4   The innocent in hands, *that is, in works*, and in (or with) a clean heart; which (or who) took not his soul in vain, neither swore in guile (or with deceit) to his neighbour.

5   He shall take (or receive) blessing of (or from) the Lord; and the mercy of God his health (or his salvation).

6   This is the generation of men (and women) seeking him; of men (and women) seeking the face of the God of Jacob.

7   Ye princes, take up your gates, (or Lift up your heads, ye gates), and ye everlasting gates, be ye raised (up); and the King of glory shall enter (in).

8   Who is this King of glory? the Lord strong and mighty, the Lord mighty in battle.

9   Ye princes, take up your gates, (or Lift up your heads, ye gates), and ye everlasting gates, be ye raised (up); and the King of glory shall enter (in).

10   Who is this King of glory? the Lord of virtues (or of hosts, or armies), he is the King of glory.

PSALM 25

1   *The song of David.* Lord, to thee I have raised (up) my soul;

2   my God, I trust in thee, be I not ashamed. Neither (let) mine enemies scorn me;

3   for all men that suffer (or wait for) thee shall not be shamed. All men doing wicked things superfluously; be they shamed.

4   Lord, show thou thy ways to me; and teach thou me thy paths.

5   Address thou (or Direct) me in thy truth, and teach thou me, for thou art God, my saviour; and I suffered (or waited for) thee all day.

6   Lord, have thou mind of (or remember) thy merciful doings; and of thy mercies that be from the world (or from long ago).

7   Have thou not mind on (or Do not remember) the trespasses of my youth; and on mine unknowings (or ignorances). Thou, Lord, have mind on (or remember) me by (or with) thy mercy; for thy goodness.

8   The Lord *is* sweet and rightful (or upright); for this *cause* he shall give a law to men trespassing in (or on) the way.

9   He shall address (or direct) meek men in doom (or in their judgement); he shall teach mild (or humble) men his ways.

10   (Let) all the ways of the Lord be mercy and truth; to men seeking his testament (or covenant), and his witnessings (or testimonies).

11   Lord, for thy name, thou shalt do mercy to (or on) my sin; for it is much.

12   Who is a man, that dreadeth (or feareth, or revereth) the Lord? he ordaineth to him a law in the way which he (should) choose.

13   His soul shall dwell in goods (or with good things); and his seed shall inherit the land.

14   The Lord is a firmness to men dreading him; and his testament (or covenant) is, that it be showed to them.

15   Mine eyes *be* evermore toward (or upon) the Lord; for he shall pull away my feet from the snare.

16   Behold thou to me, and have thou mercy on me; for I am one (or all) alone and poor.

17   The tribulations of mine heart be multiplied; deliver thou me of my needs (or from all my troubles).

18   See thou my meekness and my travail (or my troubles); and forgive thou all my trespasses (or all my sins).

19   Behold thou mine enemies, for they be multiplied; and they hate me by (or with such) wicked hatred.

20   Keep thou (safe) my soul, and deliver me; be I not ashamed, for I hoped (or trusted) in thee.

21   Innocent men and rightful cleaved to me; for I suffered (or waited for) thee.

22   God, deliver thou Israel; from all his tribulations (or from all their troubles).

PROVERBS CHAPTER 4

1   Sons, hear ye the teaching of *your* father; and perceive ye (or understand), (so) that ye know prudence.

2   I shall give to you a good gift; forsake ye not my law (or my instructions).

3   For why and I was the son of my father, a tender son, and one begotten, before my mother (or her only child).

4   And *my father* taught me, and said, Thine heart receive my words; keep thou my behests (or obey my commands), and thou shalt live.

5   Wield thou wisdom, wield thou prudence; forget thou not, neither bow thou away from the words of my mouth.

6   Forsake thou not it, and it shall keep thee (safe); love thou it, and it shall keep thee (safe).

7   The beginning of wisdom, (is to) wield thou (or to get) wisdom; and in (or of) all thy possessions, get thou prudence.

8   Take thou (or receive) it, and it shall enhance thee (or raise thee up); thou shalt be glorified of (or by) it (or honoured), when thou hast embraced it.

9   It shall give increasings of graces to thine head (or bring many favours unto thee); and a noble crown shall defend (or adorn) thee.

10   My son, hear thou, and take my words (to heart); (so) that the years of (thy) life be multiplied to thee.

11   I shall show to thee the way of wisdom; and I shall lead thee by the paths of equity (or on the fair ways).

12   Into which when thou hast entered, thy goings shall not be made strait; and thou shalt run, and shalt not have hurting (or not be caused to stumble).

13   Hold thou (fast to my) teaching, and forsake thou it not; keep thou it (near), for it is thy life.

14   Delight thou not in the paths of wicked men; and the way of evil men please not thee.

15   Flee thou from it, and pass thou not thereby; bow thou away, and forsake it.

16   For they sleep not, no but (first) they have done evil; and sleep is ravished (or taken) from them, no but (first) they have deceived *simple men.*

17   They eat the bread of unpiety, and drink the wine of wickedness.

18   But the path of just or rightwise men goeth forth as light shining (or like a shining light), and increaseth till to perfect day.

19   The way of wicked men *is* dark; they know not where, (or when), they shall fall.

20   My son, hearken thou (to) my words; and bow down thine ears to my speeches.

21   Go not they away from thine eyes; keep thou them in the middle of thine heart.

22   For they be life to men finding them, and health of (or for) all (their) flesh.

23   With all (safe) keeping keep thine heart (safe), for life cometh forth of (or from) it.

24   Remove thou a shrewd mouth from thee (or speak not

depraved things); and backbiting lips be far from thee.

25　(Let) thine eyes see rightful things; and thine eyelids go before thy steps.

26　Address thou (or Direct) the paths to (or the steps of) thy feet, and all thy ways shall be stablished.

27　Bow thou not to the right side, neither to the left side; turn away thy foot from evil.

ECCLESIASTICUS CHAPTER 6

1　Do not thou for a friend (or instead of a friend) be made an enemy to *thy* neighbour; for why an evil man shall inherit upbraiding and despising, and each sinner (is) envious and double-tongued.

2　Enhance (or Exalt) thee not in the thought of thy soul, as a bull *doeth*; lest thy virtue (or thy strength) be hurtled down by folly,

3　and it eat thy leaves, and lose (or destroy) thy fruits, and thou be left as a dry tree in the desert or in the wilderness.

4　Forsooth a wicked, or shrewd (or depraved) soul shall lose or destroy him that hath it, and it giveth him into the joy of the enemy, and it shall lead forth into the part of wicked men.

5　A sweet word multiplieth friends, and assuageth enemies; and a tongue well gracious shall be plenteous or abound in a good man.

6　Many peaceable men be to thee, and (or but only) one (out) of a thousand be a counsellor to (or for) thee.

7　If thou hast a friend, have him in temptation, *that is, prove thou him in thine adversity*, and betake not lightly or not lightly open, *or trust*, thyself to him.

8　For there is a friend by (or for) his (own) time, and he shall not dwell or abide in the day of tribulation.

9　And there is a friend which (or who) is turned to enmity; and there is a friend, that shall show openly hatred, and chiding or strife, and despisings.

10　Forsooth there is a friend, a fellow of the table, and (he) dwelleth or abideth not still in the day of need.

11　If a friend dwelleth steadfast, he shall be as a man even with thee, and he shall do trustily in (or with) thy menial or home things (or domestics).

12　If he meeketh himself before thee, and hideth him(self) from thy face, thou shalt have good friendship of one accord or of one will.

13　Be thou parted from thine enemies, and take heed of thy friends.

14　A faithful friend *is* a strong defending or strong protection; forsooth he that findeth him, findeth a treasure.

15　No comparison is to a faithful friend; weighing of gold and of silver is not worthy against the goodness of his faithfulness.

16　A faithful friend *is* the medicine of life, and of undeadliness (or of immortality); and they that dread (or fear, or revere) the Lord, shall find him.

17　He that dreadeth the Lord, shall have evenly good friendship; for why his friend shall be at the likeness of him.

18　Son, from thy youth take thou doctrine, and unto thine hoar hairs thou shalt find wisdom.

19　As he that eareth (or ploweth), and that soweth, nigh thou to it, and abide thou (for) the good fruits thereof. For thou shalt travail a little in the work thereof, and thou shalt eat soon of the generations thereof or the gettings of it.

20　Wisdom is over-sharp or is full-sharp to untaught men, and an heartless man shall not dwell therein.

21　As the virtue (or the strength) of a stone, proving shall be in them; and they shall not tarry to cast away it or to throw it afar.

22   Forsooth the wisdom of teaching is by the name thereof, and it is not open to many men; but it dwelleth with them, of whom it is known, unto the sight of God.

23   Son, hear thou, and take the counsel of understanding, and cast thou not away my counsel.

24   Set-in thy foot into the stocks thereof, and thy neck into the bies (or the bands), or the collars thereof.

25   Make subject thy shoulder, and bear it, and be thou not annoyed (or harmed) in the bonds thereof.

26   In all thy will go to it, and in all thy virtue (or thy strength) keep the ways thereof or of it.

27   Inquire thou (of or about) it or ensearch it, and it shall be made open to thee; and thou made holding *wisdom* forsake not it.

28   For in the last things thou shalt find rest therein, and it shall turn or shall be turned to thee into delighting.

29   And the stocks thereof shall be to thee in(to) a defence or a protection of strength, and the foundaments (or the foundations) of virtue, and the bies (or the bands), or the collars thereof, in(to) a stole of glory.

30   For why the fairness of life is in wisdom, and the bonds thereof *be* healthful or wholesome binding.

31   Thou shalt wear it as a stole of glory, and thou shalt set or put on thee a crown of thanking.

32   Son, if thou takest heed to me, thou shalt learn wisdom; and if thou givest (to it) thy will (or thy determination), thou shalt be wise.

33   If thou bowest down thine ear, thou shalt take (or receive) teaching; and if thou lovest for to hear (it), thou shalt be wise.

34   Stand thou in the multitude of prudent priests, and be thou joined of (or in) heart to the wisdom of them;

35   (so) that thou mayest hear each telling of God, and the proverbs of praising flee not or fly not away from thee.

36   And if thou seest a wise man, wake thou to him, and thy foot often tread upon the grees (or the steps) of his doors.

37   Have thou thought in (or on) the commandments of God, and be thou most busy in his behests (or decrees); and he shall give to thee an heart *to understand and work them*, and covetousness of (or for) wisdom shall (also) be given to thee.

ECCLESIASTES CHAPTER 4

1   I turned me to other things, and I saw false challenges (or oppression), that be done under the sun, and the tears of the guiltless, and (that) no man (was a) comforter; and that they destitute, *either forsaken*, of the help of all men, may not (or cannot) against-stand the violence of them.

2   And I praised more the dead than the living;

3   and I deemed (or judged) him, that was not born yet, and saw not the evils that be done under the sun, *to be* more blessed than ever either.

4   Again I beheld all the travails (or the labours) of men, and busynesses; and I perceived that those (or they) be open to the envy of the neighbour; and therefore in this is vanity (or emptiness and futility), and superfluous busyness.

5   A fool foldeth together his hands, and eateth his flesh (or his meat),

6   and saith, Better is an handful, with rest, than ever either hand full, with travail (or labour) and torment of (or for) the soul.

7   I beheld and found also another vanity (or more emptiness and futility) under the sun;

8   one there is (or one is alone), and he hath not a second; neither a son, nor a brother; and nevertheless he ceaseth not to travail (or labour), neither his eyes be (ful)filled with (his) riches;

neither he bethinketh *to him*(*self*), and saith, To whom travail I (or For whom am I working), and deceive my soul in goods (or with good things)? In this also is vanity, and the worst torment.

9   Therefore it is better, that two be together than one; for they have profit of (or benefit from) their fellowship.

10   If one falleth down, he shall be under-set of (or helped up by) the tother; woe to him that is alone, for when he falleth, he hath none to raise him up (again).

11   And if twain (or two) sleep *together*, they shall be nourished together; (but) how shall one be made hot?

12   And if any man hath the mastery against one, twain against-stand him; a threefold cord is broken of hard (or is much harder to break).

13   A poor man and wise is better than an old king and fool(ish), that cannot before-see into the time to coming (or the time to come).

14   For sometime a man goeth out, both from prison and chains, to a realm (or and becometh a king); and another, born into a realm, is wasted by neediness.

15   I saw all men living that go under the sun, with the second young waxing (or growing) man, that shall rise (up) for him, (or and yet for each, someone young shall rise up, and shall take their place).

16   The number of people, of all that were before him, is great without measure, and they that shall come afterward, shall not be glad in him (or shall not be grateful to him); but also this *is* vanity (or empty and futile) and a torment of (or for) the spirit. Δ

DAY 5

PSALM 26

1   *The psalm of David.* Lord, deem (or judge) thou me, for I entered (or walked) in mine innocence; and I hoping (or trusting) in the Lord, shall not be made unsteadfast (or to waver).

2   Lord, prove thou me, and assay me; burn thou my reins, and mine heart.

3   For why thy mercy (or thy love) is (evermore) before mine eyes; and I (am always) pleased in (or by) thy truth.

4   I sat not with the counsel of vanity (or those who make empty and futile plans); and I shall not enter (or go along) with men doing wicked things.

5   I hated the church (or the congregation, or assembly) of evil men; and I shall not sit with wicked men.

6   I shall wash mine hands among the innocents (or in innocence); and, Lord, I shall compass (or go about) thine altar.

7   (So) that I hear the voice of praising; and (so) that I tell out all thy marvels.

8   Lord, I have loved the fairness (or the beauty) of thine house; and the place of the dwelling of thy glory.

9   God, lose (or destroy) thou not my soul (along) with unfaithful men; and my life with men of bloods (or murderers).

10   In whose hands wickednesses be; the right hand of them is full-filled with gifts (or with bribes).

11   But I entered in mine innocence; again-buy (or redeem) thou me, and have mercy on me.

12   My foot stood in rightfulness (or on level ground); Lord, I shall bless thee in the churches (or in the congregations, or the assemblies).

DAY 5

PSALM 27

1   *The holy prayer of David.* The Lord *is* my lightening, and mine health (or my salvation); whom shall I dread (or fear)? The Lord *is* the defender of my life; for whom shall I tremble or quake?

2   The while noisome men nigh on me; for to eat my fleshes. Mine enemies, that troubled me; they were made sick (or feeble), and felled down.

3   Though tents (or hosts, or armies) stand together against me; mine heart shall not dread (or fear). Though battle riseth against me; in this thing I shall have hope (or trust).

4   I asked of the Lord (only) one thing; I shall seek this thing; that I dwell in the house of the Lord all the days of my life. That I see the will (or the beauty) of the Lord; and that I visit his temple.

5   For he hid me in his tabernacle in the day of evils; he defended me in the hid place of his tabernacle. He enhanced me in (or lifted me up upon) a stone;

6   and now he enhanced (or lifted up) mine head over mine enemies. I compassed, and offered in his tabernacle a sacrifice of crying out; I shall sing, and I shall say a psalm to the Lord.

7   Lord, hear thou my voice, by which I cried to thee; have thou mercy on me, and hear (or answer) me.

8   Mine heart said to thee, My face sought thee; Lord, I shall seek again thy face. (And thou saidest, Seek ye my face; and my heart said to thee, Lord, I shall seek thy face.)

9   Turn thou not away thy face from me; bow thou not away in wrath from thy servant. Lord, be thou mine helper, forsake thou not me; and, God, mine health (or my salvation), despise thou not me.

10   For my father and my mother have forsaken me; but the Lord hath taken me (up) (or shall still take care of me).

11   Lord, set thou a law to me in (or on) thy way; and address (or direct) thou me in a rightful path, for (or because of) mine enemies.

12   Betake thou not me into (or unto) the souls of them, that trouble me; for wicked witnesses have risen against me, and wickedness lied to itself (or the wicked lie even to themselves!).

13   I believe to see the good(ness) of the Lord; in the land of living men.

14   Abide thou (or wait for) the Lord, do thou manly; and thine heart be comforted (or strengthened), and suffer thou (or wait for) the Lord.

PSALM 28

1   *The psalm to this David.* Lord, I shall cry to thee; my God, be thou not still from me (or deaf to me), be thou not still any time from me; and (or) I shall be made like to them, that go down into the pit.

2   Lord, hear thou the voice (or the words) of my beseeching, while I pray to thee; while I raise (up) mine hands to(ward) thine holy temple.

3   Betake thou not me together with sinners; and lose (or destroy) thou not me with them that work wickedness. Which speak peace to their neighbour(s); but evils *be* in their hearts.

4   Give thou to them after (or according to) the works of them; and after the wickedness of their findings. Give thou to them after the works of their hands; yield thou their yielding to them.

5   For (or Because) they understood not the works of the Lord, and by the works of his hands thou shalt destroy them; and thou shalt not build them.

6   Blessed *be* the Lord; for he heard the voice of my beseeching (or plea).

7   The Lord *is* mine helper and my defender; and mine heart hoped (or trusted) in him, and I am helped. And my flesh flowered again; and (out) of my will (or from my heart) I shall acknowledge to him.

8   The Lord *is* the strength of his people; and he is the defender of the savings of his christ (or his anointed *king*).

9   Lord, make thou safe (or save) thy people, and bless thou thine heritage (or thy inheritance); and rule thou them, and enhance thou them (or lift them up) till into without end (or forevermore).

PSALM 29

1   *The psalm of David.* Ye sons of God, bring to the Lord; bring ye to the Lord, the sons of rams. Bring ye to the Lord glory and honour;

2   bring ye to the Lord glory to his name; praise ye the Lord in his holy large place (or in his holy Temple).

3   The voice of the Lord (is heard) upon the waters, God of majesty thundered; the Lord (is heard) upon many waters.

4   The voice of the Lord in virtue (or in strength); the voice of the Lord in great doing.

5   The voice of the Lord breaking cedars; and the Lord shall break the cedars of Lebanon.

6   And he shall all-break them (un)to dust, as a calf of the Lebanon; and the darling *was* as the son of an unicorn.

7   The voice of the Lord parting the flames of fire (or the flashes of lightning);

8   the voice of the Lord shaking the desert; and the Lord shall stir

(or shake) altogether the desert of Kadesh.

9   The voice of the Lord making ready harts (to calve), and he shall show thick things (or bringeth the goat kids early to their birth); and in his temple all men shall say (or shout) glory(!).

10   The Lord maketh to inhabit (or ruleth over) the great flood; and the Lord shall sit (as) King (into) without end (or forever).

11   The Lord shall give virtue (or strength) to his people; the Lord shall bless his people in (or with) peace.

PSALM 30

1   *The psalm of the song, for the hallowing (or the dedication) of the house of David.* Lord, I shall enhance (or exalt) thee, for thou hast up-taken me; and thou delightedest not mine enemies on me.

2   My Lord God, I cried to thee; and thou madest me whole.

3   Lord, thou leddest out my soul from hell (or the grave); thou savedest me from them that go down into the pit.

4   Ye saints of the Lord, sing to the Lord; and acknowledge ye to the mind of (or the remembrance of) his holiness.

5   For ire (or anger) *is* in his indignation; and life *is* in his will (or favour). Weeping shall dwell at eventide; and gladness at (or in) the morrowtide.

6   Forsooth I said in my plenty; I shall not be moved (or shaken) without end.

7   Lord, in thy will; thou hast given virtue to my fairness (or thou hast protected me). (But then) thou turnedest away thy face from me; and I am made troubled.

8   Lord, I shall cry to thee; and I shall pray to my God.

9   (And I said), What profit *is* in my blood; while I go down into corruption? Whether dust shall acknowledge to (or praise) thee;

either it shall tell (out) thy truth?

10   The Lord heard, and had mercy on me; the Lord is made mine helper.

11   Thou hast turned my wailing into joy to me; thou hast rent my sackcloth, and hast encompassed me with gladness.

12   (So) that my glory sing to thee, and I be not compunct; my Lord God, I shall acknowledge to (or praise) thee without end.

PSALM 31

1   *To victory, the psalm of David.* Lord, I have hoped in (or trusted) thee, be I not shamed without end; deliver thou me in thy rightwiseness.

2   Bow down thine ear to me; hasten thou to deliver me. Be thou to me into God a defender, and into an house of refuge; (so) that thou make me safe (or save me).

3   For thou art my strength and my refuge; and for thy name, thou shalt lead me forth, and shalt nourish me.

4   Thou shalt lead me out of the snare, which they hid to (or for) me; for thou art my defender.

5   I betake (or entrust) my spirit into thine hands; Lord God of truth, thou hast again-bought (or redeemed) me.

6   Thou hatest them that keep vanities superfluously (or worship useless idols). Forsooth I hoped in (or trusted) the Lord;

7   I shall have full out joy, and shall be glad in thy mercy (or love). For thou beheldest my meekness; thou savedest my life from needs (or distress).

8   And thou enclosedest not me altogether within the hands of the enemy; thou hast set my feet in a large (or broad) place.

9   Lord, have thou mercy on me, for I am troubled; mine eye is troubled in ire (or anger), my soul and my womb *also*.

10   For why my life failed in sorrow; and my years in wailings. My virtue (or strength) is made feeble in poverty; and my bones be troubled (or diseased).

11   Over all mine enemies I am made a shame, and greatly to my neighbours; and (an object of) dread to my known (or my acquaintances). They that saw me withoutforth (or outside), fled from me;

12   I am given to forgetting (or I am forgotten), as a dead man from the heart. I am made as a forlorn vessel;

13   for I heard despising of (or from) many men dwelling in compass. In that thing while they came together against me; they counselled (or planned) to take my life.

14   But, Lord, I hoped (or put my trust) in thee; I said, Thou art my God;

15   my times *be* (or my life *is*) in thine hands. Deliver thou me from the hands of mine enemies; and from them that pursue (or persecute) me.

16   Make thou clear thy face (or Make thy face to shine) upon thy servant; Lord, make thou me safe in thy mercy (or save me in thy love);

17   be I not shamed, for I inwardly called thee. Unpious men be ashamed, and be they led forth into hell (or the grave);

18   (let) guileful (or deceitful) lips be made dumb. (They) that speak wickedness against the rightwise; in pride, and in mis-using or abusing.

19   Lord, the multitude of thy sweetness *is* full great; which thou hast hid to men dreading (or fearing) thee. Thou hast made a perfect thing to them that hope (or trust) in thee; in the sight of (or before) the sons of men.

20   Thou shalt hide them in the private of thy face (or in the secret of thy presence); from the troubling of men. Thou shalt

defend them in thy tabernacle; from the against-saying of tongues.

21   Blessed *be* the Lord; for he hath made wonderful (or shown) his mercy (or love) to me in a strengthened (or fortified) city.

22   Forsooth I said in the out-passing (or going forth) of my soul; I am cast out from the face of thine eyes (or from before thee). There-fore thou heardest the voice of my prayer; while (or when) I cried to thee.

23   All ye holy men of the Lord, love him; for the Lord shall seek truth (or preserve the faithful), and he shall yield plenteously to them that do pride.

24   All ye that hope (or trust) in the Lord, do ye manly; and your heart be comforted (or strengthened).

PROVERBS   CHAPTER 5

1   My son, perceive thou my wisdom, and bow down thine ear to my prudence;

2   (so) that thou keep thy thoughts (proper), and thy lips keep teaching (or guard knowledge).

3   Give thou not attention to the falseness of a woman; for the lips of an whore *be* (like) an honeycomb dropping (or dripping), and her throat *is* clearer than oil;

4   but the last things of her *be* (as) bitter as wormwood, and her tongue *is* (as) sharp as a sword carving, (*or cutting*), on each side.

5   Her feet go down(ward) into (or unto) death; and her steps pierce to hell (or shall lead thee to the grave).

6   They go not by (or on) the path of life; her steps be uncertain, and may not be sought out (or should not be followed).

7   Now therefore, my son, hear thou me (or listen to me), and go thou not away from the words of my mouth.

8   Make far thy way from her, and nigh thou not to the doors of

her house.

9   Give thou not thine honour to aliens (or strangers), and thy years to the cruel;

10   lest peradventure strangers be filled with thy strengths (or thy wealth), and lest (the rewards of) thy travails be in an alien's house;

11   and thou bewail in the last days, when thou hast wasted thy flesh, and thy body;

12   and (thou) say, Why loathed I teaching or discipline, and mine heart assented not to blamings (or to rebukes);

13   neither I heard the voice of men teaching me, and I bowed not down mine ear to masters?

14   Almost I was in all-evil, in the midst of the church (or the congregation), and of the synagogue (or the assembly).

15   Drink thou water of (or from) thy cistern, and the floods of thy well (or the out-flowings from thy own well).

16   Thy wells be streamed (or floweth) forth; and part thy waters in the streets.

17   Have thou alone them; and aliens (or strangers) be not thy partners.

18   (Let) thy vein (or thy fountain) be blessed; and be thou glad with the woman of thy young waxing (or growing) age.

19   An hind (or deer) most dearworthy; and an hart calf most acceptable. Her teats (ful)fill thee in all time; and delight thou continually in the love of her.

20   My son, why art thou deceived of (or by) an alien (or foreign) woman; and art fostered (or comforted) in the bosom of another?

21   The Lord seeth the ways of a man; and he beholdeth all his steps.

22   The wickednesses of a wicked man take (hold of) him; and he is bound with the ropes of his sins.

23   He shall die, for he had not learning; and he shall be

deceived or beguiled in the muchliness or multitude of his folly.

ECCLESIASTICUS CHAPTER 7

1   Do not thou do evils, and they shall not take or catch thee.

2   Depart thou from wickedness or Go away from the wicked, and evils shall fail from thee.

3   Sow thou not evils in the furrows of unrightwiseness, and thou shalt not reap them in sevenfold.

4   Do not thou seek of (or from) a man the leading or the dignity of a leader, neither of (or from) a king the chair of honour.

5   Justify thou not thee (or thyself) before God, for he is the knower of the heart; and do not thou desire to be seen wise with (or before) the king.

6   Do not thou seek to be made a judge, no but thou mayest break wickednesses by (thy) virtue; lest thou dread (or fear) the face of a mighty man, and set slander (or a cause of stumbling) in thy swiftness.

7   Do not thou sin in (or against) the multitude of a city, neither send thee (or thyself) (down) into the people;

8   neither bind thou to double sins, for thou shalt not be guiltless in one.

9   Do not thou be a coward in thy soul, to pray; and despise thou not to do alms-deeds.

10   Say thou not, God shall behold in the multitude of my gifts; and when I shall offer to God alder-highest or to the highest God, he shall take my gifts.

11   Scorn thou not a man in the bitterness of (his) soul; for why God is the beholder, that maketh meek, and enhanceth (or exalteth).

12   Do not thou love a leasing (or a lie) against thy brother;

neither do thou in like manner against a friend.

13   Do not thou desire to lie any leasing (or any lie); for why the continuance thereof or the busyness forsooth of them is not good.

14   Do not thou be a jangler or full of words in the multitude of priests; and rehearse thou not a word in thy prayer.

15   Hate thou not travailous (or labourious) works, and earth-tilthing or churlish doing, made of (or from) the Highest.

16   Areckon thou not thee in the multitude of unlearned men. Have thou mind on (or Remember that) wrath, for it shall not tarry (long).

17   Make thou meek greatly (or Greatly humble) thy spirit, for why the vengeance of the flesh of an unpious man *is* fire, and worms.

18   Do not thou trespass against thy friend delaying money; neither despise thou a full dearworthy brother for gold.

19   Do not thou depart or go away from a wise woman, and good, whom thou hast gotten in the dread of (or because of thy reverence for) the Lord; for why the grace (or gift) of her shamefastness *is* above gold.

20   Hurt thou not a servant working in truth (or faithfully), neither an hired man giving his life.

21   A witty (or a witting, or knowing) servant be dearworthy to thee as thy (own) soul; defraud thou not him of freedom, neither forsake thou him (when) needy.

22   Beasts be to thee? take thou heed to them; and if they be profitable, dwell they still with thee.

23   Sons be to thee? teach thou them, and bow thou them *under chastising* from their childhood.

24   Daughters be to thee? keep thou (or guard) the body of them, and show thou not a glad face to them.

DAY 5

25   Give thy daughter *to marriage*, and thou doest a great work; and give thou her to a wise man.

26   If a woman is to thee after thy soul (or of like-mind), cast her not away; and (or but) betake thou not thee in all thine heart to an hateful *woman*.

27   Honour thy father; and forget thou not the wailings of thy mother.

28   Have thou mind (or Remember) that thou haddest not been, no but by them, and yield thou to them as they *did* to thee.

29   In all thy soul dread thou (or fear, or revere) God, and hallow thou his priests.

30   In all thy virtue (or strength) love thou him that made thee; and forsake thou not his ministers or servants.

31   Honour thou God of (or with) all thy soul; and honour thou priests, and cleanse thee with (thine) arms, *that is, by offerings gotten with thy travail (or labour)*. Give thou to them the part (or portion) of the first fruits, and of purging, as also it is commanded to thee; and of thy negligence purge thou thee with few men. Thou shalt offer to the Lord the gift of thine arms, and the sacrifice of hallowing, the beginnings, *that is, the first fruits and dimes (or tithes)*, of holy men or holy things.

32   And address (or direct) or put forth thine hand to the poor, (so) that thy mercy and (thy) blessing be performed.

33   Grace is given or Grace of gift in the sight of (or before) each that liveth; and forbid thou not grace to a dead man.

34   Fail thou not in (or to do) comfort to them that weep; and go thou with them that mourn.

35   Be thou not slow to visit the sick; for by these things thou shalt be made steadfast in love.

36   In all thy works have thou mind on or have in mind thy last things; and thou shalt not do sin without end.

DAY 5

ECCLESIASTES CHAPTER 5

1   Thou that enterest into the house of God, keep thy foot, and nigh thou (or approach) for to hear; for why much better is obedience, than the sacrifice of fools, that know not what evil they do.

2   Speak thou not anything follily (or foolishly), neither (let) thine heart be swift to bring forth a word before God; for God *is* in heaven, and thou art on the earth, therefore (let) thy words be few.

3   Dreams follow many busynesses, and folly shall be found in many words.

4   If thou hast vowed anything to God, tarry thou not to yield *it*; for an unfaithful and fond promise displeaseth him; but yield thou whatever thing thou hast avowed;

5   and it is much better to make not a vow, than after a vow to yield not the promises.

6   Give thou not thy mouth, that thou make thy flesh to do sin; neither say thou before an angel, No purveyance there is (or This is but a mistake); lest peradventure the Lord be wroth on (or with) thy words, and destroy all the works of thine hands.

7   Where be many dreams, *be* full many vanities (or much that *is* empty and futile), and words without number; but dread thou God.

8   If thou seest false challenges (or the oppression) of needy men, and violent dooms (or grave injustice), and that rightfulness or rightwiseness is destroyed in the province, wonder thou not on this doing; for another is higher than an high man, and also other men be more high above these men;

9   and furthermore the king of all the earth (or the whole land) commandeth to the servant.

10   An avaricious (or greedy) man shall not be fulfilled of (or

with) money; and he that loveth riches shall not take (or fully enjoy the) fruits of them; and therefore this *is* vanity (or empty and futile).

11   Where there be many riches, also many men there *be*, that eat them; and what profiteth it to the holder, but that he seeth the riches with his eyes?

12   Sleep is sweet to him that worketh, whether he eat little either much; but the fullness of a rich man suffereth not (or will not allow) him to sleep.

13   Also another sickness is full evil, which I saw under the sun; riches (that) *be* kept into the harm of their lord.

14   For they perish in the worst torment; (and so) he begat a son, that shall be (left) in sovereign neediness.

15   As he went naked out of his mother's womb, so he shall return again; and he shall take away with him nothing of his travail (or his labour).

16   Utterly *it is* a wretched sickness; as he came, so he shall return again. What profiteth it to him, that he travailed into (or only laboured for) the wind?

17   In all the days of his life he ate in darknesses, and in many busynesses, and in neediness, and sorrow.

18   Therefore this seemed good to me, that a man eat, and drink, and use gladness of his travail (or get happiness from the fruits of his labour), in which he travailed (or laboured) under the sun, in the number of days of his life, which God gave to him; and this is his part (or portion).

19   And to each man, to whom God gave riches, and chattel or substance, and gave power to him to eat of them (or to enjoy them), and to use his part (or portion), and to be glad of his travail (or happy in his work); this is the gift of God.

20   For he shall not think much on the days of his life, for God occupieth his heart with delights. Δ

DAY 6

PSALM 32

1   *The understanding of David.* Blessed (or Happy) *be* they, whose wickedness be forgiven; and whose sins be covered.

2   Blessed (or Happy) *is* the man, to whom the Lord areckoned not sin; neither guile (or deceit) is in his spirit.

3   For I was still, my bones waxed (or grew) old; while I cried all day.

4   For by day and night thine hand was made grievous (or heavy) on me; I am turned in my wretchedness, while the thorn is set in.

5   I made my sin known to thee; and I hid not my unrightfulness or unrightwiseness. I said, I shall acknowledge against me mine unrightfulness to the Lord; and thou hast forgiven the wickedness of my sin.

6   For this thing each holy man shall pray to thee; in covenable (or suitable) time. Nevertheless in the great flood of many waters; they shall not (come) nigh to thee.

7   Thou art my refuge from tribulation, that encompassed me; thou, my fully joying or my full out joy, deliver me from them that encompass me.

8   (The Lord said), I shall give understanding to thee, and I shall teach thee; in this way in which thou shalt go, I shall make steadfast mine eyes upon thee.

9   Do not ye be made as an horse and mule; to which is none understanding. Lord, constrain thou the cheeks of them with a barnacle (or a bit) and bridle; (so) that (they) nigh not to thee.

10   Many beatings be of (or to) the sinner; but mercy shall encompass him that hopeth (or trust) in the Lord.

11   Ye rightwise, be glad, and make fully joy in the Lord; and all

ye rightful of heart, have glory.

PSALM 33

1   Ye rightwise, have fully joy in the Lord; praising (him) altogether becometh rightful men.

2   Acknowledge ye to (or Praise) the Lord in (or on) an harp; sing ye to him in a psaltery (or with a lyre) of ten strings.

3   Sing ye to him a new song; say ye well a psalm to him in crying out.

4   For the word of the Lord is rightful or right (or true); and all his works be (done) in faithfulness.

5   He loveth mercy and doom (or justice); the earth is full of the mercy of the Lord.

6   The heavens be made steadfast by the word of the Lord; and all the virtue (or the host) of them by the spirit of his mouth.

7   And he gathered together the waters of the sea as in a bouget or a bottle; and he setteth deep waters in (his) treasures or treasuries (or storehouses).

8   All the earth dread (or fear) the Lord; soothly all men inhabiting the world be moved (or be in awe) of him.

9   For he said, and things were made; he commanded, and (all) things were made of nought (or out of nothing!).

10   The Lord destroyeth the counsels of the folks (or nations), forsooth he reproveth the thoughts of the peoples; and he reproveth the counsels of princes (or rulers).

11   But the counsel (or the plans) of the Lord dwelleth (into) without end; the thoughts of his heart *dwell* in generation and into generation.

12   Blessed (or Happy) *is* the folk (or nations), whose Lord is his (or their) God; the people which he chose into heritage to (or as an

inheritance for) himself.

13   The Lord beheld from heaven; he saw all the sons (and daughters) of men.

14   From his dwelling place made ready before; he beheld on all men (and women), that inhabit the earth.

15   Which made singularly, *either each by himself*, the souls of them; which understandeth all the works of them.

16   A king is not saved by much virtue (or a large army), *that is, strength*; and a giant shall not be saved in the muchliness of his virtue (or strength).

17   An horse *is* false to health (or salvation); forsooth he shall not be saved in the abundance, *either plenty*, of his virtue (or strength).

18   Lo! the eyes of the Lord *be* on men dreading (or fearing, or revering) him; and in (or on) them that hope in his mercy (or trust in his love).

19   (So) that he deliver their souls from death; and feed them in hunger.

20   Our soul suffereth the Lord, *that is, abideth patiently his will* (*to be done*); for he is our helper and defender.

21   For our hearts shall be glad in him; and we shall have hope (or trust) in his holy name.

22   Lord, thy mercy be made (or rest) upon us; as (or for) we hoped in thee.

PSALM 34

1   *To David, when he changed his mouth, or his word, or his face before Abimelech, and he drove out David, and he went forth or went away.* I shall bless the Lord in all time; evermore his praising *be* in my mouth.

2   My soul shall be praised (or glory) in the Lord; mild (or meek)

men hear, and be glad.

3   Magnify ye the Lord with me; and enhance we his name into itself (or let us exalt his name together).

4   I sought the Lord, and he heard me; and he delivered (or saved) me from all my tribulations (or troubles).

5   Nigh ye to him, and be ye lightened; and your faces shall not be shamed.

6   This poor man cried, and the Lord heard him; and saved him from all his tribulations.

7   The angel of the Lord sendeth in the compass of men dreading him, (or surroundeth and guardeth those who fear or revere him); and he shall deliver them.

8   Taste ye, and see, for the Lord is sweet (or good); blessed *is* the man, that hopeth (or trusteth) in him.

9   All ye holy men of the Lord, dread ye (or fear, or revere) him; for no neediness is to men dreading (or fearing, or revering) him.

10   Rich men were needy, and were hungry; but men that seek the Lord shall not fail of all good (or of any good thing).

11   Come, ye sons, hear ye me; I shall teach you the dread (or fear) of (or reverence for) the Lord.

12   Who is the man, that willeth (or desireth) life; *that* loveth to see good days?

13   Forbid thy tongue from evil; and thy lips speak not guile (or deceit, or deception).

14   Turn thou away from evil, and do good; seek thou peace, and perfectly pursue thou it.

15   The eyes of the Lord *be* upon the rightwise; and his ears *be* to their prayers.

16   But the cheer (or face) of the Lord *is* upon (or against) men doing evils; that he lose the mind (or destroy or blot out the memory) of them from the earth.

17   The rightwise cried, and the Lord heard them; and delivered them from all their tribulations (or troubles).

18   The Lord is nigh to them that be of troubled heart; and he shall save meek men (or the humble) in spirit.

19   Many tribulations *be* of (or to) the rightwise; and the Lord shall deliver them from all (of) these.

20   The Lord keepeth (safe, or guardeth) all the bones of them; one of them shall not be broken.

21   The death of sinners *is* the worst; and they that hate the rightwise shall trespass.

22   The Lord shall again-buy (or redeem) the souls of his servants; and all, that hope in him, shall not trespass.

PSALM 35

1   *The psalm of David.* Lord, deem (or judge) thou them, that annoy (or harm) me; overcome thou them, that fight against me.

2   Take thou (up) arms (or weapons), and shield; and rise up into help to (or for) me.

3   Hold (or Draw) out the sword, and close altogether (the way) against them that pursue me; say thou to my soul, I am thine health (or thy salvation).

4   (Let) they that seek my life; be shamed, and ashamed. (Let) they that think evils to me; be turned away backward, and be they shamed.

5   Be they made as dust before the face of the wind; and the angel of the Lord make them strait (or pursue them).

6   Their way be made darkness, and sliderness (or slippery); and the angel of the Lord pursue them.

7   For without cause they hid to me the death of their snare (or their deadly snare); in vain they despised my soul.

8   (Let) the snare which (or when) he knoweth not come to (or catch) him, and the taking which he hid take him; and fall he into the snare in that thing.

9   But my soul shall fully have joy or full out joyeth in the Lord; and shall delight on his health (or in his salvation).

10   All my bones shall say, Lord, who is like thee? Thou deliverest a poor man or the helpless from the hand of his stronger; a needy man and poor from them that diversely ravish (or oppress) him.

11   Wicked witnesses rising (up) asked me things, which I knew not.

12   They yielded to me evils for goods; barrenness to my soul.

13   But when they were dis-easeful to me; I was clothed in an hair-shirt. I meeked my soul in fasting; and my prayer shall be returned into my bosom.

14   I pleased so as (if he was) our neighbour, as our brother; I was made meek, so as (if) mourning and sorrowful.

15   And they were glad, and came together against me; torments were gathered upon me, and I knew *it* not. They were scattered, and not compunct;

16   they tempted me, they scorned me with mocking, they gnashed upon me with their teeth.

17   Lord, when thou shalt behold, restore thou my soul from the wickedness of them; mine one alone (life) from the lions.

18   I shall acknowledge to (or thank) thee in a great church (or congregation); I shall praise thee in (or before) a firm people.

19   They that be adversaries wickedly to me, have not joy upon me; that hate me without cause, and beckon with the eyes.

20   For soothly they spake (not) peaceably to me; and they speaking in wrathfulness of the earth, thought guiles (or deception, or deceitfulness).

21   And they made large their mouth upon me; (and) they said,

Well, well! (now) our eyes have seen (it all!).

22   Lord, thou hast seen, be thou not still; Lord, depart thou not from me.

23   Rise up, and give attention to my doom (or give me justice); my God and my Lord, *behold* into my cause.

24   My Lord God, deem thou me by thy rightwiseness; and have they not joy over me.

25   Say they not in their hearts, Well, well, to our soul; neither say they, We shall devour him.

26   Shame they, and dread they altogether; that joy for (or over) mine evils. Be they clothed with shame and dread; that speak evil things upon me.

27   Have they full out joy, and be they glad, that will (or desire) my rightfulness; and say they evermore, The Lord be magnified, which will (or who desireth) the peace of his servant.

28   And my tongue shall bethink (on) thy rightwiseness; all day thy praising.

PROVERBS CHAPTER 6

1   My son, if thou hast promised for thy friend, thou hast fastened thine hand at (or to) a stranger.

2   Thou art bound by the words of thy mouth; and *thou art* taken (or caught) with thine own words (or promises).

3   Therefore, my son, do thou that that I say, and deliver (or save) thyself; for thou hast fallen into the hand of thy neighbour. Run thou about, hasten thou, raise (or implore) thy friend;

4   give thou not sleep to thine eyes, neither (let) thine eyelids nap.

5   Be thou ravished (or released), as a doe from the hand; and as a bird from the ambushings of the fowler.

6   O! thou slow (or lazy) man, go to the ant; and behold thou his ways, and learn thou wisdom.

7   Which when he hath no duke, neither commander, nor prince;

8   maketh ready in summer meat to (or food for) himself, and gathereth together in harvest that, that he shall eat.

9   How long shalt thou, slow man, sleep? when shalt thou rise from thy sleep?

10   A little thou shalt sleep, a little thou shalt nap; (and) a little thou shalt join together thine hands (so) that thou sleep (again).

11   And *then* neediness, as a way-goer, shall come to thee; and poverty, as an armed man. Forsooth if thou art not slow, thy ripe corn shall come as a well; and neediness shall flee far from thee.

12   A man apostate, a man unprofitable, (is) he (who) goeth with a wayward mouth;

13   he beckoneth with the eyes, he trampeth with the foot, he speaketh with the finger,

14   by shrewd (or a depraved) heart he imagineth evil, and in all times he soweth dissensions.

15   His perdition shall come to him anon, and he shall be broken suddenly; and he shall no more have medicine.

16   Six things there be, which the Lord hateth; and his soul curseth the seventh thing.

17   High eyes, a tongue liar, *that is, accustomable to deadly leasing (or lies)*, hands shedding out innocent blood,

18   an heart imagining full wicked thoughts, feet swift to run into evil,

19   a man bringing forth leasing (or lies), a false witness; and him that soweth discord among brethren.

20   My son, keep the commandments of thy father; and forsake thou not the law (or instructions) of thy mother.

21   Bind thou those continually in (or to) thine heart; and encompass to thy throat (or about thy neck).

22   When thou goest, go they with thee; when thou sleepest, keep they thee (safe); and thou waking, speak with them.

23   For the commandment *of God* is a lantern, and the law *is* a light, and the blaming (or rebuke, or correction) of teaching *is* the way of life;

24   (so) that they keep thee from an evil woman, and from a flattering tongue of a strange woman.

25   Thine heart covet not the fairness of her; neither be thou taken (in) by the beckonings of her.

26   For the price of a whore is scarcely a gobbet (or a piece) of bread; but (such) a woman taketh (away) the precious soul of a man.

27   Whether a man may hide fire in his bosom, (so) that his clothes burn not;

28   either go upon coals, and his feet be not burnt?

29   So he that entereth to the wife of his neighbour; (he) shall not be clean, when he hath touched her.

30   It is no great sin, when a man stealeth; for he stealeth to fill an hungry soul.

31   And he (is) taken or caught, shall yield (back) the sevenfold; and he shall give all the chattel or substance of his house, and (so he) shall deliver himself.

32   But he that is an adulterer, shall lose (or destroy) his (own) soul, for the poverty of heart, *that is, (for the) wanting of reason.*

33   He gathereth filth, and scandal to himself; and his shame shall not be done away.

34   For the fervent love and strong vengeance of the man (or the husband) shall not spare (him) in the day of vengeance,

35   neither shall (the husband) assent to the prayers of any;

neither he shall take many gifts for ransom (or recompense).

ECCLESIASTICUS CHAPTER 8

1   Chide or strive thou not with a mighty man, lest thou fall into his hands.

2   Strive thou not with a rich man, lest peradventure he make a play again-ward to(wards) thee or he set strife to thee. For why gold and silver hath lost (or destroyed) many men; and it stretcheth forth unto the hearts of kings, and turneth (them).

3   Chide thou not with a man, a jangler, or Strive thou not with a tonguey man, and lay thou not trees into his fire.

4   Commune thou not with an untaught man, lest he speak evil of thy kindred.

5   Despise thou not a man turning away himself from sin, neither upbraid thou him, nor put thou reproof to him; have thou mind (or remember), that all we be in corruption.

6   Despise thou not a man in his old (age); for why (some) of us men wax (or grow) old.

7   Do not thou make joy of (or over) thine enemy (being) dead, witting that all we die (or knowing that we all die), and will (or desire) not (to) come into joy *of (or with) our enemies.*

8   Despise thou not the telling of wise priests, and be thou conversant or altogether dwell in the proverbs of them; for of (or from) them thou shalt learn wisdom, and the teaching of under-standing, and to serve without (com)plaint to great men.

9   The telling of elder men pass not (by) thee; for they have learned of (or from) their fathers. For of (or from) them thou shalt learn understanding; and in the time of need thou shalt give an answer.

10   Kindle thou not the coals of sinners, and reprove them; and

be thou not burnt with the flame of the fire of their sins.

11   Stand thou not against the face of a man full of despising or of the strifeful; lest he sit as an espyer to thy mouth.

12   Do not thou lend to a man stronger than thyself; that (or but) if thou hast lent, have thou it as lost.

13   Promise thou not above or over thy power; that (or but) if thou hast promised, bethink thou as yielding, *for thou art holden to do thy might*, (that is, thou art held to pay it back).

14   Deem thou not against a judge; for he deemeth after that, that is just.

15   Go thou not in (or on) the way with a foolhardy man, lest peradventure he aggregate (or bring together all) his evils in (or upon) thee; for he goeth after his (own) will (or desire), and thou shalt perish together with (him through) his folly.

16   Make thou not chiding or jangling with a wrathful man, and go thou not into a desert with a foolhardy man; for why blood, *that is, shedding out of innocent blood,* is as nought (or nothing) before him, and where none help is (or where there is no help), he shall hurtle thee down.

17   Have thou not counsel with fools; for they may not (or cannot) love, no but those things that please them(selves).

18   Make thou not a counsel (or a plan) before a stranger; for thou knowest not, what he shall bring forth.

19   Make not thine heart known to each man or To all men thine heart open thou not, *but only to a very (or a true) friend, and proved*; lest peradventure he bring to thee false grace, *that is, feigned friendship,* and despise thee.

ECCLESIASTICUS CHAPTER 9

1   Love thou not jealously or Be thou not jealous to the woman

of thy bosom; lest she show upon thee the malice of evil doctrine.

2   Give thou not to a woman the power of (or over) thy soul; lest she enter into thy virtue, and thou be shamed or confounded.

3   Behold thou not a woman of many wills (or desires), *that coveteth now this man, now that man*; lest peradventure thou fall into the snares of her.

4   Be thou not customable with a danceress, neither hire thou her; lest peradventure thou perish in the speedy work of her.

5   Behold thou not a virgin or a maiden; lest peradventure thou be caused to stumble in (or by) the fairness of her.

6   Give thou not thy soul to whores in anything; lest thou lose thee (or destroy thyself), and thy soul, and thine heritage (or thy inheritance).

7   Do not thou behold about in the lanes of the city; neither err thou (or wander) in the large streets thereof. [Do thou not behold about in the ways of the city; nor err thou about in the streets of it.]

8   Turn away thy face from a woman well-arrayed; and behold thou not about the fairness of another or of another *man's wife*. Many men have perished for the fairness of a woman; and thereby covetousness or lust burneth on high as fire. Each woman which is an whore, *either customable to fornication*, shall be defouled as a turd in the way (or on the road). Many men wondering on the fairness of an alien (or foreign) woman were made reprovable, for why the speech of her burneth on high as fire.

9   Sit thou not in any manner with an alien (or foreign, or unfamiliar) woman, neither rest thou with her on a bed, nor lie thou with her upon the arm; and jangle or strive thou not with her in (or over) wine, lest peradventure thine heart bow into her, or she bow down thine heart into her, and thou fall or slide into perdition by thy blood.

10   Forsake thou not an old friend; for a new friend shall not be

like him. New wine *is* (like) a new friend; (after) it shall wax (or grow) old, and (then) thou shalt drink it with sweetness.

11   Covet or Love thou not the glory and riches of a sinner; for thou knowest not, what destroying of him shall come, or what be to come (of) the turning upside-down of him.

12   The wrong of unrightwise men please not thee, and know thou that a wicked man shall not please unto hell (or the grave).

13   Be thou far from a man that hath power to slay, *that is, from a cruel tyrant*, and thou shalt not have suspicion of the dread of death; and if thou nighest to him, do not thou do any trespass, or anything do amiss, lest peradventure he take away thy life. Know thou the communing of death; for thou shalt enter into the midst of snares, and thou shalt go on the arms (or weapons) of them that sorrow.

14   By thy virtue, keep thee (away) from thy neighbour *that may speak against thee to a tyrant*; and treat thou (or talk and consult) with wise men and prudent men.

15   Just or Rightwise men be guests, *or meat*-frères, to thee (or meal companions for thee); and thy glorying be in the dread (or fear) of (or reverence for) God.

16   And the thought of God be to thee in wit, *that is, apply thy wit to think on God*; and all thy telling-out *be* in the behests (or about the commands) of the Highest.

17   Works shall be praised in (or from) the hand of craftsmen, and the prince of the people in the wisdom of his word; forsooth in the wit (or thinking) of elders a word *shall be praised*.

18   A man, a jangler or a tonguey man, is dreadful or fearful in his city; and a foolhardy man in his word shall be hateful.

ECCLESIASTES CHAPTER 6

1   Also another evil there is, which I saw under the sun; and

certainly *it is* oft used with men.

2   A man *is*, to whom God gave riches, and chattel or substance (or possessions), and honour; and nothing faileth to his soul of all the things which he desireth; and (or but) God giveth not the power to him, that he eat thereof (or to enjoy those things), but a strange man shall devour it (or enjoy them), *for God draweth him away suddenly from this present life.* This is vanity (or emptiness and futility), and a great wretchedness.

3   If a man engendereth or beget an hundred free sons, and hath many days (or years) of age, and his soul useth (or enjoyeth) not the goods of his chattel or substance (in his life), and (he) wanteth burying (or lacketh a proper burial); I pronounce of this man, that a dead-born child is better than he.

4   For he cometh in vain, and goeth to darknesses; and his name shall be done away by forgetting.

5   He saw not the sun, neither knew the diversity of good and of evil;

6   also though he live two thousand years, and useth not goods (or enjoyeth the good things in his life); whether all things hasten not to one place?

7   All the travail (or labour) of a man *is* in (or for) his mouth, but the soul of him (or his appetite) shall not be fulfilled with goods (or with enough good things).

8   What hath a wise man more than a fool? and what hath a poor *man*, but that he go thither, where is life (or with an understanding of life)?

9   It is better to see that, that thou covetest, than to desire that, that thou knowest not; but also this is vanity (or empty and futile), and presumption of spirit (or like chasing the wind).

10   The name of him that shall come, is called now, and it is known, that he is a man, and he may not (or cannot) strive in

doom (or at a judgement) against a stronger than himself.

11   Words be full many, and have much vanity (or emptiness and futility) in disputing. What need is it to (or for) a man to seek greater things than himself (or what profit is it to anyone),

12   since he knoweth not, what shall befall to him in his life, in the number of days of his pilgrimage, and in the time that passeth as a shadow? or who may (or can) show to him, what thing under the sun shall come after him? Δ

DAY 7

PSALM 36

1   *To victory, the psalm of David, the servant of the Lord.* The unjust man said, that he trespass in himself; the dread (or fear) of God (or the reverence for God) is not before his eyes.

2   For he did guilefully (or deceitfully) in the sight of (or before) God; (so) that his wickedness be found to (be) hatred (or hateful).

3   The words of his mouth *be* wickedness and guile (or deceitful); he would not understand to do well (or to do good).

4   He thought wickedness in his bed; he stood nigh (to) all ways (that be) not good; forsooth he hated not malice.

5   Lord, thy mercy *is* in the heavens; and thy truth *is* unto the clouds.

6   Thy rightwiseness *is* as (high as) the hills of God; thy dooms (or judgements) *be* (as) much depth (as) of the waters. Lord, thou shalt save men and beasts;

7   as (or for) thou, God, hast multiplied thy mercy. But the sons of men shall hope (or trust) in the covering of thy wings.

8   They shall be (ful)filled greatly of (or from) the plenty of thine house; and thou shalt give drink to them of (or from) the stiff (or flowing) stream of thy delights.

9   For the well of life is with thee; and in thy light we shall see light.

10   Lord, set forth thy mercy to them that know thee; and thy rightwiseness to them that be of rightful heart.

11   The foot of pride come not to me; and the hand of the sinner move me not.

12   There they have fallen down, that work wickedness; they be cast out, and might not stand (up again).

DAY 7

PSALM 37

1   *The psalm of David.* Do not thou pursue or follow wicked men; neither love thou men doing wickedness.

2   For they shall wax (or grow) dry swiftly as hay; and they shall fall down soon as the worts of herbs (or plants).

3   Hope (or trust) thou in the Lord, and do thou goodness (or do good); and inhabit thou the land, and thou shalt be fed with his riches.

4   Delight thou in the Lord; and he shall give to thee the askings of thine heart.

5   Show (or Give) thy ways to the Lord; and hope (or trust) in him, and he shall do (it).

6   And he shall lead out thy rightwiseness as light, and thy doom (or judgements) as midday;

7   be thou subject to the Lord, and pray thou (to) him. Do not thou pursue or follow him, that hath prosperity in his way; (nor) a man doing unrightfulness or unrightwiseness.

8   Cease thou of (or from) wrath, and forsake strong vengeance; do not thou pursue or follow, that thou do wickedly.

9   For they, that do wickedly, shall be destroyed; but they that suffer (or hope in) the Lord, shall inherit the land.

10   And yet (after) a little, and (then) a sinner shall not be; and thou shalt seek his place, and thou shalt not find *it.*

11   But mild (or meek) men shall inherit the land or the earth; and shall delight in the multitude of peace.

12   A sinner shall ambush the rightwise; and he shall gnash with his teeth on him.

13   But the Lord shall scorn the sinner; for he beholdeth that his day cometh.

14   The sinners have drawn out (their) swords; they (have) bent

their bows. To deceive the poor and the needy or helpless; to strangle rightful or right men of heart.

15 Their sword (shall) enter into the heart of themselves; and their bow (shall) be broken.

16 Better is a little thing to the rightwise; than the many riches of sinners.

17 For the arms (or the strength) of the sinners shall be all-broken; but the Lord confirmeth (or upholdeth) rightwise men.

18 The Lord knoweth the days of the unwemmed (or unblemished); and their heritage (or inheritance) shall be without end.

19 They shall not be shamed in the evil time, and they shall be fulfilled in the days of hunger;

20 for the sinners shall perish. Forsooth anon (or at once) as the enemies of the Lord be honoured, and enhanced (or exalted); they failing shall fail (or disappear) as smoke.

21 A sinner shall borrow, and shall not pay (back); but the rightwise hath mercy, and shall give (to others).

22 For they that bless (or be blessed by) the Lord shall inherit the land or the earth; but they that curse him shall perish.

23 The goings of a man shall be addressed with (or directed by) the Lord; and he shall delight in his way.

24 When he falleth, he shall not be hurtled or hurled down; for the Lord undersetteth or underputteth his hand.

25 I was younger, and soothly I waxed (or grew) old; and I saw not the rightwise forsaken, neither his seed seeking bread.

26 All day (long) he hath mercy, and lendeth; and his seed shall be in blessing.

27 Bow thou away from evil, and do good; and dwell thou into the world of world (or and thou shalt live forever).

28 For the Lord loveth doom (or justice), and shall not forsake his saints (or people); they shall be kept (safe) without end. The unright-

wise shall be punished; and the seed of wicked men shall perish.

29 But the rightwise shall inherit the land or the earth; and shall inhabit thereon or indwell upon it into the world of world (or forever).

30 The mouth of the rightwise shall bethink wisdom; and his tongue shall speak doom (or justice).

31 The law of his God *is* in his heart; and his steps shall not be deceived.

32 A sinner beholdeth the rightwise; and seeketh to slay him.

33 But the Lord shall not forsake him in his hands; neither he shall condemn him, when it shall be deemed (or judged) against him.

34 Abide thou (or Wait for) the Lord, and keep thou his way, and he shall enhance (or exalt) thee, (so) that by heritage (or inheritance) thou take the land or the earth; when the sinners shall perish, thou shalt see (it).

35 (Once) I saw the wicked man enhanced (or raised up) above (many others); and raised up as (high as) the cedars of Lebanon.

36 And I passed (by later), and lo! he was not (there); I sought him, and his place was not found.

37 Keep thou innocence (or See the innocent), and see equity (or fairness); for they be relics (or posterity) to a peaceable man.

38 Forsooth the unrightwise shall perish; the remnants or relics (or posterity) of wicked men shall perish altogether.

39 But the health (or salvation) of the rightwise is of (or from) the Lord; and he is their defender in the time of tribulation (or troubles).

40 And the Lord shall help them, and shall make them free, and he shall deliver them from the sinners; and he shall save them, for they hoped (or trusted) in him.

PSALM 38

1 *The psalm of David, to bethink on the sabbath.* Lord, reprove

thou not me in thy strong vengeance; neither chastise thou me in thy wrath.

2   For thine arrows be fixed in me; and thou hast made steadfast thine hand upon me.

3   None health is in my flesh from the face of thy wrath; no peace is to my bones from the face (or because) of my sins.

4   For my wickednesses be gone over mine head; as an heavy burden, they be made heavy upon me.

5   Mine healed wounds were rotten, and be broken; from the face (or because) of mine unwisdom (or my foolishness).

6   I am made a wretch, and I am bowed down unto the end; all day I entered (or go about) sorrowful(ly).

7   For my loins be filled with scornings; and health is not in my flesh.

8   I am tormented, and made low full greatly; I roared for the wailings of mine heart.

9   Lord, all my desire *is* before thee; and my wailing is not hid from thee.

10   Mine heart is troubled in me, my virtue (or strength) forsook me; and the light of mine eyes, and it is not with me.

11   My friends and my neighbours nighed; and stood (over) against me. And they that were beside me stood afar;

12   and they did violence, that sought my life. And they that sought evils to (or for) me, spake vanities (or gossip); and thought (up) guiles (or deceptions) all day (long).

13   But I, as a deaf man, heard not; and as a dumb man not opening his mouth.

14   And I am made as a man not hearing; and not having reprovings in his mouth.

15   For, Lord, I hoped (or trusted) in thee; my Lord God, thou shalt hear me.

16   For I said, (Hear me), lest any time mine enemies have joy (up)on or over me; and the while my feet were moved, they spake great things upon me.

17   For I am ready to (or for) beatings; and my sorrow is evermore in my sight (or before me).

18   For I shall tell (out) my wickedness; and I shall think for (or about) my sin.

19   But mine enemies live, and they be confirmed upon me; and they be multiplied, that hate me wickedly.

20   They that yield evils for goods, backbited me; for I pursued or followed goodness.

21   My Lord God, forsake thou not me; go thou not away from me.

22   Lord God of mine health (or salvation); behold thou into mine help.

PSALM 39

1   *For victory, to Jeduthun, the psalm of David.* I said, I shall keep (watch over) my ways; (so) that I trespass not in (or with) my tongue. I put keeping to my mouth; when a sinner stood against me.

2   I was dumb, and I was meeked full greatly, and was still, (even) from goods (or about good things); and my sorrow was renewed.

3   Mine heart was hot within me; and fire shall burn out (or burn forever) in my thinking. I spake in (or with) my tongue;

4   Lord, make thou mine end known to me. And the number of my days, what it is; (so) that I know, what faileth (or falleth) to me (or when I shall die).

5   Lo! thou hast set or put (or made) my days measureable; and my substance is as nought (or nothing) before thee. Nevertheless all (is) vanity (or empty and futile); each man living (or for everyone alive).

6   Nevertheless a man passeth in an image (or as a shadow); but

also he is troubled vainly. He treasureth; and he know not, to (or for) whom he shall gather those things.

7   And now which is mine abiding (or who do I wait for)? whether not the Lord? and my substance is at or with thee.

8   Deliver thou me from all my wickednesses; thou hast given me (as) a shame to the unknowing (people).

9   I was dumb, and opened not my mouth; for thou hast made (this happen),

10   remove thou thy wounds from me. From the strength of thine hand I failed in blamings (or I am failing from the strokes of thy hand);

11   for wickedness thou hast chastised a man. And thou madest his life to fail as a spider; nevertheless each man is troubled in vain (or over nothing).

12   Lord, hear thou my prayer, and my beseeching; perceive thou with ears (or listen to) my tears. Be thou not still (or silent), for I am a comeling (or a newcomer here) with thee; and a pilgrim, as (be) all my (fore)fathers.

13   Forgive thou to me, (so) that I be refreshed, before that I go (away); and (then) I shall no more be.

PROVERBS   CHAPTER 7

1   My son, keep thou my words; and keep my behests (or commands) to thee.

2   Keep thou my behests, and thou shalt live; and my law (or teaching), as the apple of thine eyes.

3   Bind thou it in (or to) thy fingers; write thou it in the tables (or on the tablets) of thine heart.

4   Say thou to wisdom, Thou art my sister; and call thou prudence thy love.

5   (So) that it keep thee (safe) from a strange woman; and from

an alien (or foreign, or unfamiliar) woman, that maketh her words sweet.

6   (For she saith), For why from the window of mine house, by the lattice, I beheld;

7   and I see little children, *that is, fools that have little wit.* I behold a young man a coward or sorry-hearted,

8   that passeth by or through the streets, beside the corner; and he goeth nigh the way of her house,

9   in a dark time, when the day draweth to night, in the darkness and mist in the night.

10   And lo! a woman, made ready with the ornaments of an whore to deceive souls, meeteth him,

11   and *she is* a jangler (or loud), and going about, and unpatient of rest, and may not (or cannot) stand in the house with her feet;

12   and now withoutforth, now in the streets, now beside the corners, she ambusheth (him).

13   And she taketh (hold of), and kisseth the young man; and flattereth (him) with wooing cheer, *that is, unrestful(ly), and without shame,* and saith,

14   I owed sacrifices for health (or I have paid my offerings for my deliverance); today I have yielded my vows.

15   Therefore I went out into thy meeting, and I desired to see thee; and I have found *thee.*

16   I have made (ready) my bed with cords (or blankets), I have arrayed *it* with tapets painted of Egypt (or tapestries from Egypt);

17   I have besprinkled my bed with myrrh, and aloes, and canel (or cinnamon).

18   Come thou, be we filled with *touching of* teats, and use we embracings *that be* coveted (or and with desired embraces); till the day begin to be clear.

19   For *mine* husband is not in his house; he is gone (away) a full

long way.

20   He took with him a bag of money; (and) he shall return again into his house in the day of the full moon.

21   She bound him with many words; and she drew forth him with flatterings of (or from her) lips.

22   Anon (or At once) he as an ox led to slain sacrifice pursueth or followeth her, and as a jolly lamb and unknowing (or ignorant); and the fool knoweth not, that he is drawn (un)to bonds,

23   till an arrow pierce his maw. As if a bird hasteth to the snare; and knoweth not, that it is done of (or at) the peril of his (or its) life.

24   Now therefore, my son, hear thou (or listen to) me; and perceive (or understand) the words of my mouth.

25   Lest thy soul be drawn away in (or by) the ways of her; neither be thou deceived in (or on) the paths of her.

26   For she hath cast down many wounded men; and (even) all the strongest men were slain of (or by) her.

27   The ways of hell (or to Sheol) *is* (through) her house; and pierce (or lead) into the inner things of death.

ECCLESIASTICUS CHAPTER 10

1   A wise judge shall deem (or judge) his people; and the princehood of a witty (or a witting, or a knowing) man shall be steadfast or stable.

2   After the judge of the people, so and his ministers or the servants of him; and what manner man is the governor of the city, such *be* also men dwelling in it.

3   An unwise king shall lose (or destroy) his people; and (or but) the cities shall be inhabited by the wit (or through the understanding) of prudent men.

4   The power of the earth *is* in the hand of God, and all the

wickedness of the heathen men or the Gentiles is abominable; and he shall raise (up) a profitable governor at a time or in (due) time on (or over) it.

5   The power of man *is* in the hand of God; and he shall set his honour on the face of a wise man in the law or the scribe.

6   Have thou not mind on (or Do not remember) all the wrongs of the neighbour; and do thou nothing in the works of wrong(doing).

7   Pride is hateful before God and men; and all the wickedness of the heathen men or the Gentiles *is* abominable.

8   A realm (or kingdom) is translated, *either taken away*, or borne over, from a folk into (another) folk for unrightwisenesses, and wrongs, and strives or despisings, and diverse treacheries.

9   Nothing is curseder than an avarice man. What (or Why) art thou proud, thou earth and ashes? Nothing is more wicked or worse, than to love money; for why this man hath, yea, his soul set to (or for) sale, or sellable, *or able to be sold*, for in his life he cast or threw away his (most) inward things.

10   Each power *is* short life (or short-lived); long sickness or infirmity grieveth the leech (or the physician). A leech (or physician) cutteth away or cutteth off, *or healeth soon*, a short *or fresh* sickness; so and a king is today or today is, and tomorrow he shall die.

11   Forsooth when a man shall die, he shall inherit serpents, and beasts, and worms.

12   The beginning of the pride of man *was* to be apostate or to go backward (or away) from God; for his heart went away from him that made him.

13   For why pride is the beginning of all sin or the beginning of all sin is pride; he that holdeth it, shall be filled with cursings, and it shall destroy him into the end. Therefore the Lord hath shamed the covents or convents (or the gatherings) of evil men, and hath destroyed them unto the end.

14   God destroyed the seats (or the thrones) of proud dukes; and made mild (or meek, or humble) men to sit for them.

15   God made dry the roots of proud folks (or nations); and planted meek men of those folks (or in their place).

16   The Lord destroyed the lands of folks or Gentiles (or the nations); and lost or destroyed them unto the foundament (or the foundation of the earth).

17   He made dry *the roots* of them, and lost (or destroyed) them; and made the mind of them (or their memory) to cease from the earth. God lost the mind of proud men; and left the mind of meek men in wit, (or God destroyed the memory of the proud; but left the memory of the humble).

18   Pride was not made to (or for) men; neither wrathfulness to (or for) the nation of women, *that is, to all men born of women.*

19   This seed of men that dreadeth (or feareth, or revereth) God, shall be honoured; but this seed shall be dishonoured, that over-passeth (or passeth over) the commandments of the Lord.

20   In the midst of brethren the governor of them *is* in honour; and they that dread (or fear, or revere) God, shall be in his eyes, *that is, shall be honourable, and please him.*

21   (This verse is omitted in the original text.)

22   The glory of rich men (and of those who be) honoured and (also) of poor men, (yea, all of them), is the dread (or fear) of (or reverence for) God.

23   Do not thou despise a rightwise poor man; and do not thou magnify a rich sinful man.

24   The judge is great, and he is mighty in honour; and (or but) he is not greater than that man that dreadeth (or feareth, or revereth) God.

25   Free children serve a witty (or a witting, or a knowing) servant; and a prudent man and learned shall not grumble, *when he is* blamed (or corrected), and an unknowing (or an ignorant)

man shall not be honored.

26   Do not thou enhance thee (or exalt thyself) in thy work to be done; and do not thou be slow or despair in the time of anguish.

27   He is better that worketh, and hath plenty or aboundeth in all things, than he that hath glory (or boasteth), and needeth bread.

28   Son, keep thy soul in mildness (or in meekness), *that holdeth due measure, and refraineth (from) excess*; and give thou honour to it, after his (or its) merit.

29   Who shall justify him that sinneth against his (own) soul? and who shall honour him that dishonoureth his (own) soul?

30   A poor man hath glory by his learning and dread (or reverence); and there is a man that is honoured for his chattel or his substance.

31   Forsooth if a man hath glory (or is honoured) in poverty, how much more in chattel or substance? and he that hath glory in chattel or in substance, dread(eth) (or feareth) poverty.

ECCLESIASTES CHAPTER 7

1   A good name is better than precious ointments; and the day of death *is better* than the day of birth.

2   It is better to go to the house of mourning, than to the house of a feast; for in that *house* the end of all men is *warned* (of), and a man living thinketh, what is to come.

3   Wrath is better than laughing; for the soul of a trespasser is amended by the heaviness of (his) cheer (or face).

4   The heart of wise men *is* where sorrow is; and the heart of fools *is* where *folly (or foolish)* gladness is.

5   It is better to be reproved of (or rebuked by) a wise man, than to be deceived by the flattering of fools;

6   for as the sound of thorns burning under a pot, so *is* the laughing of a fool. But also this *is* vanity (or empty and futile).

7   False challenge (or Lies and slander) troubleth a wise man, and it shall lose (or destroy) the strength of his heart.

8   Forsooth the end of prayer is better than the beginning. A patient man is better than a proud man.

9   Be thou not swift to be wroth; for wrath (or anger) resteth in the bosom of a fool.

10   Say thou not, What guessest thou is the cause, that the former times were better than be now? for why such asking is fond (or foolish).

11   Forsooth wisdom with riches is more profitable, and profiteth more to men seeing the sun.

12   For as wisdom defendeth, so money *defendeth*; but learning and wisdom have this moreover, that they give life to them that have them.

13   Behold thou the works of God, *and see* that no man may amend (or can correct) him, whom *God* hath despised.

14   In (or On) a good day use thou goods (or enjoy thy good things), and before eschew thou (or shun them on) an evil day; for God made so this day as that day, (so) that a man find not just complainings against him.

15   Also I saw these things in (or since) the days of my nativity (or my birth); the rightwise perisheth in his rightwiseness, and a wicked man liveth much time in his malice.

16   Do not thou be just or rightwise over much (or Do not be too good), neither understand thou more than is needful; lest thou be astonished (or regarded with contempt).

17   Do thou not (do) wickedly much (or do many wicked things), and do not thou be a fool; lest thou die in a time not thine (own) (or before thy time).

18   It is good, that thou sustain a just or rightwise man (or the one); but also withdraw thou not thine hand from him (or from the

other); for he that dreadeth (or feareth, or revereth) God, is not negligent of anything.

19   Wisdom hath strengthened a wise man, over (or more than) ten princes of a city.

20   There is not forsooth a rightwise man in (or on) the earth, that (always) doeth good, and sinneth not (or never).

21   But also give thou not thine heart to all the words, that be said; lest peradventure thou hear thy servant cursing thee;

22   for thy conscience knoweth, that also thou hast cursed oft other men.

23   I assayed all things in wisdom; I said, I shall be made wise, and (or but) it went away further from me,

24   much more than it was (before); and the depth *is* (so) low, who shall (be able to) find it?

25   I compassed all things with my soul (or I put my mind upon everything), to know, and to behold, and (to) seek (out) wisdom, and reason, and to know the wickedness of a fool, and the error of unprudent men.

26   And I found a woman bitterer than death, the which is (like) the snare of hunters, and her heart *is* (like) a net, and her hands be (like) bonds; he that pleaseth God shall escape her, but he that is a sinner, shall be taken of her (or be caught by her).

27   Lo! I found this, said Ecclesiastes, (concerning) one (thing) and another, (so) that I should find the reason,

28   which my soul seeketh yet; and (other things) I found not. I found one man (out) of a thousand; and I found not a woman (out) of all (of them).

29   I found this only, that God made a man rightful (or upright, or clear-headed); and (or but then) he meddled or mingled (or mixed) himself (in or up) with questions without number. Δ

DAY 8

PSALM 40

1   *For victory, the psalm of David.* I abiding abode (or Waiting *patiently*, I waited for) the Lord; and he gave attention to me. And he heard my prayers;

2   and he led out me from the pit of wretchedness, and from the filth of dregs. And he ordained my feet on a stone; and he addressed (or directed) my goings.

3   And he sent into my mouth a new song; a song to our God. Many men shall see, and dread (or fear); and shall hope (or trust) in the Lord.

4   Blessed *is* the man, of whom the name of the Lord is his hope; and he beheld not into vanities, and into false vengeances.

5   My Lord God, thou hast made thy marvels many; and in thy thoughts none is, that is like thee (toward us). I told and I spake (about them); and they be multiplied above number.

6   Thou wouldest (or desiredest) not sacrifice and offering; but thou madest perfectly ears to (hear) me. Thou askedest not (for) burnt sacrifice, and *other* sacrifice for sin;

7   then I said, Lo! I come. In the head of the book it is written of me (or From the beginning, the Book *of the Law* was written for me),

8   that I should do thy will; my God, I would or desired also *to do* (*it*); and thy law (is) in the midst of mine heart.

9   I told (out) thy rightwiseness in a great church; lo! I shall not refrain my lips, Lord, thou knewest (that).

10   I hid not thy rightwiseness in mine heart; I said (or spoke of) thy truth and thine health (or thy salvation). I hid not thy mercy, and thy truth, from a much council (or a great congregation).

11   But thou, Lord, make not far thy merciful doings from me; thy

mercy and thy truth evermore take (or raise) me up.

12   For why evils, of which is no number, encompassed me; my wickednesses have (over)taken me, and I might not, that I should (or could even) see. They be multiplied above the hairs of mine head; and mine heart forsook me.

13   Lord, please it to thee (or may it please thee), that thou deliver me; Lord, behold thou to help me.

14   Be they shamed, and ashamed altogether; that seek my life, to take away it. Be they turned aback, and be they shamed; that will (or desire) evils to (or for) me.

15   Bear they their confusion anon (or at once); that say to me, Well! well! *in scorn.*

16   (But let) all men that seek thee, be fully joyful, and be glad in thee; and say they, that love thine health (or thy salvation), The Lord be magnified evermore.

17   Forsooth I am a beggar and poor; the Lord is busy of me (or Lord, help thou me). Thou art mine helper and my defender; my God, tarry thou not.

PSALM 41

1   *For victory, the song of David.* Blessed *is* he that understandeth of the needy and poor; the Lord shall deliver him in the evil day.

2   The Lord (shall) keep him (safe), and quicken him, and make him blessful in the land; and betake not him into the will of his enemies.

3   The Lord (shall) bear help to him upon the bed of his sorrow; thou hast oft turned all his bedstraw in his sickness.

4   I said, Lord, have thou mercy on me; heal thou my soul, for I have sinned against thee.

5   Mine enemies said evils to me; When shall he die, and his

name shall perish?

6   And if he entered for to see (me), he spake vain things (to me); his heart gathered wickedness to himself. He went withoutforth; and spake to the same thing or the same end.

7   All mine enemies backbited privily (or secretly) against me; against me they thought (up) evils to (do to) me.

8   They ordained an evil word against me; Whether he that sleepeth, shall not lie to, that he rise again?

9   For why the man of my peace, in whom I hoped (or trusted), he that ate my loaves; made great deceit on (or against) me.

10   But thou, Lord, have mercy on me, and raise me (up) again; and I shall yield to (or repay) them.

11   In (or by) this thing I knew, that thou wouldest (or delightest in) me; for mine enemy shall not have joy on (or over) me.

12   Forsooth thou hast taken me up (or upheld me) for (or because of mine) innocence; and hast confirmed me in thy sight without end (or forever).

13   Blessed *be* the Lord God of Israel, from the world, and into the world (or forever); be it done, be it done (or amen, amen).

PSALM 42

1   *To victory, to the sons of Korah.* As an hart desireth to (or for) the wells of waters; so thou, God, my soul desireth to (or for) thee.

2   My soul thirsted to (or for) God, the quick well or the well of life; when shall I come, and appear before the face of God?

3   My tears were (my only) loaves to (or for) me day and night; while it is said to me each day, Where is thy God?

4   I bethought of (or on) these things, and I poured out in me my soul; for I shall pass into the place of the wonderful tabernacle, unto the house of God. In the voice of full out joying, and acknowledging;

is the sound of the eater (or those at the feast or festival).

5　　My soul, why art thou sorry (or so sad); and why troublest thou me? Hope thou in God, for yet I shall acknowledge to (or praise) him; *he is* the health of my cheer (or my salvation), and my God.

6　　My soul is troubled with(in) myself; therefore, *God*, I shall be mindful of (or remember) thee from the land of Jordan, and from the little hill of the Hermonites.

7　　Depth calleth depth; in the voice of thy windows (or waterfalls). All thine high things (or breakers), and thy waves; passed over me.

8　　The Lord sent (forth) his mercy (or his love) in the day; and his song in the night. With me *is* the prayer to the God of my life;

9　　I shall say to God, Thou art mine up-taker (or my defender). Why forgettest thou me; and why go I sorrowful, while the enemy tormenteth me?

10　　While my bones be broken altogether; mine enemies, that trouble me, despised me. While they say to me, by all days; Where is thy God?

11　　My soul, why art thou sorry (or so sad); and why troublest thou me? Hope thou in God, for yet I shall acknowledge to (or praise) him; *he is* the health of my cheer (or my salvation), and my God.

PSALM 43

1　　God, deem (or judge) thou me, and separate thou my cause from a folk (or a nation) not holy; deliver thou me from a wicked man, and guileful (or deceitful).

2　　For thou art God, my strength; why hast thou put me aback, and why go I sorrowful (or go about in sorrow), while the enemy tormenteth me?

3　　Send out thy light, and thy truth; those things led me forth, and brought *me* into thine holy hill, and into thy tabernacles (or into thy Temple).

4   And I shall enter (or go) to the altar of God; to God, that gladdeth my youth. God, my God, I shall acknowledge to (or praise) thee in (or on) an harp;

5   my soul, why art thou sorry (or so sad), and why troublest thou me? Hope thou in God, for yet I shall acknowledge to (or praise) him; *that is* the health of my cheer (or my salvation), and my God.

PSALM 44

1   *To victory, learning to the sons of Korah.* God, we heard with our ears; our fathers told to us. The work, which thou wroughtest in the days of them; and (or yea), in the old days.

2   Thine hand lost (or destroyed) the heathen men, and thou plantedest them (or our forefathers, there); thou tormentedest the peoples, and castedest them out.

3   For the *children of Israel* wielded the land not by their sword; and the arm of them saved not them. But thy right hand, and thine arm, and the lightening of thy cheer (or the shining of thy face); for thou were pleased in (or with) them.

4   Thou art thyself, my King, and my God; that sendest healths (or victories, or salvation) to Jacob.

5   By thee we shall winnow our enemies with the horn (or thy power); and in thy name we shall despise (or defeat) them, that rise against us.

6   For I shall not hope (or trust) in my bow; and my sword shall not save me.

7   For thou hast saved us from men tormenting us; and thou hast shamed men hating us.

8   We shall be pleased in God all day; and in thy name we shall acknowledge to (or praise) thee into the world (or forever).

9   But now thou hast put us aback, and hast shamed us; and thou, Lord, shalt not go out in our virtues (or with our hosts, or armies).

10   Thou hast turned us away behind after our enemies; and they, that hated us, ravished diversely to (or taken spoils for) themselves.

11   Thou hast given us as sheep of meats (or for food), and among the heathen men thou hast scattered us.

12   Thou hast sold thy people without price; and multitude (or profit) there was not in the exchangings of them.

13   Thou hast put (or made) us (as) a shame to our neighbours; mocking and scorn to them that be in our compass.

14   Thou hast put (or made) us into a likeness to the heathen men; and stirring or wagging of the head among the peoples.

15   All day my shame is against me; and the shame of my face covered me.

16   From the voice of the despiser, and evil speaker; from the face of the enemy, and the pursuer.

17   All these things came upon us, and we have not forgotten thee; and (or but) we did not (do) wickedly in thy testament (or thy covenant).

18   And our hearts went not away behind (thee); and thou hast (not) bowed away our paths from thy way.

19   For thou hast made us low (or humbled us) in the place of torment; and the shadow of death covered us.

20   (And) if we forgat the name of our God; and if we held forth our hands to an alien God (or to a foreign god).

21   Whether God shall not seek (out) these things? for he knoweth the hid things of the heart.

22   For why we be slain all day (long) for thee; we be deemed as

sheep of slaying (or judged like sheep for the slaughter).

23 Lord, rise up, why sleepest thou? rise up, and put not *us* away into the end (or do not shun *us* forever).

24 Why turnest thou away thy face? thou forgettest our poverty, and our tribulation (or and all our troubles?).

25 For our life is made low in the dust; our womb is glued together in the earth (or to the ground).

26 Lord, rise up thou, and help us; and again-buy (or redeem) us for thy name.

PROVERBS CHAPTER 8

1 Whether wisdom crieth not oft; and prudence giveth (forth) her voice?

2 In most sovereign and high tops (or places), above (or along) the way, in the midst of the paths,

3 and it standeth beside the gates of the city, in those enclosings, and speaketh, and saith,

4 A! ye men, I cry oft to you; and my voice *is* to (or for) the sons of men.

5 Little children, *that is, little of wit*, understand ye wisdom; and ye unwise men, perceiveth in (your) hearts.

6 Hear ye (or Listen), for I shall speak of great things; and my lips shall be opened, to preach rightful things.

7 My throat shall bethink (or tell) the truth; and my lips shall curse a wicked man.

8 My words be just or rightwise; no shrewd (or depraved, or wicked) thing, neither wayward is in them.

9 They be rightful to them that understand; and *they be* even to them that find knowing (or knowledge).

10 Take ye (or receive) my chastising, and not money, choose ye

teaching, more than treasure.

11   For wisdom is better than all riches most precious; and all desirable thing may not be comparisoned thereto.

12   I, wisdom, dwell in (good) counsel; and I am among learned thoughts.

13   The dread of the Lord hateth evil (or to fear, or to revere the Lord is to hate evil); I curse boast, and pride, and a shrewd (or a depraved, or wicked) way, and a double-tongued mouth.

14   Counsel is mine, and equity (or fairness); prudence is mine, and strength.

15   Kings reign by me; and makers of laws deem (or judge) just things *by me.*

16   Princes command by me; and mighty men deem (or judge) rightfulness or rightwiseness *by me.*

17   I love them that love me; and they that wake early to me, shall find me.

18   With me be riches, and glory; sovereign riches, and rightfulness or rightwiseness.

19   My fruit is better than gold, and precious stones; and my seeds (or my yields) *be better* than chosen silver.

20   I go in the ways of rightfulness or rightwiseness, in the midst of the paths of doom (or justice);

21   (so) that I make rich them that love me, and that I fill their treasuries.

22   The Lord wielded (or created) me in (or at) the beginning of his ways; before that he made anything, (yea), at the (very) beginning.

23   From without beginning I was ordained; and from old times, before that the earth was made.

24   The depths of waters were not yet (made); and I was conceived then. The wells of waters had not broken out yet,

25   and the hills stood not altogether yet by firm heaviness; (yea), before the little hills I was born.

26   Yet he had not made the earth; and floods (or rivers), and the earths (or soils) of the world.

27   When he made ready the heavens, I was present; (and) when he compassed or enclosed the depths of the waters by certain law and compass.

28   When he made steadfast the air above; and weighed (or created) the wells of waters.

29   When he compassed to the sea his mark (or set the boundaries for the seas); and setted the law to (or for) the waters, (so) that they should not pass their coasts. When he weighed the foundaments (or created the foundations) of the earth;

30   I was making all (these) things with him. And I delighted by (or in) all days, and played before him in all time,

31   and I played in the world; and my delights *be* to be with the sons of men.

32   Now, therefore, sons, hear ye me; blessed *be they* that keep my ways.

33   Hear ye teaching, and be ye wise men; and do not ye cast it away.

34   Blessed *is* the man that heareth me, and that watcheth at my gates all day; and keepeth (guard) at the posts of my doors.

35   He that findeth me, shall find life; and he shall draw health of (or salvation, or favour from) the Lord.

36   But he that sinneth against me shall hurt his soul; all that hate me, love death.

ECCLESIASTICUS CHAPTER 11

1   The wisdom of a man made meek shall enhance (or lift up)

his head; and shall make him to sit in the midst of great men.

2 Praise thou not a man in (or for) his fairness (or beauty); neither despise thou a man in his sight (or for his appearance).

3 A bee is little among birds; and his fruit hath the beginning of sweetness.

4 Have thou never glory in clothing, and be thou not enhanced (or exalted) in the day of thine honour; for why the works of the Highest alone *be* wonderful, and his works *be* glorious, and hid, and unseen.

5 Many tyrants have set in (or upon) a throne; and a man of whom was no supposing bare the diadem (or wore the crown).

6 Many mighty men be oppressed greatly; and glorious men be given into the hands of other men.

7 Before that thou ask, blame thou (or rebuke) not any man; and (only) when (first) thou hast asked (or inquired of him), (then) blame thou justly or chastise thou rightly.

8 Before that thou hear (or listen), answer thou not a word; and in the midst of elder men add thou not to speak.

9 Strive thou not, of (or in) that thing that dis-easeth or grieveth (or concerneth) not thee; and stand thou not in the doom (or judgement) of (or with) sinners.

10 Son, thy deeds be not in many things; and if thou art rich, thou shalt not be without part of guilt. For if thou pursuest or shalt follow (after many things), thou shalt not overtake (all of them); and thou shalt not escape, if thou runnest before.

11 There is a man travailing (or labouring), and hastening, and sorrowing, and unpious; and by so much the more he shall not have plenty or he shall not abound.

12 There is a man fading or withered, *that is, feeble, failing more than others*, needing recovering, failing more in virtue (or strength), and abounding in poverty; and the eye of God beheld

him in good (or with kindness), and raised him (up) from his lowness;

13　and enhanced (or lifted up) his head; and many men wondered or marvelled in (or about) him, and honoured or worshipped God.

14　Goods and evils, *that is, prosperities and adversities*, life and death, poverty and honesty (or honours, or riches), be of (or from) God.

15　Wisdom, and learning, and knowing (or knowledge) of the law *be* with the Lord; love or loving and the ways of good men *be* at or with (or from) him.

16　Error and darknesses be made together to (or with) sinners; forsooth they that make full out joy in evil, wax (or grow) old together into evils.

17　The gift of God dwelleth to (or with) just or rightwise men; and the increasings of him shall have prosperities without end.

18　*Some* man there is made rich in doing scarcely (or carefully investing), and this *is* the part of his meed (or reward),

19　in that that he saith, I have found rest to (or for) me, and now I alone shall eat of my goods. And he know not that time passeth him, and death nigheth (or approacheth), and he shall leave all things to other men, and shall die or and die.

20　Stand thou in thy testament (or covenant, or promise), and speak thou altogether in it; and wax thou (or grow) old in the work of thy behests (or of thy commands).

21　Dwell or abide thou not in the works of sinners; but trust thou in God, and dwell in thy place. For it is easy in the eyes of God, suddenly to make honest (or rich) a poor man.

22　The blessing of God hasteneth into the meed (or the reward) of the rightwise; and the going forth of him maketh fruit in swift honour.

23　Say thou not, What is need to me (or What do I need)? and what goods (or good things) shall be (for) me hereafter?

24   Say thou not, I am sufficient, and what (or why) shall I be made worse hereafter?

25   In the day of goods (or good times), be thou not unmindful of evils, and in the day of evils, be thou not unmindful of goods (or good times); (On a good day do not forget the bad days, and on a bad day do not forget the good days;)

26   for it is easy before God to yield in the day of death, to each man after (or according to) his ways.

27   The malice of one hour maketh forgetting of most lechery; and in the end of a man *is* making naked of his works.

28   Praise thou not any man before his death; for why a man is known in (or by) his sons.

29   Bring thou not each man into thine house; for why many treasons be of a guileful (or deceitful) man.

30   For why as the entrails of stinking things break out, and as a partridge is led into a trap, *either a net*, and as a capret is led into a snare, so and the heart of proud men; and as a beholder seeing the fall of his neighbour.

31   For he turneth goods or good things into evils, and setteth treasons, and putteth a wem (or a spot, or a blemish) upon the chosen men.

32   Fire is increased of a sparkle (or by a spark), and blood is increased of (or by) a guileful (or deceitful) man; for why a sinful man setteth treason or waiteth to (or lieth in wait for) blood.

33   Take heed to thee from a guileful (or deceitful) man, for he maketh or forgeth evils; lest peradventure he bring in upon thee scorning without end.

34   Receive thou an alien (or a foreigner, or a stranger) (un)to thee, and he shall destroy thee in a whirlwind, and he shall make thee alien (or alienated) from thine own ways.

DAY 8

ECCLESIASTES CHAPTER 8

1   Who is such as a wise man? and who knoweth the solving, *either expounding*, of a word? The wisdom of a man shineth in his cheer (or on his face); and the mightiest shall change his face, (or and shall make even the mightiest to change his expression).

2   I keep the mouth of the king, and the commandments and the swearings of God. (I counsel or advise thee to obey the king's commands, and to keep your oath or pledge to God.)

3   Hasten thou not to go away from his face, and dwell thou not in evil work. For he shall do all the things, that he will (or desireth);

4   and his word is full of power, and no man may (or can) say to him, Why doest thou so?

5   He that keepeth (or obeyeth) the commandment *of God*, shall not feel anything of evil; the heart of a wise man understandeth (or knoweth) the (proper) time and answer.

6   (The right) time and season is to (or for) each work; and much torment *is* of (or for) a man,

7   for he knoweth not the things (that be) passed, and he may not (or cannot) know by any messenger the things to come.

8   It is not in the power of man to forbid the spirit, *that is, his soul, from going out from the body*, neither he hath (any) power in the day of death, neither he is suffered (or allowed) to have rest, when the battle nigheth; neither wickedness shall save a wicked man.

9   I beheld all these things, and I gave mine heart in(to) all the works, that be done under the sun. Sometime a man is lord of a man, to his evil.

10   I saw wicked men buried, which, when they lived yet, were in the holy place; and they were praised in the city, as *men* of

rightwise works; but also this is vanity (or empty and futile).

11   Forsooth for the sentence is not brought forth soon against evil men, the sons of men do evils without any dread (or fear).

12   Nevertheless of that, that a sinner doeth evil an hundred times, and is suffered (or allowed to) by patience, I knew that good *it* shall be to (or for) men dreading (or fearing) God, that reverence his face, *or presence.*

13   (But) good (shall) be not to the wicked man, neither his days (shall) be made long; but pass they (shall) as a shadow, (for those) that dread (or fear) not the face of the Lord, (or be not reverent before the Lord).

14   There is and another vanity, that is done on the earth. There be rightwise men, to whom evils come, as if they did the works of wicked men; and there be unpious or wicked men, that be as secure, as if they had (done) the deeds of rightwise men; but I deem (or judge) also this most vain (or to be most empty and futile).

15   Therefore I praised gladness (or pleasure, or enjoyment), (yea), that no good was to a man under the sun, (no) but to eat, and drink, and to be joyful; and that he should bear (or carry) away with himself only this of his travail (or from his labour), in (all) the days of his life, which God gave to him under the sun.

16   And I setted mine heart to know wisdom, and to understand the parting or the distinction, which is turned in (or done upon) the earth. There is a man, that by days and nights, taketh not sleep with *his* eyes.

17   And I understood, that of all the works of God, a man may (or can) find no reason of (or for) those things, that be done under the sun; and inasmuch as he travaileth (or laboureth) more to seek (it out), by so much (the more) he shall find (it) less; yea, though a wise man say that he knoweth, he shall not be able to find (it out). Δ

DAY 9

PSALM 45

1   *To the overcomer, for the lilies, the most loved song of the learning of the sons of Korah.* Mine heart hath told out a good word; I say (or tell of) my works to the king. My tongue *is* (like) the pen of a writer; (yea), writing swiftly.

2   *Christ* (or *Anointed King*), *thou art* fairer in shape than the sons of men; grace is spread abroad in thy lips; therefore God blessed thee without end.

3   Be thou gird with thy sword; on thy hip most mightily. Behold thou in thy shapeliness and thy fairness (or beauty);

4   come thou forth with prosperity, and reign thou. For truth, and mildness (or humility), and rightfulness; and thy right hand shall lead forth thee wonderfully.

5   Thy sharp arrows shall fall into the hearts of the enemies of the king; peoples *shall be* (or *fall*) under thee.

6   God, thy seat (or thy throne) is into the world of world (or forever and ever); the rod of thy realm *is* a rod of right ruling, *or of equity.*

7   Thou lovedest rightfulness or rightwiseness, and hatedest wickedness; therefore thou, God, thy God, (or and so God, thy God), anointed thee with the oil of gladness, more than thy fellows.

8   Myrrh, and gum, and cassia, (be the perfumes) of thy clothes, of the ivory houses (or palaces); of which the daughters of kings delighted thee, (or and the sound of music coming forth from the ivory palace delighteth thee).

9   A queen stood nigh on thy right side, in clothing overgilded; compassed with diversity. (The daughters of kings be there among thy honourable women; the queen standeth nigh on thy right side,

in clothing overgilded with the gold of Ophir.)

10   Daughter, hear thou, and see, and bow down thine ear; and forget thy people, and the house of thy father.

11   And the King shall covet thy fairness; for he is thy Lord God, and they shall worship him. (And when the king shall covet thy fairness; for he is thy lord, thou shalt give him honour, *that is, thou shalt obey him*.)

12   And the daughters of Tyre in (or shall be there with) gifts; all the rich men of the people shall beseech thy cheer (or shall seek thy favour, or to be in thy presence, or before thee).

13   All the glory of that daughter of the king *is* within (the palace), (she is adorned) in golden hems;

14   she *is* clothed about with diversities. Virgins shall be brought to the king after her; (yea), her neighbouresses (or friends) shall be brought to thee.

15   They shall be brought in gladness, and full out joying; they shall be brought into the temple (or the palace) of the king.

16   Sons be born to thee, for thy fathers; thou shalt ordain them (to be) princes on (or rulers over) all the earth.

17   Lord, they shall be mindful of (or remember) thy name; in each generation, and into generation. Therefore the peoples shall acknowledge to (or praise) thee without end; and into the world of world (or forever and ever).

PSALM 46

1   *To the overcomer, the song of the sons of Korah, for youths.* Our God, *thou art* (our) refuge, and virtue (or strength); (our) helper in tribulations (or troubles), that have found us greatly (or who hath always found us in time).

2   Therefore we shall not dread (or fear), while the earth shall be

troubled; and the hills shall be borne over into the heart of the sea.

3   The waters of them sounded, and were troubled; hills were troubled altogether in the strength of him.

4   The fierceness of the flood (or the river) maketh glad the city of God; the highest God hath hallowed his tabernacle.

5   God (is) in the midst thereof (and the city) shall not be moved; God shall help it early in the gray morrowtide.

6   Heathen men were troubled altogether, and realms were bowed down; *God* gave his voice, the earth was moved.

7   The Lord of virtues (or of hosts, or armies) *is* with us; God of Jacob *is* our up-taker (or our refuge).

8   Come ye, and see the works of the Lord; which wonders he hath set on the earth.

9   He doing away battles till to the end of the land; shall all-bruise the bow, and he shall break altogether arms (or weapons), and he shall burn shields with fire.

10   Give ye attention, and see ye, that I am God; I shall be enhanced (or exalted) among the heathen men; and I shall be enhanced in (or over all) the earth.

11   The Lord of virtues (or of hosts, or armies) *is* with us; God of Jacob *is* our up-taker (or our refuge).

PSALM 47

1   *To victory, a psalm to the sons of Korah.* All ye folks (or nations), make joy with (your) hands; sing ye heartily to God in the voice of full out joying (or rejoicing).

2   For the Lord *is* high and fearedful; a great King on (or over) all the earth.

3   He made the peoples subject to us; and (put) heathen men under our feet.

4   He chose his heritage to us (or his inheritance for us); the fairness (or beauty) of Jacob, whom he loved.

5   God ascended in a hearty song; and the Lord in the voice (or the sound) of a trump.

6   Sing ye to our God, sing ye; sing ye to our King, sing ye.

7   For God *is* the King of all the earth; sing ye a psalm wisely.

8   God shall reign on (or over) the heathen men; God sitteth on his holy seat (or throne).

9   The princes of the peoples be gathered together with the God of Abraham; for the strong gods of the earth be raised (up) greatly.

PSALM 48

1   *The song of psalm, of the sons of Korah.* The Lord *is* great, and worthy to be praised full much; in the city of our God, in (or on) the holy hill of him.

2   It is founded in the full out joying (or rejoicing) of all the earth; the hill of Zion, the sides of the north, the city of the great King.

3   God shall be known in the houses thereof; when he shall take it. (And God is known as a refuge, *or a stronghold,* in its palaces.)

4   For lo! the kings of the earth were gathered together (against it); they came into one place.

5   They seeing, so wondered; they were troubled, they were moved altogether, (or and they ran away),

6   trembling took them. There sorrows, as of a woman travailing of (or labouring with) child;

7   in a great spirit (or with a great wind) thou shalt all-break the ships of Tarshish.

8   As we heard, so we saw, in the city of the Lord of virtues (or of hosts, or armies), in the city of our God; God hath founded that city without end (or established it forever).

9   God, we have received thy mercy (or think about thy love); in the midst of thy temple.

10   After thy name, God, so thy praising *is spread abroad* into (or unto) the ends of the earth; thy right hand is full of rightwiseness.

11   (Let) the hill of Zion be glad (or rejoice), and the daughters of Judah be fully joyful; for thy dooms (or judgements), Lord.

12   Compass ye Zion, and embrace ye it; tell ye in the towers of it.

13   Set ye your hearts in the virtue of it (or its strength); and part ye or delighteth (in) the houses of it, (so) that ye (can) tell (it) out in another generation.

14   For this is God, our God, into without end, and into the world of world; he shall govern us into worlds (or forever).

PSALM 49

1   *To victory, a psalm to the sons of Korah.* All ye folks, hear these things; all ye that dwell in the world, perceive with ears (or listen!).

2   All the sons of the earth, and the sons of men; together the rich man, and the poor into one, (or yea, the rich and the poor, together as one).

3   My mouth shall speak wisdom; and the thinking of mine heart *shall speak* prudence.

4   I shall bow down mine ear into (or listen to) a parable; I shall open my reason set forth in a psaltery (or on a lyre).

5   Why shall I dread (or fear) in the evil day? (when) the wickedness of mine heel (or my enemies) shall encompass me.

6   Which (or Who) trust in their own virtue (or wealth); and have glory in the multitude of their riches.

7   A brother again-buyeth not, shall a man again-buy? and he shall not give to God his pleasing. (No one shall ever be able to redeem himself; he shall never be able to pay God the price that

he asketh for him.)

8   And *he shall not (be able to) give* the price of ransom for his soul; and (even if) he shall travail into without end (or labour forever),

9   and he shall live yet into the end. He shall not see perishing, (so that he would live forever, and not see perishing, *or corruption*,)

10   when he shall see wise men dying; (and) the unwise man and the fool shall perish together (with them). And they (all) shall leave their riches to aliens (or to foreigners, or strangers);

11   and the sepulchres of them *be* the houses of them without end. The tabernacles of them *be* in generation and in generation; they called their names in their lands (or even though their lands were once called by their names).

12   A man or Man, when he was in honour, understood not; he is comparisoned to unwise beasts, and (soon) is made like to them.

13   This way of them *is* a cause of stumbling to them; and afterward they shall please altogether in their mouth (or what they say).

14   As sheep they be put in hell; death shall gnaw them. And just men shall be the lords of them in the morrowtide; and the help of them shall wax (or grow) old in hell, for or from the glory of them.

15   Nevertheless God shall again-buy (or redeem) my soul from the power of hell (or Sheol, or the grave); when he shall take me (away).

16   Dread thou not (or Fear not), when a man is made rich; and when the glory of his house is multiplied.

17   For when he shall die, he shall not take all things (or anything) *with him*; and his glory shall not go down with him.

18   For his soul shall be blessed in his life; he shall acknowledge to (or praise, or thank) thee, when thou hast done well to him.

19   He shall enter till into the generations of his fathers; and till into without end he shall not see the light.

DAY 9

20   A man or Man, when he was in honour, understood not; he is comparisoned to unwise beasts, and soon is made like to them.

PROVERBS CHAPTER 9

1   Wisdom builded an house to himself; he hewed out seven pillars,

2   he offered his slain sacrifices, he meddled or mingled (or mixed in spices with) the wine, and setted forth his table.

3   He sent (forth) his handmaids, that they should call to the tower; and to the walls of the city.

4   If any man is little (*in wit or understanding*), come he to me. And (then) *wisdom* spake to unwise men, (and said),

5   Come ye, eat ye my bread; and drink ye the wine, which I have meddled or mingled to you (or mixed in spices for you).

6   Forsake ye young childhood (or foolishness), and live ye; and go ye by the way of prudence.

7   He that teacheth a scorner, doeth wrong to himself; and he that reproveth a wicked man, engendereth a wem to (or begetteth a wound for) himself.

8   Do not thou reprove a scorner; lest he hate thee. Reprove thou a wise man; and he shall love thee.

9   Give thou occasion to a wise man; and wisdom shall be increased to him. Teach thou a rightwise man; and he shall hasten to take *it* (to heart).

10   The beginning of wisdom *is* the dread (or fear) of (or reverence for) the Lord; and prudence *is* the knowing of the saints (or the knowledge of the Holy One).

11   For thy days shall be multiplied by me; and the years of (thy) life shall be increased to thee.

12   If thou art wise, thou shalt be *wise* to (or for) thyself, and to

thy neighbours. Forsooth if *thou art* a scorner, thou alone shalt bear the evil.

13   A fond or foolish woman, and full of cry (or loud), and full of unleaveful (or unlawful) lusts, and that knoweth nothing utterly,

14   sitteth in (or at) the doors of her house, on a seat, in an high place of the city;

15   to call men passing by the way, and men going in (or on) their journey.

16   Who is a little man *in wit*; bow he to me (or turn he unto me). And she spake to a coward, (and said),

17   Waters of theft be sweeter, and bread hid (or eaten in secret) is sweeter. [Stolen waters be sweeter, and hid bread more sweet.]

18   And he knew not that giants be there; and the guests of her *be* in the depths of hell (or Sheol, or the grave). Soothly he that shall be applied, *either fastened*, to her, shall go down to hell. For why he that goeth away from her shall be saved.

ECCLESIASTICUS   CHAPTER 12

1   If thou doest well, know thou to whom thou doest (it); and there shall be much grace in thy goods (or favor for thy good doings).

2   Do thou well to a rightwise man, and thou shalt find great yielding; if not of (or from) him, certainly of (or from) the Lord.

3   It is not well to him that is customable or is busy in evils, and to him that giveth not alms; for why the Highest both hateth sinners, and doeth mercy to them that do penance.

4   Give thou to the merciful, and receive thou not a sinner, *that is, (one) obstinate in sins; God* shall yield vengeance both to unfaithful men and to sinners, keeping them in the day of vengeance. Give thou to a good man, and receive thou not a

sinner.

5   Do thou good or well to a meek man, and give thou not to an unpious man, *that is, (one) obstinate in sin*; forbid thou (thyself) to give loaves to him, lest in (or with) them, he be(come) mightier than thou. For (then) thou shalt find double evils in all goods (or in all the good things), whatever thou doest to (or for) him;

6   for why the Highest both hateth sinners, and shall yield vengeance to unfaithful men.

7   (This verse is omitted in the original text.)

8   A friend shall not be known in goods (or in good times), and an enemy shall not be hid in evils, *that is, adversities.*

9   In the goods (or the good times) of a man, his enemies *be sorry*; and a friend is known in the sorrow and malice of him, *that is, in the adversity of him.*

10   Believe thou never to or (do) not trust thine enemy; for his wickedness rusteth as (or like) iron.

11   Though he be made meek, and go low, cast away thy soul or throw away thy will, and keep thee from him.

12   Set thou not him beside thee, neither sit he at thy right side, lest he turn (against thee), and stand in thy place; lest peradventure he turn into thy place, and inquire (about) thy chair, and in (or at) the last time thou know (or remember) my words, and be pricked in (or with) my words.

13   Who shall do medicine to an enchanter smitten of (or by) a serpent, and to all men that nigh to (or approach) beasts,

14   and *to him* that goeth with an evil man, and is wrapped (up) in the sins of him?

15   In one hour he shall dwell with thee; soothly if thou bowest away or down, he shall not bear (thee) up.

16   The enemy maketh sweet in (or with) his lips, and in his heart he setteth treason to overturn thee into the ditch. The enemy

weepeth in (or with) his eyes; and (or but) if he findeth the time, he shall not be full-filled of (or with enough) blood.

17   If evils befall to thee, thou shalt find him the former (or the first) there. The enemy shall weep before thine eyes, and he as helping shall undermine thy feet.

18   He shall stir or move his head, and he shall beat or flap (or clap) for joy with (his) hands; and he shall speak privily many *evils* of (or about) thee, and shall change his cheer (or his face).

ECCLESIASTICUS CHAPTER 13

1   He that toucheth pitch, shall be defouled of (or by) it; and he that communeth with a proud man, shall (be) clothe(d) (with) or in pride.

2   He raiseth or taketh a weight upon himself, that communeth with a more honest (or more honoured) man than himself; and be thou not fellow to a man richer than thou. What (or How) shall a caldron commune to (or with) a pot? for when those hurtle themselves together, *the pot* shall be broken.

3   A rich man shall do unjustly, and shall gnash, *as ready yet to do worse*; but a poor man hurt shall be still or shall hold his peace.

4   If thou givest, he shall take (from) thee; and if thou hast not, he shall forsake thee.

5   If thou hast, he shall live together with thee, and shall make thee void; and he shall not have sorrow upon thee.

6   If thou art needful or necessary to him, he shall deceive or beguile thee; and he shall flatter, and shall give hope, telling to thee all goods (or every good thing); and shall say, What need is to thee?

7   And he shall shame thee in (or at) his meats, till he annihilate or extinguish thee twice and thrice, and at the last he shall scorn

thee; afterward he shall see (thee), and shall forsake thee, and he shall move his head to (or at) thee. Be thou made meek to God, and abide thou his hands.

8 Take heed, lest thou be deceived, and be made low in folly. Do not thou be low in thy wisdom, lest thou be made low, and be deceived into folly.

9 When thou art called of (or by) a mightier man, go thou away; for by this he shall more call thee.

10 Be thou not greatly pressing, lest thou be hurtled down; and be thou not far from him, lest thou go into forgetting.

11 Withhold thou not to speak with him evenly, *that is, speak thou to him without reverence*, and believe thou not to his many words; for of (or with) much speech he shall tempt thee, and he shall laugh privily, and shall ask thee of (or about) thine hid things.

12 His cruel soul shall keep thy words, and he shall not spare (thee) from malice, and from bonds.

13 Beware to thee, and take heed diligently to thine hearing; for thou goest with thy destroying. But thou hearing those things, see as in sleep, and thou shalt wake.

14 In all thy life love thou God, and inwardly call thou him in thine health, *that is, for thine health* (or *thy deliverance*), (*both*) *temporal and everlasting*.

15 Each beast loveth *a beast* like itself; so and each man *oweth* (or *ought*) *to love* his neighbour.

16 Each flesh shall be joined to *flesh* like itself, and each man shall be fellowshipped to *a man* like himself.

17 As a wolf shall commune sometime with a lamb, so a sinner with a rightwise man.

18 What communing or communication *is* of an holy man to (or with) a dog? either what good part *is* of a rich man to (or with) a poor man?

19   The hunting of a lion *is* a wild ass in the desert or the wilderness; so (in) the pastures of rich men be poor men.

20   And as meekness is an abomination to a proud man, so and a poor man is an abomination of (or to) a rich man.

21   A rich man moved, *that is, disturbed, either hurled*, is confirmed of (or by) his friends; but a meek man, when he falleth, shall be cast or put out, yea, of (his) known men (or by his friends).

22   Many recoverers (or helpers) be to a rich man deceived; he spake proudly, and they justified him. (But) a meek man is deceived, furthermore also he is reproved; he spake wisely, and no place was given to him.

23   The rich man spake, and all men were still or held their peace; and they shall bring or shall bear his words till to the clouds. (But) a poor man spake, and they say, Who is this? and if he offendeth (or if he stumble), they shall destroy him.

24   Chattel or substance is good *to him*, to whom is no sin in conscience; and the worst poverty is in the mouth of a wicked man or the unpious.

25   The heart of a man changeth his face, either in good either in evil. Of hard and with travail, *or only with much hard seeking*, thou shalt find the step of a good heart, and a good face *together*.

26   (This verse is omitted in the original text.)

ECCLESIASTES CHAPTER 9

1   I treated (or considered) all these things in mine heart (or in my mind), to understand diligently. There be rightwise and wise men, and their works be in the hand of God; and nevertheless a man knoweth not, whether he is worthy of love or of hate.

2   But all things be kept uncertain into the time to come; for all things befall evenly to the rightwise and to the wicked, to a good

man and to an evil man, to a clean man and to an unclean man, to a man offering offerings and sacrifices, and to a man despising sacrifices; as (to) a good man, so and (to) a sinner; as (to) a forsworn man, so and (to) he that greatly sweareth the truth.

3 This thing is the worst among all things, that be done under the sun, that the same thing befall to all men; wherefore and the hearts of the sons of men be filled with malice and with despising in their life (or during their lives); and after these things, they shall be led down into hell (or to the grave, or Sheol).

4 No man there is, that liveth ever, and that hath trust of this thing; better is a quick (or living) dog than a dead lion.

5 For they that live (at least) know that they shall die; but dead men know nothing more, neither have meed further (or any further reward); for their mind (or their memory) is given to forgetting.

6 Also the(ir) love, and hatred, and envy, (have) perished altogether; and they have no part in this world, and in the work that is done under the sun.

7 Therefore go thou, *just man*, and eat thy bread in gladness, and drink thy wine with joy; for thy works please God.

8 In each time thy clothes be white, and oil fail not from thine head.

9 Use thou (or Enjoy) life with the wife which thou lovest, in all the days of the life of thine unstableness (or thy changing life), that be given to thee under the sun, in all the time of thy vanity (or in all thine empty and futile time); for this is thy part in thy life and travail (or thy labour), by which thou travailest under the sun.

10 Work thou busily, (at) whatever thing thine hand may (or can) do; for neither work, neither reason, nor knowing (or knowledge), nor wisdom, shall be at hell (or in the grave, or in the land of the dead), whither thou hastenest.

11 I turned me to another thing, and I saw under the sun, that

running is not of swift men (or that the race is not always to the swift), neither battle *is* of (or to) the strong men, neither bread *is* of (or to) the wise men, neither riches *be* of (or to) the teachers, nor grace *is* of craftsmen (or favour is to the skilled); but time and hap *is* in (or *be* to) all things, *that is, uncertainty, that oweth* (or *ought*) *to refrain a man from pride.*

12   A man knoweth not his end; but as fishes be taken with an hook, and as birds be taken with a snare, so men be taken in an evil time, when it cometh suddenly upon them.

13   Also I saw this wisdom under the sun, and I proved *it* the most, (or and it greatly impressed me).

14   (There was) a little city, and (only) a few men in it; a great king came against it, and encompassed it with pales (or posts), and he builded strongholds, *either engines*, by compass; and (so) the besieging was made perfect.

15   And a poor man and a wise (one) was found in it; and he delivered (or saved) the city by his wisdom, and (or but) no man bethought afterward on (or much about) that poor man.

16   And I (have always) said, that wisdom is better than strength; how therefore (or so why then) is the wisdom of a poor man despised, and his words be not heard (or appreciated)?

17   The words of wise men (should) be heard in silence, more than the (loud) cry of a prince among fools.

18   Better is wisdom than the arms (or the weapons) of battle; and he that sinneth in one thing, shall lose many goods (or much that is good). Δ

DAY 10

PSALM 50

1 *The psalm of Asaph.* God, the Lord of gods, or the God of gods, spake; and called the earth, from the rising of the sun unto the going down.

2 The shape of his fairness (or beauty) from Zion, God shall come openly;

3 our God, and he shall not be still (or silent). Fire shall burn on high in his sight; and a strong tempest in his compass (or all around him).

4 He called heaven above; and the earth, to witness him deem (or judge) his people.

5 Gather ye to him his saints (or his people); that ordain his testament (or covenant) above sacrifices.

6 And the heavens shall show or tell (out) his rightwiseness; for God is the judge.

7 My people, hear thou, and I shall speak to Israel; and I shall witness to (or testify against) thee, I am God, thy God.

8 I shall not reprove (or rebuke) thee in (or for) thy sacrifices; and thy burnt sacrifices be evermore before me

9 I shall not take calves of (or from) thine house; neither goat bucks of (or from) thy flocks.

10 For all the wild beasts of the woods be mine; (and) the work beasts, and the oxen in (or on) the hills.

11 I have known all the volatiles (or birds) of the firmament; and the fairness of the field is with me (or is mine).

12 If I shall be hungry, I shall not say to thee; for the world and the fullness thereof is mine.

13 Whether I shall eat the flesh of bulls? either shall I drink the

blood of goat bucks? (No!)

14   Offer (or Give) thou to God the sacrifice of praising; and yield (or pay) thy vows to the highest *God.*

15   And inwardly call thou me in the day of tribulation; and I shall deliver thee, and thou shalt honour me.

16   But God said to the sinner, Why tellest thou out my rightfulnesses (or statutes); and takest my testament by (or my covenant in) thy mouth?

17   Soothly thou hatedest lore, *or discipline*; and hast cast away my words behind (thee).

18   If thou sawest a thief, thou rannest with him; and thou settedest thy part or thy portion with adulterers.

19   Thy mouth was plenteous (or full) of malice; and thy tongue meddled together guiles or treacheries (or mixed together lies).

20   Thou sitting spakest against thy brother, and thou settedest (forth) slander against the son of thy mother;

21   thou didest these things, and I was still. Thou guessedest wickedly, that I shall be like thee; I shall reprove thee, and I shall set (them) against thy face.

22   Ye that forget God, understand these things; lest sometime he ravish (or tear thee in pieces), and none be that shall deliver (thee).

23   The sacrifice of praising shall honour me; and there *is* the way, wherein I shall show to him the health (or the salvation) of God.

PSALM 51

1   *To victory, the psalm of David, when Nathan the prophet came to him, when he entered to Bathsheba.* God, have thou mercy on me; by thy great mercy (or great love). And by the muchliness of thy merciful doings; do thou away my wickedness.

2   Moreover wash thou me from my wickedness; and cleanse

thou me from my sin.

3   For I acknowledge (or confess) my wickedness; and my sin is evermore against me.

4   I have sinned to thee alone, and I have done evil before thee; (so) that thou be justified in thy words (about me), and overcome when thou art deemed (or and correct when thou judgest me).

5   For lo! I was conceived in wickednesses (or in sinfulness); and my mother conceived me in sins.

6   For lo! thou lovedest truth; thou hast showed to me the uncertain things, and privy (or secret, or private) things of thy wisdom.

7   Lord, sprinkle thou me with hyssop, and I shall be cleansed; wash thou me, and I shall be made white more than snow (or made more white than snow).

8   Give thou joy, and gladness to mine hearing; and the bones made meek (or bruised) shall full out make joy.

9   Turn away thy face from my sins; and do away all my wickednesses.

10   God, make thou a clean heart in me; and make thou new a rightful spirit in my entrails (or deep within me).

11   Cast thou me not away from thy face; and take thou not away from me thine Holy Spirit.

12   Give thou to me the gladness of thine health (or salvation); and confirm thou me with the principal (or a willing) spirit.

13   I shall teach wicked men thy ways; and unfaithful men shall be converted to thee.

14   God, the God of mine health (or salvation), deliver thou me from bloods, *or sins*; and my tongue shall joyfully sing (of) thy rightwiseness.

15   Lord, open thou my lips; and my mouth shall tell (out) thy praising.

16   For if thou haddest would (or desired) sacrifice, I had given *it*;

truly thou shalt not delight in burnt sacrifice.

17   A sacrifice to God is a spirit troubled, *that is, (one made) sorry
for sin*; God, thou shalt not despise a contrite heart, and made meek.

18   Lord, do thou benignly (or kindly) in thy good will to Zion;
(so) that the walls of Jerusalem (may) be builded.

19   Then thou shalt take pleasantly the sacrifice of rightwiseness
(or be pleased with a righteous sacrifice), (with) offerings, and
burnt sacrifices; then they shall put calves upon thine altar.

PSALM 52

1   *To victory, the psalm of David, when Doeg the Idumaean
came, and told to Saul, and said to him, David came into the
house of Ahimelech.* What (or Why) hast thou glory in malice;
which (or who) art mighty in wickedness?

2   All day (long) thy tongue thought (or spake) unrightfulness; as
a sharp razor thou hast done guile or treachery (or deception).

3   Thou lovedest malice more than benignity (or goodness); *and*
wickedness more than to speak equity (or the truth).

4   Thou lovedest all words of casting down; with a guileful (or a
deceitful) tongue.

5   Therefore God shall destroy thee into the end, he shall draw
thee out by the root, and he shall make thee to pass away from thy
tabernacle; and thy root from the land of living men.

6   Rightwise men shall see, and shall dread (or fear); and they
shall laugh on (or at) him,

7   and they shall say, Lo! the man that put not God (as) his
helper. But he hoped in the multitude of his riches; and had the
mastery in his vanity.

8   Forsooth I, as a fruitful olive tree in the house of God; hoped
in the mercy (or trusted in the love) of God without end, and into

the world of world (or forever and ever).

9   (O God), I shall acknowledge to thee into the world (or praise thee forever), for thou hast done *mercy to me*; and I shall abide (or wait upon) thy name, for it is good in the sight of thy saints (or thy people).

PSALM 53

1   *To the overcomer, by the quire, the learning of David.* The unwise man said in his heart, God is not. They be corrupt, and made abominable in their wickednesses; none is that doeth good.

2   God beheld from heaven upon the sons of men; (so) that he see, if there is any understanding, either seeking God.

3   All bowed away, they be made unprofitable altogether; none is that doeth good, there is not unto one.

4   Whether all men, that work wickedness, shall not know; which devour my people, as the meat (or the food) of bread? They called not (upon) God;

5   (and) there they trembled for dread (or fear), where no dread was. For God hath scattered the bones of them, that please men; they be shamed, for God hath forsaken (or despised) them.

6   Who shall give from Zion health (or salvation) to Israel? when the Lord hath returned the captivity (or restored the fortunes) of his people, Jacob shall full out make joy, and Israel shall be glad.

PSALM 54

1   *To victory, in organs, either in psalms, the learning of David, when the Ziphims came, and said to Saul, Whether David is not hid at (or with) us?* God, in thy name, make thou me safe (or save me); and by thy virtue (or strength), deem thou me (or judge me).

2   God, hear thou my prayer; with ears perceive thou (or listen to) the words of my mouth.

3   For aliens (or foreigners) have risen against me, and strong men sought my life; and they setted not God before their sight.

4   For lo! God helpeth me; and the Lord is the up-taker of my soul (or the Lord is my defender).

5   Return thou away evils (back) to mine enemies; and lose (or destroy) thou them in (or by) thy truth.

6   Willfully (or Willingly) I shall sacrifice to thee; and, Lord, I shall acknowledge to (or praise) thy name, for it is good.

7   For thou deliveredest me from all tribulation (or troubles); and mine eyes despised on (or saw the defeat of) mine enemies.

PSALM 55

1   *To victory, in organs (or with instruments), the learning of David.* God, hear thou my prayer, and despise thou not my beseeching;

2   give thou attention to me, and hear thou me. I am sorrowful in mine exercising (or grieved by my distress);

3   and I am disturbed of (or made afraid by) the face of the enemy, and of the tribulation of (or from) the sinner. For they bowed wickednesses into me; and in (or with) wrath they were dis-easeful to me.

4   Mine heart was troubled in me; and the dread (or fear) of death fell upon me.

5   Dread and trembling came upon me; and darknesses covered me.

6   And I said, Who shall give to me feathers, as of a culver (or wings like a dove); and I shall fly (away), and shall take rest?

7   Lo! I went far away, and fled; and I dwelled in the wilderness.

8   I abode him, that made me safe from the littleness, *either dread*, of the spirit; and from the tempest. (I would hasten, and make myself safe from the wind, and from the tempest.)

9   Lord, cast thou down, and part thou the tongues of them; for I saw wickedness and against-saying in the city.

10   By day and night wickedness shall encompass it on the walls thereof; and travail and unrightfulness *be* in the midst of them.

11   And usury and guile or treachery (or deception, or deceit) failed not; from the streets thereof.

12   For if mine enemy had cursed me; soothly I had suffered. And if he, that hated me, had spoken great (evil) things (up)on or over me; in hap I had hid me from him.

13   But thou art a man of one will (with me); my leader, and my known.

14   Which tookest together sweet meats (or who shared his good counsel) with me; we went with consent in(to) the house of God.

15   Death come upon them; and go they down quick (or alive) into hell (or Sheol, or the grave). For waywardnesses be in the dwelling places of them; (and) in the midst of them.

16   But I cried to thee, Lord; and the Lord saved (or will save) me.

17   In the eventide, and the morrowtide, and in midday, I shall tell, and show (him); and he shall hear my voice.

18   He shall again-buy (or redeem, or ransom) my soul in peace from them, that nigh to me; for among many they were with me (or for many were against me).

19   God shall hear; and he that is before the worlds (or eternal) shall make them low. For changing is not to them, and they dreaded (or feared) not God;

20   he holdeth forth his hand in yielding. They defouled his testament (or covenant, or promise),

21   they be divided from the wrath of his cheer (or his face); and

his heart nighed. The words of him were softer than oil; and (or but) they be (as sharp as) darts.

22   Cast thy care, *or thought*, (or) thy busyness, upon the Lord, and he shall fully nourish thee; and he shall not give without end fluttering to the rightwise (or he shall not allow the righteous to be moved, *or shaken*, forever).

23   But thou, God, shalt lead them forth; into the pit of death. Men-quellers (or Murderers) and beguilers (or deceivers) shall not have half their days; but, Lord, I shall hope (or trust) in thee.

PROVERBS   CHAPTER 10

1   *The parables of Solomon.* A wise son maketh glad his father; but a fond or fool(ish) son is the sorrow of his mother.

2   Treasures of wickedness shall not profit; but rightwiseness shall deliver from death.

3   The Lord shall not torment the soul of the rightwise with hunger; and he shall destroy the treasons of unpious men.

4   A slow (or lazy) hand hath wrought neediness; but the hand of strong men maketh ready riches. Forsooth he that endeavoureth *to get anything* by lies, feedeth the winds; soothly the same man pursueth or followeth (after) birds flying.

5   He that gathereth together in harvest, is a wise son; *but* he that sleepeth in summer, is a son of confusion.

6   The blessing of God *is* upon the head of the rightwise; but wickedness covereth the mouth of wicked men.

7   The mind (or The memory) of the rightwise *shall be* with praisings; and the name of wicked men shall wax (or grow) rotten.

8   A wise man shall receive (or take) commandments with (or unto his) heart; a fool is beaten with (his own) lips.

9   He that goeth simply (or honestly), goeth trustily; *but* he that

maketh shrewd (or depraved) his ways, shall be made open (or exposed).

10 He that beckoneth with the eye, shall give sorrow; a fool shall be beaten with (his own) lips.

11 The vein (or The fountain) of life *is* the mouth (or the words) of the rightwise; but the mouth of wicked men covereth wickedness.

12 Hatred raiseth up chidings; and charity (or love) covereth all sins.

13 Wisdom is found in (or on) the lips of a wise man; and a rod in (or on) the back of him that is needy of heart (or foolish).

14 Wise men hide (or store up) knowing (or knowledge); but the mouth of a fool is next to confusion.

15 The chattel or substance of a rich man *is* the city of his strength; the dread (or fear) of poor men *is* the neediness of them.

16 The work of a rightwise man *is* to life; but the fruit of a wicked man *is* to sin.

17 The way of life *is* to him that keepeth chastising (or receiveth discipline); but he that forsaketh blamings (or correction), erreth.

18 False lips hide hatred; he that bringeth forth despising is unwise.

19 Sin shall not fail (or be lacking) in (or with) much speaking; but he that measureth his lips (or his words), is most prudent.

20 Chosen silver *is* (like) the tongue of the rightwise; the heart of wicked men *is* for nought (or worth nothing).

21 The lips of the rightwise teach full many; but they that be unlearned shall die in neediness of the heart.

22 The blessing of the Lord maketh rich men; and torment shall not be fellowshipped to them.

23 A fool worketh wickedness as by laughing; but prudence is to a wise man.

24 That that a wicked man dreadeth, shall come upon him; the desire of rightwise men shall be given to them.

25   As a tempest passing, a wicked man shall not be; but the rightwise *shall be* as an everlasting foundament (or foundation).

26   As vinegar *annoyeth or harmeth* the teeth, and smoke *harmeth* the eyes; so a slow man *harmeth* them that sent him in (or on) the way.

27   The dread (or fear) of (or reverence for) the Lord increaseth days; and the years of wicked men shall be made short.

28   The abiding of the rightwise *is* gladness; but the hope of wicked men shall perish.

29   The strength of a simple (or an honest) man *is* the way of the Lord; and dread (or ruin) to them that work evil.

30   The rightwise shall not be moved without end; but wicked men shall not dwell upon the earth (or in the land).

31   The mouth of the rightwise shall bring forth wisdom; the tongue of shrews (or the depraved) shall perish (or be stopped).

32   The lips of the rightwise behold (or say) pleasant things; and the mouth of wicked men wayward or perverted things.

ECCLESIASTICUS   CHAPTER 14

1   Blessed *is* the man, that is not slid in (or slippeth by) the words from his mouth, and was not pricked in (or with) the sorrow of trespass.

2   *He is* blessed, that hath not sorrow of (or in) his soul, and falleth not down or away from his hope.

3   Chattel or substance, *that is, riches*, is without reason to a covetous man, and hard niggard (or stingy, or miserly); and whereto *is* gold to an envious man?

4   He that gathereth of his will unjustly (or by defrauding his own soul), gathereth to (or for) other men; and another man shall make waste or do lechery in (or with) his goods.

5   To what other man shall he be good, which (or who) is wicked to himself? and he shall not be merry in his goods.

6   Nothing is worse, than he that hath envy to himself; and this is the yielding of (or the recompense for) his malice.

7   And if he doeth good, he doeth (it) unwittingly, and not willfully (or willingly); and at the last he showeth his malice.

8   The eye of an envious man is wicked, and turning away the face, and despising his soul.

9   The eye of the covetous man *is* never filled; he shall not be filled into the part of wickedness, till he perform unrightfulness or unrightwiseness, and make dry his (own) soul.

10   An evil eye to evils, and the needy man shall not be filled with bread; and he shall be in sorrow on (or at) his table.

11   Son, if thou hast, do well with thyself, and offer thou worthy offerings to God.

12   Be thou mindful (or remember) that death shall not tarry, and the testament of hell (or the covenant of the grave), *that is, the ordinance of God, of the death of each man*, which is showed to thee; for why the testament of this world shall die by death.

13   Before (thy) death do thou good to (or for) thy friend, and by thy mights or strengths stretch thou forth, and give to the poor.

14   Be thou not deceived or beguiled of (or from) a good day, and a little part of a good day pass not thee (unfulfilled or unappreciated).

15   Whether thou shalt not leave to other men thy sorrows, and thy travails (or the fruit of thy labours)?

16   In the parting of lot give thou, and take, and justify thy soul.

17   Before thy death work thou rightfulness or rightwiseness; for at hell (or in the grave), it is not to find meat (or any food).

18   Each man shall wax (or grow) old as hay, and as a leaf bringing fruit in (or on) a green tree. Others be engendered, and others be cast or fall down; so the generation of flesh and blood,

another is ended, and another is born.

19   Each corruptible work shall fail in the end; and he that worketh it, shall go with it. And all chosen work shall be justified; and he that worketh it, shall be honoured in (or by) it.

20   Blessed *is* the man, that shall dwell in wisdom, and that shall bethink in rightwiseness, and shall think in wit (about) the beholding of God.

21   Who thinketh out, *either findeth out*, the ways of him in his heart, and shall be understanding in the hid things of it (or wisdom);

22   going as a searcher after it, and standing in the ways of it.

23   Who beholdeth by the windows of it, and heareth in (or at) the gates of it;

24   who resteth nigh the house of it, and setteth a stake in the walls of it.

25   He shall set his little house at the hands of it, and goods (or good things) shall rest in his little house, by the enduring of the world;

26   he shall set his sons under the covering or the roof of it, and he shall dwell under the boughs or the branches of it;

27   he shall be covered under the covering or the roof of it from heat, and he shall rest in the glory of it.

ECCLESIASTICUS   CHAPTER 15

1   He that dreadeth God, shall do good *works*; and he that holdeth rightfulness, shall take (or receive) it, *that is, wisdom.*

2   And it as a mother honoured shall meet him, and as a woman from virginity or from maidenhood it shall take (or shall receive) him.

3   It shall feed him with the bread of life, and of understanding; and it shall give drink to him with water of wholesome wisdom;

4   it shall be made steadfast in him, and he shall not be bowed (or turned away) *from the evenness of rightfulness.* And it shall

hold him, and he shall not be shamed or confounded;

5   and it shall enhance him at (or it shall exalt him above) his neighbours. And in the midst of the church it shall open his mouth; and *God* shall fill him with the spirit of wisdom, and of understanding, and shall clothe him with the stole of glory.

6   *God* shall treasure upon him mirth, and full out joying; and shall inherit him with an everlasting name.

7   Fond or fool(ish) men shall not take (or receive) that *wisdom*, and (or but) witty (or witting, or knowing) men shall meet (with) it. (Yea), fond or fool(ish) men shall not see it;

8   for why it goeth away far from pride, and guile or treachery (or deception, or deceit). Men leasing-mongers or liars shall not be mindful thereof (or see it), and (or but) soothfast men shall be found in it; and shall have prosperity unto the beholding of God.

9   Praising is not fair (or beautiful) in the mouth of a sinner, for he is not sent of the Lord (or it was not sent to him from the Lord).

10   For why wisdom went forth from God; forsooth praising shall stand nigh (to) the wisdom of God, and it shall be plenteous or abound in a faithful mouth, and the Lord shall give it to him.

11   Say thou not, It goeth away by God; for why do thou not those things (or why do thou do those things), which *God* hateth.

12   Say thou not, He made me for to err; for why wicked or unpious men be not needful to him.

13   The Lord hateth all cursedness of error, and it (also) shall not be amiable or loveful to them, that dread (or fear, or revere) him.

14   At the beginning God made or ordained man, and left him (or let him go) in the hand of his counsel.

15   He added his commandments, and laws; if thou wilt keep the commandments, they shall keep thee, and keep pleasant (or pleasing) faith without end.

16   He hath set or put to thee water and fire; address (or direct) or

put forth thine hand to that, that thou wilt.

17   Before man is life and death, good and evil; that, that pleaseth him, shall be given to him.

18   For why the wisdom of God is much, and he is strong in power, and seeth all men without ceasing.

19   The eyes of the Lord *be* to (or upon) them, that dread (or fear, or revere) him; and he knoweth all the travail or all the works of man.

20   He commanded not to any man to do wickedly or unpiously; and he gave not to any man space to do sin.

ECCLESIASTES   CHAPTER 10

1   Flies that die (in it), lose (or destroy) the sweetness of the ointment. A little folly at some time is more precious than wisdom and glory.

2   The heart of a wise man *is* in his right side (or in the right); and the heart of a fool *is* in his left side (or in the wrong).

3   But also a fool going in (or on) the way, when (or since) he is unwise, guesseth (or thinketh) that all men (be) fools.

4   If the spirit of him, that hath power, goeth upon (or against) thee, forsake thou not thy place (or do not leave thy position); for caring, *or taking heed*, shall make the greatest sins to cease.

5   An evil there is, that I saw under the sun, and going out as by error from the face of the prince;

6   a fool (is) set in high dignity, and rich men sit beneath.

7   I saw servants (riding) on horses, and princes as servants going on the earth (or walking on the ground).

8   He that diggeth a ditch, shall fall into it; and an adder (or a snake) shall bite him, that destroyeth a hedge.

9   He that beareth over (or carrieth) stones, shall be tormented in them (or can be hurt by them); and he that cutteth trees (or wood),

shall be wounded of them (or can be injured when cutting them).

10   If iron is folded again, and it *is* not as before, but is made blunt, it shall be made sharp with much travail (or much labour, or effort); and wisdom shall follow after busyness.

11   If a serpent biteth, *it biteth* in silence; he that backbiteth privily (or secretly), hath nothing less than it (or is no better than it).

12   The words of (or from) the mouth of a wise man *be* grace (or *bring him* favour); and the lips of an unwise man shall cast (or bring) him down.

13   The beginning of his words *is* folly (or foolish); and the last thing (out) of his mouth *is* the worst error (of all).

14   A fool multiplieth words; a man knoweth not, what was before him, and who may (or can) show to him that, that shall come after him?

15   The travail or labour of fools shall torment them, that know not how to (even) go into the city.

16   Land, woe to thee, whose king is a child, and whose princes eat early (and often).

17   Blessed *is* the land, whose king is noble (or refined); and whose princes eat in (or at) their (proper) time, to (only) sustain the(ir) kind (or themselves), and not (un)to lechery (or drunkenness).

18   The highness of houses shall be made low in sloths (or through laziness); and the house shall drop (rain or leak), in (or due to) the feebleness (or the weakness) of hands.

19   In (or With) laughing, they dispose (or array the table with) bread and wine, (so) that they drinking eat largely (or can enjoy the abundance); and (or yea), all things obey to money.

20   In thy thoughts backbite thou not the king, and in the private of thy bed, curse thou not a rich man; for the birds of the heavens shall bear (or carry) thy voice, and he that hath pens (or wings), shall tell the sentence. Δ

DAY 11

PSALM 56

1   *To the overcoming, on the dumb culver (or silent dove) of far drawing away, the comely song of David, when the Philistines held him in Gath.* God, have mercy on me, for a man hath defouled (or persecuted) me; all day (long) he impugned, and troubled me.

2   Mine enemies defouled me all day (long); for many fighters *were* against me.

3   Of the highness of day I shall dread (or fear); but God, I shall hope in (or trust) thee.

4   In God, I shall praise (with) my words (or whose words I praise); I hoped in (or trusted) God, I shall not dread (or fear) what thing flesh, *or man*, shall do to me.

5   All day they cursed my words; against me all their thoughts *were* into evil.

6   They shall dwell, and they shall hide; they shall ambush mine heel. As they abide (or lie in wait for) my life,

7   for nought shalt thou make them safe (or there is no reason thou shalt save them); in (or with) wrath thou shalt break altogether the peoples.

8   God, I showed my life to thee; thou hast set my tears in thy sight (or before thee). As and in thy promise, Lord;

9   then mine enemies shall be turned aback. In (or On) whatever day I shall inwardly call thee; lo! I have known, that thou art (with me), my God.

10   In God, I shall praise (with) a word (or whose word I praise); in the Lord, I shall praise (with) a word (or whose word I praise).

11   I shall hope in (or trust) God; I shall not dread (or fear) what thing man shall do to me.

12   God, thy vows be in (or binding upon) me; which I shall yield praisings to thee.

13   For thou hast delivered my life from death, and my feet from sliding (or slipping); (so) that I please before God in the light of them that live.

PSALM 57

1   *To the victory, lose (or destroy) thou not the seemly song, either the sweet song, of David, when he fled from the face of Saul into the den (or the cave).* God, have mercy on me, have thou mercy on me; for my soul trusteth in thee. And I shall hope in the shadow of thy wings; till the wickedness pass.

2   I shall cry to God alder-Highest; to God that did well (or good) to me.

3   He sent from heaven, and delivered me; he gave into shame them that defoul (or defile) me. God sent his mercy and his truth,

4   and delivered my soul from the midst of the whelps of lions; I slept troubled or disturbed. The sons of men, the teeth of them *be* arms and arrows; and their tongue *is* a sharp sword.

5   God, be thou enhanced (or exalted) above the heavens; and thy glory above all the earth.

6   They made ready a snare to (or for) my feet; and they greatly bowed (down) my life. They delved (or dug) a ditch before my face; and they felled down into it.

7   God, mine heart *is* ready, mine heart *is* ready; I shall sing, and I shall say a psalm (or I shall sing a song).

8   My glory, rise thou up; psaltery (or lyre) and harp, rise thou up; I shall rise up early (in the morning).

9   Lord, I shall acknowledge to (or praise) thee among the peoples; and I shall say (or sing) a psalm to thee among the

heathen men.

10   For thy mercy is magnified unto the heavens; and thy truth unto the clouds.

11   God, be thou enhanced (or exalted) above the heavens; and thy glory above all the earth.

PSALM 58

1   *To victory, lose (or destroy) thou not the sweet song, either the seemly psalm, of David.* Forsooth if ye speak rightfulness verily (or truly); ye sons of men, deem rightfully (or judge justly?). (No!)

2   For in heart ye work wickedness in (or upon) the earth; your hands make ready unrightfulnesses.

3   Sinners were made aliens (or go wrong) from the womb; they erred from the womb, they spake false things.

4   Strong vengeance *is* to them, by the likeness of a serpent; as of a deaf snake, and stopping his (or its) ears.

5   Which shall not hear the voice of charmers; and of a venom-maker charming (ever so) wisely.

6   God shall all-break the teeth of them in their mouth; the Lord shall break altogether the great teeth of lions.

7   They shall come to nought (or nothing), as water running away; he bent his bow, till they be made sick (or feeble).

8   As wax that floweth (or melteth) away, they shall be taken away; fire fell (from) above, and they saw not the sun.

9   Before that your thorns understood the rhamn, *either the thieve-thorn*; he swalloweth them (up) so in wrath, as (with) living men.

10   The rightwise man shall be glad, when he shall see vengeance; he shall wash his hands in the blood of a sinner.

11   And a man shall say truly, For fruit is to a rightwise man; truly

God is deeming (or judging) them in (or upon) the earth.

PSALM 59

1   *To the overcomer, lose (or destroy) thou not the seemly song
of David, when Saul sent (men) and kept (or guarded) the house,
(in order) to slay him.* My God, deliver thou me from mine
enemies; and deliver thou me from them that rise against me.

2   Deliver thou me from them that work wickedness; and save
thou me from men-quellers.

3   For lo! they have taken my soul; strong men fell in upon me.
Neither (for) my wickedness, neither (for) my sin;

4   Lord, I ran without wickedness, and (ad)dressed (or directed)
my works. Rise up into my meeting, and see;

5   and thou, Lord God of virtues (or of hosts, or armies), *art* God
of Israel. Give thou attention to visit (or to punish) all the folks (or
the nations); do thou not mercy to all (or to any) that work
wickedness.

6   They shall be returned at eventide, and they as dogs shall
suffer hunger; and they shall compass, *that is, go abegging,* (in) the
city.

7   Lo! they shall speak (insults) in (or with) their mouth, and a
sword (shall be) in their lips; for who heard (us)?

8   And thou, Lord, shalt scorn them; thou shalt bring all the folks
to nought (or all the nations down into nothing).

9   I shall keep my strength to thee (or Thou art my strength); for
God *is* mine up-taker (or defender),

10   my God, his mercy shall come before me. God showed to me
(my heart's desire) upon mine enemies,

11   (but) slay thou not them; lest any time my peoples forget.
(But) scatter thou them in thy virtue (or with thy strength); and,

Lord, my defender, put thou them down.

12   *Put down* the trespass of their mouths, and the words of their lips; and be they taken in their pride. And of cursing and of leasing (or lying); they shall be showed (up) in the ending.

13   (Destroy thou them) in the wrath of whole ending, and they shall not be; and (then) they shall know, that the Lord shall be Lord of Jacob, and of the ends of the earth.

14   They shall be returned at eventide, and they as dogs shall suffer hunger; and they shall compass, *that is, go abegging,* (in) the city.

15   They shall be scattered abroad, for to eat; soothly if they be not fulfilled, and they shall grumble.

16   But I shall sing (of) thy strength; and early I shall enhance (or exalt in) thy mercy. For thou art made mine up-taker; and my refuge, in the day of my tribulation (or troubles).

17   Mine helper, I shall sing to thee; for *thou art* God, mine up-taker (or defender), my God, my mercy.

PSALM 60

1   *To victory, on the witnessing (or testimony) of the rose, the sweet song of David, to teach men, when he fought against Aram of the floods (or the rivers), and Syria of Zobah; and Joab returned again, and smote Edom in the valley of the salt pits, twelve thousand.* God, thou hast put away us or put us aback, and thou hast destroyed us; thou were wroth, and thou hast done mercy to us.

2   Thou movedest the earth, and thou troubledest it; make thou whole (again) the sorrows of it, for it is moved.

3   Thou showedest hard things (or times) to thy people; thou gavest drink to us with the wine of compunction.

4   Thou hast given a signifying (or a warning) to them that dread (or fear) thee; (so) that they flee from the face of the bow.

5   (So) that thy darlings be delivered; make thou safe (or save us) with thy right hand, and hear thou me.

6   God spake by (or in) his holy (place); I shall be glad, and I shall part Shechem, and I shall mete (or measure out) the great valley of the tabernacles.

7   Gilead is mine, and Manasseh is mine; and Ephraim *is* the strength of mine head (or my helmet). Judah *is* my king (or my sceptre).

8   Moab *is* the pot of mine hope. Into Idumea I shall stretch forth my shoe; aliens (or foreigners) be made subject to me.

9   Who shall lead me into a city made strong; who shall lead me into Idumea (or Edom)?

10   Whether not thou, God, that hast put away us (or put us aback); and shalt thou not, God, go out in our virtues (or with our hosts)?

11   Lord, give thou to us help (out) of tribulation; for the help of man is vain (or futile).

12   In God we shall make virtue (or have the victory); and he shall bring to nought (or unto nothing) them that trouble or disturb us.

PSALM 61

1   *To victory, on organs (or instruments), to David himself.* God, hear thou my beseeching; give thou attention to my prayer.

2   From the ends of the earth I cried to thee; the while mine heart was anguished, thou enhancedest me in a stone (or thou liftedest me up on a rock). Thou leddest me forth,

3   for thou art made mine hope; a tower of strength from (or before) the face of the enemy.

4   I shall dwell in thy tabernacle into worlds (or forever); I shall

be covered in (or with) the covering of thy wings.

5   For thou, my God, hast heard my prayer; thou hast given a heritage to them that dread thy name (or thou hast given me the inheritance for those who fear or who revere thy name).

6   Thou shalt add, *either increase,* days onto the days of the king; his years unto the day of generation and of generation.

7   He dwelleth without end in the sight of God; who shall seek the mercy and truth of him? (or may thy love and faithfulness, preserve and protect him.)

8   So I shall say a psalm to thy name into the world of world (or forever and ever); (so) that I yield my vows from day into day.

PSALM 62

1   *To victory, over Jeduthun, the psalm of David.* Whether my soul shall not be subject to God; for mine health (or my salvation) *is* of (or from) him.

2   For why he *is* both my God, and mine health (or my salvation); mine up-taker, I shall no more be moved.

3   How long fall ye upon a man? all ye slain; as to a wall bowed, and *as* a wall of stone without mortar cast down.

4   Nevertheless they thought to put away my price (or to bring me down), I ran in thirst; with their mouth they blessed, and (or but) in their heart they cursed.

5   Nevertheless, my soul, be thou subject to God; for my patience *is* of him (or I wait patiently for him).

6   For *he is* my God, and my saviour; mine helper, I shall not pass out (or I shall not be shaken).

7   Mine health (or My salvation), and my glory *is* in God; God *is the giver* of mine help, and mine hope is in God.

8   All the gathering together of the people, hope (or trust) ye in

God, pour ye out your hearts before him; God *is* our helper without end.

9 Nevertheless the (lives of) the sons of men *be* (all in) vain (or futile); the sons of men *be* liars in (or with) balances, (so) that they deceive (themselves) of vanity into the same thing (or they all be deceived by the same emptiness and futility).

10 Do not ye have hope (or trust) in wickedness, and do not ye covet ravens (or spoils); if riches be plenteous, do not ye set the heart thereto (or upon them).

11 God spake once, I heard these two things; that power is of (or belongeth to) God,

12 and, thou Lord, mercy *is* to (or from) thee; for thou shalt yield to each man by (or according to) his works.

PROVERBS   CHAPTER 11

1 A guileful balance (or A deceptive scale) is an abomination with God; and an even weight *is* his will (or his desire, or delight).

2 Where pride is, there also despising shall be; but where meekness is, there also *is* wisdom.

3 The simpleness (or honesty) of just men shall address (or direct) them; and the deceiving of wayward men shall destroy them.

4 Riches shall not profit in the day of vengeance; but rightwiseness shall deliver from death.

5 The rightwiseness of a simple (or honest) man shall (ad)dress (or direct) his way; and a wicked man shall fall in his wickedness.

6 The rightwiseness of rightful men shall deliver them; and wicked men shall be taken (or caught) in their ambushings.

7 When a wicked man is dead, none hope shall be further *of* (or for) *him*; and the abiding of busy men *in evil* shall perish.

8   A rightwise man is delivered from anguish; and a wicked man shall be given for him (or shall be given to it).

9   A feigner by mouth (or A faker) deceiveth his friend; but rightwise men shall be delivered by knowing (or through knowledge or wisdom).

10   A city shall be enhanced (or lifted up) in the goods (or by the goods deeds) of rightwise men; and praising shall be in the perdition of wicked men.

11   A city shall be enhanced (or exalted) by the blessings of rightwise men; and it shall be destroyed by the mouths of wicked men.

12   He that despiseth his friend, is needy in heart; but a prudent man shall be still (or silent).

13   He that goeth guilefully, showeth privates (or He who goeth deceitfully, telleth secrets); but he that is faithful, covereth the private (matter) of a friend.

14   Where a governor is not, the people shall fall; but health (or victory) *is*, where be many counsels (or counsellors).

15   He that maketh faith, *that is, an obligation*, for a stranger, shall be tormented with evil; but he that escheweth or shunneth snares, shall be secure.

16   A gracious woman shall find glory (or receive honour); and strong (or ruthless) men shall have riches.

17   A merciful man doeth well (or good) to his (own) soul; but he that is cruel, casteth away, yea, (even his own) kinsmen.

18   A wicked man maketh unstable work; but faithful meed (or reward) *is* to (or for) him, that soweth rightwiseness.

19   Mercy shall make ready (or prepareth for) life; and the pursuing or following of evil, (is) death.

20   A shrewd (or depraved) heart *is* abominable to the Lord; and his will (or desire, or delight) *is* in them, that go simply (or do

honestly).

21   *Though* hand *be* in hand, an evil man shall not be innocent; but the seed of rightwise men shall be saved.

22   A golden *ring* in the nostrils of a sow, (*is like*) a woman fair (or beautiful) and fool(ish).

23   The desire of rightwise men is all good; (but) the abiding of wicked men *is* strong vengeance.

24   Some men part their own things, and be made richer; other men ravish (or steal) *things, that be* not theirs, and they be ever in neediness (or in need).

25   A soul that blesseth, shall be made fat; and he that filleth, shall be filled also.

26   He that hideth wheat, shall be cursed among the peoples; but blessing *shall come* upon the heads of sellers.

27   Well (be) he (who) riseth early, that seeketh good things; but he that is a searcher of evils, shall be oppressed of (or by) them.

28   He that trusteth in his riches, shall fall; but rightwise men shall burgeon (or flourish) as a green leaf.

29   He that troubleth his house, shall have the winds *in possession*; and he that is a fool, shall serve a wise man.

30   The fruit of a rightwise man *is* the tree of life; and he that taketh (or catcheth, or winneth) souls, is a wise man.

31   If a rightwise man receiveth (recompense) in (or here on) the earth, how much more an unfaithful man, and a sinner.

ECCLESIASTICUS CHAPTER 16

1   For he coveteth not the multitude of sons (who be) unfaithful and unprofitable. (Do not covet a multitude of sons, but who be unfaithful and unprofitable.)

2   Be thou not glad in wicked or unpious sons, if they be

multiplied; neither delight thou on (or in) them, if the dread (or the fear) of God (or reverence for God) is not in them.

3   Believe thou not to (or in) the life of them, and behold thou not into the travails of them. For why better is one dreading God, than a thousand wicked or unpious sons. And it is more profitable to die without sons, than to leave wicked or unpious sons.

4   A country shall be inhabited (or shall flourish) of (or by) one witty (or knowing, or knowledgeable) man; and it shall be made a desert of (or by) three wicked men.

5   Mine eye saw many other things, and mine ear heard stronger things than these.

6   Fire shall burn on high in the synagogue (or the assembly) of the sinners, and wrath shall burn on high in a folk unbelieveful (or in an unbelieving or unfaithful nation).

7   Old giants that were destroyed, trusting on their virtue (or in their own strength), prayed not for their sins;

8   and *God* spared not the pilgrimage of them, *that is, their life, which is a pilgrimage* (*here*) *on earth*, but he killed them, and cursed them, for the pride of their words.

9   He had not mercy on them, and he lost or destroying all the folk enhancing (or all the nation exalting) themselves in their sins.

10   And as *he killed* six hundred thousand of footmen, that were gathered together in the hardness of their hearts, *that is, rebelty (or in rebellion) against God*;

11   and if one had been hard-nolled, (it is a) wonder if he had been guiltless. For why mercy and wrath is with him; prayer is mighty, and the pouring out of wrath.

12   By (or According to) his mercy, so *is* the chastising of each man; he is deemed by (or judged according to) his works.

13   A sinner in (or with his) raven (or spoils) shall not escape; and the sufferance of him that doeth mercy shall not tarry.

14 All mercy shall make a place to (or for) each man, after the merit of his works, and after the understanding of his pilgrimage.

15 (This verse is omitted in the original text.)

16 (This verse is omitted in the original text.)

17 Say thou not, I shall be hid from God; and from the highest, *that is, (in) heaven*, who shall have mind on (or remember) me? *Say thou not*, I shall not be known in (such) a great (number of) people; for why what is my soul in so great a (number of) creatures?

18 Lo! heaven, and the heavens of heavens, the great ocean, *or the deepness*, and all the earth, and those things that be in them, shall be moved in his sight (or by his presence);

19 the mountains altogether, and the little hills, and the foundaments (or the foundations) of the earth; and when God beholdeth them, they shall be shaken altogether with trembling.

20 And in all these things the heart is unwise, and (or but) each heart is understood of (or by) him. And (or But) who understandeth his ways?

21 and a tempest, which the eye of man saw not? For why full many works of him be in hid things,

22 but who shall tell out the works of his rightfulness (or justice), or who shall suffer (them)? For why the testament is far from some men; and the asking (or the trial) of men is in the ending.

23 He that is made little in heart, thinketh (upon) vain things; and a man unprudent and a fool thinketh (upon) fond things or follies.

24 Son, hear thou me, and learn thou teaching or discipline of wit (or understanding), and give thou attention to my words in thine heart;

25 and I shall say teaching in equity (or of fairness), and I shall seek to tell out wisdom. And give thou attention to my words in thine heart; and I say in equity of spirit the virtues, which God hath

set on his works at the beginning, or that God put into his works from the beginning, and in truth I tell out the knowing of him (or his knowledge).

26   In the doom (or the judgement) of God *be* his works from the beginning; and in the ordinance of them, he parted or severed the parts of them, and *he parted* the beginnings of them in his folks (or among his nations).

27   He adorned without end the works of them; they hungered not, neither travailed, and they ceased not of (or from) their works.

28   Each shall not make strait or anguish the next to him, unto without end. Be thou not unbelieveful to the word of him.

29   After these things God beheld into (or looked upon) the earth, and filled it with his goods (or his good things).

30   Forsooth the soul of each living thing told before his face; and that *soul is* again the returning again of those things.

ECCLESIASTES CHAPTER 11

1   Send thy bread upon the waters passing forth, for after many times thou shalt find it (or thou shalt receive it back, *and more along with it*).

2   Give thou (thy) parts to seven, and also to eight, (*that is, do not put all thine eggs in one basket*); for thou knowest not, what evil shall come upon the earth.

3   If the clouds be filled, they shall pour out rain upon the earth; if a tree falleth down to the south, either to the north, in whatever place it falleth down, there it shall be.

4   He that espieth (or looketh for) the wind, soweth not; and he that beholdeth (or watcheth) the clouds, shall never reap (or bring in the harvest).

5   As thou knowest not, which is the way of the spirit (or the

path of the wind), and by what reason bones be joined together in the womb of a woman with child, so thou knowest not the works of God, which (or who) is the Maker of all things.

6   Early sow thy seed, and thine hand cease not in (or until) the eventide; for thou knowest not, what shall come forth more, this either that; and if ever either (or both) *come forth* together, it shall be the better.

7   The light *is* sweet, and delightable to (or for) the eyes to see the sun.

8   If a man liveth many years, and is glad in all (of) these, he (still) oweth (or ought) to have mind of (or to remember) the dark time, and of (those) many days (yet to come); and when they shall come, the things passed (away) shall be reproved of vanity (or be rebuked as but empty and futile).

9   Therefore, thou young man, be glad (or happy) in thy youth, and (let) thine heart be in goodness in the days of thy youth, and go thou in the ways of thine heart, and in the beholding of thine eyes; and (or but) know thou, that for all these things God shall bring thee into doom (or to the Judgement).

10   Do thou away wrath (or anger) from thine heart, and remove thou malice from thy flesh; for why youth and lust be vain things (or vanity, or empty and futile). Δ

DAY 12

PSALM 63

1   *The psalm of David, when he was in the desert of Judah.*
God, my God, I wake to thee full early. My soul thirsted to (or for)
thee; my flesh *thirsted* to (or for) thee full manyfold. In a land
forsaken without a way, and without water,

2   so I appeared to thee in (thy) holy (place); (so) that I should (or
could) see thy virtue (or thy power), and thy glory.

3   For thy mercy is better than lives (or thy love is better than
living, or than life itself); my lips shall praise thee.

4   So I shall bless thee in my life; and in thy name I shall raise
(up) mine hands.

5   My soul be fulfilled as with inner fatness and uttermore
fatness; and my mouth shall praise (thee) with lips of full out joying
(or with rejoicing).

6   So I had mind on (or remembered) thee upon my bed, in the
morrowtides I shall think of thee;

7   for thou hast been mine helper. And in (or under) the
covering of thy wings I shall make full out joy,

8   my soul cleaved after (or to) thee; thy right hand took (or
lifteth) me up.

9   Forsooth they sought in vain (to take away) my life, they shall
enter into the lower things of the earth (or Sheol, or the land of the
dead);

10   they shall be betaken into the hands of the sword, they shall
be made the parts of (or a portion for) foxes.

11   But the king shall be glad in God; and all men shall be praised
that swear in (or by) him; for the mouth of them, that speak wicked
things, is stopped.

DAY 12

PSALM 64

1   *To victory, the psalm of David.* God, hear thou my prayer, when I beseech; deliver thou my soul from the dread (or the fear, or the threats) of the enemy.

2   Thou hast defended me from the covent (or community) of evil-doers; from the multitude of them that work wickedness.

3   For they sharpened their tongues as a sword, they bend their bow, a bitter thing (or and shot out bitter words);

4   for to shoot in huddles, *or privates*, (or secretly attack) him that is unwemmed (or unblemished). Suddenly they shall shoot him, and they shall not dread;

5   they made steadfast to themselves a wicked word. They told (each other), that they should hide (their) snares; they said, (And) who shall see them?

6   They sought (out) wickednesses; they sought, and failed (not) in seeking. A man nighed to a deep heart;

7   and God shall be enhanced (or exalted). The arrows of little men, *that is, (of) envious men*, be made the wounds of them;

8   and the tongues of them be made sick against them (or their own undoing). All men be troubled, that saw them;

9   and each man dreaded. And they told (about) the works of God; and they understood the deeds of him.

10   The rightwise shall be glad in the Lord, and shall hope in him; and all men of rightful heart shall be praised.

PSALM 65

1   *To victory, the psalm of the song of David.* God, praising becometh to (or be due to) thee in Zion; and a vow shall be

yielded to thee in Jerusalem.

2   Hear thou my prayer; each man and woman shall come to thee.

3   The words of wicked men had the mastery over us; and thou shalt do (or show) mercy to(ward) our wickednesses.

4   Blessed *is* he, whom thou hast chosen, and hast taken; he shall dwell in thy foreyards (or courtyards). We shall be fulfilled with the goods (or good things) of thine house; thy temple is holy,

5   wonderful in equity. God, our health (or our salvation), hear thou us; *thou art* the hope of all the coasts of the earth, and in the sea afar.

6   And thou makest ready the hills in thy virtue (or by thy strength), and art girded with power;

7   which (or who) troublest the depth of the sea, the sound of the waves thereof. The folks (or The nations) shall be troubled,

8   and they that dwell in the ends (of the earth) shall dread of (or have awe at) thy signs; thou shalt delight the out-goings of the morrowtide and eventide.

9   Thou hast visited the land, and hast greatly filled it; thou hast multiplied (it) to make it rich. The flood (or The river) of God was full-filled with waters; thou madest ready the meat (or the food) of them, for the making ready of it is so.

10   Thou filling greatly the streams thereof, multiply the fruits thereof; *the land* bringing forth fruits shall be glad in the gutters of it (or for all this water).

11   Thou shalt bless the crown of the year of thy good will; and thy fields shall be full-filled with plenty of fruits.

12   The fair things of the desert shall wax (or grow) fat; and little hills shall be encompassed with full out joying.

13   The wethers (or The rams) of sheep be clothed, and the valleys shall be plenteous of (or with) wheat; they shall cry (out), and soothly they shall say praising or a psalm.

DAY 12

PSALM 66

1   *To victory, the song of the psalm.* All the earth, make ye joy heartily to God,

2   say ye (or sing) a psalm to his name; give ye glory to his praising.

3   Say ye to God, Lord, thy works be full dreadful (or so awesome); in the multitude of thy virtue (or great strength) thine enemies shall lie (down) to (or before) thee.

4   God, all the earth worship thee, and sing to thee; say it (or sing) a psalm to thy name.

5   Come ye and see ye the works of God; fearedful in counsels on (or towards) the sons (and daughters) of men.

6   Which (or Who) turned the sea into dry land; in the flood (or the river) they shall pass through with (or on) foot, there we shall be glad in him.

7   The which is Lord in his virtue (or might) without end, his eyes behold on the folks (or the nations); they that make sharp (or rebel) be not enhanced (or exalted) in themselves.

8   Ye heathen men, bless our God; and make ye heard the voice of his praising (or the sound of your praises).

9   That hath set my soul to life, and gave not my feet into stirring (or slipping, or stumbling).

10   For thou, God, hast proved us; thou hast examined (or assayed) us by fire, as silver is examined (or assayed).

11   Thou leddest us into a snare, thou puttedest tribulations in (or on) our back;

12   thou settedest men upon our heads. We passed by (or through) fire and water; and (then) thou leddest us out into refreshing.

13   I shall enter into thine house in (or with) burnt sacrifices; I

shall yield to thee my vows (or I shall pay my vows to thee),

14   which my lips spake distinctly. And my mouth spake in my tribulation (or trouble);

15   I shall offer to thee burnt sacrifices full of marrow, with the burning of rams; I shall offer to thee oxen with the bucks of goats.

16   All ye that dread (or fear, or revere) God, come and hear, and I shall tell; how great things he hath done to (or for) my soul.

17   I cried to him with my mouth; and I joyed fully under (or with) my tongue.

18   If I beheld (or had) wickedness in mine heart; the Lord shall not hear (me).

19   Therefore (or But) God heard (me); and he perceived the voice of my beseeching.

20   Blessed *be* God; that removed not my prayer, *nor* his mercy from me.

PSALM 67

1   *To victory in organs (or on instruments), the psalm of the song.* God have mercy on us, and bless us; lighten he his cheer (or his face) upon us, and have he mercy on us.

2   (So) that we know thy way on the earth; thine health in all folks (or thy salvation among all the nations).

3   God, (may) the peoples acknowledge to (or praise) thee; all the peoples acknowledge to (or praise) thee.

4   Heathen men be glad, and make full out joy, for thou deemest the peoples in equity (or with fairness); and addressest (or directest) the heathen men in (or upon) the earth.

5   God, the peoples acknowledge to (or praise) thee, all the peoples acknowledge to (or praise) thee;

6   the earth hath given his (or its) fruit. God, our God, bless us,

7   God bless us; and all the coasts (or the ends) of the earth dread (or revere) him.

PSALM 68

1   *To victory, the psalm of the song of David.* (May) God rise up, and his enemies be scattered; and they that hate him, flee from his face.

2   As smoke faileth (or vanisheth), fail (or vanish) they; as wax floateth (away, or melteth) from the face of the fire, so perish the sinners from the face of God.

3   And rightwise men eat, and make they full out joy in the sight of God; and delight they in gladness.

4   Sing ye to God, say ye (or sing) a psalm to his name; make ye a way to (or for) him, that ascendeth or went up upon the going down, the Lord *is* the name of him. Make ye full out joy in his sight, (*his*) *enemies* shall be troubled from the face of (or before) him,

5   *which* (or *who*) *is* the father of fatherless and motherless children; and the judge of widows. God *is* in his holy place;

6   God that maketh *men* of one will to dwell in the house. Which (or Who) leadeth out by strength them that be bound; in like manner them that make sharp (or rebel), that dwell in sepulchres.

7   God, when thou wentest out in the sight of (or before) thy people; when thou passedest forth in the desert.

8   The earth was moved, for the heavens dropped (or poured) down (rain) from the face of God of Sinai; from the face of the God of Israel.

9   God, thou shalt (im)part willful (or plentiful) rain to thine heritage (or thy inheritance), and it was sick; but thou madest it perfect.

10   Thy beasts (or Thy creatures, or Thy people) shall dwell in it;

God, thou hast made (it) ready in thy sweetness to (or for) the poor.

11   The Lord shall give a word; to them that preach the gospel (or the good news) with much virtue (or strength).

12   The kings of virtues *be made* loved of the darling; and to the fairness of the house to part spoils. (The kings and hosts flee, flee away; the women at home part the spoils.)

13   If ye sleep among the midst of sorts, *either heritages*, (or the pots), (yet ye shall be as) the feathers of the culver (or the dove that) be (covered) of (or with) silver; and the hinder things of the his back *be* in the shining of gold.

14   While (or When) *the King* of heaven deemeth the kings upon (or over) it, they shall be made whiter than the snow in Salmon;

15   the hill of God *is* a fat hill. The crudded (or curdled) hill *is* a fat hill;

16   whereto believe ye falsely, (ye) crudded (or curdled) hills? The hill in which it pleaseth well God to dwell in (or on) it; for the Lord shall dwell (there) into the end (or forever).

17   The chariot of God is manyfold with ten thousand, a thousand of them that be glad; the Lord was in (or among) them, in (or from) Sinai, in the holy (place).

18   Thou ascendedest on high, thou tookest the captivity (captive); thou receivedest gifts among men. For why *thou tookest* (also from) them that believed not; for to dwell in (or with) the Lord God.

19   Blessed *be* the Lord each day; the God of our healths (or our salvation) shall make an easy way to (or for) us.

20   Our God *is* the God to make men safe; and the out-going from death (or our escape) *is* of (or from) the Lord God.

21   Nevertheless God shall break the heads of his enemies; the top of the hair of them that go in their trespasses.

22   The Lord said, I shall return (them) from Bashan; I shall return (them) into (or from) the depth of the sea.

23   (So) that thy foot be dipped in blood; the tongue of thy dogs *be dipped in the blood* of the enemies of him.

24   God, they saw thy goings-in; the goings-in of my God, of my King, which is in the holy (place).

25   The princes joined with the singers came before; in the middle or the midst of the young damsels singing in (or with) tympans.

26   In the churches bless ye God; *bless ye* the Lord from the wells of Israel. (Bless ye God in the congregations; *bless* the Lord all *ye* tribes of Israel.)

27   There (is) Benjamin, a young man; in the ravishing of mind (or in the lead). The princes (or The leaders) of Judah *were* the dukes of them; the princes of Zebulun, the princes of Naphtali.

28   God, command thou to thy virtue (or thy power); God, confirm thou this thing, which thou hast wrought in us.

29   From thy temple, which is in Jerusalem; the kings shall offer gifts to thee.

30   Blame thou the wild beasts of (or among) the reeds, the gathering together of the bulls is among the kine (or the cattle) of the peoples; (so) that they exclude them that be proved by silver. Destroy thou the folks that will (or the nations that desire) battles,

31   the legates (or the ambassadors) shall come from Egypt; Ethiopia shall come before the hands thereof to God.

32   The realms (or The kingdoms) of the earth, sing ye to God; say ye (or sing) a psalm to the Lord. Sing ye to God;

33   that ascended or went up upon the heaven of heaven at the east. Lo! he shall give to his voice the voice of virtue (or of power),

34   give ye glory to the God upon (or over) Israel; his great doing and his virtue (or his power) *is* in the clouds.

35   God *is* wonderful in his saints (or among his people); God of Israel, he shall give virtue (or power), and strength, to his people; blessed be God.

DAY 12

PROVERBS CHAPTER 12

1   He that loveth chastising or discipline, loveth knowing (or knowledge); but he that hateth blamings (or reproofs), is unwise.

2   He that is good, shall draw to himself the grace (or favour) of the Lord; but he that trusteth in his (own) thoughts, doeth wickedly.

3   A man shall not be made strong by wickedness; and the root of rightwise men shall not be moved.

4   A diligent woman is a crown to her husband; and rot is in the bones of that *woman*, that doeth things worthy of confusion (or shameful things).

5   The thoughts of rightwise men *be* dooms (or just sentences); and the counsels of wicked men *be* guileful (or deceitful, or deceptive).

6   The words of wicked men set treason to (or lie in wait for) blood; the mouth of just men shall deliver (or save) them.

7   (Over)turn thou wicked men, and they shall not be; but the houses of rightwise men shall dwell perfectly.

8   A man shall be known by his teaching; but he that is vain and heartless, shall be open to despising.

9   Better is a poor man, and sufficient unto himself, than (to be) a (self)-glorious (or boastful) man, and needy of bread.

10   A rightwise man knoweth the lives of his work beasts; but the entrails (or bowels, or innermost thoughts) of wicked men *be* cruel.

11   He that worketh his land, shall be filled with loaves; but he that pursueth or followeth idleness, is most fool(ish). He that is sweet, *that is mild*, liveth in temperances; and in his admonishings he forsaketh despisings.

12   The desire of a wicked man is the memorial of worst things; but the roots of rightwise men shall increase (or go deeper).

13   For the sins of (his) lips, falling down nigheth to an evil man;

but a rightwise man shall escape from anguish.

14   Of the fruit of his mouth each man shall be fulfilled with goods (or good things); and by the works of his hands it shall be yielded to him.

15   The way of a fool *is* rightful in his eyes; but he that is wise, heareth counsels (or listeneth to good advice).

16   A fool showeth anon his wrath (or his anger at once); but he that dissembleth wrongs, is wise.

17   He that speaketh that, that he knoweth, is a judge of rightfulness; but he that lieth, is a guileful (or deceitful) witness.

18   A man is that promiseth, and he is pricked as with the sword of conscience; but the tongue of wise men is health.

19   The lip of truth shall be steadfast without end; but he that is a sudden witness, maketh ready the tongue of leasing (or haveth a lying tongue).

20   Guile (or Deceit, or Deception) *is* in the heart of them that think evils; but joy followeth them that make counsels of peace.

21   Whatever befalleth to a rightwise man, it shall not make him sorry; but wicked men shall be filled with evil.

22   False (or Lying) lips is an abomination to the Lord; but they that do faithfully, please him.

23   A fell (or prudent) man covereth knowing (or keepeth his knowledge discreet); and the heart of unwise men stirreth folly.

24   The hand of strong men shall have lordship; but the hand that is slow, shall serve to tributes (or forced labour).

25   Mourning in the heart of a just man shall make him meek; and he shall be made glad by a good word.

26   He that despiseth harm for a friend, is a rightwise man; but the way of wicked men shall deceive them.

27   A guileful (or deceitful) man shall not find winning; and the substance of (a diligent) man shall be (equal to) the price of gold,

that is, preciouser than gold.

28   Life *is* in the path of rightwiseness; but the wrong way leadeth to death.

ECCLESIASTICUS   CHAPTER 17

1   God formed man (out) of the earth; and after his image he made man.

2   And again he turned man into that *image*; and after himself he clothed him with virtue (or with strength).

3   He gave to him the number of days, and (a short) time; and he gave to him power of (or over) those things that be upon the earth.

4   He put the dread (or fear) of man upon all flesh, and he was the lord of beasts and of flying birds.

5   He formed of man an help(er) like himself;

6   he gave to them counsel, and tongue, and eyes, and ears, and heart to think out (things); and he filled them with the teaching or discipline of understanding.

7   He made to them the knowing (or knowledge) of spirit (or spiritual understanding), he filled the heart of them with wit (or understanding); and he showed to them evils and goods.

8   He setted the eye of them (or He set his eye) on the hearts of them, to show to them the great things of his works, (so) that they praise altogether the name of hallowing;

9   and to have glory in his marvels, (so) that they tell out the great things of his works.

10   (This verse is omitted in the original text.)

11   He added to them teaching; and he inherited them with the law of life.

12   He ordained an everlasting testament (or covenant) with them; and he showed to them his rightfulness or rightwiseness, and dooms.

13   And the eyes of them saw the great things of his honour, and the ears of them heard the honour of (his) voice;

14   and he said to them, Take heed to you from all wicked thing. And he commanded to them, to each man of his neighbour.

15   The ways of them be ever before him; they be not hid from his eyes.

16   (This verse is omitted in the original text.)

17   On each folk (or Over each nation) he made sovereign a governor; and Israel was made the open part of God (or God's portion).

18   (This verse is omitted in the original text.)

19   And all the works of them *be* as the sun in the sight of God; and his eyes behold without ceasing in (or on) the ways of them.

20   The testaments were not hid from the wickedness of them; and all the wickednesses of them *were* in the sight of God.

21   (This verse is omitted in the original text.)

22   The alms of a man *is* as a bag or a little sack with him, and it shall keep the grace of a man as the apple of the eye;

23   and afterward *man* shall rise again, and it shall yield to them a yielding, to each *man* into (or onto) the head of them; and (it) shall return into the lower parts of the earth.

24   Forsooth it gave to men repenting the way of rightfulness or rightwiseness, and confirmed men failing to suffer, and ordained to them the part (or their portion) of the truth.

25   Return thou to the Lord, and forsake thy sins; pray thou before the face of the Lord, and make thou less hurtings or the occasions of guilts.

26   Turn thou again to the Lord, and turn thou away from thine unrightfulness, and hate thou greatly cursing, *that is, cursed sin.*

27   And know thou the rightfulnesses, and the dooms (or judgements) of God; and stand thou in the part of good purpose, and

of prayer of (or to) the highest God. Go thou into the parts of the holy world, with men alive, and giving acknowledging (or thanks) to God.

28 Dwell thou not in the error of wicked men. Acknowledge thou before death; acknowledging or confession perisheth from a dead man, as nothing. Living thou shalt acknowledge (or confess), living and whole thou shalt acknowledge, and shalt praise God; and thou shalt have glory in the merciful doings of him.

29 The mercy of God *is* full great, and his help to them that convert to him.

30 For why not all things may (or can) be in men; for why the son of man is not undeadly (or immortal), and malices pleased into vanity.

31 What *is* more clear than the sun? and this shall fail; or what *is* worse than that, that flesh and blood thought out? and of this he shall be reproved.

32 He beholdeth the virtue (or the strength) of the highness of heaven; and all men *be* (but) earth and ashes.

ECCLESIASTES CHAPTER 12

1 Have thou mind on (or Remember) thy Creator in the days of thy youth, before that the time of thy torment come, and the years *of thy death* nigh, of which thou shalt say, They (or These days) please not me.

2 Before that the sun be (made) dark, and the light, and the stars, and the moon; and (before) the clouds return again after the rain.

3 When the (door)keepers (or the guards) of the house shall be moved (or shaken), and the strongest men shall tremble; and the grinders shall be idle, when the(ir) number shall be made less, and the seers by the holes shall wax (or grow) dark;

4 and (they) shall close the doors in (or to) the streets, in the lowness of the voice of a grinder; and they shall rise (up) at the voice

of a bird, and all the daughters of song shall wax (or grow) deaf.

5   And high things shall dread (or When they shall fear the high places), and shall be afeared in (or on) the way; and an almond tree shall flower, a locust shall be made fat, and the capers shall be destroyed; for a man shall go into the house of his everlastingness, and the wailers shall go about in the street.

6   *Have thou mind on* (or *Remember*) *thy Creator*, before that a silveren rope be broken, and a golden lace run against (or a gold bowl is broken), and a water pot be all-broken on (or at) the well, and a wheel be broken altogether on (or at) the cistern;

7   and the dust return again into his earth (or the earth), whereof it was, and the spirit return again to God, that gave it.

8   Vanity of vanities (or Emptiness and futility), said Ecclesiastes, vanity of vanities, and all things *be* vanity (or empty and futile).

9   And when (or for) Ecclesiastes was most wise, he taught the people, and he told out the things which he did, and he sought out *wisdom*, and made many parables;

10   he sought (out) profitable words, and he wrote most rightful words, and full of truth.

11   The words of wise men *be* as pricks, and as nails fastened (or driven) deep, which be given of (or from) the one Shepherd by the counsels of masters (or for the counsel of us all).

12   My son, seek thou no more than these; none end there is to make (or the making of) many books, and oft thinking is a torment of (or for) the flesh.

13   All we hear together the end of the speaking. Dread thou (or Fear or Revere) God, and keep his behests (or commands); that is *(for) to know*, every man.

14   *God* shall bring all things into doom (or to the Judgement), that be done; for each thing covered, *either privy*, (or secret, or private), whether it be good, or evil. Δ

DAY 13

PSALM 69

1   *To victory, on the roses of David.* God, make thou me safe (or save me); for the waters have entered unto my soul.

2   I am set or in-fixed (or sinking) in the slime of the depth; and there is no substance. I came into the depth of the sea; and the tempest drowned me down.

3   I (am) travailed (from) crying, my cheeks were made hoarse; mine eyes failed, the while I hope/d into my God.

4   They that hated me without cause; were multiplied above the hairs of mine head. Mine enemies that pursued me unjustly were comforted (or strengthened); I paid then (for) those things, which I ravished (or stole) not.

5   God, thou knowest mine unwisdom or unknowing (or my foolishness or ignorance); and my trespasses be not hid from thee.

6   Lord, Lord of virtues (or of hosts, or armies); they, that abide thee, be not ashamed in me. God of Israel; they, that seek thee, be not shamed on (or by) me.

7   For I suffered shame for thee; shame covered my face.

8   I am made a stranger to my brethren; and a pilgrim to the sons of my mother.

9   For the (or my) fervent love of thine house ate me (up, or devoured me); and the shames of men saying shames to thee fell upon me.

10   And I covered (or humbled) my soul with fasting; and it was made into shame to me (or and I was reproached even for that!).

11   And I putted (for) my cloth (or my cloak) an hair-shirt; and I am made to them into a parable.

12   They, that sat in (or by) the gate, spake against me; and they,

that drank wine, sang of (or about) me.

13   But Lord, *I address* (*or direct*) my prayer to thee; God, *I abide* (*or wait for*) the time of good pleasance. Hear thou me in the multitude of thy mercy; in the truth of thine health (or thy salvation).

14   Deliver thou me from the clay, (so) that I be not fast set-in; deliver thou me from them that hate me, and from the depths or deepness of the waters.

15   (Let) the tempest of water drown not me down, neither the depth swallow me; neither the pit make strait (or close) his (or its) mouth upon me.

16   Lord, hear thou me, for thy mercy is benign; after the multitude of thy merciful doings behold thou into me.

17   And turn not away thy face from thy servant; for I am in tribulation, (so) hear (or answer) thou me swiftly.

18   Give thou attention to my soul, and deliver thou it (or and save me); for mine enemies, deliver thou me.

19   Thou knowest my reproof, and my despising; and my shame. All that trouble me be in thy sight;

20   mine heart abode (in) shame, and wretchedness. And I abode (or waited for) him, that was sorry (or sad) together (with me), and none was; and that should comfort *me*, and I found not.

21   And they gave gall into my meat (or for my food); and in my thirst they gave to me drink with vinegar.

22   The board (or The table) of them be made before them into a snare; and into yieldings, and into a cause of stumbling.

23   Their eyes be made dark (or dim), (so) that they see not; and evermore bow down the back of them.

24   Pour out thy wrath upon them; and the strong vengeance of thy wrath take them.

25   (May) the habitation of them be made forsaken; and be there

none that dwell in the tabernacles of them.

26   For they pursued him, whom thou hast smitten; and they added on(to) the sorrow of my wounds.

27   Add thou wickedness on(to) the wickedness of them; and enter they not into thy rightwiseness.

28   Be they done away from the book of living men; and be they not written with rightwise men.

29   I am poor and sorrowful; God, thine health took me up (or thy salvation lift me up).

30   I shall praise the name of God with song; and I shall magnify him with praising.

31   And it shall please God more than a new calf bringing forth horns and claws (or hooves).

32   (Let) poor men see, and be glad; seek ye God, and your soul shall live.

33   For the Lord heard poor men; and despised not his bound men.

34   (Let) the heavens and the earth, praise him; (let) the sea, and all creeping beasts in those (or them), *praise him.*

35   For God shall make safe (or save) Zion; and the cities of Judah shall be builded. And they shall dwell there; and they shall get it by heritage (or by inheritance).

36   And the seed of his servants shall have it in possession; and they that love his name, shall dwell therein.

PSALM 70

1   *To the victory, the psalm of David, to have mind (or to remember).* God, behold thou into mine help (or look to help me); Lord, hasten thou to help me.

2   Be they shamed, and ashamed; that seek my life. Be they

turned aback; and shame they, that will evils to me.

3   Be they turned away anon (or at once), and shame they; that say to me, Well! well!

4   (Let) all men that seek thee, make fully joy (or rejoice), and be glad in thee; and they that love thine health (or thy salvation), say evermore, The Lord be magnified.

5   Forsooth I am a needy man, and poor; God help thou me. Thou art mine helper and my deliverer; Lord, tarry thou not.

PSALM 71

1   Lord, I hoped (or trusted) in thee; be I not shamed without end;

2   in thy rightwiseness deliver thou me, and ravish (or snatch) me out. Bow down thine ear to me; and make me safe (or save me).

3   Be thou to me into God a defender; and into a strengthened place, (so) that thou make me safe. For thou art my steadfastness; and my refuge.

4   My God, deliver thou me from the hand of the sinner; and from the hand (or power) of a man doing against the law, and (the hand) of the wicked man.

5   For thou, Lord, art my patience, (or whom I put my trust in); Lord, *thou art* mine hope from my youth.

6   In thee I am confirmed, *that is, defended*, from the womb; thou art my defender from the womb of my mother. My singing *is* evermore in (or of) thee;

7   I am made as a great wonder to many men; and thou *art* a strong helper.

8   My mouth (shall) be filled with praising; (so) that I sing (of) thy glory, (yea), all day (long about) thy greatness.

9   Cast thou not away me in the time of eld (age) or oldness;

when my strength faileth, forsake thou not me.

10   For mine enemies said of me; and they that kept (or laid wait, or ambush for) my life made counsel (or plotted) together.

11   Saying, God hath forsaken him; pursue ye, and take (hold of) him; for none there is that shall deliver (him).

12   God, be thou not made afar from me; my God, behold thou into mine help (or hasten thou to help me).

13   (Let) men that backbite my soul, be shamed, and fail they; and be they covered with reproof (or reproach) and shame, that seek evils to (or for) me.

14   But I shall hope evermore; and I shall add to ever over all thy praising.

15   My mouth shall tell (out) thy rightwiseness; all day (long) thine health (or thy salvation). For I knew not (by) literature, *that is, by man's teaching, but by God's revelation,*

16   I shall enter into the powers of the Lord; Lord, I shall bethink on thy rightwiseness alone.

17   God, thou hast taught me from my youth, and unto now; I shall tell out thy marvels (or marvellous deeds).

18   And till into eld (age) or oldness, and the last age; God, forsake thou not me. Till I tell thine arm, *or power,* to each generation that shall come.

19   *Till I tell* (of) thy might, and thy rightwiseness, God, unto the highest great deeds which thou hast done; God, who is like thee?

20   How (or What) great tribulations, many and evil, hast thou showed to me; and thou converted, hast quickened (or revived) me, and hast again-brought me again from the depths of the earth.

21   Thou hast multiplied thy great doing; and thou converted (or thou turned), hast comforted me.

22   For why and I shall acknowledge to (or praise) thee, thou God, thy truth in (or with) the instruments of a psalm; I shall sing in

(or with) an harp to thee, *that art* the Holy (One) of Israel.

23   My lips shall make fully joy, when I shall sing to thee; and my soul, which thou again-boughtest (or hast bought back, or redeemed).

24   But and my tongue shall think all day on (or shall talk all day long about) thy rightwiseness; when they shall be shamed and ashamed, that seek evils to (or for) me.

PSALM 72

1   *To Solomon.* God, give thy doom (or thy judgement) to the king; and thy rightwiseness to the son of the king.

2   To deem thy people in (or with) rightwiseness; and thy poor men in doom (or with judgement).

3   (May) the mountains receive (or bring) peace to the people; and the little hills *receive (or bring)* rightwiseness.

4   He shall deem (or judge) the poor men of the people, and he shall make safe (or shall save) the sons of poor men; and he shall make low (or bring down) the false challenger.

5   And he shall dwell with the sun, and before the moon, *that is, without beginning, and end*; in generation and into generation (or in all generations).

6   He shall come down as rain into a fleece (or onto a field); and as gutters dropping (or dripping) on the earth.

7   Rightwiseness shall come forth in his days; and the abundance of peace, till the moon be taken away.

8   And he shall be lord from the sea unto the sea; and from the flood (or the River) unto the ends of the world.

9   The Ethiopians shall fall down before him; and his enemies shall lick the earth (or the dust).

10   The kings of Tarshish and the isles shall offer gifts (or tribute); the kings of Arabia and of Seba shall (also) bring gifts.

11   And all kings shall worship him; all folks (or nations) shall serve him.

12   For he shall deliver a poor man from the mighty; and a poor man to (or for) whom there was none helper.

13   He shall spare a poor man and needy; and he shall make safe (or shall save) the souls of poor men.

14   He shall again-buy the souls of them from usuries, and wickedness; and the name of them *is* honourable before him.

15   And he shall live (long), and men shall give to him of the gold of Arabia; and they shall ever worship of (or pray for) him, all day they shall bless him.

16   Steadfastness shall be in the earth, in the highest place of the mountains; the fruit thereof shall be enhanced (or flourish) above the Lebanon; and they shall blossom from the city, as the hay of the earth doeth.

17   His name be blessed into worlds (or forever); his name dwell before the sun. And all the lineages (or the tribes) of the earth shall be blessed in him; all the folks (or the nations) shall magnify him.

18   Blessed be the Lord God of Israel; which alone maketh (or doeth) marvels.

19   And blessed be the name of his majesty without end; and all the earth shall be filled with his majesty; be it done, be it done (or amen, amen).

20   *The prayers, or praisings, or hymns, of David, the son of Jesse, be ended.*

PROVERBS CHAPTER 13

1   A wise son *is* (or *heareth*) the teaching of the father; but he that is a scorner, heareth not, when he is reproved (or rebuked).

2   A man shall be filled with the goods (or the good things) of

the fruit of his mouth; but the soul of unpious men *is* wicked.

3   He that keepeth (or guardeth) his mouth, keepeth his soul; but he that is unwary to speak, shall feel evils.

4   A slow man will, and will not; but the soul of them that work shall be made fat (or shall prosper).

5   A rightwise man shall loathe a false word; but a wicked man shameth, and shall be shamed.

6   Rightwiseness keepeth (safe) the way of an innocent man; but wickedness deceiveth a sinner.

7   A man is as rich, when he hath nothing; and a man is as poor, when he is in many riches.

8   The redemption of the soul of a man *is* his riches; but he that is poor, suffereth not blaming.

9   The light of rightwise men maketh glad; but the lantern of wicked men shall be quenched.

10   Strives be ever among proud men; but they that do all things with counsel, be governed by wisdom.

11   Hastened chattel or substance, *that is, gotten hastily*, shall be made less; but that that is gathered little and little with hand, shall be multiplied.

12   Hope which is delayed, tormenteth the soul; a tree of life *is* a desire (that is) coming.

13   He that backbiteth anything, bindeth himself into the time to come; but he that dreadeth the commandment, shall live in peace.

14   The law of a wise man *is* a well of life; (so) that he bow away from the falling of death, *that is, of sin, and of hell.*

15   Good teaching shall give grace; a swallow (or a pit, or destruction) *is* in the way of despisers.

16   A fell man doeth all things with counsel; but he that is a fool, shall open folly (or show his foolishness for all to see).

17   The messenger of a wicked man shall fall into evil; a faithful

messenger is health (or salvation, or deliverance).

18   Neediness and shame *is* to him that forsaketh teaching; but he that assenteth to a blamer (or correction), shall be glorified.

19   Desire, if it is fulfilled, delighteth the soul; fools loathe them that flee evils.

20   He that goeth with wise men, shall be wise; the friend of fools shall be made like them.

21   Evil pursueth sinners; and good things shall be given to rightwise men.

22   A good man shall leave *after him* heirs, sons, and the sons of sons; and the chattel or the substance of a sinner is kept to (or for) the rightwise.

23   Many meats (or Much food) *be* in the newly-tilled fields of the (fore)fathers; and be gathered to (or for) other men without doom.

24   He that spareth the rod, hateth his son; but he that loveth him, teacheth busily (or busily teacheth him).

25   The rightwise man eateth, and fulfilleth his soul; but the womb of wicked men *is* unable to be filled.

ECCLESIASTICUS CHAPTER 18

1   He that liveth without beginning and end, made of nought (or out of nothing) all things together;

2   God alone shall be justified,

3   and he dwelleth a King unovercome or unvanquished without end.

4   Who shall suffice to tell out his works? for why who shall seek (out) the great (and) worthy things of him?

5   But who shall tell out the virtue (or the strength) of his greatness? or who shall lay to for to tell out his mercy?

6   It is not to make less, neither to lay to or to add to; neither it is

to find the great (and) worthy things of God.

7   When a man hath ended, then he shall begin or beginneth; and when he hath rested, (then) he shall work.

8   What is a man, and what is the glory of him? and what is the good, or (and) what is the wicked thing of him?

9   The number of the days of men, *that be* commonly or as much (as) an hundred years,

10   be areckoned as the drops of the water of the sea; and as the stone (or a stone) of gravel, so a few years in the day of everlasting-ness or the spiritual world.

11   For this thing God is patient in (or with) them, and he shall pour out upon them his mercy.

12   He saw the presumption, *or the pride*, of their heart, for it was evil; and he knew the destroying of them, for it was wicked or shrewd (or depraved). Therefore he filled his mercy in(to) them (or had compassion), and showed to them the way of equity.

13   The merciful doing of man *is* about his neighbour; but the mercy of the Lord *is* over each flesh or upon all flesh. He that hath mercy, and teacheth, and chastiseth as a shepherd his flock,

14   do *he* mercy, taking the teaching of merciful doing; and he that hasteneth in the dooms of him (or his judgements).

15   Son, in good things give thou not (com)plaint, and in (or with) each gift give thou not heaviness of an evil word.

16   Whether dew shall not cool heat? so and a word *is* better than a gift.

17   Lo! whether a word *is* not above or over a good gift? but ever either *is* with a justified man.

18   A fool shall upbraid sharply or shall give reproof; and the gift of an untaught man maketh the eyes to fail.

19   Before the doom (or the Judgement) make thou ready rightfulness to thee; and learn thou, before that thou speak. Before

sickness give thou (to thyself) or take medicine;

20   and before the doom (or the Judgement) ask thyself, and thou shalt find mercy in the sight of God.

21   Before sickness make thee meek (or humble), and in the time of sickness or infirmity show thy living (or repent for thy sins).

22   Be thou not hindered to pray evermore, and dread thou not to be justified unto the death; for why the meed (or the reward) of God dwelleth without end.

23   Before prayer make ready or prepare thy soul; and do not thou be as a man that tempteth God, *that is, that a man betake himself to peril, and believe that that he may do reasonably, and (then) abide to be delivered of (or by) God.*

24   Have thou mind of (or Remember) the wrath in the day of ending; and make thou in living the time of yielding.

25   Have thou mind of (or Remember) poverty in the day of abundance or the time of plenty; and the need of poverty in the time or the day of riches.

26   From the morrowtide unto the eventide the time shall be changed; and all these things *be* swift in the eyes of God.

27   A wise man shall dread (or fear) in all things; and in the days of trespasses he shall flee from unknowing, *either sloth.*

28   Each fell or witty (or witting, or knowing) man, *that is, attentive to eschew evils, by God's dread,* knoweth wisdom; and to him that findeth it, he shall give acknowledging (to it).

29   Witty (or Witting or Knowing) men in words also they did wisely, and understood truth, and rightfulness or rightwiseness; and besought proverbs and dooms (or judgements).

30   Go thou not after thy covetousnesses or thy lusts; and be thou turned away from thy will.

31   If thou givest to thy soul the covetousnesses thereof or (its) lusts, it shall make thee into joy to thine enemies.

32   Delight thou not in companies (or crowds), neither in little *companies* or in small things; for why the sinning or the trespassing of them is continual.

33   Be thou not mean in the striving of (or for) love or for money, and something is not to thee in the bag; for why thou shalt be envious to thy (own) soul.

WISDOM OF SOLOMON   CHAPTER 1

1   Ye that deem (or judge) the earth, love rightwiseness; feel ye of the Lord in goodness, and seek ye him in the simpleness of (your) heart.

2   For he is found of (or by) them, that tempt (or test) him not; forsooth he appeareth to them, that have faith into him.

3   For why wayward thoughts part or sever (one) from God; but proved virtue reproveth unwise men.

4   For why wisdom shall not enter into an evil-willed soul; neither *it* shall dwell in a body subject to sins.

5   Forsooth the Holy Ghost of wisdom shall fly away from a feigning thing (or deception), *or from a feigned man*, and he shall take away himself from thoughts, that be without understanding; and *the unwise man* shall be punished of (or by) wickedness coming above (or upon him). [An holy spirit forsooth shall flee the feigner or the feigned thing of discipline, and shall take himself away from thoughts, that be without understanding; and he shall be chastised from the overcoming wickedness.]

6   For the Spirit of Wisdom is benign, and he shall not deliver a cursed man from his lips; for why God is witness of his reins, and the searcher of (whether) his heart is true, and the hearer of his tongue.

7   For why the Spirit of the Lord hath filled the world; and this

thing, that containeth all things, hath the knowing (or the knowledge) of the voice.

8   Therefore this he that speaketh wicked thing, may not (or cannot) be hid; and doom (or judgement) and punishing shall not pass (by) him.

9   For why asking shall be in the thoughts of a wicked man or the unpious. Forsooth the hearing of his words shall come to God, and to the punishing or the correction of his wickednesses;

10   for the ear of fervent love or the ear of the jealous heareth all things, and the noise of grumblings shall not be hid.

11   Therefore keep ye you from grumbling, that profiteth nothing, and from backbiting spare ye the tongue; for a dark word shall not go into vain; forsooth the mouth that lieth, slayeth the soul.

12   Do not ye covet death, in the error of your life, neither get ye perdition in (or with) the works of your hands;

13   for God made not death, neither he is glad in the perdition of living men.

14   For why God made of nought (or out of nothing) all things, that those (or they) should be; and he made the nations of the world able to be healed. For why the medicine of destroying is not in those men, neither the realm (or the kingdom) of hell is in (or on) the earth.

15   For rightwiseness is everlasting, and undeadly (or immortal); but unrightwiseness *is* the getting or the purchasing of death.

16   Forsooth wicked or unpious men called that *unrightfulness* (unto themselves) by (their own) hands and words, and they guessed or esteemed it a friend, and (then) flowed away, and they putted promises to it; for they be worthy (of) the death, that be of the part of it. Δ

DAY 14

PSALM 73

1 *The psalm of Asaph.* The God of Israel *is* full good; to them that be of a rightful (or an upright) heart.

2 But my feet were moved almost; my steps were shed out (or slipped) almost.

3 For I envied upon (or I envied) wicked men; seeing the peace (or the prosperity) of sinners.

4 For beholding is not to the death of them; and steadfastness in the sickness of them. (For it seemed that they never die; yea, they always be strong, and never get sick.)

5 They be not in travail of (or have troubles like other) men; and they shall not be beaten (down) with (or like other) men.

6 Therefore pride hath held them; they were covered with their wickedness and unfaithfulness.

7 The wickedness of them came forth as of fatness; they went into (or in the) desire of (their) hearts.

8 They thought and spake waywardness; they spake wickedness on high.

9 They putted their mouth into (or against) heaven; and their tongue passed in (or went about over all) the earth.

10 Therefore my people shall be returned again here; and full days shall be found in them.

11 And they said, How knoweth God; and whether (any) knowing is on high?

12 Lo! those sinners and having abundance in the world; (they) held riches.

13 And I said, Therefore without cause I justified mine heart; and washed mine hands among the innocents.

14   And I was beaten all day (long); and my chastising *was* in the morrowtides.

15   If I said, I shall tell thus; lo! I have reproved (or betrayed) the nation of thy sons.

16   I guessed, that I should know this; (but too much) travail is before me.

17   Till I enter into the saintuary of God; and (I) understand in the last things of them, *that is, their end.*

18   Nevertheless for the guiles (or deceits, or deceptions) thou hast put to them; thou castedest them down, while they were raised (up).

19   How be they made into desolation; they failed suddenly, they perished for their wickedness or their waywardness.

20   As the dream of men that arise; Lord, thou shalt drive their image to nought (or into nothing), in thy city (until they disappear).

21   For mine heart is enflamed, and my reins be changed (or my feelings be hurt);

22   and I am driven (in)to nought, and I knew not. As (or Like) a work beast I am made with (or before) thee;

23   and (or but still) I am ever with thee. Thou heldest my right hand,

24   and in thy will (or by thy counsel) thou leddest me forth; and with glory (or honour) thou tookest me up (or in).

25   For why what is to me in heaven; and what would I of thee (or what would I desire besides thee) upon the earth?

26   My flesh and mine heart failed; God of mine heart, and my part (or portion) *is* God without end.

27   For lo (or behold)! they that draw away far themselves from thee shall perish; thou hast lost (or shalt destroy) all men that do fornication from (or be unfaithful to) thee.

28   But it is good to (or for) me to cleave to God; and to set mine hope (or trust) in the Lord God. (So) that I tell all thy preachings, in

the gates of the daughter of Zion.

PSALM 74

1   *The learning of Asaph.* God, why hast thou put (us) away (or deserted us) into the end; thy strong vengeance is wroth upon the sheep of thy pasture?

2   Be thou mindful of (or Remember) thy gathering together; which thou haddest in possession from the beginning. Thou again-boughtest the rod of thine heritage (or thy inheritance); the hill of Zion, in which thou dwelledest therein.

3   Raise (up) thine hands into the prides of them; how great things the enemy did wickedly in the holy (place).

4   And they that hated thee; had glory in the midst of thy solemnity. They setted their signs, *either banners, to be* signs upon the highest (place), as in the out-going; and they knew not.

5   As in a wood of trees, they hewed down with axes the gates thereof into itself (or as if they were woodsmen);

6   they casted down it (or them) with an ax, and a broad falling ax.

7   They burnt with fire thy saintuary (or sanctuary); they defouled the tabernacle of thy name in the earth (or they razed it to the ground).

8   The kindred of them said together in their heart; Make we all the feast days of God to cease in the earth.

9   We have not seen our signs, (that is, the future), now there is no prophet; and he shall no more know us.

10   God, how long shall the enemy say despite (or show despising)? the adversary stirreth to ire thy name into the end.

11   Why turnest thou away thine hand, and *to (not) draw out* thy right hand from the midst of thy bosom, till into the end?

12   Forsooth God our King before worlds, wrought health (or hath

given salvation) in the midst of the earth.

13   Thou madest firm the sea by thy virtue (or thy strength); thou hast troubled the heads of the dragons in the waters.

14   Thou hast broken the heads of the dragon; thou hast given him to *be* meat to (or food for) the peoples of the Ethiopians.

15   Thou hast broken wells, and streams; thou madest dry the floods (or the rivers) of Eitan.

16   The day is thine, and the night is thine; thou madest the morrowtide and the sun.

17   Thou madest all the ends of the earth; summer, and ver time, *either springing* (or spring) *time*, thou formedest them.

18   Be thou mindful of (or Remember) this thing, the enemy hath said shame or put reproof to the Lord; and the unwise (or foolish) people hath excited to ire (or scorned) thy name.

19   Betake thou not (over) to beasts the men acknowledging to (or confessing) thee; and forget thou not into the end the souls (or suffering) of thy poor men.

20   Behold into thy testament (or Remember thy covenant); for they that be made (in) the dark of the earth, be full-filled with the houses of wickednesses.

21   A meek man be not turned away made ashamed; a poor man and needy shall praise thy name.

22   God, rise up, deem (or defend) thou thy cause; be thou mindful of thy shames, *either upbraidings*, of (or by) them that be all day of the unwise man (or who be unwise all the day long).

23   Forget thou not the voices of thine enemies; the pride of them that hate thee ascendeth or goeth up evermore.

PSALM 75

1   *To the overcomer, lose thou (or destroy) not the psalm of the*

song of Asaph. God, we shall acknowledge to (or praise) thee, we shall acknowledge (or thank thee); and we shall inwardly call thy name. We shall tell (out all) thy marvels;

2   when I shall take (hold of) the time, I shall deem (with) rightfulnesses (or judge with fairness).

3   The earth is melted (or shaken), and all that dwell therein; I confirmed (or made firm) the pillars thereof.

4   I said to wicked men, Do not ye do wickedly; and to trespassers, Do not ye enhance (or lift up) the horn.

5   Do not ye raise on high your horn; do not ye speak wickedness against God.

6   For neither from the east, neither from the west, neither from the desert hills;

7   for God is the judge. He meeketh this *man,* and enhanceth him (or humbleth this *one,* and raiseth up that *one*);

8   for a cup of clean (or clear) wine, full of meddling (or mixing) *is* in the hand of the Lord. And he bowed (some) of this into that; nevertheless the dregs thereof is not diminished, *either made less,* (for) all the sinners of the earth shall drink thereof.

9   Forsooth I shall tell (this) into the world (or forever); I shall sing to the God of Jacob.

10   And I shall break all the horns of the sinners; and the horns of the rightwise shall be enhanced (or lifted up).

PSALM 76

1   *To the victory in organs (or on the instruments), the psalm of the song of Asaph.* God is known in Judah; his name is great in Israel.

2   And his place is made in peace (or Salem); and his dwelling *is* in Zion.

3   There he brake the powers; bow, shield, sword, and battle.

4   And thou, *God*, lightenest wonderfully (coming back) from the everlasting hills;

5   all unwise (or foolish) men of heart were troubled. They slept their sleep, *that is, were dead*; and all men found nothing of riches in their hands.

6   They that ascended or went upon horses; slept for thy blaming, thou God of Jacob.

7   Thou art fearful, and who shall against-stand thee? from that time (of) thy wrath (or when thou art angry?).

8   From heaven thou madest doom (or your judgement) heard; the earth trembled, and rested.

9   When God rose up into doom (or to judge); to make safe all the mild men (or to save all the humble) of the earth.

10   For the thought of man shall acknowledge to (or praise) thee; and the remnants or the leavings of thought shall make a feast day to thee.

11   Make ye a vow, and yield ye to your Lord God; all that bring gifts in the compass of it. To God fearedful (or revered),

12   and to him that taketh away the spirit of princes; to the fearedful (or revered one) at (or by all) the kings of the earth.

PROVERBS   CHAPTER 14

1   A wise woman buildeth her house; and an unwise woman shall destroy with hands, *that is, with her evil works*, an house builded.

2   A man going in rightful way, and dreading (or fearing, or revering) God, is despised of (or by) him that goeth in the way of evil fame.

3   The rod of pride *is* in the mouth of a fool; the lips of wise men

keep them (safe).

4   Where oxen be not, the cratch is void (or the stall is empty); but where full many corns appear, there the strength of the ox is made open.

5   A faithful witness shall not lie; a guileful (or deceitful) witness bringeth forth a leasing (or many lies).

6   A scorner seeketh wisdom, and he findeth *it* not; the teaching of prudent men *is* easy.

7   Go thou against a man a fool; and he shall not know the lips of prudence.

8   The wisdom of a fell (or a prudent) man is to understand his way; and the unwariness of fools erreth.

9   A fool scorneth sin; grace shall dwell among just men.

10   The heart that knoweth the bitterness of his (or its) soul; a stranger shall not be meddled or mingled (or mixed) in the joy thereof.

11   The house of wicked men shall be done away; the tabernacles of just men shall burgeon (or flourish).

12   Soothly a way is, that seemeth just to a man; but the last things of it lead forth to death.

13   Laughing shall be meddled or mingled (or mixed) with sorrow; and mourning occupieth the last things of joy.

14   A fool shall be filled with his ways; and a good man shall be above him.

15   An innocent man believeth to each word; a fell or witting (or knowing) man beholdeth his goings.

16   A wise man dreadeth, and boweth away from evil; a fool skippeth over, and trusteth.

17   A man unpatient shall work folly; and a guileful (or a deceitful) man is odious.

18   Little men *of wit* (or Those with little wit, or low intelligence)

shall hold (fast to) folly; and fell or witting (or knowing) men shall abide knowing.

19   Evil men shall lie (down) before good men; and unpious men before the gates of rightwise men.

20   A poor man shall be (thought) hateful, yea, (even) to his neighbour; but many men *be* the friends of rich men.

21   He that despiseth his neighbour, doeth sin; but he that doeth mercy to a poor man, shall be blessed.

22   He that believeth in the Lord, loveth mercy; they err that work evil. Mercy and truth make ready goods (or bring forth good things);

23   abundance shall be in each or in every good work. Soothly where full many words be, there neediness is oft.

24   The crown of wise men *is* the riches of them; the folly of fools *is* unwariness (or their recklessness).

25   A faithful witness delivereth souls; and a false man bringeth forth leasings (or lies).

26   In the dread (or fear) of (or reverence for) the Lord *is* trust of strength; and hope shall be to the sons of him.

27   The dread of (or reverence for) the Lord *is* a well of life; (so) that it (or thou) bow away from the falling of death (or deadly traps).

28   The dignity of the king *is* in the multitude of (his) people; and the shame of a prince *is* in the fewness of (his) people.

29   He that is patient, is governed by much wisdom; but he that is unpatient, enhanceth his folly.

30   The health of the heart *is* the life of the flesh; envy *is* the rot of the bones.

31   He that falsely challengeth (or oppresseth) a needy man, despiseth his maker; but he that hath mercy on a poor man, honoureth his maker.

32   A wicked man is put out for (or brought down by) his malice; but the rightwise hopeth (or hath hope) in his (own) death.

33   Wisdom resteth in the heart of a wise man; and he shall teach all unlearned men.

34   Rightwiseness raiseth up a folk (or a nation); sin maketh peoples wretches.

35   A servant understanding is acceptable to a king; a *servant* unprofitable shall suffer the wrathfulness of him.

ECCLESIASTICUS CHAPTER 19

1   A drunken workman shall not be made rich; and he that chargeth not (or careth not about) little *sins*, falleth down *into grievouser sins*, little and little.

2   Wine and women make to be apostates, yea, wise men, or Wine and women make also wise men to go backward; and they reprove witty (or witting, or knowing) men. And he that joineth himself to whores, shall be wicked;

3   rot and worms shall inherit him, and he shall be set on high into more ensample, and his soul shall be taken away from the number *of chosen men.*

4   He that believeth soon, is unstable or light in heart, and shall be made less; and he that trespasseth against his (own) soul, shall be had furthermore.

5   He that joyeth in wickedness, shall be cursed; and he that hateth blaming or correction, shall be made less in life;

6   and he that hateth jangling or much speech, quencheth malice. (But) he that sinneth against his (own) soul, shall not repent or do penance; and that is merry in malice, shall be cursed or reproved.

7   Rehearse thou (or Repeat) not an hard word, and wicked; and thou shalt not be made less.

8   Do not thou tell thy wit to a friend and (or) to an enemy; and if trespass is to thee, do not thou make (it) naked (or open).

9   For he shall hear thee, and shall keep thee, and (or but) he as defending the sin shall hate thee; and so he shall be ever(more) with thee.

10   Thou hast heard a word against thy neighbour; die it altogether in (or with) thee, and trust thou that it shall not break thee (to keep it secret).

11   A fool travaileth (or laboureth) greatly of (or in) the face of a word, as the sorrow of the bearing, or the wailing of the birth, of a child.

12   An arrow fastened or fixed in the hip of a dog, so a word in the heart of a fool.

13   Reprove thou or chastise a friend, lest peradventure he understand not, and say, I did (it) not; either if he hath done (it), lest he add to do (it) again.

14   Reprove thou or chastise a neighbour, lest peradventure he say (it) not; and if he said (it), lest peradventure he rehearse (or repeat it).

15   Reprove thou or chastise a friend, for why trespassing is done often; and believe thou not to each word.

16   There is a man that falleth or that slideth by his tongue, but not of will, *that is, wittingly and of (or on) purpose.* For why who is he, that trespasseth not in (or with) his tongue?

17   Reprove thou or chastise a neighbour, *betwixt thee and him,* before that thou threaten (him); and give thou place to the dread (or fear) of (or reverence for) the Highest.

18   (This verse is omitted in the original text.)

19   (This verse is omitted in the original text.)

20   For why all wisdom *is* the dread of God, and in that *wisdom* for to dread God; and the ordinance or the disposing of the law *is* in all wisdom.

21   (This verse is omitted in the original text.)

22   And the teaching of wickedness or shrewdness (or depravity) is not wisdom; and the prudence of sins is not good thought, or good thinking is not the prudence of sins.

23   There is wickedness or shrewdness (or depravity) of prudence, and cursedness *is* therein; and there is an unwise man, which is made little or is lessened in wisdom.

24   Better is a man that hath a little wisdom, and failing in wit, in the dread (or the fear) of (or reverence for) God, than he that hath plenty of wit, and breaketh the law of the Highest.

25   There is a certain subtlety or slyness, and it is wicked. And there is a man, that sendeth out a certain word, telling out the truth.

26   There is a man that meeketh himself wickedly or that shrewdly meeketh himself *to deceive men the more*; and his inner things or the entrails of him be full of guile or of treachery.

27   And there is a just or rightwise man, that maketh low greatly or under-putteth himself of (or by) much meekness (or humility); and there is a just or rightwise man, that boweth the face, and feigneth him(self) to see not that, that is unknown.

28   (Even) though he is forbidden of (or by the) feebleness or infirmity of strengths to do sin; if he findeth the time to do evil, he shall do evil.

29   A man is known by (his) sight (or by his appearance); and a witty (or a witting, or a knowing) man is known by meeting of face.

30   The clothing of the body, and the laughing of teeth, and the entering or the going in of a man, tell out of him.

WISDOM OF SOLOMON   CHAPTER 2

1   Forsooth wicked men said, thinking with(in) themselves not rightfully, The time of our life is little, and with annoyance; no

refreshing is in the end of a man, and none there is, that is known, that returned again from hell (or from the grave).

2   For we were born of nought (or out of nothing), and after this *time* we shall be, as if we had not been; for why smoke is blown out in (or of) our nostrils, and a word of sparkle (or of spark) to stir our heart.

3   For our body shall be quenched ashes, and the spirit shall be scattered abroad as soft air; and our life shall pass as the step of a cloud, and it shall be departed as a mist, which is driven away of (or by) the beams of the sun, and is grieved of (or by) the heart of it.

4   And our name shall take forgetting by *the passing of* time; and no man shall have mind (or a remembrance) of our works.

5   For why our time is the passing of a shadow, and there is not returning again of (or after) our end; for it is asealed, and no man returneth again.

6   Therefore come ye, and use we the goods (or good things) that be, and use we a creature, as in (our) youth, swiftly.

7   Fill we us with precious wine and ointments; and the flower of time pass not (by) us.

8   Crown we us with roses, before that they wither; no meadow be, that our lechery pass not by or through.

9   No man of us be there without (his) part of (or in) our lechery; everywhere leave we the signs of gladness; for this is our part, and this is our heritage (or our inheritance) or our lot.

10   Oppress we a poor rightwise man, and spare we not a widow, neither reverence we hoar hairs of an old man of much time.

11   But our strength be the law of rightfulness; for why that that is feeble, is found unprofitable.

12   Therefore deceive we a rightwise man, for he is unprofitable to us, and *he is* contrary to our works; and he upbraideth or

reprovingly putteth to us the sins of the law, and he defameth on or against us the sins of our teaching.

13   He promiseth that he hath the knowing (or the knowledge) of God, and he nameth himself the son of God.

14   He is made to us into showing of our thoughts.

15   He is grievous to us, yea, to see; for why his life is unlike to other men, and his ways be changed.

16   We be guessed of (or by) him *to be* triflers, *that is, men of no virtue*, and he abstaineth himself from our ways, as from uncleannesses; and he telleth before the last things of just men, and he hath glory, that he hath God (as) *his* father.

17   Therefore see we, if his words be true; and assay we, what things shall come to him; and we shall know, what shall be the last things of him.

18   For if he is the very (or the true) son of God, he shall up-take him (or take him up), and shall deliver him from the hands of them that be contrary *to him*.

19   Ask we him by despising and torment, (so) that we know his reverence, and that we prove his patience.

20   By most foul death condemn we him, for why beholding or respect shall be of his words.

21   They thought these things, and they erred; for why their malice blinded them.

22   And they knew not the sacraments of God, neither they hoped (for) the meed (or the reward) of rightwiseness, neither they deemed the honour of holy souls.

23   For why God made man unable to be destroyed or undeadly, (or immortal), and *God* made man to (or in) the image of his (own) likeness.

24   But by envy of (or from) the Devil death entered into the world; forsooth they pursue or follow him, that be of his part. ∆

DAY 15

PSALM 77

1   *To the victory on Jeduthun, the psalm of Asaph.* With my
voice I cried to the Lord, with my voice to God; and he gave
attention to me.

2   In the day of my tribulation I sought God with mine hands
(raised up); in the night before (or toward) him, and I am not
deceived. My soul forsook to be comforted;

3   I was mindful of (or remembered) God, and I delighted, and I
was exercised (or upset); and my spirit failed.

4   Mine eyes before took wakings; I was troubled, and I spake not.

5   I thought (about the) old days; and I had in mind everlasting
years.

6   And I thought (deeply) in the night with mine heart; and I was
exercised (or was upset), and I cleansed my spirit.

7   Whether God shall cast away without end; either shall he not
lay to (or add), that he be more pleased yet?

8   Or shall he cut (or take) away his mercy (or his love) into the
end; from generation into generation (or for all generations)?

9   Or shall God forget to do mercy (to us); either shall he
withhold his mercies in his wrath (or anger)?

10   And I said, Now I began; this *is* the changing of the right hand
of the high *God.*

11   I had mind on (or remembered) the works of the Lord; for I
shall have mind (or remember) from the beginning of thy marvels.

12   And I shall think on all thy works; and I shall be exercised,
either occupied, in thy findings (or thy deeds).

13   God, thy way *was* in the holy (place); what God (or god) *is*
great as our God?

201

14   thou art God, that doest marvels. Thou madest thy virtue (or thy strength) known among the peoples;

15   thou again-boughtest (or redeemed) in (or with) thine arm thy people, the sons of Jacob and of Joseph.

16   God, the waters saw thee, the waters saw thee, and dreaded; and the depths of waters were troubled.

17   The multitude of the sound of waters; the clouds gave voice. For why thine arrows pass through (them);

18   the voice of thy thunder *was* in a wheel (or a whirlwind). Thy lightnings shined to the world; the earth was moved (or shaken), and trembled.

19   Thy way in the sea, and thy paths in many waters; and thy steps shall not be known.

20   Thou leddest forth thy people as sheep; in the hand of Moses and Aaron.

PSALM 78

1   *The learning of Asaph.* My people, perceive ye my law; bow your ear into the words of my mouth.

2   I shall open my mouth in parables; I shall speak perfect reasons (or reasoning) from the beginning (or the old days).

3   How (or What) great things have we heard, and we have known them; and our fathers told to us.

4   They be not hid from the sons of them; in another generation. And they told the praisings of the Lord, and the virtues of him (or and his strength and power); and his marvels, which he did.

5   And he raised (up) witnessing (or a testimony) in Jacob; and he setted or put law in Israel. How great things commanded he to our (fore)fathers, to make those things known to their sons;

6   (so) that another generation know. Sons, that shall be born,

and shall rise up; shall tell out to their sons.

7   That they set or put their hope (or trust) in God, and forget not the works of God; and that they seek his commandments.

8   Lest they be made a shrewd (or depraved) generation; and (one) stirring to wrath, as the fathers of them. A generation that addressed (or directed) not his (or its) heart; and his (or its) spirit was not believed with God.

9   The sons of Ephraim, bending a bow, and sending *arrows*; were turned (aback) in the day of battle.

10   They kept not the testament (or the covenant) of God; and they would not go in his law.

11   And they forgat his benificences or benefits (or good gifts); and his marvels, which he showed to them.

12   He did marvels before the fathers of them, in the land of Egypt; in the field of Tanis (or on the plain of Zoan).

13   He brake the sea, and led them through *it*; and he ordained the waters as in a bouget (or a bottle).

14   And he led them forth in (or by) a cloud of the day; and all night in (or by) the lightening of fire.

15   He brake a stone in the desert or the wilderness; and he gave water to them as in a much depth.

16   And he led or brought water out of the stone; and he led forth waters as floods (or rivers).

17   And they putted yet to do sin against him; they excited the high *God* into wrath, in a place without water.

18   And they tempted God in their hearts; that they asked meats to their lives (or so that they demanded the food that they craved).

19   And they spake evil of God; they said, Whether God may make ready a board (or can prepare a table here) in the desert?

20   For he smote a stone, and waters flowed; and streams went out in abundance. Whether also he may (or can) give bread; or

make ready a board to (or prepare a table for) his people?

21 Therefore the Lord heard, and delayed; and fire was kindled in Jacob, and the wrath of God ascended upon Israel.

22 For they believed not in God; neither hoped in his health (or trusted in his salvation).

23 And he commanded to the clouds above; and he opened the gates of heaven.

24 And he rained (down) to them manna for to eat; and he gave to them the bread of heaven.

25 Man ate the bread of angels; he sent to them meats (or food) in abundance.

26 He turned over the south wind from the heavens; and he brought in by his virtue (or his power) the west wind.

27 And he rained (down) fleshes as dust on them; and *also* volatiles (or birds) feathered, as the gravel (or the sand) of the sea.

28 And they fell in the middle of the tents of them (or their camp); about their tabernacles (or their tents).

29 And they ate, and were full-filled greatly, and he brought their desire to them;

30 (but) they were not defrauded (or quenched) of their desire. Yet their meats (or their foods) were in their mouth(s);

31 and the wrath of God ascended upon them. And he killed the fat men of them; and he hindered (or struck down) the chosen men of Israel.

32 In all these things they sinned yet; and believed not in the marvels of God.

33 And (so) the days of them failed in vanity (or he ended their days like a breath); and the years of them *failed* with haste (or with sudden disaster).

34 When (or After) he killed them, (then) they sought him; and they turned again, and early they came to him.

35   And they bethought (again) or remembered, that God is the helper of them; and the high God is the again-buyer of them (or their redeemer).

36   And they loved him in (or with) their mouths; and (or but) with their tongues they lied to him.

37   Forsooth the heart of them was not rightful with him; neither they were had faithful in his testament (or his covenant).

38   But he is merciful, and he shall be made merciful to the sins of them; and he shall not destroy them. And he did greatly, to turn away his wrath; and he kindled not all his wrath.

39   And he bethought, that they be flesh; a spirit going (or like the wind passing by), and not returning again.

40   How oft made they him wroth (or angry) in the desert; they stirred him into wrath in a place without water.

41   And they were turned (again), and tempted God; and they wrathed (or angered) the Holy (One) of Israel.

42   They bethought not on his hand; in the day in which he again-bought (or redeemed) them from the hand of the troubler.

43   As he put his signs in Egypt; and his great wonders in the field of Tanis.

44   And he turned the floods (or the rivers) of them, and the rains of them, into blood; (so) that they should (or could) not drink.

45   He sent a flesh fly into them, and it ate them; and *he sent* a paddock or a frog, and it lost them (or ruined their land).

46   And he gave the fruits of them (un)to rust (or their crops over to mildew); and *he gave* the travails (or labours) of them to locusts.

47   And he killed the vines of them with hail; and the (syca)more trees of them with frost.

48   And he betook the beasts of them (un)to hail; and the possessions of them (un)to fire.

49   He sent into them the wrath of his indignation; indignation,

and wrath, and tribulation, sendings-in by evil angels.

50   He made a way to the path of his wrath, and he spared not from the death of their lives; and he enclosed altogether in death the beasts of them.

51   And he smote all the first engendered or begotten things in the land of Egypt; the first fruits of all the travail (or the labour) of them in the tabernacles (or tents) of Ham.

52   And he took away (from there) his people as sheep; and he led them forth as a flock in the desert.

53   And he led them forth in hope (or safety), and they dreaded not; and the sea covered the enemies of them.

54   And he brought them into the hill of his hallowing (or unto his holy hill); unto the hill which his right hand (had) gat.

55   And he casted out heathen men from the face of them; and by lot he parted to them the land in a cord of dealing (or with a measuring cord). And he made the lineages (or tribes) of Israel to dwell in the tabernacles of them (or in their tents).

56   And (still) they tempted, and wrathed the high God; and they kept not his witnessings (or testimonies, or teachings).

57   And they turned away themselves, and they kept not covenant; as their fathers, (they) were turned (or bent) into a shrewd (or crooked) bow.

58   They stirred him into wrath in their little hills (or with their high places); and they stirred him to indignation in their graven images (or with their carved idols).

59   God heard, and forsook (them); and brought to nought Israel greatly.

60   And he put away (or deserted) the tabernacle of Shiloh; his tabernacle in which he dwelled among men.

61   And he betook the virtue of them (or their strength) into captivity; and the fairness of them into the hands of the enemy.

62   And he enclosed altogether his people in (or with) the sword; and he despised his heritage (or his inheritance).

63   Fire ate (up) the young men of them; and the virgins of them were not bewailed or bewept.

64   The priests of them fell down by the sword; and the widows of them were not bewept.

65   And the Lord was raised up, as sleeping; as mighty greatly filled of or drunk (with) wine or.

66   And he smote his enemies on the hinder parts (or backsides); he gave to them everlasting shame.

67   And he put away (or rejected) the tabernacle of Joseph; and he chose not the lineage (or tribe) of Ephraim.

68   But he chose the lineage (or tribe) of Judah; *he chose* the hill of Zion (or Mount Zion), which he loved.

69   And he as an unicorn builded his holy place; in the land, which he founded into worlds (or forever).

70   And he chose David (to be) his servant, and took him up (or away) from the flocks of sheep;

71   he took him from behind sheep with lambs. To feed Jacob his servant; and Israel his heritage (or his inheritance).

72   And he fed them in the innocence of his heart; and he led them forth in the understandings of his hands.

PSALM 79

1   *The psalm of Asaph.* God, heathen men came into thine heritage (or thy inheritance); they defouled (or defiled) thine holy temple, they put Jerusalem into the keeping of apples.

2   They put the slain bodies of thy servants *to be* meats to the volatiles (or food for the birds) of the heavens; the fleshes of thy saints to (or for) the beasts of the earth.

3   They poured out the blood of them, as water in the compass of (or all around) Jerusalem; and none there was that buried (them).

4   We be made a shame to our neighbours; mocking and scorning to them, that be in our compass.

5   Lord, how long shalt thou be wroth, into the end? shall thy vengeance be kindled as fire?

6   Pour out thine wrath into (or onto) the heathen men, that know not thee; and into realms, that called not thy name.

7   For they ate (or devoured) Jacob; and made desolate his place.

8   Have thou not mind on (or Do not remember) our old wickednesses; thy mercies before take us soon, for we be made poor greatly.

9   God, our health (or our salvation), help thou us, and, Lord, for the glory of thy name, deliver thou us; and be thou merciful to our sins, for thy name.

10   Lest peradventure they say among the heathen men, Where is the God of them? and be he known among the nations before our eyes. The vengeance of the blood of thy servants, which is poured out;

11   the wailing of fettered men enter into thy sight. After the greatness of thine arm (or thy power); wield thou the sons of slain men.

12   And yield thou to our neighbours sevenfold in(to) the bosom of them; the shame of them (or the same rebuke), which they did shamefully to thee, thou Lord.

13   But we *that be* thy people, and the sheep of thy pasture; shall acknowledge to (or thank) thee into the world (or forever). In generation and into generation, we shall tell out thy praising.

PROVERBS CHAPTER 15

1   A soft answer breaketh wrath; an hard word raiseth strong

vengeance.

2   The tongue of wise men honoureth knowing (or knowledge); the mouth of fools boileth out folly (or foolishness).

3   In each place the eyes of the Lord behold good men, and evil men.

4   A pleasant tongue *is* the tree of life; but the tongue that is unmeasurable or untempered, shall defoul (or defile) the spirit.

5   A fool scorneth the teaching of his father; but he that keepeth blamings (or receiveth rebukes), shall be made wiser. Most virtue shall be in plenteous rightfulness or rightwiseness; but the thoughts of wicked men shall be drawn up by the root.

6   (In) the house of the rightwise *is* full great strength; and troubling *is* in the fruits of a wicked man.

7   The lips of wise men shall sow abroad knowing (or knowledge); (but) the hearts of fools shall be unlike (them).

8   The sacrifices of wicked men *be* abominable to the Lord; the vows of just men *be* pleasant (or pleasing to him).

9   The life of the unpious man is an abomination to the Lord; he that pursueth rightfulness or followeth rightwiseness, shall be loved of (or by) the Lord.

10   Evil teaching is of (or from) men that forsake the way of life; he that hateth blamings (or rebukes) shall die.

11   Hell and perdition *be open* before the Lord; how much more the hearts of the sons and daughters of men.

12   A man full of pestilence loveth not him that reproveth him; and he goeth not to wise men.

13   A joyful heart maketh glad the face; (but) the spirit is cast down in the mourning of the soul.

14   The heart of a wise man seeketh teaching; and the mouth of fools is fed with unknowing (or ignorance).

15   All the days of a poor man *be* evil; (the life of) a secure soul *is*

a continual feast.

16   Better is a little with the dread of (or reverence for) the Lord, than many treasures and unfillable (or with trouble and turmoil).

17   It is better to be called to worts with charity (or to herbs with love), than with hatred to a calf made fat (or a fattened calf).

18   A wrathful man raiseth chidings; he that is patient, assuageth *chidings that were* raised.

19   The way of slow (or lazy) men *is* as an hedge of thorns; the way of just men *is* without a thing of hurting.

20   A wise son maketh glad *his* father; but a fond (or foolish) man despiseth his mother.

21   Folly is joy to a fool; but a prudent man shall address (or direct) his steps.

22   Thoughts (or Plans) be destroyed, where no counsel is; but where many counsellors be, they be confirmed.

23   A man is glad in the sentence of his mouth; and (or but) a covenable (or a suitable) word is (always) best.

24   The path of life *is* on (or *leadeth* upward for) a learned man; (so) that he bow (or turn) away from the last hell, (or from Sheol, *that is, the land of the dead*, which is below).

25   The Lord shall destroy the house of proud men; and he shall make steadfast the coasts of a widow, (or but he shall make firm the property lines, *or the boundary stones*, of a widow).

26   Evil thoughts *is* an abomination of (or to) the Lord; and a clean word most fair shall be made steadfast of him (or but a most fair and clean word is his delight).

27   He that pursueth or followeth avarice, troubleth his house; but he that hateth gifts shall live (long). Sins be purged by mercy (or be cleansed by love) and faith; each man boweth away from evil by the dread (or fear) of (or reverence for) the Lord.

28   The soul of a rightwise man bethinketh obedience; the mouth

of wicked men is full of evils.

29   The Lord is far from wicked men; and (or but) he shall hear the prayers of rightwise men.

30   The light of the eyes maketh glad the soul; good fame maketh fat the bones.

31   The ear that heareth the blamings (or rebukes) of life, shall dwell in the midst of wise men.

32   He that casteth away chastising or discipline, despiseth his (own) soul; but he that assenteth to blamings (or rebukes), is a peaceable holder of the heart (or shall become wiser).

33   The dread (or fear) of (or reverence for) the Lord *is* the teaching of wisdom; and meekness (or humility) goeth before glory.

ECCLESIASTICUS CHAPTER 20

1   There is false reproving in the ire of a man full of despising or There is lying correction in the wrath of the wrongful; and there is doom (or judgement) which is not proved to be good; and there is a still man, and he is prudent.

2   It is full good to reprove or How good (it) is to reprove, *more* than to be wroth, and to forbid not a man acknowledging (or confessing) in prayer.

3   The covetousness or lust of a gelding hath defouled the maidenhood of a young woman, so (or is as) he that maketh wicked doom by violence. [The lust of the gelding deflowered the young woman, or (made her) bereft of her maidenhood, so he that doeth by force wicked doom.]

4   It is full good, that a man *that is* reproved, show openly penance; for so thou shalt escape willful sin. [How good (it) is, the chastised to show penance; so forsooth thou shalt flee away (from) willful sin.]

5   There is a still man, which (or who) is found wise; and he (that) is hateful, which (or who) is foolhardy to speak.

6   Soothly there is a still man, not having wit of speech; and there is a still man, knowing the season of covenable (or of suitable, or opportune) time.

7   A wise man shall be still till to the (right) time; but a jolly or reckless, *or wild*, man and an unprudent man shall not keep time.

8   He that useth many words, hurteth his (own) soul; and he that taketh power to himself unjustly or wrongfully, shall be hated.

9   There is going forth in evils to (or for) a man unlearned or undisciplined; and there is finding into (im)pairing or into harm.

10   There is a gift, which is not profitable; and there is a gift, whose yielding (or recompense) is double.

11   There is making less for glory; and there is a man, which shall raise the head (up) from meekness (or low status).

12   There is a man, that again-buyeth many *sins* for a little price or that many things again-buy for little price, and (or but) restoreth them in sevenfold.

13   A wise man in words maketh himself amiable or lovable; but the graces of fools shall be poured out.

14   The gift of an unwise man shall not be profitable to thee; for his eyes be sevenfold, *that is, his intent is manyfold and diverse*.

15   He shall give little things or few things, and he shall up-braid many things; and the opening of his mouth is enflaming. Today a man lendeth, and tomorrow he asketh (for) it (again); and such a man is hateful.

16   A friend shall not be to a fool, and grace shall not be to his goods (or thanks shall not be for his good deeds). For they that eat his bread, be of false tongue, *that is, flatterers praising his follies*;

17   how often, and how many men shall scorn him?(!) For he parteth or he dealed not by even wit that, that was worthy to be

had; in like manner and that, that was not worthy to be had.

18 The falling or sliding of a false tongue *is* as he that falleth in (or on) the pavement; so the falls of evil men shall come hastily.

19 A man without grace or unkind *is* as a vain fable; and it shall be customable in the mouth of unlearned men, or it shall be often in the mouth of the undisciplined.

20 A parable, *that is, a true sentence and great,* shall be reproved (when it cometh out) of the mouth of a fool; for he saith it not in his (or its) time.

21 There is a man, that is forbidden to do sin, for (or because of) poverty; and he shall (not) be pricked in his rest.

22 There is a man, that shall lose (or destroy) his (own) soul for shame; and for the unprudence of a person he shall lose it. Forsooth he shall lose (or destroy) himself for the taking (or the favouring) of a person.

23 There is a man, that for shame promiseth to a friend; and (then) he hath gotten or won him(self) an enemy without cause or willfully (or willingly).

24 Leasing (or Lying) *is* a wicked shame in a man; and it shall be customably or busily in the mouths of unlearned men or the undisciplined.

25 Better, *or less evil,* is a thief than the customableness of a man, a leasing-monger, *that is, a man accustomed to lying,* or a liar; forsooth both they (or both of them) shall inherit perdition.

26 The manners of men leasing-mongers or liars *be* without honour; and their shame *is* with them without ceasing.

27 A wise man in words shall bring forth himself; and a prudent man shall please great men.

28 He that worketh his land, shall make high the heap of fruits; and he that worketh rightfulness or rightwiseness, shall be enhanced (or exalted). Soothly he that pleaseth great men, shall

escape wickedness.

29   Presents and gifts blind the eyes of judges; and as (one) dumb in the mouth it turneth away the chastisings of them.

30   Wisdom hid, and treasure unseen, what profit *is* in ever either?

31   He is better, that hideth his unwisdom, than a man that hideth his wisdom.

32   (This verse is omitted in the original text.)

WISDOM OF SOLOMON   CHAPTER 3

1   Forsooth the souls of rightwise men be in the hand of God; and the torment of death shall not touch them.

2   They seemed to the eyes of unwise men to die; and torment was deemed the outgoing of them (or their demise).

3   And from a just way they went into destroying, and that that is of (or for) us the way of destroying or destruction; but they be in (or at) peace.

4   Though they suffered torments before men, the hope of them is full of undeadliness (or for immortality).

5   They *were* travailed (or tormented) in a few things, *and they* shall be disposed well in many things; for why God assayed them, and found them worthy to (or for) himself.

6   He proved them as gold in a furnace, and he took them as the offering of a burnt sacrifice;

7   and the beholding of them shall be in the time *of yielding.* Just men shall shine, and they shall run about as sparkles (or sparks) in a place of reeds. [and in time shall be the beholding of them. They shall shine rightwise, and as sparkles in reedy places they shall run hither and thither.]

8   They shall deem (or judge) the nations, and shall be lords of the peoples; and the Lord of them shall reign without end (or forever).

9   They that trust on (or in) him, shall understand the truth; and faithful men in love shall assent to him; for why (free) gift and peace is to (or for) his chosen men and women.

10   But wicked men, by or after those things that they thought (or did), shall have punishing or corrections; which (or who) despised just things or the rightwise, and went away from the Lord.

11   For he that casteth away wisdom and lore or discipline, is cursed or unhappy; and the hope of wicked men is void, and their travails *be* without fruit, and their works *be* unhabitable, and unprofitable.

12   The women of them be unwitty or unwise, and the sons of them *be* full wayward or most wicked.

13   The creature (or The offspring) of them *is* cursed; for why *the woman* barren and undefouled is blessed (or happy), that hath not known the bed in trespass; she shall have fruit in the beholding of holy souls.

14   And a man unmighty to engender or to beget, that is, a gelding, *is blessed*, that hath not wrought wickedness by (or with) his hands, neither thought most wayward or wicked things against the Lord; for why a chosen free gift of faith shall be given to him, and a most acceptable heritage (or inheritance) in the temple of God.

15   For why the fruits of good travails (or labour) is glorious, and the root of wisdom that falleth not down.

16   But the sons of adulterers shall be in destroying, and the seed of a wicked bed shall be destroyed or outlawed.

17   And soothly though they shall be of long life, they shall be areckoned into nought (or into nothing); and the last old (age) of them shall be without honour.

18   And if they be dead swiftlier, they shall not have hope, neither allowing in the day of knowing (or of trial).

19   Forsooth wicked nations be of hard ending (or meet a horrible end). Δ

DAY 16

PSALM 80

1   *To victory; this psalm is the witnessing of Asaph for lilies.* Thou that governest Israel, give attention; that leadest forth Joseph as a sheep. Thou that sittest on (or above) the cherubim, be showed

2   before Ephraim, Benjamin, and Manasseh. Stir thy power, and come thou, that thou make us safe (or save us).

3   God of virtues (or of hosts, or armies), turn thou us (again); and show thy face, and we shall be safe (or shall be saved).

4   Lord God of virtues (or of hosts), how long shalt thou be wroth on (or with) the prayer of thy servants?

5   *How long* shalt thou feed us with the bread of tears; and shalt give drink to us with tears in (great) measure?

6   Thou hast set us into against-saying to (or by) our neighbours; and our enemies have scorned us.

7   God of virtues, turn thou us (again), (or God of hosts, bring us back); and show thy face, and we shall be safe (or saved).

8   Thou translatedest (or broughtest out) a vine from Egypt; thou castedest out heathen men, and plantedest it.

9   Thou were the leader of the way in the sight thereof; and thou plantedest the roots thereof, and it filled the land.

10   The shadow thereof covered the hills; and the branches thereof *filled* (or *were thick like*) the cedars of God.

11   It stretched forth his scions or (its) branches unto the sea, and the generations thereof unto the flood (or the river).

12   Why hast thou destroyed the wall thereof; and all men that go forth by the way, gather away the grapes thereof?

13   A boar of the wood destroyed it; and a singular wild beast devoured it.

14   God of virtues (or of hosts), be thou turned (again to us); behold from heaven, and see, and visit (or care for) this vine.

15   And make thou it perfect, which (or what) thy right hand planted; and *behold thou* on the son of man, which thou hast confirmed to (or for) thee.

16   (These) things (were) burnt with fire, and undermined; (they who did this thing) shall perish for the blaming of thy cheer (or from the look on thy face).

17   Thine hand be made upon the man of (or at) thy right hand; and upon the son of man, whom thou hast confirmed to thee (or hast made strong for thyself).

18   And we departed not from thee; thou shalt quicken us, and we shall inwardly call (upon) thy name.

19   Lord God of virtues, turn thou us (again); and show thy face, and we shall be safe. (Lord God of hosts, bring us back; and shine thy face upon us, and we shall be saved.)

PSALM 81

1   *To the overcomer, on the pressers or the (wine) presses, the psalm of Asaph.* Make ye fully joy or full out joyeth to God, our helper; sing ye heartily to the God of Jacob.

2   Take ye a psalm, and give ye a tympan; a merry psaltery (or a lyre) with an harp.

3   Blow ye with a trump in the new moon; in (or on) the noble day of your solemnity (or our feast day).

4   For why (this) commandment is in Israel; and doom (or judgement) *is* to God of Jacob.

5   He put that witnessing in (or put that testimony, or command on) Joseph; when he went out of the land of Egypt, he heard a language, that he knew not.

6   He turned away his back from (his) burdens; his hands served in a coffin (or were freed from carrying the baskets).

7   In tribulation thou inwardly calledest me, and I delivered thee; I heard thee in the hid place of tempest, I proved thee at the waters of against-saying.

8   My people, hear thou *me*, and I shall be witness against (or to) thee; Israel, if thou hearest (or listenest to) me,

9   a fresh God shall not be in (or among) thee; and thou shalt not worship an alien (or foreign) god.

10   For I am thy Lord God, that led thee out of the land of Egypt; make large thy mouth, and I shall fill it.

11   And my people heard not my voice; and Israel gave not attention to me.

12   And I let them go after the desires of their hearts; they shall go (forth) in their findings (or in their own ways).

13   If (only) my people had heard me; if (only) Israel had gone in my ways.

14   For not in hap I had made low their enemies; and I had sent mine hand upon the men doing tribulation to them.

15   The enemies of the Lord lied (down) to (or would fall down before) him; and their time shall be into worlds (or forever).

16   And he fed them with the fatness of wheat; and he fulfilled them with honey of the stone (or with wild honey).

PSALM 82

1   *The psalm of Asaph.* God stood in the synagogue of gods; forsooth he deemeth (or judgeth among) the gods in the middle.

2   How long deem ye (with) wickedness; and take the faces of (or show favour to) the sinners?

3   Deem ye (or Judge) to (or for) the needy, and to (or for) the

motherless child; justify ye the meek and the poor.

4   Ravish ye out (or Rescue) the poor; and deliver ye the needy
from the hand (or the power) of the sinners.

5   They know not, neither understand, they go in darknesses; all
the foundaments (or the foundations) of the earth shall be moved.

6   I said, Ye be gods; and all ye be the sons of the (most) high
God.

7   But ye shall die as men; and ye shall fall down as one of the
princes.

8   Rise (up), thou God, deem thou the earth; for thou shalt have
heritage in all folks (or all the nations shall be thy inheritance).

PSALM 83

1   *The song of the psalm of Asaph.* God, who shall be like thee?
God, be thou not still (or silent), neither be thou peaced (or do not
hold thy peace).

2   For lo! thine enemies sounded; and they that hate thee raised
up the(ir) heads.

3   They made a wicked counsel on (or plotted against) thy
people; and they thought (together) against thy saints.

4   They said, Come ye, and lose (or destroy) we them from the
folk (or and let us utterly destroy them as a nation); and the name
of Israel be no more had in mind (or remembered).

5   For they thought with one accord;

6   the tabernacles of the Idumeans, and the men of Ishmael
disposed a testament (or agreed to a covenant) together against
thee. Moab, and the Hagarenes,

7   Gebal, and Ammon, and Amalek; (and) the aliens (or
foreigners) with them that dwell in Tyre.

8   For Assur cometh with them; they be made into help to the

sons of Lot.

9   Make (or Do) thou to them as (thou did) to Midian, and Sisera; as to Jabin, in the stream of Kishon.

10   They perished in Endor; they were made as a turd of (or upon the) earth.

11   Put (or Make) thou the princes of them as Oreb and Zeeb; and Zebah and Zalmunna.

12   All the princes of them, that said, Hold we by heritage the saintuary of God, (or Let us take for ourselves the land that belongeth to God, or his people).

13   My God, put thou them as a wheel (or into a whirlwind); and as stubble before the face of the wind.

14   As fire that burneth a wood; and as a flame burning the hills.

15   So thou shalt pursue them in (or with) thy tempest; and thou shalt trouble them in (or with) thine wrath.

16   Lord, fill thou the faces of them with shame; and they shall seek thy name.

17   Be they ashamed, and be they troubled into the world of world (or forever and ever); and be they shamed, and perish they.

18   And know they, that Lord is the name to thee (or The Lord is thy name); thou alone art the Highest in every land.

PROVERBS   CHAPTER 16

1   It pertaineth to man to make ready the soul; and *it pertaineth* to the Lord to govern the tongue.

2   All the ways of men be open to the eyes of God; the Lord is a weigher of spirits, *that is, of wills, yielding to man after his deservings.*

3   Show thy works to the Lord; and thy thoughts shall be addressed (or directed).

4   The Lord wrought all things for himself; and he *made ready* a wicked man to the evil day. (The Lord made everything for its own purpose; and he *made* the wicked for the day of evil.)

5   An abomination of (or to) the Lord is each proud man; yea, though the hand is to the hand, he shall not be innocent. The beginning of the good way *is* to do rightwiseness; forsooth it is more acceptable with God, than to offer sacrifices.

6   Wickedness is again-bought (or redeemed) by mercy and truth; and men boweth away from evil by the dread (or fear) of (or reverence for) the Lord.

7   When the ways of a man please the Lord, he shall convert, yea, his enemies to peace.

8   Better is a little with rightwiseness, than many fruits with wickedness.

9   The heart of a man shall dispose (or plan) his way; but it pertaineth to the Lord to address (or direct) his steps.

10   Divining *is* in the lips of a king; his mouth shall not err in doom (or judgement, or justice).

11   The dooms (or justice) of the Lord be weight and balance; and his works *be* all the stones (or the weights) of the world.

12   They that do wickedly *be* abominable to the king; for the throne *of the realm* is made steadfast by rightwiseness.

13   The will of kings *is* rightwise lips; he that speaketh rightful things, shall be addressed (or directed, or favoured).

14   The indignation of the king *is* (like) messengers of death; and a wise man shall please him.

15   Life *is* in the gladness of the king's cheer (or face); and his mercy *is* as rain coming late.

16   Wield thou wisdom, for it is better than gold; and get thou prudence, for it is more precious than silver.

17   The path of just men boweth away (from) evils; the keeper of

his soul keepeth his way (safe).

18   Pride goeth before sorrow; and the spirit shall be enhanced (or exalted, or raised up) before falling.

19   It is better to be made meek with mild (or humble) men, than to part spoils with proud men.

20   A learned man in word shall find goods (or obtain good things); and he that hopeth (or trusteth) in the Lord is blessed.

21   He that is wise in heart, shall be called prudent; and he that is sweet in speech, shall find greater things.

22   The well of life *is* the learning of him that wieldeth (it); the teaching of fools *is* folly.

23   The heart of a wise man shall teach his mouth; and shall increase grace (or favour) to his lips.

24   Words well-set together *is* a comb of honey; the health of the bones is the sweetness of the soul.

25   A way there is that seemeth rightful or right to a man; and the last things thereof lead to death.

26   The soul of a man travailing (or labouring) travaileth to (or for) himself; for his mouth (or his hunger) compelled him.

27   An unwise man diggeth (up) evil; and fire burneth in his lips.

28   A wayward man raiseth strives; and a man full of words separateth princes.

29   A wicked man flattereth his friend; and leadeth him by a way not good.

30   He that thinketh shrewd (or depraved) things with eyes astonished, biteth his lips, and performeth evil.

31   A crown of dignity *is* old (age), that shall be found in the ways of rightwiseness.

32   A patient man is better than a strong man; and he that is lord of his soul, *is better* than an overcomer of cities.

33   Lots be sent into the bosom; but they be tempered of (or by)

the Lord.

ECCLESIASTICUS CHAPTER 21

1   Son, thou hast done sin? or Son, hast thou sinned? add thou (to it) not again; but beseech thou for the former *sins*, (so) that they be forgiven to thee.

2   As from the face of a serpent or a shadow adder, flee thou sins; and if thou nighest (or approachest) to them, they shall take thee. The teeth of a lion *be* (as) the teeth of it, that slay the souls of men.

3   All wickedness *is* as a sharp sword on either side; health (or healing) is not to the wound of it.

4   Chidings and wrongs shall destroy chattel or substance; and an house that is over-rich, shall be destroyed by pride; so the chattel or substance of a proud man shall be drawn up by the root.

5   The prayer of a poor man shall come from the mouth unto the ears *of God*; and doom (or judgement, or justice) shall come to him hastily.

6   He that hateth reproving, is (in) a step of the sinner; and (or but) he that dreadeth (or feareth, or revereth) God, shall be turned or converted to (him in) his heart.

7   A mighty man with an hardy tongue is known afar; and a witty (or a witting, or a knowing) man knoweth how to keep himself or how to slide from that *man*.

8   He that buildeth his house with other men's costs, *is* as he that gathereth his stones in winter.

9   Sheaves, or stubble, or flax tops, gathered together *is* the synagogue of sinners; and the ending of them *is* the flame of fire.

10   The way of sinners *is* set altogether or planted with stones; and in the end of them *be* hell, and darknesses, and pains.

11   He that keepeth rightfulness, shall hold the wit (or the under-

standing) thereof. The perfection of God's dread (or the fear of or reverence for God) *is* wisdom and wit (or understanding).

12   He shall not be taught, which is not wise in (what is) good. Forsooth unwisdom is, which is plenteous or aboundeth in evil; and wit (or clear thinking) is not, where (there) is bitterness.

13   The knowing (or the knowledge) of a wise man shall be (as) plenteous (or abundant) as flowing (water); and the counsel of him dwelleth as a well of life.

14   The heart of a fool *is* as a broken vessel; and it shall not hold any wisdom.

15   Whatever wise word a knowing man heareth, he shall praise (it), and lay to (or add to it). A lecherous man heard (it), and it shall displease him; and he shall cast or throw it away behind his back.

16   The telling of a fool *is* as a burden in (or on) the way; for why grace (or favour) shall be found in (or on) the lips of a wise man.

17   The mouth of a prudent man is sought in the church (or congregation); and *men* shall think (on) his words in their hearts.

18   As an house destroyed, so *is* wisdom to a fool; and the knowing (or knowledge) of an unwise man *is* words that may not (or cannot) be told out or (that be) untellable.

19   Stocks in (or on) the feet *is* teaching or doctrine to a fool; and as bonds of the hands on the right hand.

20   A fool enhanceth (or lifteth up) his voice in laughing; but a wise man shall laugh scarcely still (or very seldom).

21   Teaching *is* a golden ornament to a prudent man; and as an ornament of the arm or an arm-circle (or a bracelet) in (or on) the right arm.

22   The foot of a fool *is* light (or easily) into the house of a neighbour; and a wise man shall be ashamed of the person of a mighty man (or shall be ashamed of that fool).

23   A fool beholdeth from the window into the house; but a

learned man shall stand withoutforth.

24   It *is* folly of (or for) a man to harken by the door; and a prudent man shall be grieved by despising or with strife.

25   The lips of unprudent men shall tell fond things or follies; but the words of prudent men shall be weighed in a balance.

26   The heart of fools *is* in their mouth; and the mouth of wise men *is* in their heart.

27   When a wicked man curseth the devil, he curseth his own soul.

28   A privy backbiter (or whisperer) shall defoul (or defile) his (own) soul, and in all things he shall be hated, and he that dwelleth, shall (also) be hated; a still (or silent) man and wise shall be honoured.

ECCLESIASTICUS   CHAPTER 22

1   A slow man is (as) stunned in (or as) a stone of clay; and all men shall speak on or of the great despising of him.

2   A slow man is (as) stunned of (or as) the dung or drit of oxen; and each man that toucheth him, shall shake the hands.

3   The shame of a father is of a son unlearned or undisciplined; but a fond or a fool(ish) daughter shall be in (or to) the decreasing or the diminishing *of the honour of father and mother.*

4   A prudent daughter *is* heritage to (or an inheritance for) her husband; for (or but) she that shameth *her husband,* is in despising or reproof of (or by) the father.

5   A bold *woman, that is, shameless,* shameth the father and (her) husband, and shall not be made less than unfaithful men; forsooth she shall not be honoured of (or by) ever either.

6   Melody in mourning *is* uncovenable (or unsuitable) telling; beatings or scourges and teaching or doctrine, (be) in all times with wisdom.

7   He that teacheth a fool, (is) as he that glueth together a tilestone or a shard. He that telleth a word to him that heareth not, *is* as he that raiseth a man sleeping from a grievous or a heavy sleep.

8   He that telleth wisdom to a fool, speaketh with a man sleeping; and in the end of the telling he shall say, Who is this?

9   (This verse is omitted in the original text.)

10   (This verse is omitted in the original text.)

11   Weep thou on (or for) a dead man, for why his light failed; and weep thou on (or for) a fool, for he failed of wit. Weep thou a little on (or for) a dead man, for he hath rested. Forsooth the life of a full wicked man *is* full wicked, more than the death of a fool.

12   The mourning of (or for) a dead man *is* seven days; but *the mourning* of (or for) a fool and of (or for) a wicked man *is* all the days of their life.

13   Speak thou not much with a fool, and go thou not with an unwise man. Keep thee from him, (so) that thou have not dis-ease or grief; and thou shalt not be defouled (or defiled) in the sin of him. Bow thou away from him, and thou shalt find rest; and be thou not annoyed (or harmed) by his folly.

14   What shall be made heavier than lead? and what other name than a fool *is* to him?

15   It is lighter (or easier) to bear gravel, and salt, and a gobbet (or a piece) of iron, than an imprudent man, and a fool, and unfaithful.

16   As an heap or a joining of trees, bound together in the foundament (or foundation) of the building, shall not be unbound or unloosed, so and an heart confirmed in the thought of counsel.

17   The thought of a wise man shall not be made shrewd (or depraved) in any time, neither dreaded.

18   As chaffs in high places, and sand without meddling of him (or the mixing of it) or mortar without due cost, set against the face

of the wind, shall not dwell; so and a dreadful heart in the thought or in the thinking of a fool against-standeth not against the fierceness of dread (or fear). As adorning, *either pargeting*, full of gravel in a clear wall, so and a fearedful heart in the thought of a fool or the trembling heart in the thinking of a fool shall not dread in (or fear at) any time; so and he that dwelleth evermore in the behests (or the commands) of God.

19 He that pricketh the eye, shall lead out tears; and he that pricketh the heart, bringeth forth wit (or understanding).

20 He that casteth or throwing a stone to (or at) birds, shall cast down them; so and he that doeth wrong to a friend, departeth or loseth friendship.

21 Though thou bringest forth a sword to a friend, despair thou not; for there is going again to the friend.

22 If he openeth a sorrowful mouth, dread thou (or fear) not; for why there is according, except (for) despising, and shame, and pride, and showing or opening of privates (or of secrets), and a treacherous wound; in all these things a friend shall fly away.

23 Have thou faith with a friend in his poverty, (so) that thou be glad also in his goods (or good times). In the time of his tribulations (or troubles), dwell thou or abide still faithful to him, (so) that also thou be even-heir in the heritage of him (or in his inheritance).

24 Heat and smoke of fire *is* made high before the fire of a chimney; so and curses, and despisings or wrongs, and threats, *come* before blood.

25 I shall not be ashamed for to greet a friend, and I shall not hide me from his face;

26 (even) though evils come to me by him, I shall suffer (it). Each man that shall hear, shall keep warily himself from him.

27 Who shall give keeping or ward to (or keep watch over) my mouth, and a certain sealing or mark upon my lips, (so) that I fall

not by them, and that my tongue lose (or destroy) not me?

WISDOM OF SOLOMON CHAPTER 4

1   How fair is a chaste generation with clearness or clarity; for the mind thereof is undeadly (or the remembrance of them is immortal or forever), for it is known, both with God, and with men.

2   When it is present, they follow it; and they desire it, when it hath led out itself, and it overcoming getteth by victory the meed (or the reward) of battles undefouled, and is crowned without end.

3   But the manyfold engendered multitude of wicked or unpious men shall not be profitable; and (as) plantings of adultery they shall not give deep roots, neither shall set stable steadfastness.

4   Though they burgeon in boughs or (in) branches for a time, they set unsteadfastly shall be moved of (or by) the wind, and they shall be drawn out or pulled up by the roots of (or by) the greatness of the winds.

5   For why boughs or branches unperfect shall be broken altogether; and the fruits of them *be* unprofitable, and sour to eat, and covenable to (or suitable for) nothing.

6   For why all the sons, that be born of wicked men, be witnesses of wickedness against (their) fathers and mothers, in their asking.

7   But the rightwise man, though he be before-occupied by death, shall be in refreshing (or at rest).

8   For why worshipful old (age) is not of long time or long enduring, neither it is reckoned by the number of years;

9   the wits of a man be hoary, and the age of old (or old age) *is* life without wem (or spot, or blemish), or undefouled.

10   He pleased God, and was made dearworthy or loved, and he living among sinners was translated, *or borne over;*

11   he was ravished (or taken away), lest malice should change

his understanding, either lest feigning should deceive or beguile his soul.

12　For why deceiving of trifling maketh dark good things, and the unstableness of covetousness overturneth the wit without malice, (or confuseth even the simple or most honest person).

13　He was ended in short time, and fulfilled many times;

14　for why his soul was pleasant to or pleased God; for this thing *God* hastened to lead him out from the midst of wickednesses;

15　but the peoples saw and understood not, neither putted such things in their hearts or entrails. For the grace and mercy of God is on (or with) his saints (or his people), and the beholding or the respect *of God is* on (or for) his chosen men.

16　Forsooth the rightwise dead condemneth quick wicked men or unpious men alive (or living); and youth ended swiftlier *condemneth* the long life of the unrightwise.

17　For they shall see the end of a wise man, and they shall not understand, what thing God thought of him, and why the Lord made him less or diminished him.

18　For they shall see, and shall despise him; but the Lord shall scorn them. And after these things they shall be falling down without honour, and in despising among the dead into without end (or forever).

19　For he shall all-break them swollen without a voice, and he shall move them from the foundaments (or the foundations); and they shall be desolate unto the last thing. And they shall be wailing, and the mind (or the memory) of them shall perish.

20　They shall come fearedful in the thought of their sins; and their wickednesses on the contrary side shall lead them over. Δ

DAY 17

PSALM 84

1   *To victory, on the pressers. The psalm of the sons of Korah.*
Lord of virtues (or of hosts, or armies), thy tabernacles be greatly
loved;

2   my soul coveteth, and faileth into (or longeth for) the porches
of the Lord. Mine heart, and my flesh; full out joyed into the quick
(or in the living) God.

3   For why a sparrow findeth an house to (or for) itself; and a
turtle(dove) *findeth* a nest to (or for) itself, where it shall keep his
(or its) birds. Lord of virtues (or of hosts, or armies), thine altars; my
King, and my God.

4   Lord, blessed *be* they that dwell in thine house; they shall
praise thee into the worlds of worlds (or forever and ever).

5   Blessed (or Happy) *is* the man, whose help is of (or in) thee;
he hath ordained (thy) goings (or thy ways) in his heart,

6   in the valley of tears, in the place which he hath set. For the
giver of the law shall give a blessing,

7   they shall go from virtue into virtue (or from strength to
strength); the God of gods shall be seen in Zion.

8   Lord God of virtues (or of hosts, or armies), hear thou my prayer;
God of Jacob, perceive thou with ears (or *please* listen *to me*).

9   God, our defender, behold thou; and behold into the face of
thy christ (or thine anointed one).

10   For why one day in thine halls is better; than a thousand (days
elsewhere). I (would) choose to be abject, *either an outcast*, in the
house of my God; more than to dwell in the tabernacles of sinners.

11   For God loveth mercy and truth; the Lord shall give grace and
glory. He shall not deprive them from goods (or good things), that

go in innocence (or they who do what is right).

12   Lord of virtues (or of hosts, or armies), blessed *is* the man, that hopeth in (or trusteth) thee.

PSALM 85

1   *To the overcomer, the song of the sons of Korah.* Lord, thou hast blessed thy land; thou hast turned away the captivity of (or returned prosperity to) Jacob.

2   Thou hast forgiven the wickedness of thy people; thou hast covered all the sins of them.

3   Thou hast assuaged all thy wrath; thou hast turned (thyself) away from the wrath of thine indignation.

4   God, our health (or our salvation), convert thou us; and turn away thy wrath from us.

5   Whether thou shalt be wroth to us without end (or forever); or shalt thou hold forth or stretch out thy wrath (or anger) from generation into generation?

6   God, thou converted, shalt quicken us; and thy people shall be glad (or shall rejoice) in thee.

7   Lord, show thy mercy to us; and give thine health (or thy salvation) to us.

8   I shall hear what the Lord God shall speak in (or say to) me; for he shall speak peace to his people. And upon his holy men; and upon them that be turned to (or in their) hearts.

9   Nevertheless his health (or his salvation) *is* nigh (to) men dreading (or fearing, or revering) him; (so) that glory (can) dwell in our land.

10   Mercy and truth met themselves; rightwiseness and peace were kissed.

11   Truth came forth (out) of the earth; and rightwiseness beheld

from heaven.

12 For the Lord shall give benignity (or what is good); and our earth shall give his (or its) fruit.

13 Rightwiseness shall go before him; and shall put his steps in (or on) the (right) way (for us to go).

PSALM 86

1 *A prayer of David.* Lord, bow (down) thine ear, and hear me; for I am needy and poor.

2 Keep thou my life (safe), for I am holy; my God, make thou safe (or save) thy servant hoping (or trusting) in thee.

3 Lord, have thou mercy on me, for I cried all day (long) to thee;

4 make thou glad the soul of thy servant; for why, Lord, I have raised (up) my soul to thee.

5 For thou, Lord, *art* sweet and mild; and of much mercy to all men inwardly calling thee.

6 Lord, perceive thou my prayer with ears (or *please* listen to my prayer); and give thou attention to the voice of my beseeching.

7 In the day of my tribulation I cried to thee; for thou heardest me.

8 Lord, none among the gods is like thee; and none is even to thy works.

9 Lord, all the folks (or the nations), whichever thou madest, shall come, and worship before thee; and they shall glorify thy name.

10 For thou art full great, and making marvels; thou art God alone.

11 Lord, lead thou me forth in (or on) thy way, and I shall enter in thy truth; mine heart be glad, that it dread (or revere) thy name.

12 My Lord God, I shall acknowledge to (or praise) thee in (or with) all mine heart; and I shall glorify thy name without end.

13 For thy mercy is great on (or towards) me; and thou deliveredest my soul from the lower hell (or Sheol).

14   God, wicked men have risen upon (or against) me; and the synagogue (or assembly) of mighty men have sought my life; and they have not set forth thee in their sight.

15   And thou, Lord God, doing mercy, and merciful; patient, and of much mercy, and soothfast (or faithful).

16   Behold upon me, and have mercy on me, give thou the empire (or thy strength) to thy servant; and make thou safe (or save) the son of thine handmaid.

17   Make thou with me a sign in(to) good (or show me a sign of thy goodness), (so) that they see, that hate me, and be ashamed; (yea), for thou, Lord, hast helped me, and hast comforted me.

PSALM 87

1   *The psalm of the song of the sons of Korah.* The foundaments of him *be* in holy hills (or His foundations *be* upon the holy hill/s);

2   the Lord loveth the gates of Zion, more than all the tabernacles of Jacob.

3   Thou city of God, without end; glorious things be said of thee.

4   I shall be mindful of (or remember the people of) Rahab, and Babylon; knowing me. Lo! Aliens (or Foreigners), and Tyre, and the people of Ethiopians; they (all) were there.

5   Whether a man shall say to Zion, And a man is born therein; and that man, the alder-Highest, founded it?

6   The Lord shall tell in the scriptures of (these) peoples; and of these princes (or their leaders), that were in it.

7   As the dwelling of all that be glad; is in thee.

PSALM 88

1   *The song of the psalm, to the sons of Korah, to victory on*

Mahalath, for to answer the learning of Heman, the Ezrahite. Lord God of mine health (or my salvation); I cried in day and night before thee.

2   (Let) my prayer enter before thy sight (or into thy presence); bow down thine ear to my prayer.

3   For my soul is full-filled with evils; and my life nighed to hell (or the grave).

4   I am guessed with them that go down into the pit; I am made as a man without help,

5   and free among dead men. As men wounded sleeping in sepulchres, of which men none (thou) is mindful (of) after; and they be put away from thine hand (or cut off from thy help).

6   They have put me in the lower pit; in dark places, and in the shadow of death.

7   Thy strong vengeance is confirmed on me (or Thy fury hath raged against me); and thou hast brought in all thy waves upon me.

8   Thou hast made far from me my known (or my friends); they have put (or made) me an abomination unto themselves. I am taken (in), and I went not out;

9   mine eyes were sick for poverty (or weakened from suffering). Lord, I cried to thee; all day I spreaded abroad mine hands to thee.

10   Whether thou shalt do marvels to (or for) dead men; or leeches (or physicians) shall raise (them up), and they shall acknowledge to (or shall praise) thee?

11   Whether any man in a sepulchre shall tell (of) thy mercy; and (of) thy truth (or thy faithfulness) in perdition?

12   Whether thy marvels shall be known in darknesses; and thy rightwiseness in the land of forgetting?

13   And, Lord, I cried to thee; and early my prayer shall before come to thee.

14   Lord, why puttest thou away my prayer; thou turnest away thy

face from me?

15   I am poor, and in travails (or torment) from my youth; soothly I am enhanced (or lifted up), and I am made low, and troubled.

16   Thy wraths passed on (or over) me; and thy dreads troubled me.

17   They encompassed me as water all day (long); they encompassed me altogether.

18   Thou madest far from me a friend and neighbour; and my known from wretchedness (or and now wretchedness is my only companion).

PROVERBS CHAPTER 17

1   Better is a dry morsel with joy, than an house full of sacrifices with chiding (or with arguments).

2   A wise servant shall be the lord of fond or foolish sons; and he shall (have) part (of) the heritage (or share the inheritance) among (all) the brethren.

3   As silver is proved by fire, and gold *is proved* by a chimney, so the Lord proveth hearts.

4   An evil man obeyeth to a wicked tongue; and a false man obeyeth to false lips (or a liar obeyeth lies).

5   He that despiseth a poor man, reproveth his Maker; and he that is glad in the falling of another man, shall not be (or go) unpunished.

6   The crown of old men *is* the sons of sons; and the glory of sons *is* the fathers of them.

7   Words well-set together (or put together well) beseem not a fool; and a lying lip *becometh* not a prince.

8   A precious stone most acceptable *is* the abiding of him that seeketh; whither ever he turneth himself, he understandeth prudently.

9   He that covereth trespass, seeketh friendships; he that rehearseth by an high word (or who remembereth a wrong), separateth them that (should) be knit together in peace.

10   A blaming (or A rebuke) profiteth more at (or to) a prudent man, than an hundred wounds at (or to) a fool.

11   Ever an evil man seeketh strives; forsooth a cruel angel (or messenger) shall be sent against him.

12   It speedeth more to meet a female bear, when her whelps be ravished (or snatched away), than a fool trusting to himself in his folly (or trusting in his own foolishness).

13   Evil shall not go away from the house of him, that yieldeth evils for goods (or who giveth evil for good).

14   He that letteth (out) water, is the head of strives (or quarrels); and before that he suffereth wrong, he forsaketh doom (or deserteth judgement).

15   Both he that justifieth a wicked man, and he that condemneth a just man, ever either is abominable to God.

16   What profiteth it to a fool to have riches, since he may not (or cannot) buy wisdom? He that maketh his house high, seeketh falling; and he that escheweth to learn, shall fall into evils.

17   He that is a friend, loveth in (or at) all times; and a brother is proved in anguishes.

18   A fond or foolish man shall make joy (or clap) with (his) hands, when he hath promised for his friend.

19   He that bethinketh discords, loveth chidings or strife; and he that enhanceth his (own) mouth, seeketh (his own) falling.

20   He that is of wayward heart, shall not find good; and he that (mis)-turneth the tongue, shall fall into evil.

21   A fool is born in his shame; but not the father shall be glad in a fool (or to have a fool for a son).

22   A joyful soul maketh liking age (or maketh a good life); a

sorrowful spirit maketh dry bones.

23 A wicked man taketh (secret) gifts from the bosom, to mis-turn the paths of doom (or to pervert the course of justice).

24 Wisdom shineth in the face of a prudent man; the eyes of fools *be* in (or wander unto) the ends of the earth.

25 A fond or foolish son *is* the wrath of the father, and the sorrow of the mother that bare him.

26 It is not good to bring in harm to a just or rightwise man; neither to smite the prince that deemeth (or judgeth) rightfully.

27 He that measureth his words, is wise and prudent; and a learned man is of (or hath a) precious spirit.

28 Also a fool, if he is still (or silent), shall be guessed a wise man; and, if he presseth together his lips, *he is guessed* an understanding man.

ECCLESIASTICUS   CHAPTER 23

1 Lord, Father, and lordly governor of my life, forsake thou me not in the thought or in the thinking and the counsel of them, *that is, of fools and unfaithful men*; neither suffer (or allow) thou me to fall in that shame.

2 Who setteth above in my thoughts beatings or Who putteth upon in my thinking scourges, and in mine heart the teaching of wisdom, (so) that in the unknowings (or ignorances) of them he spare not me, and (so) that the trespasses of them appear not?

3 Lest mine unknowings (or ignorances) increase, and my trespasses be multiplied, and my sins be plenteous or abound; and lest I fall in the sight of mine adversaries, and mine enemy have joy.

4 Lord, Father, and God of my life, forsake thou not me in the thoughts of them. Give thou not to me enhancing of mine eyes, *yea, suffer not (or do not allow) that pride be lord over me*;

5   and turn thou away from me all shrewd (or depraved) desire.

6   Do thou away from me the covetousnesses of the womb, and the covetousnesses of lechery or of lust take me not; and give thou not me (over) (un)to a soul unreverent and undiscreet, or unsavoury.

7   Sons, hear ye the teaching of the mouth; and he that keepeth it, shall not perish by his lips, neither shall be caused to stumble in worst works.

8   A sinner and proud man shall be taken or caught in his vanity; and a cursed man shall be caused to stumble in them.

9   Thy mouth be not customable (or accustomed) to swearing; for why many fallings *be* therein. [To swearing use not thy mouth; many forsooth fallings be in it.]

10   Forsooth the naming of God be not customable or continual in thy mouth, and be thou not meddled to, or mingled, (or mixed with) the names of saints; for thou shalt not be guiltless of them.

11   For as a servant *that is* asked busily, shall not want (or lack) wanness, *or envy*; so each man swearing and naming shall not be purged of sin in all. A man swearing much shall be filled with wickedness; and vengeance shall not go away from his house. And if he deceiveth a brother, his trespass shall be upon him; and if he feigneth, he shall trespass doubly. And if he sweareth in vain, he shall not be justified; for why his house shall be filled with the worst yielding.

12   Also again-ward another speech is into death; be it not found in the heritage (or the inheritance) of Jacob. For why all these things shall be done away from merciful men; and they shall not delight in trespasses.

13   Thy mouth be not customable (or accustomed) to unreverent speech; for why a word of sin is in it. [To the undisciplined speech use not thy mouth; forsooth there is in it the word of sin.]

14   Have thou mind on (or Think upon) thy father and mother; for

(or when) thou standest in the midst of great men. Lest peradventure God forget thee in the sight of them; and lest thou made a fool by thus customableness or busyness, suffer shame, *either scorning*, or reproof, and haddest rather to be not born, and curse the day of thy birth.

15   A man customable in (or accustomed to using) the words of shame or reproof, in all (his) days shall not be taught.

16   Two kinds be plenteous or abound in sins, and the third bringeth wrath and perdition. An hot soul burning as fire shall not be quenched, till it swallow something; and a wicked man in the mouth of his flesh shall not fail, till he kindle a fire.

17   Each bread *is* sweet to a lecherous man; he shall not be made weary, trespassing till to the end.

18   Each man that passeth or that over-goeth his bed, doeth despite against his soul, and saith, Who seeth me? Darknesses encompass me, and the walls cover me, and no man beholdeth me. Whom dread I? The Highest shall not have mind on my sins.

19   And he understandeth not, that the eye of him, *that is, of God*, seeth all things; for why the dread of such a man putteth away from him(self) the dread of God, and the eyes of men that dread him *put away from him God's dread*. And he knew not, that the eyes of the Lord be much more clearer than the sun, and behold all the ways of men, and the depth of the sea, and they behold the hearts of men into hid parts.

20   For why all things were known to the Lord, before that they were made or formed of nought (or out of nothing); so and after the making, he beholdeth all things.

21   This *man* shall be punished in the streets of the city; he shall be driven away as an horse colt, and he shall be taken or caught, where he hopeth not. And he shall be (in) shame to all men; for he understood not the dread (or the fear) of (or reverence for) the

Lord.

22   So and each woman forsaking her husband shall do sin, and ordaining heritage, *that is, an heir of her husband,* of (or by) an alien matrimony (or another man).

23   For first she was unbelieveful in (or of) the law of the Highest, and the second time she forsook her husband; and the third time she was defouled in adultery, and ordained to him sons of (or by) another man.

24   She, this *woman,* shall be brought into the church, and men shall behold on her sons.

25   Her sons shall not give or take roots, and her branches shall not give fruit.

26   They shall leave the mind (or the memory) of her into cursing, and the shame of her shall not be done away.

27   And they that be left shall know, that nothing *is* better than the dread (or fear) of God (or reverence for God), and nothing *is* sweeter than to behold in the commandments of the Lord.

28   It is great glory to follow the Lord; for why the length of days shall be taken of (or received from) him.

WISDOM OF SOLOMON   CHAPTER 5

1   Then rightwise men shall stand in great steadfastness against them that anguished them, and which took away their travails.

2   They shall see (it), and shall be disturbed (or troubled) with horrible dread, and they shall wonder in the suddenty or marvel in the suddenness of *their* health (or of *their* deliverance) unhoped (for);

3   and they shall wail for anguish of spirit, and they shall say, doing penance within themselves, and wailing for the anguish of spirit, These men it be, which we had sometime into scorn, and into likeness of upbraiding.

4   We mad men guessed their life madness, and the end of them without honour;

5   how therefore be they reckoned or counted among the sons of God, and their part or their lot is among the saints?(!)

6   Therefore we erred from the way of truth, and the light of rightwiseness shined not to us, and the sun of understanding rose not up (un)to (or upon) us.

7   We were made weary in the way of wickedness and of perdition; and we have gone hard ways. But we knew not the way of the Lord;

8   what profited pride to us, either what brought or gave the boast of riches to us?

9   All those things passed as a shadow, and as a messenger running before.

10   And as a ship, that passeth through the flowing water, of the which when it hath passed, a step is not to find (or to be found), neither the path of the bottom thereof in the waves.

11   Or as a bird, that flyeth over in the air, of which no proof or evidence is found of his way, but only the sound of wings beating the light wind, and carving or cutting the air by the might of the way, and with wings moved together it flew over, and after this no sign is found of his way.

12   Or as an arrow shot out into a place ordained, the air is parted, and is closed again anon (or at once), (so) that the passing thereof be not known.

13   Right so we born ceased anon (or at once) to be, and soothly we might show no sign of virtue; but we were wasted in our malice. They that sinned, said such things in hell (or in the grave).

14   For the hope of a wicked man or the unpious is as the flower of a briar, *or a thistledown*, which is taken away of (or by) the wind, and as small froth or foam which is scattered abroad of (or

by) a tempest, and as smoke which is spread abroad of (or by) the wind, and as the mind (or memory) of a guest of one day, that passeth forth (or goeth away).

15 But rightwise men shall live without end (or forever), and the meed of them (or their reward) is with the Lord; and the thought of them *is* with the Highest.

16 Therefore they shall take of (or receive from) the hand of the Lord the realm of fairness, and a diadem of comeliness; for he shall govern or cover them with his right hand, and he shall defend them with his holy arm.

17 And his fervent love or the jealousy of him shall take armour, and he shall arm the creature to the vengeance of (his) enemies.

18 He shall clothe rightwiseness for the breastplate, and he shall take certain doom (or true judgement) for the helmet;

19 he shall take (for) the shield unquenchable equity, *either evenness*;

20 forsooth he shall whet or sharpen hard wrath into a spear, and the world shall fight with him against unwitty (or unwitting) men or the unwise.

21 Straight sendings-out of lightnings shall go, and as the sides of a rainbow, when the bow of clouds is crooked or bent, they shall be destroyed; and they shall skip into a certain place.

22 And full hailstones shall be sent from a stony wrath, and the water of the sea shall wax (or grow) white against them, and the floods (or rivers) shall run altogether hard.

23 The spirit of virtue (or a strong wind) shall stand against them, and as the whirling of wind (or a whirlwind) it shall depart them; and the wickedness of them shall bring all the land (un)to desert or wilderness, and malice shall destroy the seats of mighty men. Wisdom is better than strengths (or strongholds), and a prudent man doeth more than a strong man. Δ

DAY 18

PSALM 89

1   *The learning of Ethan, the Ezrahite.* I shall sing without end; the mercies of the Lord. In generation and into generation; I shall tell (out) thy truth (or thy faithfulness) with my mouth.

2   For thou saidest, Without end mercy shall be builded in heavens; thy truth shall be made ready in them.

3   (Thou saidest), I disposed a testament (or a covenant) to my chosen men; I swore to David, my servant,

4   till into without end I shall make ready thy seed. And I shall build thy seat (or thy throne); in generation, and into generation.

5   Lord, heavens shall acknowledge (or praise) thy marvels; and thy truth in the church of the saints (or and the assembly of God's people *shall praise* thy faithfulness).

6   For who in the clouds shall be made even (or equal) to the Lord; shall be like God among the sons of God?

7   God, that is glorified in the council of the saints; *is* great, and dreadful (or fearful) over all that be in his compass.

8   Lord God of virtues (or of hosts, or armies), who *is* like thee? Lord, thou art mighty, and thy truth (or faithfulness) *is* in thy compass.

9   Thou art Lord of the power of the sea; forsooth thou assuagest the stirring of the waves thereof.

10   Thou madest low the proud, as (those who be) wounded (and slain); in the arm (or power) of thy strength thou hast scattered thine enemies.

11   The heavens be thine, and the earth is thine; thou hast founded the world, and the fullness thereof;

12   thou madest of nought (or out of nothing) the north and the

sea. Tabor and Hermon shall make full out joy in thy name;

13 thine arm with (or hath) power. (Let) thine hand be made steadfast, and thy right hand be enhanced (or exalted);

14 rightwiseness and doom (or judgement) *is* the making ready of thy seat. Mercy and truth shall go before thy face (or in thy presence);

15 blessed *is* the people that know a hearty song. Lord, they shall go in the light of thy cheer (or thy face);

16 and in thy name they shall make full out joy all day; and they shall be enhanced (or exalted) in thy rightwiseness.

17 For thou art the glory of the virtue (or strength) of them; and in thy good pleasance our horn shall be enhanced (or exalted).

18 For our taking up is of (or from) the Lord; and of (or from) the Holy (One) of Israel our King.

19 Then thou spakest in revelation to thy saints, and saidest, I have put help in the mighty (man); and I have enhanced (or exalted, or raised up) the chosen man of my people.

20 I found David, my servant; I anointed him with mine holy oil.

21 For mine hand shall help him; and mine arm shall confirm him (or make him strong).

22 The enemy shall nothing profit in him (or gain any advantage over him); and the son of wickedness shall not put to, for to harm him.

23 And I shall slay his enemies from (before) his face; and I shall turn into flight them that hate him.

24 And my truth and mercy *shall be* with him; and his horn shall be enhanced (or exalted) in my name.

25 And I shall put his hand in (or over) the sea; and his right hand in the floods (or over the rivers).

26 He shall inwardly call me, (saying), Thou art my father; my God, and the up-taker of mine health (or my salvation).

27 And I shall set him the first begotten son; higher than the

kings of the earth.

28   Without end I shall keep my mercy to (or love for) him; and my testament (or my covenant) faithful to him.

29   And I shall set his seed into the world of world (or forever and ever); and his throne as (long as) the days of heaven.

30   Forsooth (or But) if his sons forsake my law; and go not in my dooms (or judgements).

31   If they make unholy my rightfulnesses (or statutes); and keep not my commandments.

32   I shall visit in (or with) a rod the wickednesses of them; and in (or with) beatings the sins of them.

33   But I shall not scatter (or take away) my mercy from him; and in my truth I shall not annoy (or harm) him.

34   Neither I shall make unholy my testament; and I shall not make void those things that come forth of (or from) my lips.

35   Once I swore in (or by) mine holiness, (that) I shall not lie to David;

36   his seed (or descendants) shall dwell without end. And his throne as the sun in my sight,

37   and as a perfect moon without end; and a faithful witness in the heavens.

38   But thou hast put away, and despised; and hast delayed thy christ (or thine anointed one).

39   Thou hast turned away the testament of thy servant; thou madest unholy his saintuary in the earth (or thou hast cast his crown down into the dirt).

40   Thou destroyedest all the hedges thereof; thou hast set the steadfastness thereof (into) dread (or thou hast brought down his strongholds into ruin).

41   All men passing by the way ravished (or robbed) him; he is made a shame to his neighbours.

42   Thou hast enhanced (or exalted) the right hand of men oppressing him; thou hast gladdened all his enemies.

43   Thou hast turned away the help of (or from) his sword; and thou helpedest not him in battle.

44   Thou destroyedest him from cleansing; and thou hast hurled down his seat in earth (or cast his throne down to the ground).

45   Thou hast made less the days of his time; thou coveredest him with shame.

46   Lord, how long turnest thou away, into the end (or forever?); shall thy wrath burn out as a fire?

47   Bethink thou what *is* my substance; for whether thou hast ordained vainly (or in vain) all the sons of men?

48   Who is a man, that shall live, and shall not see death; shall (he) deliver his soul from the hand (or power) of hell (or the grave)?

49   Lord, where be thine old (acts of) mercies; as thou hast sworn to David in thy truth (or faithfulness)?

50   Lord, be thou mindful of (or remember) the shame of thy servants; (of the curses) of many heathen men, which I held together in my bosom (or carried in my heart).

51   Which thine enemies, Lord, did (or spoke) shamefully (to me); for they despised the changing of thy christ (or the successors of thine anointed *king*).

52   Blessed *be* the Lord without end; be it done, be it done (or amen).

PSALM 90

1   *The prayer of Moses, the man of God.* Lord, thou art made a help to us; from generation into generation.

2   Before that the hills were made, either the earth and the world was formed; from the world and into the world, thou art God.

3   Turn thou not away a man into lowness; and thou saidest, Ye sons of men, be turned again (or return to dust).

4   For a thousand years *be* before thine eyes; as yesterday, which is passed, and as the keeping in the night.

5   The years of them shall be; that be had for nought. Early pass he (along), as an herb,

6   (yea), early flourish he, and pass (along); (then) in the eventide fall he down, be he hard, and wax (or grow) he dry.

7   For we have failed in (or brought to an end by) thy wrath; and we be troubled in (or by) thy strong vengeance.

8   Thou hast put our wickednesses in thy sight (or before thee); our world in the lightening of thy cheer (or in the full light of thy face).

9   For all our days have failed; and we have failed in thy wrath. Our years (we) shall bethink upon as a spider (or shall end with a sigh);

10   the days of our years *be* those seventy years. Forsooth, if fourscore or eighty years *be* in mighty men; and (yet) the more time of them is travail (or labour, or trouble) and sorrow. For mildness came above; and we shall be chastised.

11   Who knew the power of thy wrath; and *durst* number (or count) thy wrath for thy dread (or equal to thy fear)?

12   Make thy right hand so known; and *make* men learned in heart by wisdom.

13   Lord, be thou converted some-deal; and be thou able to be prayed of (or petitioned by) thy servants.

14   We were fulfilled early with thy mercy; (so) we made full out joy, and we delighted in all our days.

15   We were glad for the days in which thou madest us meek; for the years in which we saw evils.

16   Lord, behold thou into thy servants, and into thy works (or let

thy servants see thy mighty works); and address (or direct) thou the sons of them.

17   And the shining of our Lord God be upon us; and address (or direct) thou the works of our hands on (or for) us; and address (or direct) thou the works of our hands.

PSALM 91

1   He that dwelleth in the help of the highest *God*; shall dwell in (or under) the protection of the God of heaven.

2   He shall say to the Lord, Thou art mine up-taker (or defender), and my refuge; my God, I shall hope (or trust) in him.

3   For he delivered me from the snare of hunters; and from a sharp word.

4   With his shoulders he shall make a shadow to (or for) thee; and thou shalt have hope under his feathers. His truth shall encompass thee with a shield;

5   thou shalt not dread of (or fear) the night's dread. Of an arrow flying in the day,

6   of a goblin going in darknesses; of assailing, and of a midday fiend.

7   A thousand shall fall down from thy side, and ten thousand from thy right side; forsooth it shall not nigh (or come close) to thee.

8   Nevertheless thou shalt behold (or see) with thine eyes; and thou shalt see the yielding (or the punishment) of sinners.

9   For thou, Lord, art mine hope; thou hast set thine help (to be the) alder-Highest (or the Most High).

10   Evil shall not come to thee; and a scourge shall not (come) nigh to thy tabernacle.

11   For *God* hath commanded to his angels of (or to be all around) thee; (so) that they keep thee (safe) in all thy ways.

12   They shall bear thee in (or lift thee up with) the hands; lest peradventure thou hurt thy foot at (or on) a stone.

13   Thou shalt go upon a snake, and a cockatrice; and thou shalt defoul (or trample upon) a lion, and a dragon.

14   (For God saith), For he hoped (or trusted) in me, I shall deliver him, (or Because he loved me, I shall save him); I shall defend him, for he knew my name.

15   He cried to me, and I shall hear him; I am with him in tribulation; I shall deliver him, and I shall glorify him.

16   I shall fulfill him with the length of days; and I shall show mine health (or give my salvation) to him.

PROVERBS CHAPTER 18

1   He that will go away from a friend, seeketh occasions, *that is, feigneth causes (or looketh for reasons)*; in all time he shall be despisable.

2   A fool receiveth not the words of prudence; no but thou say those things, that be turned (over) in his heart.

3   A wicked man, when he cometh into the depth of sins, despiseth *wholesome lore (or discipline), and commandment*; but scandal and shame pursueth or followeth him.

4   Deep water *is* the words of the mouth of a man; and a stream floating (or flowing) over *is* the well of wisdom.

5   It is not good to take (or favour) the person of a wicked man in doom (or judging), (so) that thou bow away from the truth of doom (or judgement).

6   The lips of a fool meddle or mingle themselves with chidings; and his mouth stirreth strives.

7   The mouth of a fool *is* the defouling of him; and his lips *be* the falling of his soul.

8   The words of a double-tongued man *be* as simple; and they come unto the inner things of the womb. Dread (or Fear) casteth down a slow man; forsooth the souls of men turned into women's condition shall have hunger.

9   He that is nesh (or soft), and dissolute, *either unsteadfast,* in his work, is the brother of a man destroying his works.

10   A full strong tower *is* the name of the Lord; a rightwise man runneth to him, and he shall be enhanced (or be safe).

11   The chattel or substance of a rich man *is* the city of his strength; and as a strong wall compassing him, (*or so he thinketh*).

12   The heart of man is enhanced (or raised up), before that it be broken; and it is made meek, before that it be glorified.

13   He that answereth before that he heareth, showeth himself to be a fool; and worthy of shame.

14   The spirit of a man sustaineth (him in) his feebleness; but who may sustain a spirit light to be wroth (or easy to be angered)?

15   The heart of a prudent man shall hold steadfastly knowing (or knowledge); and the ear of wise men seeketh (out) teaching.

16   The gift of a man alargeth (or smootheth) his way; and maketh space (or an opening) to him before princes.

17   A just or rightwise man is the first accuser of himself; his friend cometh, and shall search him (out).

18   (Casting) the lot ceaseth against-sayings; and deemeth also among mighty men.

19   A brother that is helped of (or by) a brother, *is* as a steadfast city; and dooms (or arguments) *be* as the bars of cities.

20   A man's womb (or belly) shall be fulfilled of (or by) the fruit of his mouth; and the seeds of his lips shall fill him.

21   Death and life *be* in the works of the tongue; they that love (or nurture) it, shall eat the fruits thereof.

22   He that findeth a good woman, findeth a good thing; and of

the Lord he shall draw up mirth (or shall receive favour from the Lord). He that putteth away a good woman, putteth away a good thing; but he that holdeth (onto) an adulteress, is a fool and unwise.

23   A poor man shall speak with beseechings (or pleadings); and a rich man shall speak sternly.

24   A man friendly to fellowship shall more be a friend, than a brother.

ECCLESIASTICUS CHAPTER 24

1   Wisdom shall praise his soul (or praise himself), and he shall be honoured in (or before) God; and he shall have glory in the midst of his people.

2   And he shall open his mouth in the churches of the Highest; and he shall have glory in the sight of his virtue (or in the presence of his power). And he shall be enhanced (or exalted) in the midst of his people; and he shall much wonder in holy fullness, *either plenty*. And in the multitude of chosen men he shall have praising; and among blessed men he shall be blessed, and say,

3   I, the first engendered or begotten before each creature, came forth from or (out) of the mouth of the Highest. I (was) made in the heavens, that (or where) light never failing rose up, and as a cloud I covered all the earth,

4   I dwelled in the highest things, and my throne (is) in a pillar of a cloud.

5   I alone went about the compass or the circle of the heavens, and I pierced the depths of the sea;

6   and I went in the waves of the sea, and I stood in (or on) all the land or all the earth. And I had the first dignity in each people, and in each folk (or nation); and I trod by virtue (or power) upon the necks of all excellent men and meek or upon all high and low;

7   and in all these *men* I sought rest, and I shall dwell in the heritage (or the inheritance) of the Lord.

8   Then the Creator or the Former of all things commanded, and said to me; (yea), and he that formed me, rested in my tabernacle; and he said to me, Dwell thou in Jacob, and take thou heritage (or inheritance) in Israel, and send thou roots in(to) my chosen.

9   I was engendered from the beginning and before worlds, and I shall not fail or cease to be unto the world to come;

10   and I ministered or served in an holy dwelling before him. And so I was made steadfast in Zion,

11   and in like manner I rested in an hallowed city, and my power *was* in Jerusalem.

12   And I rooted in a people honoured (or an honourable people); and the heritage thereof into the parts of my God, and my withholding in the plenty or the fullness of the saints (or God's people).

13   I was enhanced (or exalted) as a cedar in Lebanon, and as a cypress tree in the hill of Zion (or on Mount Zion).

14   I was enhanced (or exalted) as a palm tree in Cades (or Engedi), and as the planting of a rose in Jericho. And as a fair olive tree in fields; and I was enhanced (or exalted) as a plane tree besides the water in (or along the) streets.

15   As canel and balm giving great smell, I gave odour; as chosen myrrh I gave the sweetness of odour. And as storax, and galbanum, and ungulam, and gum, and as Lebanon not cut down, I made hot or I smoked my dwelling place; and mine odour as balm not meddled or mingled (or mixed).

16   I as terebinth stretched forth my boughs or branches; and my boughs or branches *be* boughs (or branches) of honour, and of glory or grace.

17   I as a vine made fruit the sweetness of odour; and my flowers

be the fruits of honour, and of honesty (or riches).

18   I *am* a mother of fair love, and of dread (or fear), and of knowing (or knowledge), and of holy hope. In me *is* all the grace of the way, and of truth; in me *is* all the hope of life and of virtue.

19   All ye that covet me, pass (along, or come) to me; and be ye filled of (or with) my generations.

20   For why my spirit *is* sweet above or over honey; and mine heritage (or my inheritance) *is* above or over honey, and honey-comb. My mind *is* in(to) the generation of worlds (or I shall always be remembered).

21   They that eat me, shall hunger yet; and they that drink me, shall thirst yet.

22   He that heareth me, shall not be shamed; and they that work in me, shall not do sin; and they that declare me, shall have everlasting life.

23   All these things *is* the book of life, and the testament (or the covenant) of the Highest, and the knowing or acknowledging of the truth. Moses commanded a law in the commandments of rightwisenesses, and (for an) heritage to the house of Jacob, and the promises to Israel.

24   He setted, *that is, ordained, either promised,* to David, his child, to raise up of (or from) him a king most strong, and sitting without end in the throne of honour.

25   Which *king* filleth wisdom, as Pishon *sheddeth out water;* and as Tigris in the days of new things.

26   Which, as the Euphrates, full-filleth wit; which multiplieth, as the Jordan in the time of harvest or reap(ing).

27   Which sendeth teaching as the light; and is nigh *all men,* as Gihon in the day of vintage.

28   Which maketh perfectly first to know that *wisdom;* and a feebler man shall not ensearch it.

29   For why the thoughts thereof shall be (as) plenteous of (or as) the sea, *that is, his knowing is more plenteous than the sea*; and his counsel in the great ocean or the great deepness *is uncomprehensible.* I wisdom poured out floods (or rivers); I as a way, *that is, a strong running,* of full great water or water without measure of the flood.

30   I as the flood (or river) Dorix, and as a water conduit I went out of (or from) paradise.

31   I said, I shall water my garden of plantings; and I shall greatly fill the fruit of my child-bearing. And lo! a plenteous way of water is made to (or for) me; and my flood (or river) nighed to the sea.

32   For I enlighten teaching as the morrowtide light to all men; and I shall tell out it unto far. I shall pierce all the lower or nether parts of the earth, and I shall behold all that sleep; and I shall (en)lighten all that hope (or trust) in the Lord.

33   Yet I shall pour out teaching as prophecy, and I shall leave it to them that seek wisdom; and I shall not fail into the generations or progenies of them, till into the holy world.

34   See ye, that I travailed (or laboured) not to (or for) me alone, but to (or for) all that seek out the truth.

WISDOM OF SOLOMON   CHAPTER 6

1   Therefore, ye kings, hear, and understand; and ye judges of the coasts of the earth, learn.

2   Ye that hold together multitudes, and please you(rselves) in the companies of nations, give ears;

3   for why power is given of (or from) the Lord to you, and virtue (or strength) *is given* of (or from) the Highest, that shall ask (about) your works, and shall search (your) thoughts.

4   For when ye were ministers of his realm, ye deemed not

rightly, neither ye kept the law of rightfulness, neither ye went by the will of God.

5   Hideously or Horribly and soon he shall appear to you; for why the harshest or most hard doom (or judgement) shall be made in (or upon) them, that be sovereigns.

6   Forsooth mercy is granted to a little man; but mighty men shall suffer torments mightily.

7   For the Lord, which (or who) is lord of all things, shall not withdraw the person of any man, neither he shall dread the greatness of any man; for he made both the little man and the great man, and charge or care is to him evenly of (or for) all men.

8   But stronger torment nigheth (or approacheth) to stronger men.

9   Therefore, ye kings, these my words be to you, (so) that ye learn wisdom, and that ye fall not down.

10   For they that keep rightfulness or rightwiseness, shall be deemed rightfully; and they, that learn just things, shall find, what they shall answer.

11   Therefore covet ye my words, and loveth them; and ye shall have teaching.

12   Wisdom is clear, and that shall never fade; and it is seen lightly of (or easily by) them that love it, and it is found of (or by) them that seek it.

13   It before-occupieth them that covet it, (so) that it show itself the former (or the first) to them.

14   He or Who that waketh by light to it, shall not travail (or labour); forsooth he shall find it sitting nigh his gates.

15   Therefore to think on wisdom is perfect wit (or thinking), and he that waketh (or watcheth) for it, shall soon be secure.

16   For why it goeth about, and seeketh men worthy to (or of) it; and in their ways it shall show itself gladly to them, and in all purveyance it shall meet them.

17   For why the beginning of wisdom is the veriest (or truest) covetousness of learning. Therefore the busyness of learning is love or the care of discipline is loving;

18   and love is the keeping of his laws. Soothly the keeping of laws is the perfection of uncorruption;

19   forsooth uncorruption maketh (us) to be next to God.

20   Therefore the covetousness of wisdom shall bring (one) to (an) everlasting realm or kingdom.

21   Therefore if ye, kings of the people, delight in seats (or thrones), and in kings' rods (or sceptres), or kings' dignities, *or regalties*, love ye wisdom, (so) that ye reign without end. All ye, that be sovereigns to the peoples, love the light of wisdom.

22   Soothly what is wisdom, and how it is made, I shall tell (you); and I shall not hide from you the sacraments (or the secrets) of God; but from the beginning of birth I shall seek (for it), and I shall put into the light the knowing of it, and I shall not pass (by) or beside the truth.

23   And I shall not have (or go) the way with envy waxing (or growing) rotten; for such a man shall not be a partner of (or with) wisdom.

24   Forsooth the multitude of wise men is the health (or the deliverance) of the world; and a wise king is the establishing or the stability of the people.

25   Therefore take ye teaching or discipline by my words, and it shall profit to you. Δ

DAY 19

PSALM 92

1   *The psalm of song, in the day of sabbath.* It is good to acknowledge (or to give praise, or thanks) to the Lord; and to sing to thy name, thou Highest.

2   To show early thy mercy; and thy truth by (or thy faithfulness every) night.

3   In a psaltery (or On a lyre) of ten cords; with a song in (or on) a harp.

4   For thou, Lord, hast delighted me in (or with the works of) thy making; and I shall make full out joy in (or over) the works of thine hands.

5   Lord, thy works be magnified greatly; thy thoughts be made full deep.

6   An unwise man shall not know; and a fool shall not understand these things.

7   When sinners come forth, as hay; and all they appear, that work wickedness. (So) that they perish into the world of world (or forever and ever);

8   forsooth thou, Lord, *art* the Highest, without end (or forever).

9   For lo! Lord, thine enemies, for lo! thine enemies shall perish; and all they shall be scattered that work wickedness.

10   And mine horn (or head) shall be raised (up) as an unicorn; and mine old (age shall be) in plenteous mercy.

11   And mine eye despised (or saw the defeat of) mine enemies; and when wicked men rise against me, mine ear shall hear (their downfall).

12   A just or rightwise man shall flower as a palm tree; he shall be multiplied as a cedar of Lebanon.

257

13   Men planted in the house of the Lord; shall flower in the porches (or the courtyards) of the house of our God.

14   Yet they shall be multiplied in plenteous old (age); and they shall be suffering well (or will be strong and vigorous).

15   (So) that they tell (out), that our Lord God is rightful; and no wickedness is in him.

PSALM 93

1   The Lord hath reigned, he is clothed with fairness (or beauty); the Lord is clothed with strength, and hath girded himself. For he made steadfast the world; (so) that (it) shall not be moved.

2   God, thy seat (or thy throne) was made ready from that time; thou art from the world (or eternal).

3   Lord, the floods (or the rivers) have raised (up); the floods have raised (up) their voices (or roar). Floods (or The seas) have raised (up) their waves; of the voices of many waters.

4   The raisings of the sea *be* wonderful; the Lord *is* wonderful in high things (or high places).

5   Thy witnessings (or Thy testimonies) be made able to be believed greatly; Lord, holiness becometh thine house, into the length of days (or forever).

PSALM 94

1   God *is* the Lord of vengeances; the God of vengeance did freely.

2   Be thou enhanced (or exalted) that deemest the earth; yield thou a yielding (or a punishment) to proud men.

3   Lord, how long (shall the) sinners; how long shall the sinners have glory (or boast)?

4   They shall tell out, and shall speak wickedness; all men shall speak that work unrightfulness or unrightwiseness.

5   Lord, they have made low (or beaten down) thy people; and they have dis-eased (or distressed) thine heritage (or thy inheritance).

6   They killed a widow and a comeling (or a newcomer); and they have slain fatherless children and motherless (or orphans).

7   And they said, The Lord shall not see (it); and, The God of Jacob shall not understand.

8   Ye unwise men in the people, understand; and, ye fools, learn sometime.

9   Shall not he hear, that planted (or who formed) the ear; either beholdeth not he, that made the eye?

10   Shall not he reprove, that chastiseth folks (or the nations); (shall he not know), which teacheth man knowing?

11   The Lord knoweth the thoughts of men; that they be (in) vain (or empty and futile).

12   Blessed *is* the man, whom thou, Lord, hast learned (or taught); and hast taught him of thy law.

13   (So) that thou assuage him from the evil days; till a ditch be digged to (or for) the sinner.

14   For the Lord shall not put away (or reject) his people; and he shall not forsake his heritage (or inheritance).

15   Till rightwiseness be turned (again) into doom (or judgement); and who be nigh it, all that be of rightful heart.

16   Who shall rise with me against mis-doers; either who shall stand with me against them that work wickedness?

17   No but for the Lord helped me; almost my soul had dwelled in hell.

18   If I said, My foot was stirred (or slipping); Lord, thy mercy helped me.

19   After the multitude of my sorrows (gathered together) in mine

heart; thy comforts made glad my soul.

20　Whether the seat (or throne) of wickedness cleaveth to thee; that makest travail (or trespass) in (or by) the commandments?

21　They shall take (hold) against the soul of the rightwise; and they shall condemn innocent blood.

22　And (or But) the Lord was made to me into a refuge; and my God *was made* into the help of mine hope.

23　And he shall yield to them the (same) wickedness of them; and in the malice of them he shall lose (or destroy) them, our Lord God shall lose (or destroy) them.

PSALM 95

1　Come ye, make ye full out joy to the Lord; heartily sing we to God, our health (or our salvation, or our deliverer).

2　Before-occupy we his face in acknowledging (or with thanksgiving); and heartily sing we to him in psalms.

3　For God *is* a great Lord, and a great King above all gods; for the Lord shall not put away his people.

4　For all the ends of the earth be in his hand; and the highness, or the heights of the hills be his.

5　For the sea is his, and he made it; and his hands formed the dry land.

6　Come ye, praise we, and fall we down before God; weep we (or let us kneel) before the Lord that made us;

7　for he is our Lord God. And we *be* the people of his pasture; and the sheep of his hand. If ye have heard (or will but listen to) his voice today;

8　do not ye make hard your hearts. As in the stirring to wrath (at Meribah); by the day of temptation in the desert.

9　Where your fathers tempted me; they proved and saw my

works.

10   Forty years I was offended to this (or by that) generation; and I said, (For) evermore they err in heart. And these men knew not my ways;

11   to whom I swore in my wrath (or anger), they shall not enter into my rest.

PROVERBS CHAPTER 19

1   Better is a poor man, that goeth in his simpleness (or honesty, or integrity), than a rich man biting his lips, and unwise.

2   Where is not knowing of the soul, there is not good; and he that is hasty, in (or with his) feet hurteth (or sinneth).

3   The folly of a man deceiveth his steps (or perverteth his own way); and he burneth in his soul against God.

4   Riches increase full many friends; forsooth (or but) also they, (his friends), be departed from a poor man, which he had.

5   A false (or lying) witness shall not be unpunished; and he that speaketh leasings (or lies), shall not escape.

6   Many men honour the person of a mighty man; and they be friends of him that dealeth (out) gifts.

7   The brethren of a poor man hate him; furthermore and the friends went away far from him. He that pursueth or followeth words only, shall (soon) have nothing;

8   but he that holdeth stably the mind, loveth his soul, and the keeper of prudence shall find goods (or good things).

9   A false (or lying) witness shall not be (or go) unpunished; and he that speaketh leasings (or lies), shall perish.

10   Delights become not a fool; neither *it becometh* a servant to be the lord of princes.

11   The teaching of a man is known by patience; and his glory is

to pass over wicked things (or to overlook a wrong).

12   As the gnashing of a lion, so and the wrath of the king; and as dew on herb, so and the gladness of the king.

13   The sorrow of the father *is* a fond or foolish son; and roofs dropping (or dripping) continually *is* a woman full of chiding.

14   Houses and riches be given of (or from) the father and the mother; but a prudent wife *is given* properly of (or only from) the Lord.

15   Sloth bringeth in sleep; and a negligent soul shall have hunger.

16   He that keepeth the commandment *of God*, keepeth his soul; but he that chargeth not his way, shall be slain.

17   He that hath mercy on (or for) a poor man, lendeth to the Lord; and he shall yield his while to him.

18   Teach thy son, and despair thou not; but put thou not thy soul to the slaying of him (or but do not beat him).

19   Forsooth he that is unpatient, shall suffer harm; and when he hath ravished (or stolen one thing), he shall lay to another thing.

20   Hear thou counsel, and take thou doctrine; (so) that thou be wise in thy last things (or until thy last breath).

21   Many thoughts there *be* in the heart of a man; but the will of the Lord shall dwell (or shall stand, *yea, it shall prevail*).

22   A needy man is merciful; and better *is* a poor (but) just man, than a man (who is a) liar.

23   The dread (or fear) of (or reverence for) the Lord *leadeth* to life; and he *that dreadeth God* shall dwell in plenty, without the visiting of the worst, or without full evil visiting.

24   A slow man, (*that is, a lazy person*), hideth his hand under *his* armpit, and putteth it not to his mouth.

25   When a man full of pestilence is beaten, a fool shall be the wiser, (*if he will but learn from his experience*). (But) if thou

blamest a wise man, he shall understand the teaching.

26   He that tormenteth *his* father, and fleeth from *his* mother, shall be full of evil fame or shall be shameful, and *shall be* cursed.

27   Son, cease thou not to hear teaching; and know thou the words of knowing (or knowledge).

28   A wicked witness scorneth doom (or judgement); and the mouth of unpious men devoureth wickedness.

29   Dooms (or Judgements) be made ready to (or for) scorners; and hammers smiting *be made ready* to (or for) the bodies of fools.

ECCLESIASTICUS CHAPTER 25

1   In three things it is pleased to my spirit, which be approved before God and men; the according of brethren, and the love of neighbours, and a man and woman well consenting to themselves (or to each other, or living happily together).

2   My soul hated three species (or kinds of things), and I am grieved greatly to (or by) the soul of them; a poor man proud, and a rich man (that is a) liar, and an old man (that is) a fool and unwitty (or unwise) or doted.

3   How shalt thou find in thine old (age) those things, which thou gathered not in thy youth?

4   Doom *of* (or Judgement *with*) *discretion is* full fair in hoariness, *either an old man,* and to (or for) priests to know counsel.

5   Wisdom *is* full fair to (or for) old men, and glorious understanding, and counsel.

6   The crown of old men *is* in much knowing (or knowledge); and the glory of them *is* the dread (or fear) of (or reverence for) God.

7   I magnified nine things unsuspected of the heart; and I shall

say the tenth thing by (or with my) tongue to men. A man which (or whose) living is (made) merry in (or by) sons, and seeing the destroying of his enemies.

8   *He is* blessed that dwelleth with a witty (or with a wise) woman, and he that fell not or (is) not slidden by his tongue, and he that served not to men unworthy to himself.

9   *He is* blessed that findeth a very (or a true) friend, and he that telleth out rightfulness to an ear hearing.

10   *He is* full great that findeth wisdom and knowing (or knowledge); but *he is* not above or over him that dreadeth (or feareth, or revereth) God.

11   The dread of God hath set itself above or over all things. Blessed *is* the man to whom it is given to have the dread of God; to whom shall he be likened, that holdeth that dread?

12   The dread of God *is* the beginning of his love; forsooth the beginning of faith is to be fast-joined (un)to him.

13   The sorrow of the heart is each wound; and the wickedness of a woman is all malice. *A leech (or A physician)* shall see each wound, and (or but) not the wound of the heart; and all wickedness, and (or but) not the wickedness of a woman[1];

---

[1] This verse, and those which follow to the end of this chapter, about a "woman of malice" or a "wicked woman", are only found in *some* early copies of this book. I would suggest they are more a result of *that copyist's* bitter personal experience, than an expression of divine inspiration. There is NOT a comparable chapter (or two!) regarding living with a "troublesome" or "contentious" man. But we all know that one could easily fashion a list of comparable (or worse) grievances regarding life with a wicked or brutal man. The reader is at liberty to omit reading these verses if they so desire; they are only here in the interest of completeness. T.P.N.

14 and each covering or all hid thing, *that is, the colouring of malice*, and (or but) not the covering or the hid thing of haters; and each or all vengeance, and (or but) not the vengeance of enemies.

15 None head is worse or wickeder than the head of an adder dwelling in a shadow; and none ire or wrath is above or over the ire or wrath of a (wicked) woman.

16 It shall please more to dwell with a lion and a dragon, than to dwell with a wicked woman.

17 The wickedness of a woman changeth her face; and she blinded her cheer (or her face) as a bear *doeth*, and she shall show as a sack(cloth) in the midst of (her) neighbours.

18 Her husband greatly wailed; and hearing (her), sighed a little.

19 All malice *is* short on (or is little compared to) the malice of a (wicked) woman; the part or the lot of sinners, *that is, the pain of hell*, fall on her.

20 As a going-up (or an ascent) full of gravel in (or to) the feet of an old man, so *is* a woman (that is) a great jangler to a peaceable or quiet man.

21 Behold thou not the fairness of a woman, and covet thou not a woman for (her) fairness.

22 The wrath and unreverence of a woman *to her husband is* a great shame (or reproof). If a woman hath the first dignity or the mastery, *either chief governail*, she is contrary to her husband.

23 A low heart, and a sorrowful face, and a wound of death, *is* (from) a wicked woman. Feeble hands and knees unbound, (resulteth from) a woman that blesseth not her husband.

24 The beginning of sin was made of (or by) a woman; and all we die by her.

25 Give thou not issue to thy water, yea, not a little issue; neither to a wicked woman freedom, *or leave*, of going forth or going out.

26 If she goeth not at thine hand, she shall shame thee in the

sight of (thine) enemies. Cut her away from thy fleshes, lest evermore she mis-use thee.

ECCLESIASTICUS CHAPTER 26

1   The husband of a good woman is blessed; for why the number of their years *is* double or the number forsooth of the years of him (is) double.

2   A strong woman, *that is, against sins*, delighteth her husband; and (he) shall fulfill in peace the years of his life.

3   A good woman *is* a good part (or partner); in the good part of them that dread (or fear, or revere) God, she shall be given to a man for his good deeds.

4   Forsooth (if) the heart of a rich man and (or) of a poor man *is* good; in all time their cheer (or his face) *is* glad.

5   Mine heart dreaded of three things, and my face dreaded or was afeared in (or of) the fourth thing. Betraying of a city, and the gathering together of people, *that is, in conspiring of the people against the prince*, and false challenge; all (these) things (be more) grievous on (or worse than) death.

6   The sorrow of heart, and mourning, *is* a jealous woman. In a jealous woman *is* a beating or a scourge of (or from) the tongue, and she communeth with (or to) all men.

7   As a yoke of oxen which is moved, so and a wicked woman; he that holdeth her, *is* as he that taketh or caught (hold of) a scorpion.

8   A drunken woman *is* great wrath, and despising or strife; and her filth(hood) (or nakedness) shall not be covered.

9   The fornication of a woman *is* in the raising of (her) eyes; and she shall be known in (or by) the eyelids of her.

10   Make thou firm the keeping in (or of) a daughter not turning

away herself; lest she mis-use herself, if she findeth (an) occasion.

11   Be thou ware of all the unreverence of her eyes; and wonder thou not, if she despiseth thee.

12   As a way-goer thirsting shall open the mouth at a well, and shall drink of each water next; and *the foresaid daughter* shall sit against each pale, and shall open the arrow case (or her legs) against each arrow, or against all arrows shall open the quiver, till she fail.

13   The grace of a busy woman shall delight her husband; and shall make fat his bones.

14   The knowing of her (or Her knowledge) is the gift of God. A wise woman and a still (one) is not the changing of a learned or the taught soul.

15   Grace upon grace is an holy woman, and shamefast. Forsooth all weighing is not worth a continent soul.

16   As the sun rising in the world in the highest things of God, so the fairness of a good woman *is* into the ornament or the adornment of her house.

17   A lantern shining on an holy candlestick, and the fairness of a face on (or in) the steadfast age, *that is, as such a lantern lighteneth the church, and such a face maketh fair (or beautiful) ripe age, so a good woman maketh fair her house.*

18   Golden pillars on silvern foundaments (or foundations), and steadfast feet on the soles of a steadfast or stable woman. Everlasting foundaments on a firm stone, and the behests (or the commands) or the commandments of God in the heart of an holy woman.

19-27 (These verses omitted in the original text.)

28   In two things mine heart was made sorry or is made sorrowful, and in the third thing wrathfulness came to me. A man warrior failing by neediness, and a wise man despised. And God hath made him ready to (or for) the sword, that passeth over or over-

goeth from rightwiseness to sin.

29   Two species appeared hard and perilous to me; a merchant is delivered of hard (or with great difficulty) from his negligence, and a taverner shall not be justified of or from the sins of lips.

WISDOM OF SOLOMON   CHAPTER 7

1   Forsooth and I am a deadly (or a mortal) man, like *other* men, and of the earthly kind of him that was made first,

2   and in the womb of *my* mother I was formed flesh. In the time of ten months I was crudded (or curdled) together in blood, of (or from) the seed of man, and by the according delight of (or with) sleep.

3   And I was born, and took common air, and in like manner I fell down into (or onto) the earth made; and I weeping sent out the first voice, like all men.

4   I was nursed in wrappings or swathing (or swaddling) clothes, and in great busynesses;

5   for why no man of kings had (any) other beginning of birth.

6   Therefore one entering or entry (or entrance) to life is to (or for) all men, and like going out.

7   Wherefore I desired, and wit (or understanding) was given to me; and I inwardly called, and the spirit of wisdom came into me.

8   And I put wisdom before realms (or kingdoms), and seats (or thrones); and I said, that riches be nought (or be nothing) in comparison thereof,

9   and I comparisoned not a precious stone to it; for why all gold in comparison thereof is (but) a little gravel (or sand), and silver shall be areckoned as clay in the sight thereof.

10   I loved wisdom more than health and fairness (or beauty); and I purposed to have it for light, for the light thereof may not (or

cannot) be quenched or unquenchable is the light of it.

11 Forsooth all goods (or all good things) came together to me with it; and unnumberable honesty (or innumerable riches) *is* by the works thereof or by the hands of it.

12 And I was glad in all things; for this wisdom went before me, and I knew not, for it is the mother of all goods (or that she is the mother of all good things).

13 Which *wisdom* I learned without feigning, and I commune without envy; and I hide not the honesty (or the riches) thereof.

14 For it is treasure without number to men, and they, that used that treasure, were made partners of God's friendship, and were praised for the gifts of knowing (or knowledge) or discipline.

15 Forsooth God gave to me to say of (or with) sentence, and to take before the worthy things of these things that be given to me; for he is the leader of wisdom, and the amender of wise men.

16 For why both we, and our words, and all wisdom, and learning or discipline of knowing (or of knowledge) of works *be* in his hand.

17 Forsooth he gave to me the very (or the true) knowing of these things that be, (so) that I know the disposition of the world, and the virtues of the elements;

18 the beginning, and the ending, and the middle of times; the changings of whiles, and the endings of times; the changings of manners, and the partings or the divisions of times;

19 the courses of the year, and the dispositions of the stars;

20 the kinds of beasts, and the wraths of wild beasts; the strength of the winds, and the thoughts of men; the differences of trees, and the virtues of roots.

21 And I learned whatever things be hid and unpurveyed;

22 for why wisdom, the craftsmaker of all things, taught me. For in that *wisdom unmade* is the spirit of understanding, holy, manyfold, one alone or only, subtle, temperate or mannerly, wise,

moveable, undefouled, certain, sweet, loving a good deed, which *spirit* forbiddeth or forfendeth (or prevented, or hindered) nothing to do well;

23   courteous, benign, stable, secure, having all virtue, beholding all things, and which taketh (or receiveth) all spirits able to understand or all intelligible spirits, *he is* clean, and subtle.

24   For why wisdom is more movable than all movable things; forsooth it stretcheth forth everywhere or it attaineth over all, for his cleanness (or pureness).

25   For it is a breathing of God's virtue (or of God's power), and it is some clean coming forth of the clearness of Almighty God; and therefore no defouled thing runneth into it.

26   For it is the brightness of everlasting light, and *it is* a mirror without wem of the majesty of God, and *it is* an image of his goodness.

27   And when or since it is one, it may (or it can do) all things; and it dwelleth in itself, and reneweth all things, and by nations it beareth over itself into holy souls; it maketh the friends of God, and prophets.

28   For God loveth no man, but him that dwelleth with wisdom.

29   For why this *wisdom* is fairer than the sun, and *is* above all the disposition of the stars; wisdom comparisoned to light, it is found the former (or it is better, or before it).

30   For why night cometh after the light; but wisdom overcometh malice. Δ

DAY 20

PSALM 96

1   Sing ye a new song to the Lord; all the earth, sing ye to the Lord.

2   Sing ye to the Lord, and bless ye his name; tell ye his health (or about his salvation) from day into day.

3   Tell ye (about) his glory among the heathen men; his marvels among all the peoples.

4   For the Lord *is* great, and worthy to be praised full much; he is fearedful above all gods.

5   For all the gods of the heathen men *be* fiends; but the Lord made the heavens.

6   Acknowledging and fairness *is* in his sight (or Praising and beauty *is* before him); holiness and worthy doing *is* in his hallowing (or in his sanctuary).

7   Ye countries of the heathen men, bring (or ascribe) to the Lord, bring ye (or ascribe) glory and honour to the Lord;

8   bring ye (or ascribe) to the Lord glory to his name. Take ye sacrifices, and enter ye into the halls of him (or his courtyards);

9   praise ye the Lord in his holy hall. All the earth be moved of his face (or before him);

10   say ye among the heathen men, that the Lord hath reigned. And he hath amended the world, that shall not be moved; he shall deem (or judge) the peoples in equity (or with fairness).

11   The heavens be glad, and the earth make full out joy, the sea and the fullness thereof be moved altogether;

12   fields shall make joy, and all things that be in them. Then all the trees of the woods shall make full out joy (or rejoice),

13   for the face of (or before) the Lord, for he cometh; for he

cometh to deem (or judge) the earth. He shall deem the world in equity (or with fairness); and the peoples in his truth.

PSALM 97

1   The Lord hath reigned, the earth make full out joy (or rejoice); many isles be glad.

2   Cloud and darkness (be) in his compass; rightwiseness and doom (or judgement) *is* the amending or correction of his seat (or his throne).

3   Fire shall go before him; and shall enflame, *either set afire*, his enemies in compass (or all around him).

4   His lightnings shined to the world; the earth saw (it), and was moved.

5   The hills as wax flowed down from the face of (or before) the Lord; (over) all the earth from the face of (or before) the Lord.

6   The heavens told (out) his rightwiseness; and all the peoples saw his glory.

7   All they that worship graven things, *or (carved) images*, be a/shamed, and they that have glory in their simulacra (or idols); all ye angels of the Lord, worship him.

8   Zion heard, and was glad; and the daughters of Judah made full out joy (or rejoiced), for thy dooms (or judgements), Lord.

9   For thou, Lord, *art* the Highest on (or the Most High over) all the earth; thou art greatly enhanced (or exalted) over all gods.

10   Ye that love the Lord, hate evil; the Lord keepeth (safe) the souls of his saints; he shall deliver them from the hand of the sinner.

11   Light is risen to the rightwise; and gladness to rightful men of heart.

12   Ye rightwise, be ye glad in the Lord; and acknowledge ye to the mind of his hallowing, (or and give praise, or give thanks at the

remembrance of his holiness).

PSALM 98

1   *A psalm.* Sing ye a new song to the Lord; for he hath done marvels (or wonders). His right hand and his holy arm; hath made health to him (or hath won him the victory).

2   The Lord hath made known his health (or salvation); in the sight of (or before) heathen men he hath showed his rightwiseness.

3   He bethought on his mercy; and on his truth, to the house of Israel. All the ends of the earth; saw the health (or the victory, or the salvation) of our God.

4   All the earth, make ye heartily joy to God; sing ye, and make ye full out joy, and say (or sing) ye a psalm.

5   Sing ye to the Lord in (or with) an harp, in (or with) a harp and in (or with) the voice of a psalm;

6   in trumps beaten out with a hammer, and in voice of a trump of a horn (or with the sound of trumpets and horns). Heartily sing ye in the sight of (or before) the Lord, the King;

7   (let) the sea and the fullness thereof be moved (or roar); the world, and they that dwell therein.

8   The floods (or rivers) shall make joy with (their) hands; together the hills shall make full out joy,

9   for the sight of (or before) the Lord; for he cometh to deem the earth. He shall deem the world in (or with) rightwiseness; and peoples in equity (or with justice).

PSALM 99

1   The Lord hath reigned, (let) the peoples be wroth (or tremble); thou that sittest on (or above) the cherubim, (let) the earth be

moved (or shaken!).

2   The Lord *is* great in Zion; and high above all the peoples.

3   Acknowledge they to (or Praise) thy great name, for it is fearedful and holy;

4   and the honour of the king loveth doom (or justice, or judgement). Thou hast made ready addressings (or directions) or rulings; thou hast made doom and rightwiseness in Jacob.

5   Enhance ye (or Exalt) our Lord God; and worship ye (at) the stool of his feet, for it (or He) is holy.

6   Moses and Aaron *were* among his priests; and Samuel *was* among them that inwardly call his name. They inwardly called the Lord, and he heard them;

7   in a pillar of cloud he spake to them. They kept his witnessings (or testimonies); and the commandment which he gave to them.

8   Our Lord God, thou heardest them; God, thou were merciful to them, and (or but) thou tookest vengeance on all their findings (or for all their sins).

9   Enhance (or Exalt) ye our Lord God, and worship ye in (or at) his holy hill; for our Lord God *is* holy.

PSALM 100

1   *A psalm to acknowledge (or to give praise, or thanks).* All the earth, sing ye heartily to God;

2   serve ye the Lord in gladness. Enter ye in his sight (or before Him) in full out joying (or with rejoicing).

3   Know ye, that the Lord himself is God; he made us, and not we made us (or and we belong to him). (So let) his people, and the sheep of his pasture,

4   enter ye into his gates in acknowledging (or with thanksgiving); *enter ye into* his porches, acknowledge ye to him in hymns. Praise

ye his name,

5   for the Lord is sweet, his mercy (or love) *is* without end; and his truth *is* in generation and into generation (or eternal).

PROVERBS CHAPTER 20

1   Wine *is* a lecherous thing, and drunkenness *is* full of noise; whoever delighteth in these, shall not be wise.

2   As the roaring of a lion, so and the dread (or fearfulness) of a king; he that stirreth him to wrath, sinneth against his (own) soul.

3   It is an honour to a man that separateth himself from strivings; but fond men or fools be meddled or mingled (or mixed in) with despisings.

4   A slow man would not ear (or plow) for cold; therefore he shall beg in summer, and men shall not give to him.

5   As deep water, so counsel *is* in the heart of a man; but a wise man shall draw it out.

6   Many men be called merciful; but who shall find a faithful man?

7   Forsooth a rightwise man that goeth in his simpleness, shall leave blessed sons after him.

8   A king that sitteth in the seat of doom (or judgement), destroyeth all evil by his looking (or discernment).

9   Who may say, Mine heart is clean; I am clean of sin?

10   A weight, *greater in buying*, and a weight, *less(er) in selling*, a measure and a measure, ever either is abominable at God.

11   A child is understood by his studies (or his deeds), if his works be rightful and clean.

12   An ear hearing, and an eye seeing, God made ever either.

13   Do not thou love sleep, lest neediness oppress thee; open thine eyes, and be thou fulfilled with loaves.

14   Each buyer saith, It is evil, it is evil; and when he hath gone

away, then he shall have glory.

15　Gold, and the multitude of gems, and a precious vessel, *be* the lips of knowing (or lips that speak wise words).

16　Take thou away the cloth (or the cloak) of him that was a borrow of (or a guarantee for) another man; and for strangers take thou away a wed (or a pledge) from him.

17　The bread of a leasing (or a lie), *that is, gotten by a leasing (or a lie)*, is sweet to a man; and afterward his mouth shall be filled with reckoning or with little pebble stones.

18　Thoughts be made strong by counsels; and battles shall be treated by governances.

19　Be thou not meddled or mingled (or mixed in) with him that showeth privates (or secrets), and goeth guilefully (or deceitfully), and alargeth (or flappeth) his lips.

20　The light of him that curseth his father and mother, shall be quenched in the midst of darknesses.

21　Heritage (or An inheritance) to which men hasteneth (to get) in the beginning (or too early), shall want blessing in the last *time.*

22　Say thou not, I shall yield evil for evil; abide thou (or wait for) the Lord, and he shall deliver thee.

23　An abomination with God is weight and weight; a guileful (or deceitful, or deceptive) balance is not good.

24　The steps of man be addressed of (or directed by) the Lord; who forsooth of men may (or can) understand his way?

25　A falling of a man is to make a vow to the saints (or to God's people), and (then) afterward to withdraw the vows.

26　A wise king scattereth wicked men; and boweth a bow of victory, *that is, a stone bow,* over them.

27　The lantern of the Lord *is* the spirit of man, that seeketh out all the privates (or the secrets) of the womb.

28　Mercy and truth keep a king; and his throne is made strong by meekness (or humility).

29   The full out joying of young men *is* the strength of them; and the dignity of old men *is* hoariness (or their white hair).

30   The wanness of a wound shall wipe away evils, and (so do) wounds in the privier things of the womb.

ECCLESIASTICUS CHAPTER 27

1   Many men have trespassed for neediness; and he that seeketh to be made rich, turneth away his eye.

2   As a stake or a pale is fastened in the midst of a heap or a joining of stones, so and *a man* shall be anguished by sins betwixt the midst of selling and buying. Trespass shall be all-broken with him that trespasseth.

3   If thou holdest not thee diligently in the dread of (or reverence for) the Lord, thine house shall soon be turned upside down.

4   As dust shall dwell in the holes of a riddle, so the anguish of a man *shall dwell* in the thoughts of him.

5   A furnace proveth the vessels of a potter; and the temptation of tribulation *proveth* just or rightwise men.

6   As churl-like travail or earth-working about a tree showeth the fruit thereof, so a word of thought *showeth* the heart of man.

7   Praise thou not a man before a word *fully ended*; for why this is the temptation, *that is, the proving*, of men.

8   If thou pursuest rightfulness or followest rightwiseness, thou shalt take (or get) it; thou shalt clothe (or wear) it as a long cloth (or overcoat) or an aube of honour, and thou shalt dwell with it, and it shall defend thee without end, and in the day of knowing thou shalt find steadfastness.

9   Volatiles or fowls come together to *birds* like themselves; and truth shall return again to them that work it.

10   (As) a lion setteth espies or waiteth (or lieth in wait) evermore to (or for) hunting; so sins to them that work wickedness.

11   An holy man dwelleth in wisdom, as the sun *dwelleth*; for why a fool is changed as (or changeth like) the moon.

12   In the midst of unwise men keep thou a word to the time; but be thou busy in the midst of them that think (upon) the law of God.

13   The telling of sinners *is* hateful; and the laughing of them *is* in the trespasses of sin.

14   Speech swearing much shall make (for) standing up of hairs, for astonishing, to the head; and the irreverence of it is the stopping of the ears.

15   The shedding out of blood *is* in the chiding or jangling of proud men; and the cursing of them *is* grievous hearing, *for in their chiding they blaspheme God often, and it is full grievous to (or for) faithful ears to hear such blasphemy of God.*

16   He that showeth openly the privates (or the secrets) of a friend, loseth (or destroyeth his) faithfulness; and he shall not find a friend to (or for) his soul.

17   Love thou a neighbour, and be thou joined with him in faith. For (or But) if thou showest openly the privates (or the secrets) of him, thou shalt not (any more) perfectly pursue (or follow) after him.

18   For as a man that loseth his friend, so he that loseth the friendship of his neighbour.

19   And as a man that letteth go a bird from or out of his hand, so thou that hast forsaken thy neighbour, and thou shalt not take (or receive, or get) him (again).

20   Thou shalt not pursue or follow him, for he is far absent or far he is away; for he escaped as a capret from a snare, for the soul of him is wounded.

21   Thou shalt no more be able to bind him together; but of (or after) evil saying is according. Soothly to show openly the privates

(or the secrets) of a friend, is the despair of a soul unblessed or unfaithful.

22   He that twinkleth with the eye, maketh or forgeth wicked things; and no man shall (not) cast him away.

23   In the sight of thine eyes he shall (not) defoul his mouth, and he shall wonder on (or at) thy words; but at the last he shall turn waywardly or pervert his mouth, and in his word, or in (or regarding) thy words, he shall give slander.

24   I have heard many things, *that is, evils*, and I made (them) not even to him, *yea, I areckoned not another malice even to the malice of this man*; and the Lord shall hate him.

25   If a man casteth a stone on high, it shall fall on his (own) head; and the guileful wound of a guileful or treacherous man shall part (or make) wounds.

26   And he that diggeth a ditch, shall fall into it; and he that setteth a stone to a neighbour, shall offend therein, or shall stumble in (or on) it; and he that setteth a snare to another man, shall perish therein.

27   If a man maketh the worst or wicked counsel, it shall be turned upon him; and he shall not know from whence it shall come to him.

28   The scorning and despising of proud men and vengeance shall set espy to (or lieth in wait for) him, as a lion doeth.

29   They that delight in the fall of just men or the rightwise, shall perish by a snare; forsooth sorrow shall waste them, before that they die.

30   Wrath and madness or rage, ever either be abominable; and a sinful man shall hold (onto) them.

ECCLESIASTICUS CHAPTER 28

1   He that will be avenged, shall find of (or from) the Lord

vengeance; and he keeping shall keep his sins (in remembrance).

2 Forgive thou to thy neighbour that annoyeth (or harmeth) thee, and then (thy) sins shall be released or be forgiven to thee (after) praying.

3 A man keepeth wrath to (or for a) man; and seeketh he of (or from) God medicine (or remedy)?

4 He hath no mercy on a man like himself; and (yet) beseecheth he the Highest for his own sins?

5 He the while he is flesh, reserveth ire (or wrath); and asketh he of God mercy? who shall pray for his sins?

6 Have thou mind on (or Remember) thy last things, and cease thou or leave (off) to be (anyone's) enemy. For why failing and death nigh not in the commandments *of God*.

7 Have thou mind on (or Remember) the dread of the Lord, and be not wroth to the neighbour. Have thou mind on the testament (or Remember the covenant) of the Highest, and despise thou the ignorance of thy neighbour.

8 Abstain thee from strife, and thou shalt decrease, *either abridge*, (thy) sins. For why a wrathful man kindleth strife;

9 and a sinful man, *that is, a sower of discords*, shall disturb (or shall trouble) friends, and he shall send in enmity in(to) the midst of men having peace.

10 For why after the trees of the wood, so the fire shall burn on high; and after the might of a man, so his wrathfulness shall be, and after his chattel or his substance he shall enhance (or raise up) his wrath.

11 Hasty striving shall kindle fire, and hasty chiding shall shed out blood; and a tongue bearing witnessing shall bring death.

12 If thou blowest, as fire it shall burn on high; and if thou spittest upon it, it shall be quenched; ever either, *that is, a word kindling ire, and a word refraining it*, come forth (out) of the

mouth.

13   A privy backbiter, and a double-tongued man, *yea, he that speaketh fair before a man, and evil behind him, is* cursed; for he disturbed (or troubled) many men having peace.

14   The third tongue hath stirred many men, and hath scattered them from folk into folk (or nation to nation). It hath destroyed walled cities of rich men, and hath mined down (or undermined) the houses of great men. It hath cut down the virtues (or the strength) of (the) peoples, and hath unknit strong folks.

15   The third tongue hath cast out wedded, or honest, women, and hath deprived them of their travails (or labours).

16   He that beholdeth *the third tongue,* shall not have rest; neither shall have a friend, in whom he shall rest.

17   The wound of a beating maketh wanness (or marks on the skin); but the wound of the tongue shall make less or break the bones.

18   Many men fell down by the sharpness of the sword; but not so (many, or not as many) as they that perished or died by their tongue.

19   *He is* blessed that is covered from a wicked or a shrewd (or a depraved) tongue; and he that passed not in the wrathfulness thereof, and he that drew not the yoke thereof, and was not bound in the bonds thereof.

20   For why the yoke thereof is an iron yoke, and the bond thereof is a brazen (or bronze) bond.

21   The death thereof *is* the worst death; and hell *is* more profitable, *that is, the pain of hell is less evil,* then it.

22   The perseverance thereof shall not dwell, but it shall hold the ways of unjust men; in his flame it shall not burn just or rightwise men.

23   They that forsake God, shall fall into it; and it shall burn

greatly in them, and it shall not be quenched; and as a lion it shall be sent into them, and as a (leo)pard it shall hurt them.

24   Beset thine ears with thorns, and do not thou hear a wicked tongue; and make thou doors to (or for) thy mouth, and locks to (or for) thine ears. Well thou or melt together, *or temper thou*, thy gold, and thy silver;

25   and make thou a balance to (or for) thy words, and rightful bridles to (or for) thy mouth.

26   And take heed, lest peradventure thou slide in (or with thy) tongue, and fall in the sight of (thine) enemies, setting treason or waiting (or lying in wait) to (or for) thee, and thy fall be uncurable or unhealable unto death.

WISDOM OF SOLOMON   CHAPTER 8

1   Therefore wisdom stretcheth forth from the end unto the end strongly, and disposeth all things sweetly.

2   I loved this *wisdom made*, or This I loved, and I sought it out from my youth; and I sought to take it (as) a spousess to me, and I am made a lover of the fairness thereof, or of the form of it.

3   It having the company of God, glorifieth the gentleness of it; but also the Lord of all things loved it.

4   For it is the teacheress of the learning or the discipline of God, and the chooseress of his works.

5   And if riches be coveted or be desired in life, what *is* richer than wisdom, that worketh all things?

6   Soothly if wit (or prudence) worketh, who is a craftsmaker or craftsman more than wisdom, of these things that be?

7   And if a man loveth rightwiseness, the travails (or labours) of this *wisdom* have great virtues; for it teacheth soberness, and prudence, and rightfulness or rightwiseness, and virtue; and

nothing is more profitable than these in life to men.

8   And if a man desireth a multitude of knowing (or much knowledge), wisdom knoweth things (which have) passed (by), and guesseth of things to coming; it knoweth the fellnesses or falsenesses of words, and the assoilings (or solvings, or solutions) of arguments; it knoweth signs and showings of things to coming or wonders, before that they be made or ere they be done; and the befallings or chances of times and of worlds.

9   Therefore I purposed to bring to me this *wisdom*, to live together (with me); witting that it shall commune with me of goods (or about good things), and speaking together of (or about) my thoughts, and of mine annoyances (or my troubles), shall be.

10   For this *wisdom* I shall have clearness at (or with) companies (or crowds), and honour at (or with) the elder men;

11   I shall be found young and sharp in doom (or in judgement), and in the sight of mighty men I shall be wonderful, and the faces of princes shall worship (or honour) me, or shall marvel (at) me.

12   They shall abide me, being still, and they shall behold me, speaking; and the while I speak many things, they shall set (their) hands on their mouths.

13   Furthermore by this *wisdom* I shall have undeadliness (or immortality); and I shall leave an everlasting mind (or memorial) to them, that shall come after me.

14   I shall dispose peoples; and nations shall be subject to me.

15   Hideous kings hearing me shall dread (or fear); and in the multitude I shall be seen (as) good, and strong in battle.

16   I shall enter into mine house, and I shall rest with wisdom; for the conversation thereof hath no bitterness, and the dwelling together thereof hath none annoyance (or troubles), but gladness and joy.

17   I thought these things at (or within) me, and I remembered in mine heart; for why wisdom is undeadly (or immortal) in thought,

DAY 20

18   and good delighting *is* in the friendship thereof; and in the works of the hands of it honesty (or riches) without failing; and wisdom *is* in the strife of the speech thereof; and great clearness *is* in the communing of the words thereof; I went about, seeking to take *wisdom* (un)to me.

19   Forsooth I was a witty (or knowing) child, and I got a good soul.

20   And when (or for) I was more good, I came to a body undefouled.

21   And as I knew, that else I may not (or cannot) be chaste or continent, no but God give it, and this same thing was wisdom, to know whose this gift was; I went to the Lord, and I besought him, and I said, of (or with) all mine entrails of mine heart. Δ

DAY 21

PSALM 101

1   *The psalm of David.* Lord, I shall sing to thee; (of) mercy and doom (or judgement). I shall sing,

2   and I shall understand (or go) in a way without wem (or blemish); when thou shalt come to me. I went perfectly in the innocence of mine heart; in the middle of mine house.

3   I setted not forth before mine eyes an unjust (or impure) thing; I hated them that made trespassings.

4   A shrewd (or depraved) heart cleaved not to me; I knew not a wicked man bowing away from me.

5   I pursued him that backbited privily (or secretly) his neighbour. With the proud eye and an heart unable to be filled or unfillable; I ate not with (such as) this.

6   Mine eyes *were* to the faithful men of the earth, that they sit with me; he that went in a way without wem (or blemish, or fault), ministered to or served me.

7   He that doeth pride, shall not dwell in the middle of mine house; he that speaketh wicked things, served not in the sight of mine eyes (or before me).

8   In the morrowtide I killed all the sinners of the earth; (so) that I should lose (or destroy) from the city of the Lord all men working wickedness.

PSALM 102

1   *The prayer of a poor man, when he was anguished, and poured out his speech before the Lord.* Lord, hear thou my prayer; and my cry come to thee.

285

2   Turn not away thy face from me; in whatever day I am troubled, bow down thine ear to me. In whatever day I shall inwardly call thee; hear thou me swiftly (or *please* swiftly answer me).

3   For my days have failed (or vanished) as smoke; and my bones have dried up as croutons or cracklings, *either the leavings of frying.*

4   I am smitten (or beaten down) as hay, and mine heart (hath) dried up; for I have forgotten to eat my bread.

5   (Out) of the voice of my wailing; (for) my bones cleaved to my flesh.

6   I am made like a pelican of the wilderness; I am made as a night crow in an house.

7   I waked; and I am made as a solitary sparrow in (or on) the roof(top).

8   All day (long) mine enemies despised me; and they that praised me, swore (or conspired) against me.

9   For I ate ashes as bread; and I meddled or mingled my drink with weeping (or I mixed my drink with my tears).

10   From the face of the wrath of thine indignation; for (first) thou raising me up, (then) hast hurtled me down.

11   My days bowed away as a shadow; and I waxed (or grew) dry as hay.

12   But, Lord, thou dwellest without end; and thy memorial in generation and into generation (or for all generations).

13   Lord, thou rising up, shalt have mercy upon Zion; for the time to have mercy thereof cometh, for the time cometh.

14   For the stones thereof pleased thy servants; and they shall have mercy upon the land thereof (or love even its dust).

15   And, Lord, the heathen men shall dread (or fear) thy name; and all the kings of the earth *shall dread (or revere)* thy glory.

16   For the Lord hath built up Zion; and he shall be seen in (all) his glory.

17   He beheld on the prayer of meek (or humble) men; and he despised not the prayer of them.

18   Be these things written in (or for) another generation; and the people that shall be made shall praise the Lord.

19   For he beheld from his high holy place; the Lord looked (down) from heaven into (or onto) the earth.

20   For to hear the wailings of fettered men; and for to unbind the sons of slain men.

21   (So) that they tell in Zion the name of the Lord; and his praising in Jerusalem.

22   In gathering together the peoples into one; and the kings, (so) that they serve the Lord.

23   It or He answered to him in the way of his virtue (or strength); Tell thou to me the fewness of my days.

24   (Please) again-call thou not me in the middle of my days; thy years *be* in generation and into generation (or for all generations).

25   Lord, thou foundedest the earth in the beginning; and the heavens be the works of thine hands.

26   They shall perish, but thou dwellest perfectly; and all shall wax eld as a cloth (or grow old as a cloak). And thou shalt change them as a covering, and they shall be changed;

27   but thou art the same thyself, and thy years shall not fail (or have no end).

28   The sons of thy servants shall dwell; and the seed of them shall be addressed (or directed) into the world (or forever).

PSALM 103

1   *A psalm of (or by) David.* My soul, bless thou the Lord, and

all things that be within me, *bless* his holy name.

2   My soul, bless thou the Lord; and do not thou forget all the yieldings of (or gifts from) him.

3   Which doeth (or Who showeth) mercy to all thy wickednesses; which healeth all thy sicknesses.

4   Which again-buyeth (or Who redeemeth) thy life from death; which crowneth thee in (or with) mercy and merciful doings.

5   Which fulfilleth thy desire in goods (or with good things); thy youth shall be renewed as *the youth* of an eagle.

6   The Lord doing mercies; and doom (or judgement), to all men suffering wrong.

7   He made his ways known to Moses; his wills (or his deeds) to the sons of Israel.

8   The Lord *is* a merciful doer, and merciful in will; long abiding, and much merciful.

9   He shall not be wroth without end; and he shall not threaten without end.

10   He did not to us after (or according to) our sins; neither he yielded to us after (or according to) our wickednesses.

11   For by the highness of heaven (or as high as the heavens be) from the earth; he made strong his mercy on men dreading (or fearing, or revering) him.

12   As much as the east is from the west; he made afar our wickednesses from us.

13   As a father hath mercy on *his* sons (and daughters), the Lord had mercy on men (and women) dreading (or revering) him;

14   for he knew our making. He bethought (or knew) that we be dust,

15   a man *is* as hay; his days shall flower out so as a flower of the field.

16   For the spirit shall pass in him (or the wind passeth over it),

and *it* shall not abide (there long); and *it* shall no more know his (or its) place.

17   But the mercy of the Lord *is* from without beginning, and till into without end; on men dreading (or fearing, or revering) him. And his rightwiseness *is* into the sons of sons;

18   to them that keep his testament (or covenant). And be mindful of (or remember) his commandments; to do them.

19   The Lord hath made ready his seat (or his throne) in heaven; and his realm shall be lord of all (or he shall rule over all as King).

20   Angels of the Lord, bless ye the Lord; ye mighty in virtue (or strength, or power), doing his word, to hear the voice of his words.

21   All the virtues (or the hosts, or the armies) of the Lord, bless ye the Lord; ye ministers (or servants) of him, that do his will.

22   All the works of the Lord, bless ye the Lord, in each place of his lordship; my soul, bless thou the Lord.

PROVERBS CHAPTER 21

1   As the partings of waters, so the heart of the king *is* in the power of the Lord; whither ever he will (or desireth), he shall bow it.

2   Each way of a man seemeth rightful or right to himself; but the Lord weigheth the hearts.

3   To do mercy and doom (or judgement, or justice), pleaseth more the Lord, than sacrifices.

4   The enhancing (or The raising up) of the eyes is the alarging of the heart; the lantern of wicked men *is* sin.

5   The thoughts of a strong man *be* ever in abundance; but each slow man is ever in neediness.

6   He that gathereth treasures by the tongue of a leasing- (or a lie-)*maker* (or a liar), is vain (or futile), and without heart; and he

shall be hurled to the snares of death.

7   The ravens (or The robberies) of unpious men shall draw them down; for they would not do doom (or judgement, or justice).

8   The wayward way of a man is alien from (or foreign to) God; but the work of him that is clean of sin, is rightful or right.

9   It is better to sit in the corner of an house without (a) roof, than with a woman full of chiding, and in a common house.

10   The soul of an unpious man desireth evil; he shall not have mercy on his neighbour.

11   When a man full of pestilence is punished, (even) a little man *of wit* (or a man *of* little *wit or understanding*) shall be (made) wiser; and if he pursueth or follow a wise man, he shall take knowing (or receive knowledge).

12   The rightwise (one) of (or in) the house of a wicked man thinketh, to withdraw wicked men from evil.

13   He that stoppeth his ear at the cry of the poor, shall cry also (or shall also cry), and he shall not be heard.

14   A gift hid quencheth chidings; and a gift in the bosom *quencheth* most indignation.

15   It is joy to the rightwise to make doom (or judgement, or justice); and *it is* dread to (or fear for) them that work wickedness.

16   A man that erreth from the way of doctrine, shall dwell in the company of giants, *that is, of men evil ruled, either of fiends* (or demons).

17   He that loveth meats (or food), shall be in neediness; he that loveth wine and fat things, shall not be made rich.

18   An unpious man shall be given for a rightwise man; and a wicked man *shall be given* for a rightful man.

19   It is better to dwell in a desert land, than with a woman full of chiding, and wrathful.

20   Desirable treasure and oil *is* in the dwelling place of a just man; and an unprudent man shall destroy or scatter it.

21   He that pursueth or followeth rightwiseness or rightfulness and mercy, shall find life, and rightwiseness, and glory.

22   A wise man ascended or went up into the city of the strong men, and destroyed the strength of the trust thereof (or their trust in their stronghold).

23   He that keepeth his mouth and his tongue (under control), keepeth his soul from anguishes.

24   A proud man and a boaster is called a fool, (for) that (he) worketh (his) pride in wrath.

25   Desires slay a slow man; for his hands would not (do) work (of) anything.

26   All day he coveteth and desireth; who forsooth is rightwise, shall give, and shall not cease.

27   The offerings of wicked men, that be offered (out) of great trespass, *be* abominable.

28   A false witness shall perish; a man obedient shall speak (and get) victory.

29   A wicked man maketh firm his cheer (or face) unshamefastly; but he that is rightful, amendeth his way.

30   No wisdom there is, no prudence there is, no counsel there is, against the Lord.

31   An horse is made ready to (or for) the day of battle; but the Lord shall give health (or victory, or salvation).

ECCLESIASTICUS CHAPTER 29

1   He that doeth mercy, lendeth to his neighbour; and he that is full mighty in hand, keepeth the commandments.

2   Lend thou to thy neighbour in the time of his need; and again

yield thou to a neighbour in his time.

3   Confirm thou a word, and do thou faithfully with him; and in all time thou shalt find that, that is needful to thee.

4   Many men guessed borrowing as finding, and gave dis-ease or grief to those men that helped them.

5   Till they take (or receive), they kiss the hands of the giver; and in promises they make meek their voice. And in (or at) the time of yielding, he shall ask (for more) time, or delaying, and he shall speak words of annoy(ance) (or of hurt), and of grumblings, and he shall challenge falsely, or plead (for), or complain (about) the time, *to tarry the paying of the debt.*

6   Forsooth if he may (or can) yield, he shall be an adversary or an enemy; scarcely of the whole he shall yield the half, and he shall reckon that as (re)funding. Else he shall defraud him in (or of) his money, and *the lender* shall have him (as) an enemy without cause. And he shall yield to him, *that is, to the lender*, wrongs and cursings; and for honour and benefit, he shall yield to him despising.

7   Many men lend not, not for cause of wickedness, but they dreaded to be defrauded without cause or willfully.

8   Nevertheless on (or for) a meek man in soul, *that is, a full poor debtor*, be thou stronger; and for alms-deeds draw thou not him (along).

9   For the commandment *of God* take (or receive) thou a poor man; and for his neediness leave thou not him void (or do not let him go away empty-handed).

10   Lose thou money for a brother and friend, and hide thou not it under a stone, into perdition.

11   Put thy treasure in the commandments of the Highest; and it shall profit to thee more than gold.

12   Enclose thou alms in the bosom of a poor man; and this *alms*

shall pray for thee *to be delivered of* (*or by*) *God* from all evil. The alms of a man *is* as a bag or a little sack with him; and it shall keep the grace of a man, *that is, God's grace* (*or favour*), *given to man,* as the apple of the eye. And afterward it shall rise again, and shall yield to them a yielding, to each man into (or onto) the head of them.

13   Above or over (or better than) the shield of a mighty man, and above or over (or better than) a spear it shall fight against thine enemy.

14   A good man maketh faith to (or for) his neighbour *in becoming a borrower* (*or a guarantor*) *for him in need*; and he that loseth, shall leave shame to him.

15   Forget thou not the grace of the borrower (or of the guarantor); for he gave his life for thee.

16   A sinful man and unclean fleeth the promiser. A sinner areckoneth unto himself the good words of the borrower (or of the guarantor);

17   and the unkind man in wit forsaketh a man delivering him.

18   A man promiseth for his neighbour; and when *he* hath lost reverence, *that is, shamefastness before God and man, the borrower* shall be forsaken of (or by) him. The worst or most shrewd (or depraved) promise, *by which the neighbour promised falsely to deliver his borrow*, hath lost or spoiled many loving men, and hath moved them as the waves of the sea. It going in compass made mighty men to pass over or to go out (or to go away); and (then) they wandered about among alien folks (or foreign nations).

19   A sinner breaking or overpassing the commandment of the Lord shall fall into a wicked promise; and he that endeavoureth to do many things, shall fall into doom (or judgement).

20   Recover thy neighbour by thy virtue (or according to thy power); and take heed to thyself, lest thou fall (in the same manner).

21   The beginning of the life of a man *is* water, and bread, and

clothing, and a house covering filthhood (or nakedness).

22   Better is the lifelode (or the livelihood) of a poor man under the covering of spars, than plenteous shining feasts in pilgrimage without a house,

23   The least thing pleaseth thee for a great thing, and thou shalt not hear the shame or the reproof of pilgrimage.

24   *It is* a wicked life to seek harbour from house into house; and where he shall be harboured, he shall not do trustily, neither he shall open the mouth.

25   He shall be harboured, and he shall feed, and give drink to unkind men; and yet he shall hear bitter things.

26   Pass, thou that art harboured, or go, guest, and array a table; and give thou meats (or food) to other men, (of) those things that thou hast in the hand.

27   Go thou out from the face of the honour of my friends, for the friendship, *either affinity*, or the need of mine house; by harbouring thou art made a brother to me.

28   These things *be* grievous to a man having wit (or understanding); the reproving of house, and the despising of the usurer or the lender.

ECCLESIASTICUS CHAPTER 30

1   He that loveth his son, giveth busily beatings to him, (so) that he be glad in his last thing, and (so) that *the son* touch not the doors of neighbours.

2   He that teacheth his son, shall be praised in (or for) him; and shall have glory in him in the midst of (his) menials (or underlings).

3   He that teacheth his son, sendeth the enemy into envy; and in the midst of friends he shall have glory in that *son*.

4   (And though) the father of him is dead, and (yet) he is as not dead; for he hath left after him *a son* like him.

5   He saw in his life, and was glad in (or over) him; and in his death he was not sorry or sorrowed not, neither was ashamed before (his) enemies.

6   For he left a defender of the house against (his) enemies; and (one) yielding grace to (his) friends.

7   For *defending* the souls (or the lives) of *his* sons, he shall bind together his wounds; and his entrails or the bowels of him shall be disturbed (or troubled) on (or over) each voice.

8   An horse untamed, *either unchastised*, shall escape hard, and a son unchastised shall escape heady (or shall become headstrong).

9   Flatter thou the son, and he shall make thee dreading; play thou with him, and he shall make thee sorry or sorrow(ful).

10   Laugh thou not with him *of (or about) his follies*, lest thou have sorrow together, and at the last thy teeth shall be astonished.

11   Give thou not power to him in youth, and despise thou not his thoughts.

12   Bow thou (down) his neck in youth, and beat thou his sides, while he is a young child; lest peradventure he wax (or grow) hard or inwardly harden, and believe not to thee, and he shall be a sorrow of (or to thy) soul to thee.

13   Teach thy son, and work in him; lest thou offend into the filth of him (or lest his filthy behaviour offend thee).

14   Better is a poor man whole, and strong in mights or strengths, than a rich man feeble, and beaten with malice.

15   The health of the soul (or of the body) *is* in the holiness of rightfulness or rightwiseness, and it is better than any gold and silver; and a strong body *is better* than full much chattel or than money without measure.

16   No chattel is above the chattel of the health of the body; and no liking is above the joy of the heart. [There is not money over the money of the health of the body; and there is not liking over

the joy of the heart.]

17　Better is death than a bitter life, and everlasting rest *is better* than sickness dwelling continually or enduring.

18　Goods hid in a closed mouth *be* as the settings forth of meats (or food) set about a sepulchre.

19　What shall sacrifice profit to an idol? for why it shall not eat, neither shall smell. So he that is driven away from the Lord,

20　and beareth the meeds (or the rewards) of wickedness or shrewdness (or depravity), seeing with eyes, and wailing inwardly, as a gelding embracing a virgin or a maiden, and sighing.

21　Give thou not sorrow to thy soul, *that is, unreasonable sorrow, that annoyeth (or harmeth) both body and soul,* and torment not thyself in (or with) thy (own) counsel, *as they do that despair through sorrow, and then slay themselves.*

22　Mirth of heart, this is the life of man, and *is* a treasure of holiness without failing; and full out joying of a man is long life.

23　Have thou mercy on thy soul, and please thou God; and hold together and gather together thine heart in the holiness of him, and put far away sorrow from thee. For why sorrow hath slain many men; and none health is therein or there is not profit in it.

24　Envy and wrathfulness shall make (for) less days or Envy and wrath shall lessen days; and thoughts shall bring oldness before the time.

25　A shining or bright heart *is* good in meats (or for meals, or digestion); for why the meats (or foods) thereof be made diligently.

WISDOM OF SOLOMON   CHAPTER 9

1　God of my fathers, and Lord of mercy, that madest all things by or with thy word,

2　and ordainedest man by thy wisdom, that he should be lord

of the creatures, which is made of (or by) thee,

3   that he dispose the world in equity and rightwiseness, and deem doom (or judge judgement) in right ruling of the heart;

4   give thou to me wisdom, that standeth nigh (to) thy seats; and do not thou reprove me from (among) thy children.

5   For I am thy servant, and the son of thine handmaid; *I am* a sick or feeble man, and of little time, and less to the understanding of doom (or judgement) and of laws.

6   And if any man is perfect among the sons of me, if thy wisdom fleeth away from him, he shall be reckoned into nought (or nothing).

7   Forsooth thou hast chosen me (to be a) king to thy people, and a judge or a doomsman of thy sons and daughters;

8   and thou saidest, that I should build a temple in thine holy hill, and an altar in the city of thy dwelling place; the likeness of thine holy tabernacle, which thou madest ready at or preparedest from the beginning.

9   And thy wisdom *is* with thee, that knoweth thy works, which also was present then, when thou madest the world, and knew what was pleasant (or pleasing) to thine eyes, and what was addressed (or directed) or right in thy commandments.

10   Send thou that *wisdom* from thine holy heavens, and from the seat (or throne) of thy greatness, (so) that it be with me, and travail (or labour) with me; and (so) that I know what is acceptable or allowed with thee.

11   For why that *wisdom* knoweth and understandeth all things; and it shall lead me forth in my works soberly, and it shall keep me in his (or its) power.

12   And my works shall be acceptable, and I shall dispose thy people justly or rightwisely, and I shall be worthy of the seat (or the throne) of my father.

13 For who of men may know the counsel of God? either who may think, what (is the) will (of) God?

14 For why the thoughts of deadly (or of mortal) men *be* dreadful (or fearful), and our purveyances *be* uncertain.

15 For why the body that is corrupted, grieveth the soul; and the earthly dwelling presseth down the wit (or understanding), thinking many things.

16 And of hard we guess *those things*, that be in (or on) the earth; and we find with travail *those things*, that be in beholding. But who shall search *those things*, that be in the heavens?

17 But who shall know thy wit (or mind, or understanding), no but thou give wisdom, and send thine Holy Spirit from the highest things?

18 And if the paths of them, that be in lands, be amended, and if men have learned *those things*, that please thee. For why, Lord, whichever (or whomever) pleased thee from the beginning, were made whole by wisdom. ∆

DAY 22

PSALM 104

1   My soul, bless thou the Lord; my Lord God, thou art magnified greatly. Thou hast clothed acknowledging and fairness (or Thou art clothed with majesty and glory);

2   and thou art clothed with light, as with a cloth (or a cloak). And thou stretchest forth the heavens as a skin (or a tent);

3   and thou coverest with waters the higher parts thereof. Which puttest (or Who makest) a cloud thy ascending; which goest on the feathers (or Who goest on the wings) of the winds.

4   Which (or Who) makest spirits thine angels; and thy ministers a burning fire.

5   Which (or Who) hast founded the earth on his stableness (or its foundation); it shall not be bowed into the world of world (or forever and ever).

6   The depth of the waters as a cloth (or a cloak) is the clothing thereof; the waters shall stand on (or shall rise above the) hills.

7   They shall flee from thy blaming; men shall be afeared of the voice (or the sound) of thy thunder.

8   The hills go up, and the fields go down; into the place which thou hast founded to or (prepared for) them.

9   Thou hast set a term, which they shall not pass (over); neither they shall be turned (again), for to cover the earth.

10   And thou sendest out wells into the great valleys; and the waters shall pass betwixt the midst of the hills.

11   All the beasts of the field shall drink; the wild asses shall abide in their thirst, *that is, to be filled in their thirst.*

12   The birds of the air shall dwell on those things; from the midst of the stones they shall give (out their) voices.

13   And thou moistenest the hills of their higher things; the earth shall be fulfilled of (or with) the fruit of thy works.

14   And thou bringest forth hay to (or for) the beasts; and herb to (or plants for) the service of (or to) men. (So) that thou bring forth bread (out) of the earth;

15   and that wine make glad the heart of men. That he make glad (or shine) the face with oil; and that bread make steadfast (or strong) the heart of man.

16   The trees of the field shall be full-filled (with sap), and the cedars of the Lebanon, which he planted;

17   sparrows shall make nest there. The house of the gyrfalcon is the leader or (be on the tops) of them;

18   the high hills *be refuge* to (or for) the harts; the stone *is* refuge to urchins (or for the badgers).

19   He made the moon into (telling) times; the sun knew his (or its) going down.

20   Thou hast set darknesses, and night is made; all the beasts of the woods shall go therein.

21   The lions' whelps roaring for to ravish (prey); and to seek of (or from) God meat to (or food for) themselves.

22   The sun is risen, and they be gathered together; and they shall be set (down) in their couches (or dens).

23   A man shall go out to his work; and to his working, unto the eventide.

24   Lord, thy works be magnified full much, thou hast made all things in (or by thy) wisdom; the earth is filled with thy possessions (or thy creatures).

25   This sea *is* great and (too) large to (or for) hands (to hold); there *be* creeping beasts, of which (there) is no number. Little beasts with the great;

26   ships shall pass there. This dragon (or Leviathan) which thou

DAY 22

hast formed, for to scorn him.

27　All things abide of (or wait for) thee; (so) that thou give to them meat (or food) in (or at its proper) time.

28　When (or What) thou shalt give to them, they shall gather (up); when thou shalt open thine hands, all things shall be filled with goodness.

29　But when thou shalt turn away thy face, they shall be troubled; thou shalt take away the spirit (or the breath) of them, and they shall fail; and (then) they shall return again into their dust.

30　Send out thy spirit (or thy breath), and they shall be formed of the new (or anew); and thou shalt renew the face of the earth.

31　(May) the glory of the Lord be into the world (or forever); the Lord shall be glad in (or about) his works.

32　Which (or Who) beholdeth the earth, and maketh it to tremble; which (or who) toucheth the hills, and they smoke.

33　I shall sing to the Lord in my life; I shall say (or sing) a psalm to my God, as long as I am.

34　(May) my speech (or words) be merry or mirth to him; forsooth I shall delight in the Lord.

35　(May) sinners fail (or perish) from the earth, and wicked men *fail*, so that they be not; my soul, bless thou the Lord.

PROVERBS CHAPTER 22

1　Better is a good name, than many riches; for good grace *is* above (or more valuable than) silver and gold.

2　A rich man and a poor man met themselves; the Lord is the worker of ever either.

3　A fell man seeth evil, and hideth himself; and an innocent man passed (by), and he was tormented by harm.

4　The end of temperance *is* the dread (or the fear) of (or

reverence for) the Lord; riches, and glory, and life.

5 Armours and swords *be* in (or on) the way of a wayward man; but the keeper of his soul goeth away far from them.

6 It is a proverb, (Start) a young waxing (or growing) man after (or on) his way, and when he hath waxed (or grown) old, he shall not go away from it.

7 A rich man commandeth to poor men; and he that taketh borrowing, is the servant of the lender.

8 He that soweth wickedness shall reap evils; and the rod of his wrath shall be ended.

9 He that is ready to (give) mercy shall be blessed; for (out) of his loaves he gave (some) to the poor.

10 Cast thou out a scorner, and strife shall go out with him; and causes and despisings shall cease.

11 He that loveth the cleanness of heart, shall have the king (for) a friend, for the grace of (or favour from) his lips.

12 The eyes of the Lord keep knowing (or knowledge); and the words of a wicked man be deceived (or deceiving, or deceitful).

13 A slow (or lazy) man shall say, A lion is withoutforth; I shall be slain in the midst of the streets.

14 The mouth of an alien (or foreign, or unfamiliar) woman *is* a deep ditch; he to whom the Lord is wroth shall fall into it.

15 Folly is bound together in the heart of a child; and a rod of chastising or of discipline shall drive it away.

16 He that falsely challengeth (or oppresseth) the poor, to increase his own riches, shall give to a richer man, and (then) he shall be needy.

17 My son, bow down thine ear, and hear thou the words of wise men; but set thou the heart to my teaching.

18 That shall be fair to (or pleasing for) thee, when thou hast kept it in thine heart, and it shall flow again in (or on) thy lips.

19   (So) that thy trust be in the Lord; wherefore and I have showed it to thee today.

20   Lo! I have described it in three manners, *that is, in the three parts of the Old Testament, that be, the law (or Torah), the holy stories, and the prophets,* in thoughts and knowing,

21   (so) that I should show to thee the firmness and speeches of truth; to answer (out) of these things to them that sent (unto) thee.

22   Do thou not violence to a poor man, for he is poor; neither defoul thou a needy man in (or at) the gate.

23   For the Lord shall deem (or judge) his cause (or his case), and he shall torment them that tormented his soul.

24   Do not thou be a friend to a wrathful man, neither go thou with a wrathful man;

25   lest peradventure thou learn his ways, and take cause of stumbling unto thy soul.

26   Do not thou be with them that fasten, *or bind,* their hands, and that proffer themselves *to be* borrows (or security) for debts;

27   for if he hath not whereof he shall restore (to thee), what of cause is, that thou (should) take away the covering from (off) thy (own) bed?

28   Go thou not over the old marks (or the boundary stones), which thy fathers have set.

29   Thou hast seen a man smart in his work; he shall stand before kings, and he shall not be before unnoble men.

ECCLESIASTICUS CHAPTER 31

1   Waking of honesty shall make fleshes to fail (or Wailing for or Watching over riches shall make the flesh to pine away); and (the much) thought thereof (or about it) shall take away sleep.

2   Thoughts of before-knowing (or worry) turneth away wit (or

understanding); and grievous sickness maketh sober the soul.

3　A rich man travailed (or laboured) in the gathering of (his) chattel or (his) substance; and in his rest he shall be filled with his goods (or his good things).

4　A poor man travailed in the decreasing or the lessening of (his) lifelode; and in the end he is made needy. (A poor man worked hard, even though his livelihood continued to decrease; and in the end, he is still needy.)

5　He that loveth gold, shall not be justified; and he that pursueth or followeth (after) wasting, *or corruption*, shall be full-filled of it.

6　Many men be given into the fallings of gold, *that is, many men felled into sins for gold*; and the perdition or the loss of them was made in the fairness of it.

7　A tree of offension (or of offence, or a stumbling block) is the gold of them that make sacrifice; woe to them that pursue or follow it, and each unprudent man shall perish in it.

8　Blessed is a rich man, which is found without the wem (or the blemish) *of covetousness and avarice*; and that went not after gold, neither hoped in money, and treasures.

9　Who is this, and we shall praise him? for he did marvels in his life.

10　Which or Who is proved (or tried, or tested) in (or by) it, and is found perfect, and everlasting glory shall be to him? which (or who) might trespass, and trespassed not, and do evils, and did not.

11　Therefore his goods (or good deeds) be established in (or with) the Lord; and all the church of the saints (or Gods people) shall tell out his alms-deeds.

12　Thou hast set at a great board (or a bountiful table); open thou not first thy cheek on it, *that is, begin thou not to eat first*. And say thou not, whether those be many things, that be on it.

13   Have thou mind (or Remember), that an evil eye is a wayward, or shrewd (or depraved) (thing). What thing worse, than an eye is made? therefore of all his face he (or it) shall weep, when he seeth.

14   Stretch thou not forth first thine hand; and thou defouled by envy, be ashamed. Be thou not oppressed of (or by) wine in (or at) a feast.

15   Understand of thyself the things, that be of thy neighbour. [Understand what be of thy neighbour, of thyself.]

16   Use thou as a discreet and temperate man these things that be set forth to thee; and (so) be thou not hated, when thou eatest (too) much.

17   Cease thou first because of learning, *either nurture*; and do not thou be outrageous or be too much, lest peradventure thou offend.

18   And if thou hast set in the midst of many men, stretch not forth or out thine hand sooner than they; and ask thou not first for to drink.

19   A little wine is fully sufficient to (or for) a learned man; and in sleeping thou shalt not travail (or labour) for that *wine*, and thou shalt not feel travail.

20   Waking, and choler, *either bitter moisture*, and gnawing or anguish to an undiscreet and untemperate man. But the sleep of health *is* in a scarce (or a moderate) man; he shall sleep unto the morrowtide; and his soul (or his body) shall delight with him.

21   And if thou art constrained in eating too much, rise thou from the midst, and spew thou; and it shall refresh thee, and thou shalt not bring sickness to thy body.

22   Son, hear thou me, and despise thou not me; and at the last thou shalt find (that) my words (be true). In all thy works be thou swift; and all sickness shall not come to thee.

23   The lips of many men shall bless a shining man in loaves (or hospitable); and the witnessing of his truth *is* faithful.

24   The city shall grumble in (or for) the worst bread; and the witnessing of wickedness thereof is sooth (or true).

25   Do not thou excite or stir (up) them that be diligent or busy in (or with) wine; for why wine hath destroyed many men.

26   Fire proveth hard iron; so wine drunken in drunkenness shall reprove the hearts of proud men.

27   Even life to men *is* wine *drunken* in soberness; if thou drinkest it measurably, thou shalt be sober. What is the life which is made less by wine? What defraudeth life? death. Wine was made in gladness, not in drunkenness, at or from the beginning.

28   Wine drunken measurably *is* full out joying of soul and of body. Sober drink is the health of the soul and of the body.

29   Wine drunken much maketh voiding, and wrath, and many fallings, *or mischiefs.*

30   Wine drunken much *is* (*or bringeth out*) bitterness of the soul. Strength of drunkenness and hurting of (or by) an unprudent man maketh virtue (or strength) less, and making wounds (or injuries).

31   In the feast of wine, reprove thou not a neighbour; and despise thou not him in his mirth. Say thou not words of shame or of reproof to him; and oppress thou not him in again-asking.

ECCLESIASTICUS CHAPTER 32

1   They have set thee a governor, do not thou be enhanced (or exalted, or raised up); be thou among them as one of them. Have thou the care of them, and so behold thou; and when all thy care is filled, sit thou to meat or (to) rest.

2   (So) that thou be glad for them, and take the ornament of grace; and get a crown, and the dignity of the congregation (or the assembly).

3   Speak thou, the greater man in birth (or elder); for why the

word of him that loveth knowing (or knowledge) become thee first; and hinder thou not the music.

4   Where hearing (or quiet) is not, pour thou not out a word; and do not thou be enhanced uncovenably (or lifted up unsuitably) in thy wisdom.

5   A gem of carbuncle in the ornament of gold; and comparison of musics in the feast of wine.

6   As in the making or the forging of gold is a signet of smaragdus (or emerald), so the number of musics *is* in merry and measurable or temperate wine.

7   Hear thou (while) being still, and good grace (or favour) shall come to thee for reverence. Young man, speak thou scarcely in (or for) thy cause, (only) when the need is. If thou art asked twice, the head have thine answer.

8   In many things be thou as unknowing (or ignorant), and hear thou (or listen, while) being still altogether, and asking or seeking.

9   And presume thou not to speak in the midst of great men; and where old men be, speak thou not much.

10   Lightning shall go before hail, and grace (or favour) shall go before shamefastness, and good grace shall come to thee for reverence.

11   And in the hour of rising, trifle thee not, *that is, make thee no tarrying in arraying, either trifling of hairs, as women do*; forsooth run thou before first into thine house, and there call thou thee to *answer*, or and there be thou called to, and there play thou.

12   And do thy conceits or thy conceivings, *that is, perform thy good purpose conceived there*, and not in sins, and in a proud word.

13   On (or In) all these things, bless thou the Lord, that made thee, and filling thee greatly of (or with) all his goods (or good things).

14   He that dreadeth (or feareth, or revereth) God, shall take his teaching; and they that wake to him, shall find blessing.

15   He that seeketh the law, shall be filled thereof; and he that doeth traitorously, shall be caused to stumble therein.

16   They that dread God, shall find just doom (or judgement); and shall kindle rightfulness or rightwisenesses as a light.

17   A sinful man, *that is, obstinate in sin*, shall eschew blaming or shall shun correction; and after his will (or according to his desire), he shall find comparison.

18   A man of counsel shall not lose or destroy understanding; (but) a man alien and proud shall not dread dreading. Yea, after that he hath done with that *dread* without counsel, and he shall be reproved by his pursuings or his followings.

19   Son, do thou nothing without counsel; and after the deed thou shalt not repent.

20   Go thou not in the way of falling, and offend (or stumble) thou not against the stones or and thou shalt not offend (or stumble) against the stones.

21   Betake thou not thee to a travailous way, lest thou set slander to thy soul (or thou cause thy own soul to stumble);

22   and be thou ware of thy sons, and perceive thou or take heed of thy menials (or servants, or underlings).

23   In all thy work believe thou by (or in) the faith of thy soul; for why this is the keeping of the commandments.

24   He that believeth to (or in) God, taketh heed to the commandments; and he that trusteth in him, shall not be made less, *either deceived*.

WISDOM OF SOLOMON CHAPTER 10

1   This *wisdom of God* kept him, that was formed first of (or by) God, the father of the world, when he alone was made of nought (or out of nothing). And *this wisdom* led him out of his trespass,

and brought him out of the slime of the earth,

2   and gave to him virtue (or power) to hold together all things,
that is, gave to him the lordship over all lower things.

3   As the unrightwise man in his wrath went away from this
wisdom, brotherhood or fraternity perished by the wrath of manslaughter.

4   For which thing when the water did away the earth, wisdom
healed (it) again; governing the rightwise man by a despisable tree.

5   This *wisdom* also in the consent of pride, when nations had
raised themselves, knew the rightwise man, and kept (him) without
complaint or blame to God; and *this wisdom* kept strong mercy in
sons.

6   And it delivered the rightwise fleeing from wicked or unpious
men (who were) perishing, when fire came down into the place of
five cities.

7   For which *wicked men* the land smoking is made a desert,
into witnessing (or a testimony) of waywardness or shrewdness (or
depravity), and trees having fruits in uncertain time; and the mind
(or memorial) of an unbelieveful soul standing (as) an image of salt.

8   For why men passing (by or ignoring) wisdom, not only fell in
this, that they knew not the good things, but also they left to men
the mind (or the memory) of their unwisdom, (so) that in these
sins, which they did, they might not be hid.

9   Forsooth wisdom delivered them from sorrows, that keep it.

10   Soothly this *wisdom* led forth a rightwise man by right ways,
that fled from the wrath of his brother; and it showed him the
realm or the kingdom of God, and gave to him the knowing or
knowledge of saints; it made him honest (or rich) in (his) travels,
and fulfilled his travails (or multiplied the fruit of his labours).

11   It helped him in (or contend with) the fraud of deceivers or the
guile of the men coming about to him, and made him honest (or

honourable, or rich).

12   It kept him (safe) from *his* enemies, and defended him from deceivers; and it gave to him a strong battle, (so) that he should overcome, and know, that wisdom is the mightiest of all.

13   This *wisdom* forsook not the rightwise man (when he was) sold, *that is Joseph, when his brothers sold him to men of Ishmael,* but delivered him from the sinners; and it went down with him into a ditch, *that is, (in)to the prison of the king of Egypt;*

14   and it forsook not him in bonds, till it brought to him the sceptre of the realm, and power against them that oppressed him; and it showed them (to be) liars, that defouled him, and it gave to him everlasting clearness (or glory).

15   This *wisdom* delivered a rightwise people, and wholly without (com)plaint or blame, from the nations that oppressed it.

16   *It* entered into the soul of God's servant, and he stood against hideous kings, in (or with) great wonders and miracles or signs.

17   And it yielded to the rightwise men the meed of their travails (or the reward for their labour), and led them forth in (or on) a wonderful or a marvellous way; and it was to them in(to) a covering of (or for) the day, and in the light of stars by night.

18   And it translated, *either led over,* them through the Red Sea or the Sea of Reeds; and bare them over through full much water.

19   But it drowned down the enemies of them into the sea; and led them out from the depth or the deepness of hell, *that is, from the bottom of the sea.*

20   Therefore rightwise men take away the spoils of wicked or unpious men; and, Lord, they magnified in song thine holy name, and praised altogether thine hand, (their) overcomer.

21   For why wisdom opened the mouth of dumb men, and made the tongues of young children not speaking to be wise or (to be) made fair speaking. ∆

DAY 23

PSALM 105

1   *Alleluia.* Acknowledge ye to (or Praise) the Lord, and inwardly call ye his name; tell ye his works among the heathen men.

2   Sing ye to him, and say ye a psalm to him, and tell ye all his marvels;

3   be ye praised (or glory) in his holy name. (Let) the heart of men seeking the Lord be glad;

4   seek ye the Lord, and be ye confirmed; seek ye evermore his face.

5   Have ye mind on (or Remember) his marvels, which he did; on his great wonders, and dooms of (or judgements from) his mouth.

6   The seed of Abraham, his servant; the sons of Jacob, his chosen man.

7   He *is* our Lord God; his dooms (or his judgements) *be* in (or for) all the earth.

8   He was mindful of his testament into the world (or He remembered his covenant forever); of the word which he commanded into a thousand generations.

9   Which he disposed to (or made with) Abraham; and of his oath to Isaac.

10   And he ordained it to Jacob into (or for) a commandment; and to Israel into (or for an) everlasting testament.

11   And he said, I shall give to thee the land of Canaan; the cord of your heritage (or your inheritance, or possession).

12   When they were in a little number (or were little in number); and the comelings (or the newcomers) of them were full few.

13   And they passed from folk into folk (or from nation to nation);

311

and from a realm (or one kingdom) into another people.

14   He left not a man to annoy (or harm) them; and he chastised kings for them.

15   (Saying), Do not ye touch my christs (or my anointed ones); and do not ye do wickedly among my prophets.

16   And *God* called (for) hunger on the earth; and he wasted all the steadfastness of bread.

17   He sent a man before them; Joseph was sold into a servant (or as a slave).

18   They made low his feet in fetters, iron passed by his soul (or an iron collar around his neck);

19   till the word of him came. The speech of the Lord enflamed him;

20   (then) the king sent and unbound him; the prince of the peoples *sent* (*word*) and delivered him.

21   He ordained him the lord of his house; and the prince of all his possessions.

22   That he should learn his princes as himself, (or And that he should teach his leaders, *or officials*, as he desired); and that he should teach his old men prudence.

23   And Israel entered into Egypt; and Jacob was a comeling (or a newcomer) in the land of Ham.

24   And *God* increased his people greatly; and made them steadfast on (or stronger than) his enemies.

25   (And then) he turned the hearts of them, (so) that they hated his people; and did guile against (or dealt deceitfully with) his servants.

26   He sent Moses, his servant; and that Aaron, whom he chose.

27   He put in them (to tell and to do) the words of his miracles; and of his great wonders in the land of Ham.

28   He sent darknesses, and made (it) dark; and he made not

bitter his words.

29   He turned the waters of them into blood; and he killed the fishes of them.

30   And the land of them gave paddocks (or brought forth frogs); (even) in the privy places of the kings of them.

31   *God* said, and a flesh fly came; and gnats in all the coasts of them.

32   He put their rains (into) hail; (and) fire burning in the land of them.

33   And he smote the vines of them, and the fig trees of them; and all-brake the trees of the coasts of them.

34   He said, and the locusts came; and a bruchus of which (there) was no number (or innumerable bruchi).

35   And it ate all the hay (or all the plants) in the land of them; and it ate all the fruit of the land of them.

36   And he killed each the first engendered (or begotten) thing in the land of them; the first fruits of all the travail (or labour) of them.

37   And he led out them with silver and gold; and none was sick (or weak) in the lineages (or the tribes) of them.

38   Egypt was glad in the going out of them (or that they had left); for the dread (or fear) of them lay on the Egyptians.

39   He spreaded abroad a cloud, into the covering of them (or for their covering); and a fire, (so) that it shined to them by night.

40   They asked (for food), and a curlew came; and he fulfilled them with the bread of heaven (or with manna).

41   He brake the stone, and waters flowed; floods (or rivers) went forth in the dry place.

42   For he was mindful of his holy word (or solemn promise); which he had (said) to Abraham, his servant.

43   And (so) he led out his people in full out joying; and his chosen men in gladness.

DAY 23

44   And he gave to them the countries of the heathen men; and they had in possession the travails (or labours) of (other) peoples.

45   (So) that they keep his justifyings (or statutes); and keep (or obey) his law.

PSALM 106

1   *Alleluia.* Acknowledge ye to (or Praise) the Lord, for *he is* good; for his mercy *is* without end (or his love *is* forever).

2   Who shall speak (of) the powers of the Lord; (who) shall make known all his praisings (or the praises that he is due)?

3   Blessed *be* they that keep doom (or obey judgement, or act justly); and do rightwiseness in (or at) all times.

4   Lord, have thou mind on (or remember) us, in the good pleasance of thy people; visit thou us in thine health (or thy salvation).

5   To see in the goodness of thy chosen men, to be glad in the gladness of thy folk; (so) that thou be praised with (or by) thine heritage (or thy inheritance).

6   We have sinned with (or like) our fathers; we (all) have done unjustly, we (all) have done wickedness.

7   Our fathers in Egypt understood not thy marvels; they were not mindful of (or did not remember) the multitude of thy mercy. And they going into the sea, into the Red Sea (or the Sea of Reeds), stirred (him) to wrath;

8   and he saved them for his name, (so) that he should make known his power.

9   And he parted the Red Sea, and it was dried (up); and he led forth them in the depths of waters, as in the desert.

10   And he saved them from the hand of haters; and he again-bought them from the hand (or the power) of the enemy.

314

11   And the waters covered men troubling them; one of them abode not.

12   And they believed to his words; and they praised (or sang) the praising of him.

13   (But) they had soon done, (that) they forgat his works; and they abided not (or did not wait for) his counsel.

14   And they coveted covetousness in the desert (or were utterly insatiable in the wilderness); and tempted God in a place without water.

15   And he gave to them the asking of them; and he sent fullness into the souls of them, (or leanness, *or sickness*, into their bodies).

16   And they wrathed (against) Moses in the castles (or in their tents); (and against) Aaron, the holy (man) of the Lord.

17   The earth was opened, and swallowed down Dathan; and covered on (or up) the congregation of Abiram.

18   And fire burnt on high in the synagogue (or the congregation, or assembly) of them; the flames burnt (up) the sinners.

19   And they made a calf in Horeb; and worshipped a molten image.

20   And they (ex)changed their glory; into (or·for) the likeness of a calf eating hay.

21   They forgat God, that saved them, that did great works in Egypt,

22   marvels in the land of Ham; fearedful things in the Red Sea.

23   And *God* said, that he would lose (or destroy) them; (and he would have), if Moses, his chosen man, had not stood in the breaking of his sight. (So) that he should turn away his wrath; lest he lost (or destroyed) them.

24   And they had (or valued) the desirable land for nought (or as nothing), (for) they believed not to his word,

25   and they grumbled in their tabernacles (or tents); (and) they

heard not the voice of the Lord.

26   And he raised (up) his hand upon them; to cast down them in the desert.

27   And to cast away their seed in(to) the nations; and to lose (or destroy) them in the countries.

28   And they made sacrifice to Baal-peor; and they ate the sacrifices of dead beasts (or offered to dead gods).

29   And they wrathed *God* in (or with) their findings (or deeds); and falling, *either death*, was multiplied in them.

30   And Phinehas stood, and pleased *God*; and the vengeance ceased.

31   And it was areckoned to him to rightwiseness; in generation and into generation (or for all generations), till into without end.

32   And they wrathed *God* at the waters of against-saying (or Meribah); and Moses was travailed for them, *that is, troubled in soul,*

33   for they made (so) bitter his spirit, and he parted in his lips (or so that he spoke rashly with his lips).

34   They lost not (or did not destroy) the heathen men; which the Lord said to them (to do).

35   And they were meddled or mingled together (or mixed in) among the heathen men, and learned the works (or all the ways) of them;

36   and served the graven images (or the carved idols) of them; and it was made to them into a cause of stumbling.

37   And they offered (or sacrificed) their sons, and their daughters, to fiends.

38   And they shedded out innocent blood, the blood of their sons and of their daughters; which they sacrificed to the graven images (or carved idols) of Canaan. And the earth was slain in (or filled with) bloods,

39   and was defouled (or defiled) in the works of them; and they did fornication in their findings (or with their deeds).

40   And the Lord was wroth by strong vengeance against his people; and he had abomination of (or for) his heritage (or inheritance).

41   And he betook them into the hands of heathen men; and they that hated them, were the lords of them.

42   And their enemies did tribulation to (or troubled) them, and they were meeked under the hands of (their) enemies;

43   oft he delivered them. But they wrathed (or angered) him in their counsel; and they were made low in their wickednesses.

44   And he saw, when they were set in tribulation; and he heard the prayer of them (or their prayers).

45   And he was mindful of his testament; and it repented him by the multitude of his mercy. (And he remembered his covenant with them; and he relented because of his great love.)

46   And he gave them into mercies (or pity); in the sight of (or before) all the men, that had taken them (captive).

47   Our Lord God, make thou us safe (or save us); and gather together us from the nations. That we acknowledge to (or So that we can praise) thine holy name; and have glory in thy praising.

48   Blessed be the Lord God of Israel from the world and till into the world (or forever); and all the people shall say, Be it done, be it done (or Amen, amen).

PROVERBS CHAPTER 23

1   When thou sittest to eat with the prince, perceive thou diligently what things be set before thy face,

2   and set thou a coulter (or a knife) in thy throat (or guard what thou sayest). If nevertheless thou hast power on (or over) thy soul,

3   desire thou not of his meats, in whom is the bread of lying.

4   Do not thou travail (or labour) to be made rich, but set thou a measure to thy prudence.

5   Raise not thine eyes unto riches, which thou mayest not have; for they shall make to themselves pens (or wings), as of an eagle, and they shall fly into the heavens.

6   Eat thou not with an envious man, and desire thou not his meats (or food);

7   for at the likeness of a false diviner, and of a conjecturer, *that is, an expounder of dreams,* he guesseth that, that he knoweth not. He shall say to thee, Eat thou and drink; and his soul is not with thee.

8   Thou shalt spew out the meat, which thou hast eaten; and thou shalt lose thy fair words (or compliments).

9   Speak thou not in the ears of unwise men; for they shall despise the teaching of thy speech.

10   Touch thou not the terms (or the boundary stones of the property) of little children; and enter thou not into the field of fatherless and motherless children.

11   For the neighbour of them is strong, and he shall deem (or judge) their cause against thee.

12   (Let) thine heart enter to teaching, and thine ears to the words of knowing (or of knowledge).

13   Do not thou withdraw chastising or discipline from a child; for though thou smitest him with a rod, he shall not die.

14   Thou shalt smite him with a rod, and thou shalt deliver his soul from hell.

15   My son, if thy soul is wise, mine heart shall have joy with thee;

16   and my reins shall make full out joy, when thy lips speak rightful things.

17   (Let) thine heart pursue (or follow) not sinners; but be thou in the dread (or the fear) of (or reverence for) the Lord all day (long).

18   For thou shalt have hope at the last, and thine abiding shall not be done away.

19   My son, hear thou, and be wise, and address thy soul in the way (or direct thy soul to the right way).

20   Do not thou be in the feasts of drinkers, neither in the oft eatings of them, that bring together fleshes (or meat) to eat.

21   For men giving attention to drinks, and giving morsels together, shall be wasted, and napping shall be clothed with clothes rent (or torn).

22   Hear thy father, that begat thee; and despise not thy mother, when she is old.

23   Buy thou truth, and do not thou sell (off) wisdom, and doctrine, and understanding.

24   The father of the rightwise joyeth full out with joy; he that begat a wise man, shall be glad in him.

25   Thy father and thy mother have joy, and he that begat thee, make full out joy.

26   My son, give thine heart to me, and thine eyes keep my ways.

27   For a whore is a deep ditch, and an alien (or foreign, or unfamiliar) *woman*, is a strait pit.

28   She setteth ambush in (or on) the way, as a thief; and shall add despisers in men, *that is, (she) shall multiply the despisers of God among men.*

29   To whom *is* woe? to whose father *is* woe? to whom *be* chidings? to whom *be* ditches? to whom *be* wounds without cause? to whom *is* putting out of eyes?

30   Whether not to them, that dwell in wine, and study to drink up all of the cups?

31   Behold thou not the wine, when it sparkleth, when the colour

thereof shineth in a glass cup. It entereth sweetly,

32   but at the last it shall bite as an adder, and as a cockatrice it shall shed abroad venoms.

33   Thine eyes shall see strange (or unfamiliar) women, and thy heart shall speak wayward things.

34   And thou shalt be as a man sleeping in the midst of the sea, and as a governor asleeped, when the steer(ing), *either the instrument of governance*, is lost.

35   And thou shalt say, They beat me, but I had not sorrow; they drew me, and I feeled not; when shall I wake out, and I shall find wines again?

ECCLESIASTICUS CHAPTER 33

1   Evils shall not come to him that dreadeth God; but God shall keep (or shall guard) him in temptation, and shall deliver him from evils.

2   A wise man hateth not the commandments, and rightfulnesses or rightwisenesses; and he shall not be hurtled down, as in the tempest of a ship (or as a ship in a tempest).

3   A wise man believeth in the law of God, and the law *is* faithful to him.

4   He that maketh open asking, shall make ready or shall prepare a word; and so he shall pray, and shall be heard, and he shall keep (or obey) the teaching, and then he shall answer.

5   The entrails of a fool *be* as a wheel of a cart, and his thoughts as an axle able to turn about.

6   An horse a stallion, so and a friend a scorner, neigheth under each (one) sitting above.

7   Why a day overcometh a day, and again the light *overcometh* light, and a year *overcometh* a year, (and) the sun *overcometh* the

sun?

8   They be parted or severed of (or separated by) the knowing (or the knowledge) of the Lord, by the sun made, and keeping the commandment of God.

9   And he shall change the times and the feast days of them, and in those *times the Jews* hallowed holy days or holidays, at an hour. God enhanced (or raised up) and magnified of those *holy days* or *holidays*; and of them he put into the number of days;

10   and *God made* all men (out) of firm earth, and (out) of nesh earth or soil, whereof Adam was formed.

11   In the multitude of the knowing (or the knowledge) of the Lord, he parted (or separated) them, and changed the ways of them.

12   (Some) of them *God* blessed, and enhanced (or exalted); and (some) of them he hallowed, and chose or presented to (or for) himself; (some) of them he cursed, and made low, and turned them (out) from the departing of them (or from their places).

13   As the clay of a potter *is* in the hand of him, to make or to form and dispose, (so) that all the ways thereof *be* after the ordinance of him or after his disposition; so a man *is* in the hand of him that made him; and he shall yield to him by his doom (or according to his judgement).

14   Against evil is good, and against life *is* death; so and a sinner *is* against the rightwise.

15   And so behold thou into all the works of the Highest; two things against twain, and one thing against one, or two against two, one against one.

16   And I the last waked, and as he that gathereth the dregs of grapes, after the gatherers of grapes. And I hoped (or trusted) in the blessing of God; and as he that gathereth grapes, I filled the presser or the (wine)press.

17   Behold ye, for I travailed (or laboured) not for me alone, but

for all that seek knowing (or knowledge).

18   Great men, and all the peoples hear ye me; and ye governors of the church (or the congregation), perceive with ears (or listen).

19   Give thou not power over thee in thy life to a son, and to a woman or a wife, to a brother, and to a friend; and give thou not thy possessions to another man, lest peradventure it repent thee, and thou beseech for them (back again).

20   While thou art alive, *or livest*, and breathest yet, each man shall not change thee.

21   For it is better, that thy sons pray (or beseech) thee, than that thou behold into the hands of (or request from) thy sons.

22   In all thy works be thou the sovereign (or the ruler); give thou not a wem into (or a blemish onto) thy glory.

23   In the day of the ending of the days of thy life, and in the time of thy going out or thy death, part or deal (out) thine heritage (or thy inheritance).

24   Meats (or Food), and a rod, and a burden to (or for) an ass; bread, and chastising or discipline, and work to (or for) a servant.

25   He worketh in, *or under*, chastising, and seeketh to have rest; slack thou (thine) hands unto him, and he seeketh freedom.

26   A yoke and bridle bow down an hard neck; and busy workings bow down a servant. Torment and stocks to (or for) an evil-willed servant;

27   send thou him into working, lest he be idle; for why idleness hath taught much malice.

28   Ordain thou or Set him in work, for so it becometh him; (so) that if he obeyeth not, bow thou down him in stocks,

29   and make thou not *him* large over any man, *that is, give thou not to him power over any man*, but without doom (or good judgement), do thou nothing grievous or heavy.

30   If a faithful servant is to thee, be he as thy soul or thy life to

thee; treat thou him so as a brother, for thou hast bought him in (or with) the blood of life.

31   If thou hurtest him unjustly, he shall be turned into fleeing away or into flight; and if he enhancing (or rising up) goeth away, thou knowest not whom thou shalt seek, and in what way thou shalt seek him.

WISDOM OF SOLOMON   CHAPTER 11

1   He or It addressed (or directed) the works of them, in the hands of the holy prophet.

2   They made journey by the deserts, that were not inhabited; and they made little houses, *or cottages*, in the desert places.

3   They stood against (their) enemies, and avenged them(selves) of (or upon their) enemies.

4   They thirsted, and they inwardly called thee; and water (out) of (or from) a full high stone was given to them, and the rest of thirst *was given to them* (out) of (or from) an hard stone.

5   For by which things the enemies of them suffered pains, for the defaulting of their drink, and the sons of Israel were glad, when they had plenty; by these things, when these failed to those *enemies*, it was done well with them.

6   For soothly for the well of everlasting flood, thou gavest man's blood to unjust men.

7   And when they were made less or diminished, in the leading away of young children slain, thou gavest suddenly plenteous water to them, or thou gave to them abounding water in manner not hoped (for);

8   and showedest by the thirst, that was then, how thou wouldest enhance (or raise up) thy *servants*, and wouldest slay the adversaries of them.

9   For when they were assayed, soothly they took chastising or discipline with mercy; they knew, how wicked or unpious men deemed with wrath, should suffer torments.

10   Soothly thou admonishing as a father, provedest these men; but thou as an hard king asking condemnedest them (or the others).

11   For why men absent and *men* present were tormented in like manner.

12   For why double annoyance (or troubles) had taken them, and wailing with the mind (or the remembrance) of things passed.

13   Soothly when they heard, that it was done well with themselves by their torments, they bethought on the Lord, and wondered on the end of the out-going.

14   For at the end of the befalling, they worshipped (or honoured) him, whom they scorned (had) cast out in shrewd (or depraved) putting forth; and thou didest not in like manner to just men.

15   Forsooth for unwise thoughts the wickednesses of them *were punished*; for some men erring worshipped dumb serpents or adders (or snakes), and superfluous beasts, thou sentest into them a multitude of dumb beasts, into vengeance;

16   (so) that they should know, that by what things a man sinneth, by those things also he shall be tormented.

17   For why thine almighty hand, that made the world of matter unseen, was not unmighty to send into them a multitude of bears, or hardy lions,

18   or of a new kind of unknown beasts, and full of wrath, or spitting breathings of fires, or bringing forth the smell or odour of smoke, or sending out hideous sparkles or grizzly sparks from the eyes;

19   of which *beasts* not only the hurting might destroy them, but also the sight or the looking might slay by dread (or out of fear).

20   For why and without these *beasts* they might be slain by one

spirit, and suffer persecution of those (or by them for) their own deeds, and be scattered by the spirit of thy virtue (or by the breath of thy power). But also thou hast disposed all things in measure, and in number, and in weight;

21   for it was left ever to thee alone to be able to do much; and who shall against-stand the virtue (or the power) of thine arm?

22   For as the tongue (or a pointer) of a balance, so is the world before thee; and as a drop of dew rising before the light, or as a drop of morrowtide dew, that cometh down into (or onto) the earth.

23   And thou hast mercy of (or for) all things (or for all), for thou mayest (or thou can do) all things; and thou dissemblest, *either forbearest*, the sins of men, for penance (or repentance).

24   For thou lovest all things that be, and thou hatest nothing of them, that thou madest; for thou not hating anything ordainedest, either madest.

25   But how might anything dwell, or but if thou wouldest (it)? (or if thou haddest not willed or desirest it?) either how should *a thing* be kept, that were not called of (or by) thee?

26   But, Lord, thou lovest (all) souls, thou sparest all things; for those things be thine. Δ

DAY 24

PSALM 107

1 *Alleluia.* Acknowledge ye (or Give thanks) to the Lord, for *he is* good; for his mercy *is* into the world (or forever).

2 Say they, that be again-bought (or redeemed) by the Lord; which he again-bought from the hand of the enemy,

3 from all the countries he gathered them together. From the rising of the sun, and from the going down; from the north, and from the sea.

4 They erred (or wandered) in the wilderness, in a place without water; they found not a way to the city for a dwelling place.

5 They *were* hungry and thirsty; their souls failed in them.

6 And they cried to the Lord, when they were set in tribulation; and he delivered them from their needinesses.

7 And he led forth them by the right way; so that they should go into the city of their dwelling.

8 For the mercies of the Lord, acknowledge to (or praise) him; and for his marvels *acknowledge* to (*or praise*) him the sons of men.

9 For he fulfilled a void man; and he filled with goods (or good things) an hungry man.

10 *God delivered* men sitting in darkness, and in the shadow of death; and men imprisoned in beggary, and in iron.

11 For they (were) made bitter (or rebelled against) the speeches of God; and wrathed the counsel of the Highest.

12 And the heart of them was made meek in travails (or by hard labour); and they were sick (or weak), and none was that helped them.

13 And they cried to the Lord, when they were set in tribulation; and he delivered them from their needinesses.

14   And he led them out of darknesses, and the shadow of death; and brake the bonds of them.

15   For the mercies of the Lord, acknowledge to (or praise) him; and for his marvels, *acknowledge* to (*or praise*) him the sons of men.

16   For he all-brake the brazen (or the bronze) gates; and he brake the iron bars.

17   He up-took them from the way of their wickedness; for they were made low for their unrightfulnesses or unrightwisenesses.

18   The soul of them loathed all meat (or they hated all kinds of food); and they nighed unto the gates of death.

19   And they cried to the Lord, when they were set in tribulation; and he delivered them from their needinesses.

20   He sent his word, and healed them; and delivered them from the perishings of them (or he saved them from death).

21   For the mercies of the Lord, acknowledge to (or praise) him; and for his marvels praise him the sons of men.

22   And offer they the sacrifice of praising; and tell they about his works with full out joying (or rejoicing).

23   They that go down into the sea in ships; and make working (or ply their trade) in many waters.

24   They saw the works of the Lord; and his marvels in the depth of the sea.

25   He said, and the spirit (or the wind) of the tempest stood still; and the waves thereof were areared (or lifted up).

26   They ascend or go up (or be lifted up) till to the heavens, and (then) go down unto the depths; the soul of them failed in evils.

27   They were troubled, and they were moved as a drunken man; and all the wisdom of them was devoured.

28   And they cried to the Lord, when they were set in tribulation; and he led them out of their needinesses.

29   And he ordained the tempest thereof into a soft wind, *either*

peaceability; and the waves thereof were still(ed).

30 And they were glad, for they were still; and he led them forth into the haven of their will (or a safe harbour).

31 (For) the mercies of the Lord, acknowledge (or give thanks) to him; and (for) his marvels to (or for) the sons of men.

32 And enhance they (or exalt) him in the church (or the congregation) of the people; and praise they him in the chairs of the elder men (or in the council of the elders).

33 He hath set floods (or turned rivers) into desert; and the outgoings of waters (or springs) into thirst(y) (ground).

34 *He hath set* fruitful land into saltiness (or wasteland); for (or because of) the malice of men dwelling therein.

35 He hath set the desert into ponds of waters; and the earth without water into the outgoings of waters (or springs).

36 And he set (or put) there hungry men; and they made a city of dwelling.

37 And they sowed fields, and planted vines; and (they) made fruit of birth (or a bountiful harvest).

38 And he blessed them, and they were multiplied greatly; and he made not less their work beasts.

39 And they were made few; and were travailed of tribulation (or troubled with trials) of evils and of sorrow.

40 Strife was poured out on princes (or their leaders); and he made them for to err without the way, and not in the way.

41 And he helped the poor man from (or out of) poverty; and put families as a sheep *bringing forth lambs.*

42 Rightful men shall see, and shall be glad; and all wickedness shall stop his mouth (or and the wicked shall close their mouths).

43 Who *is* wise, and shall keep these things; and shall understand the mercies of the Lord? (or and then they shall comprehend the Lord's constant love.)

D A Y 2 4

P S A L M 1 0 8

1   *The song of the psalm of David.* Mine heart is ready, God, mine heart is ready; I shall sing, and I shall say a psalm (or sing a song) in my glory.

2   My glory, rise thou up, psaltery (or lyre) and harp, rise thou up; I shall rise up early (in the morning).

3   Lord, I shall acknowledge to (or praise) thee among the peoples; and I shall say (or sing) a psalm to thee among the nations.

4   For why, God, thy mercy *is* great on (or reacheth above) the heavens; and thy truth *is* unto the clouds.

5   God, be thou enhanced (or exalted) above the heavens; and thy glory over all the earth.

6   (So) that thy darlings (or beloved) be delivered, make thou safe (or save us) with thy right hand, and hear (or answer) thou me;

7   God spake in his holy (place). I shall make full out joy, and I shall part Shechem; and I shall mete (or measure) the great valley of tabernacles.

8   Gilead is mine, and Manasseh is mine; and Ephraim *is* the up-taking (or the helmet) of mine head. Judah *is* my king;

9   Moab *is* the cauldron of mine hope. Into Idumea I shall stretch forth my shoe; aliens (or foreigners) be made friends to me.

10   Who shall lead me forth into a strong city; who shall lead me forth till into Idumea (or unto Edom)?

11   Whether not thou, God, that hast put us away (or rejected us); and, God, shalt thou not go out in our virtues (or with our hosts)?

12   Give thou help to us (out) of (our) tribulation; for the help of man is vain (or empty and futile).

13   We shall make virtue in God (or gain victory through God);

and he shall bring our enemies to nought (or unto nothing).

PROVERBS CHAPTER 24

1 Follow thou not evil men, desire thou not to be with them.

2 For the soul of them bethinketh (on) ravens (or robberies), and their lips speak frauds.

3 An house shall be builded by wisdom, and *it* shall be made strong by prudence (or by understanding).

4 The cellars shall be filled in teaching, *with* all riches precious and full fair.

5 A wise man is strong, and a learned man is stalworthy and mighty.

6 For why battle is begun with ordinance; and health (or victory) shall be, where many counsels be.

7 Wisdom *is* high to a fool; in the gate he shall not open his mouth.

8 He that thinketh to do evils, shall be called a fool.

9 The thought of a fool is a sin; and a backbiter *is* (an) abomination of (or to) men.

10 If thou hast slid, despairest (thou) in the day of anguish, (for) thy strength shall be made less.

11 Deliver thou them, that be led to death; and cease thou not to deliver them, that be drawn to death.

12 If thou sayest, Strengths (or Strongholds) suffice not; he that is the beholder of the heart, understandeth, and nothing deceiveth the keeper of thy soul, and he shall yield to a man after his works.

13 My son, eat thou honey, for *it is* good; and the honeycomb *for it is* full sweet to thy throat.

14 So and the teaching of wisdom *is good* to (or for) thy soul; and when thou hast found it, thou shalt have hope in the last

things, and thine hope shall not perish.

15 Ambush thou not, and seek not (to bring) wickedness in(to) the house of the rightwise, neither waste thou, his rest(ing) (place).

16 For the rightwise man shall fall seven times *in the day*, and shall rise again; but wicked men shall fall into evil.

17 When thine enemy falleth, have thou not joy; and thine heart have not full out joying in his falling;

18 lest peradventure the Lord see, and it displease him, and he take away his wrath from him.

19 Strive thou not with the worst men, neither follow thou wicked men.

20 For why evil men have not hope of things to come, and the lantern of wicked men shall be quenched.

21 My son, dread thou (or fear, or revere) God, and the king; and be thou not meddled or mingled (or mixed in) with backbiters.

22 For their perdition shall rise altogether suddenly, and who knoweth the fall of ever either?

23 Also these things *that follow* be to wise men. It is not good to know a person in doom (or whom thou is judging).

24 The peoples shall curse them that say to a wicked man, Thou art just or rightwise; and the lineages (or the tribes) shall hold them (as) abominable.

25 They that reprove *justly sinners*, shall be praised; and blessing shall come upon them.

26 He that answereth (with) rightful words, shall kiss lips.

27 Make ready thy work withoutforth, and work thy field diligently, (so) that thou build thine house afterward.

28 Be thou not a witness without reasonable cause against thy neighbour; neither flatter thou any man with thy lips.

29 Say thou not, As he did to me, so I shall do to him, and I shall yield to each man after his works.

30 I passed by the field of a slow man, and by the vinery (or the vineyard) of a fond or foolish man;

31 and lo! nettles had filled all (the places), thorns had covered the higher part thereof, and the wall of stones without mortar was destroyed.

32 And when I had seen this thing, I put (it) in mine heart, and by ensample, I learned the teaching.

33 How long sleepest thou, slow man? when shalt thou rise from sleep? Soothly thou shalt sleep a little, thou shalt nap a little, thou shalt join together the hands a little, to take rest;

34 and *then* thy neediness as a courier shall come to thee, and thy beggary as an armed man.

ECCLESIASTICUS CHAPTER 34

1 Vain hope and a leasing (or a lie), to an unwise man; and dreams enhance (or lift up) unprudent men.

2 As he that taketh or catcheth (at) a shadow, and pursueth wind, so and he that taketh heed to leasings (or lies) seen, (that is, to vain dreams).

3 After this thing *is* the sight of dreams; before the face of a man *is* the likeness of another man (or one thing resembles another).

4 What shall be cleansed of him that is unclean or of the unclean, what shall be cleansed, and what true thing shall be said of a liar?

5 False divining of error, and false divinings by chittering (or chattering, or twittering) of birds, and dreams of witches, (all) is vanity (or empty and futile). And as *the heart* of a woman travailing of or bearing a child, thine heart suffereth fantasies;

6 no but (or unless) the visitation is sent out of (or from) the Highest, give thou not thine heart in (or to) those *dreams.*

7   For why dreams have made many men for to err, and men hoping (or trusting) in them fell down or fell away.

8   The word of the law *of God and of his prophets*, shall be made perfect without leasing (or without lies); and wisdom in the mouth of a faithful man shall be made plain.

9   What knoweth he, that is not assayed? A man assayed in many things, shall think many things; and he that learned many things, shall tell out understanding.

10   He that is not assayed or is not expert (or experienced), knoweth few things; forsooth he that is a fool in many things, shall multiply malice.

11   What manner things know he, that is not assayed? He that is not planted, *that is, hath not set root of* (or in) *understanding, and desire in* (or for) *good*, shall be plenteous in wickedness or shall abound (in) shrewdness (or in depravity). I saw many things in telling out, and full many customs of words.

12   Sometime I was in peril unto death, for the cause of these things; and I was delivered by the grace of God.

13   The spirit of them that dread God is sought, and shall be blessed in the beholding of him. For why the hope of them *is* into *God* saving them; and the eyes of the Lord *be* into (or upon) them, that love him.

14   He that dreadeth (or revereth) God, shall not tremble or quake for anything, and he shall not dread; for why *God* is his hope.

15   The soul of him that dreadeth the Lord, is blessed. To whom beholdeth he, and who is his strength?

16   The eyes of the Lord *be* on them that dread him. *God is* a defender of might, a steadfastness or a firmament of virtue (or strength), a covering of (or from) the heat, and a shadowing place of (or at) midday; beseeching of offending, *that is, hearing beseeching for offenses*, and a help of (or from) falling,

17   enhancing (or lifting up) the soul, and lightening the eyes, and giving health, and life, and blessing.

18   The offering of him that offereth of wicked thing, *that is, of a thing gotten unjustly*, is defouled (or defiled); and the scornings of unjust men be not well pleasant or well-pleasing.

19   The Lord alone *is* to them that abide him in the way of truth, and of rightfulness or rightwiseness. The Highest approveth not (of) the gifts of wicked men, neither beholdeth in (or on) the offerings of wicked men, neither in (or for) the multitude of their sacrifices he shall do or have mercy to (or for their) sins.

20   He that offereth sacrifice of the chattel or substance of poor men, *is* as he that slayeth the son in the sight of his father.

21   The bread of needy men is the life of a poor man; he that defraudeth him, is a man of blood (or a blood-shedder).

22   He that taketh away bread (earned) in (or with) sweat, *is* as he that slayeth his neighbour. He that sheddeth out blood, and he that doeth fraud to an hired man, be brethren.

23   One building, and one destroying; what profiteth it to them, no but travail (except their labour)?

24   One praying, and one cursing; whose voice shall the Lord hear?

25   What profiteth the washing of him, that is washed for a dead body, and toucheth again a dead body?

26   So a man that fasteth in his sins, and again doing the same sins, what profiteth he in meeking himself? who shall hear his prayer?

ECCLESIASTICUS CHAPTER 35

1   He that keepeth the word *of God*, multiplieth prayer. Wholesome sacrifice is to take heed to (or of) the commandments, and to depart or go away from all wickedness. And to offer the pleasing of

sacrifice for unrightfulnesses or unrightwisenesses, and beseeching for sins, *is* to go away from unrightfulness or unrightwiseness.

2	He that offereth purest flour of wheat, shall yield grace, *that is, shall give a pleasant (or a pleasing) service to God*; and he that doeth mercy, offereth a sacrifice.

3	It is well pleasant or well-pleasing to the Lord, to go away from wickedness; and prayer *is* to go away from unrightwiseness.

4	Thou shalt not appear void (or empty) before the sight of God;

5	for why all these things be done for the behests (or for the commands, or the commandments) of God.

6	The offering of the rightwise maketh fat the altar, and is the odour of sweetness in the sight of (or before) the Highest.

7	The sacrifice of a just man or the rightwise is acceptable, and the Lord shall not forget the mind (or the memory) of him.

8	With good will yield thou glory to God, and make thou not less the first fruits of thine hands.

9	In each gift or In all gifts make glad thy cheer (or thy face), and in full out joying hallow thy tithes.

10	Give thou to the Highest after his free gift, *that is, after the quantity of thy goods (or good things), which thou hast of (or from) God*; and with good eye make thou the findings of thine hands, *that is, with rightful intent, ordain thy good works, to the praising of God and not of man.*

11	For why the Lord is a yielder, and he shall yield sevenfold as much to thee.

12	Do not thou offer shrewd (or depraved) gifts; for he shall not receive them. And do not thou behold (or trust in) an unrightwise sacrifice; for the Lord is judge, and glory, *or taking*, (or favouring) of persons is not with him.

13	The Lord shall not take a person against a poor man (or favour some person over a poor person); and he shall hear the prayer of him that is hurt (or oppressed).

14   He shall not despise the prayers of a fatherless child, neither a widow, if she poured out the speech of wailing.

15   Whether the tears of a widow go not down to the cheek, and the crying of her on (or against) him that leadeth forth those *tears*? For why they ascend or go up from the cheek unto heaven, and the Lord hearing shall not delight in them.

16   He that worshippeth God in delighting, shall be received; and his prayer shall nigh unto the clouds.

17   The prayer of him that meeketh (or humbleth) himself shall pierce the clouds, and till it nigheth (or approacheth), he shall not be comforted, and he shall not go away, till the Highest behold (him). And the Lord shall not be far or long away, but he shall judge just or rightwise men, and shall make doom (or judgement);

18   and the Strongest shall not have patience in (or towards) them, that (or till) he trouble the backs of them. And he shall yield vengeance to the folks or the Gentiles, till he take away the fullness or the plenty of (or from) proud men, and trouble altogether the sceptres of wicked men;

19   till he yield to men after their deeds, and after the works of Adam[1], and after the presumption of him; till he deem the doom (or judgement) of his people, and shall delight just or rightwise men in his mercy.

20   The mercy of God *is* fair in the time of tribulation, as clouds of rain in the time of dryness or of drought.

WISDOM OF SOLOMON   CHAPTER 12

1   Lord, how good, and how sweet is thy Spirit in all things;

---

[1] *By (or For) Hebrews, this word 'Adam' signifieth man commonly.*

2   and therefore thou chastisest by parts these men that err; and
thou admonishest or warnest of which things they sin, and thou
speakest *to them*, so that when they have forsaken their malice,
they believe in thee, Lord.

3   For *thou wouldest lose (or destroy)* those old dwellers of thine
holy land, which thou loathest;

4   for they did works hateful to thee, by medicines, *that is, by*
witchcrafts, and false divinings, and sacrifices offered to fiends,
and unrightwise sacrifices;

5   and the slayers of their sons, without mercy, and the eaters of
the entrails or the bowels of men, and the devourers of blood;

6   and by the hands of our fathers thou wouldest lose (or
destroy) from thy middle sacrament, *that is, from Judea*, fathers and
mothers, authors of souls, *that is, of their children*, unhelped;

7   (so) that our fathers should take the worthy pilgrimage of
God's children, which is to thee the dearworthiest land of all.

8   But also thou sparedest these as men, and thou sentest wasps,
the before-goers of thine host, (so) that they should destroy them
(by) little and little.

9   Not for thou were unmighty to make wicked men subject to
rightwise men in battle, either to destroy at once, by cruel beasts,
either by an hard word;

10   but thou deemedest (or judgest) by parts, and gavest place to
penance, and knewest, that the nation of them was wayward or
shrewd (or depraved), and their malice *was* kindly (or by kind),
that is, made hard by long custom, and that their thought might
not be changed into without end or forevermore.

11   For it was a cursed seed at or from the beginning. And thou
not dreading any man, gavest forgiveness to the sins of them.

12   For why who shall say to thee, What hast thou done? or who
shall stand against thy doom (or thy judgment)? or who shall come

in thy sight, *to be* the avenger of wicked men? either who shall areckon to thee, if the nations perish, which thou madest?

13 Forsooth there is none other God than thou, to whom is care of all things, (so) that thou show, that thou deemest doom (or judgest judgement, or justice) not unjustly.

14 Neither king neither tyrant in thy sight (or before thee) shall inquire (or be able to defend any) of these men, which thou hast destroyed.

15 Therefore since thou art just or rightwise, thou disposest justly or rightwisely all things; also Father, thou condemnest him, that ought not to be punished[2], and thou guessest him a stranger from thy virtue (or thy power).

16 For why thy virtue (or thy power) is the beginning of rightwiseness; and for this (or because of this), that thou art lord (or the Lord) of all men, thou (or it) makest thee to spare all men.

17 For thou, that art not believed to be perfect or full ended in virtue (or in strength), thou showest virtue (or thy strength); and thou leadest over these men, that know not thee, in hardiness (or with boldness).

18 But thou, lord of virtue (or of power), deemest (or judgest) with peaceableness, and disposest us with great reverence; for it is subject to thee to be able to, when thou wilt.

19 Forsooth thou hast taught thy people by such works, that it behooveth *a judge* to be just, and benign, *either merciful*; and thou madest thy sons (to be) of good hope, for thou deemest, and givest place to (or for) penance in (or repentance for) sins.

20 For if thou tormentedest the enemies of thy servants, and men due to death with so great perceiving, *either attentiveness*, and deliveredest, giving time and place, by which they might be

---

2 *That is, punishest sometime, to (or for the) proving of his patience, (as) it is open(ly) (seen) of saint Job.*

changed from malice;

21 with how great diligence deemest thou (or judgest) thy sons, to whose fathers thou gavest oaths and covenants of good promises?

22 Therefore when thou givest chastising or discipline to us, thou beatest or thou scourgest manyfold our enemies, (so) that we, (when) deeming (or judging), think (of) thy goodness; and when it is deemed of us, that we hope (for) thy mercy.

23 Wherefore and to them, that lived unwisely, and unjustly or unrightfully in their life, thou gavest sovereign torments, by those things which they worshipped.

24 For they erred full long in the way of error, and guessed *to be* gods those things that be superfluous in beasts, and lived by custom or manner of unwise young children.

25 For this thing thou gavest doom (or judgement), into scorn, as to unwise children;

26 but they, that were not amended by scornings or reproofs and blamings, feeled the worthy doom (or judgement) of God.

27 For they bare heavily in these things, which they suffered, in which things they suffering had indignation; they seeing him, whom they denied sometime them to know, knew *him* as the very (or the true) God, by these things which they guessed to be gods among them, when they were destroyed; for which thing and the end of their condemnation shall come upon them. Δ

DAY 25

PSALM 109

1 *To victory, the psalm of David.* God, hold thou not still (or remain not silent to) my praising;

2 for the mouth of the sinner, and the mouth of the guileful or treacherous (or deceitful) man, is opened upon me. They spake against me with a guileful (or lying) tongue,

3 and they encompassed me with words of hatred; and fought against me without cause (or for no reason).

4 For that thing that they should love me (for), they backbited me; but I prayed (for them).

5 And they setted against me evils for goods (or returned evil for good to me); and hatred for my love.

6 Ordain thou a sinner on (or over) him; and the devil stand on his right half.

7 When he is deemed (or judged), go he out condemned; and (let) his prayer be made into sin.

8 (Let) his days be made few; and another take his bishopric (or his office).

9 (Let) his sons be made fatherless; and his wife a widow.

10 (Let) his sons trembling be borne over (or be made vagrants), and beg; and be they cast out of their habitations.

11 An usurer seek (or take away) all his chattel or substance; and aliens ravish his travails (or foreigners, or strangers, snatch the fruits of his labour).

12 None helper be to him; neither any(one) be that have mercy on his motherless children.

13 His sons be made into perishing (or all die); (and) the name of him be done away in one generation.

14   (Let) the wickedness of his fathers come again into mind in the sight of the Lord; and the sin of his mother be not done away (or wiped out).

15   Be they made evermore against the Lord; and the mind (or the memory) of them perish from the earth.

16   For that thing that he thought not to do mercy, and he pursued a poor man and a beggar; and to slay a man compunct in heart (or broken-hearted).

17   And he loved cursing, and it shall come to him; and he would not (or did not delight in) a blessing, and it shall be made far from him.

18   And he clothed cursing as a cloth (or a cloak), and it entered as water into his inner things; and as oil in(to) his bones.

19   Be it made to him as a cloth (or a cloak), with which he is covered; and as a girdle, with which he is evermore girded.

20   This is the work (or the reward) of them that backbite me with the Lord; and that speak evils against my life.

21   And thou, Lord God, do with me for thy name; for thy mercy is sweet (or thy love is good). Deliver thou me,

22   for I am needy and poor; and mine heart is troubled within me.

23   I am taken (or fade) away as a shadow, when it boweth away; and I am shaken away as locusts (or a bug).

24   My knees be made feeble with fasting; and my flesh was changed for oil.

25   And I am made a shame to them; they saw me, and moved (or shook) their heads.

26   My Lord God, help thou me; make thou me safe by thy mercy (or save me by thy love).

27   And they shall know, that this is thine hand; and (that) thou, Lord, hast done it.

28   And they shall curse, and thou shalt bless, they that rise

against me, be shamed; but thy servant shall be glad.

29   They that backbite me, be clothed with shame; and be they covered with their shame, as with a double cloth.

30   I shall acknowledge to (or thank) the Lord greatly with my mouth; and I shall praise him in the middle of many men.

31   Which (or Who) stood nigh on the right half (or at the right hand) of a poor man; to make safe my soul from pursuers (or persecutors).

PSALM 110

1   *The psalm of David.* The Lord said to my Lord; Sit thou on my right side. Till I put (or make) thine enemies a stool of thy feet.

2   The Lord shall send out from Zion the rod of thy virtue (or thy strength); be thou lord in the midst of thine enemies.

3   The beginning *is* with thee in the day of thy virtue (or thy strength), in the brightnesses of the saints; I begat thee of (or from) the womb, before the day star.

4   The Lord swore, and it shall not repent him; Thou art a priest without end, by the order of Melchizedek.

5   The Lord on (or at) thy right side; hath broken kings in the day of his vengeance.

6   He shall deem (or judge) among the nations, he shall fill (the land with) fallings; he shall shake heads in the land of many men (or wound leaders in many lands).

7   He drank of (or from) the stream in (or on) the way; therefore he enhanced the head (or shall hold his head up high).

PSALM 111

1   *Alleluia.* Lord, I shall acknowledge to (or praise, or thank)

thee in (or with) all mine heart; in the council, and the congregation of just men.

2   The works of the Lord *be* great; sought out into all his wills (or by all who take delight in them).

3   His work *is* acknowledging and great doing; and his rightfulness or rightwiseness dwelleth into the world of world (or forever and ever).

4   The Lord, merciful in will, and a merciful doer, hath made a mind of (or is remembered for) his marvels;

5   he hath given meat (or food) to men dreading him. He shall be mindful of his testament into the world (or shall remember his covenant forever);

6   he shall tell (or show) to his people the strength of his works. That he give to them the heritage of folks (or the inheritance of the nations);

7   the works of his hands *be* truth and doom (or justice, or judgement). All his commandments *be* faithful,

8   confirmed into the world of world (or forever and ever); made in truth and equity.

9   The Lord sent redemption to his people; he commanded his testament (or covenant) without end. His name *is* holy and dreadful (or fearful);

10   the beginning of wisdom *is* the dread (or the fear) of (or reverence for) the Lord. Good understanding *is* to all that do it; his praising dwelleth into the world of world (or forever and ever).

PSALM 112

1   *Alleluia.* Blessed (or Happy) *is* the man that dreadeth the Lord; he shall delight full much in his commandments.

2   His seed (or His children) shall be mighty in the earth; the

generation of rightful (or upright) men shall be blessed.

3   Glory and riches *be* in his house; and his rightfulness or rightwiseness dwelleth into the world of world (or forever and ever).

4   Light is risen up in darknesses to rightful men; *the Lord* is merciful in will, and a merciful doer, and rightful or rightwise.

5   The man *is* merry, that doeth mercy, and lendeth; he disposeth his words in doom (or his deeds with justice);

6   for he shall not be moved without end (or nothing shall shake him). A just man shall be in everlasting mind (or remembered forever);

7   he shall not dread of an evil hearing (or fear to hear bad news). His heart *is* ready for to hope (or to trust) in the Lord;

8   his heart is confirmed, he shall not be moved, till he despise his enemies.

9   He spreaded abroad (much money), he gave to poor men; his rightwiseness dwelleth into the world of world (or forever and ever); his horn shall be raised (up) in glory.

10   A sinner shall see (it), and shall be wroth; he shall gnash with his teeth, and shall fail, *either shall wax (or grow) rotten*; the desire of sinners shall perish.

PROVERBS CHAPTER 25

1   Also these *be* the Parables of Solomon, which the men of Hezekiah, king of Judah, translated.

2   The glory of God is to cover a word; and the glory of kings *is* to seek out a word.

3   Heaven above, and the earth beneath, and the heart of kings *is* unsearchable.

4   Do thou away rust from silver, and a full clean vessel shall go

out.

5   Do thou away unpiety from the cheer (or the face) of the king, and his throne shall be made steadfast by rightfulness or rightwiseness.

6   Appear thou not glorious before the king, and stand thou not in the place of great men.

7   For it is better, that it be said to thee, Ascend thou or Go up hither, than that thou be made low before the prince.

8   Bring thou not forth soon those things in strife, which thine eyes saw; lest afterward thou mayest not amend, when thou hast made thy friend unhonest (or he hath shamed thee).

9   Treat thy cause with thy friend, and show thou not a private (matter) to a strange man;

10   lest peradventure he have joy of thy fall, when he hath heard (of it), and cease not to do shame to thee.

11   (As) a golden pomme (or apple) or pommel in beds of silver *is he*, that speaketh a word in his time.

12   (As) a golden earring, and a shining pearl *is he*, that reproveth a wise man, and an ear obeying.

13   As the cold of snow in the day of harvest, so a faithful messenger to him that sent him, maketh his soul to have rest.

14   (As) a cloud and wind, and (then) rain not pursuing or following, *is* a glorious man, and not fulfilling promises.

15   A prince shall be made soft by patience; and a soft tongue shall break hardness.

16   Thou hast found honey, eat thou (only) that that sufficeth to thee; lest peradventure thou be (over)-filled, and spew it out.

17   Withdraw thy foot from the house of thy neighbour; lest sometime he be filled (of thee), *that is, annoyed (by thee)*, and hate thee.

18   (Like) a dart, and a sword, and a sharp arrow, (*is*) a man that

speaketh false witnessing against his neighbour.

19   (As) a rotten tooth, and a faint foot *is* he, that hopeth on (or trusteth in) an unfaithful man in the day of anguish,

20   and loseth his mantle in the day of cold. Vinegar in a vessel of salt *is* he, that singeth songs to the worst heart. As a moth *annoyeth or harmeth* a cloth (or a cloak), and a worm *harmeth* a tree, so the sorrow of a man *harmeth* the heart.

21   If thine enemy hungereth, feed thou him; if he thirsteth, give thou him water to drink;

22   for thou shalt gather together coals upon his head; and the Lord shall yield to thee.

23   The north wind scattereth *abroad* rains; and a sorrowful face *destroyeth* a tongue backbiting.

24   It is better to sit in the corner of an house without a roof, than with a woman full of chiding, and in a common house.

25   Cold water to a thirsty man; and a good messenger from a far land.

26   (As) a well disturbed with foot, and a vein (or spring) broken, (*is*) a just man falling before a wicked man.

27   As it is not good to him that eateth much honey; so he that is a searcher of majesty, shall be put down from glory.

28   As a city open, and without compass of walls; so *is* a man that may not (or cannot) refrain his spirit in speaking.

ECCLESIASTICUS   CHAPTER 36

1   God of all things, have thou mercy on us; and behold thou us, and show to us the light of thy merciful doings.

2   And send thy dread (or thy fear) upon heathen men, that sought not thee, (so) that they know that no God is, no but thou; (so) that they tell out thy great (and) worthy deeds.

3   Raise up thine hand upon heathen men aliens, (so) that they see thy power.

4   For as thou were hallowed in us in the sight of them, so in our sight thou shalt be magnified in them;

5   (so) that they know thee, as and we have known (thee), that none other is God, except thee, Lord.

6   Make thou new signs, and change thou marvels; glorify the hand, and the right arm.

7   Raise up thou strong vengeance, and pour out wrath; take away the adversary, and torment the enemy.

8   Haste thou the time, and have thou mind on (or remember) the end, (so) that they tell out thy marvels.

9   And he that is saved, be devoured in the ire of flame; and they that treat worst thy people, find perdition.

10   All-break thou the heads of princes, and of enemies, saying, There is none other, except us.

11   Gather thou together all the lineages (or the tribes) of Jacob, and know they that there is no God but thou, (so) that they tell out thy great deeds; and thou shalt inherit them, as at the beginning.

12   Have thou mercy on thy people, on which thy name is called in to help; and on Israel, whom thou madest even to thy first engendered or begotten son.

13   Have thou mercy on Jerusalem, the city of thine hallowing, on the city of thy rest.

14   Full-fill thou Zion with thy virtues, that may not be told out or untellable, and *fill* thy people with thy glory.

15   Give thou witnessing, that at or from the beginning they were thy creatures; and raise thou the prayers, which the former prophets spake in thy name.

16   Lord, give thou meed (or reward) to them that abide thee, (so) that thy prophets be found true or faithful;

17   and hear thou the prayer of thy servants. After the blessing of Aaron give thou to thy people, and address (or direct) thou us into the way of rightfulness; (so) that all men know, that dwell in (or on the) earth, that thou art God, the beholder of worlds.

18   The womb shall eat all meats, and *one* meat is better than *another* meat.

19   Cheeks touch meat almost (or taste many kinds of meat), and an unwise heart *receiveth* false or leasing (or lying) words.

20   A shrewd (or depraved) heart shall give heaviness, and a wise man shall against-stand or withstand it.

21   A woman shall take each knave or male child, and (or but) a daughter is or there is a daughter better than a son.

22   The fairness of a woman maketh glad the face of her husband, and (so) she shall bring desire (for herself) over all the covetousness or the lust of (her) man.

23   If there is a tongue of healing or of curing (or of caring), there is also (one) of assuaging, and of mercy; (and) the husband of her is not after (or like most of) the (other) sons of men.

24   He that hath in possession a good woman, beginneth a possession; she is an help like (to) him(self), and a pillar as (or of) rest.

25   Where an hedge (or a wall) is not, the possession shall be ravished (or snatched) away; and where a woman is not, a needy man waileth.

26   To whom believeth he that hath no nest, and boweth down wherever it is dark, as a thief girded up, skipping out from city into city?

ECCLESIASTICUS CHAPTER 37

1   Each friend shall say, And I have coupled friendship; but that

or there is a friend, a friend by name alone (or in name only).

2   Whether sorrow is not till to death? Forsooth a fellow of the table and a friend shall be turned to enmity.

3   O! the worst or most shrewd (or depraved) presumption, whereof art thou made to cover dry malice, and the guilefulness thereof or the treachery of it?

4   A fellow of the table shall be merry with a friend in delightings, and in the day of tribulation he shall be an adversary.

5   A fellow of the table shall have sorrow with a friend, for cause or because of the womb (or the belly); and he shall take (up) a shield against an enemy.

6   Forget thou not thy friend in thy soul, and be thou not unmindful of him in thy works. Do not thou take counsel with the father of thy wife; and hide thou counsel from them that have envy to thee.

7   Each counsellor showeth counsel, but there is a counsellor to, or in (or only for) himself.

8   Keep thy soul from an evil counsellor; first know thou, what is his need, and what he shall think in his soul; lest peradventure he send a stake or put a pole, or a pale, into the earth,

9   and say to thee, Thy way is good, and (then) he stand again-ward, to see what shall befall to thee.

10   With an unreligious man, treat thou[1] (**not**) of (or about) holiness, and with an unjust or unrightwise man, (**not**) of (or about) rightfulness or rightwiseness, [Do thou not counsel with him that hath thee suspect, and from men envying to thee, hide thou thy counsel,]

11   and with a woman, (**not**) of (or about) these things which she hateth or envieth. With a fearedful man, treat thou (**not**) of (or

---

[1] *The author of this book speaketh here (and also in verse 11) in scorn, and understandeth the contrary of his saying.*

about) battle, with a merchant, (**not**) of (or about) carrying over of merchandises *to chapping* or (about) (ex)changing; with a buyer, (**not**) of (or about) selling, with an envious man, (**not**) of (or about) graces to be done; with an unpiteous man, (**not**) of (or about) pity, with an unhonest man, (**not**) of (or about) honesty, with a workman of the field or the field worker, (**not**) of (or about) each work; with a workman hired by the year or the annual worker, (**not**) of (or about) the ending of the year, with a slow servant, (**not**) of (or about) much working. Give thou not attention or Take thou not heed to these men in all counsel,

12   but be thou busy with an holy man, whomever thou knowest (is) keeping God's dread, whose soul is after thy soul. Whoever doubteth in darknesses, shall not have sorrow with thee.

13   And establish thou the heart of good counsel with thee; for why another thing is not more than it (is) to thee.

14   The soul of an holy man telleth out truths sometime; more than seven beholders or lookers about, sitting on high for to behold.

15   And in all these things beseech thou the Highest, that he address (or direct) thy way in truth.

16   Before all works a soothfast (or a true) word go before thee; and a steadfast counsel *go* before each deed.

17   A wicked or shrewd (or depraved) word shall change the heart,

18   of which *heart* four parts come forth; good and evil, life and death; and a busy tongue is lord of those or these.

19   A wise man hath taught many men, and (or but) he is (not) sweet to his (own) soul.

20   He that speaketh sophistically, *either by sophism*, is hateful; he shall be defrauded in each thing.

21   For why grace (or favour) is not given of (or from) the Lord to him, for he is defrauded of all wisdom.

22   A wise man is wise to his (own) soul, and the fruits of his wit (or understanding) be worthy to be praised.

23   A wise man teacheth his people, and the fruits of his wit (or understanding) be faithful.

24   A wise man shall be filled with blessings, and they that see him shall praise *him.*

25   The life of a man *is* in the number of days; but the days of Israel be unnumberable.

26   A wise man in the people shall inherit honour, and his name shall be living without end.

27   Son, assay thy soul in thy life; and if it is wicked, give thou not power to it;

28   for why not all things speed to (or be expedient for) all men, and not each kind (or thing) pleaseth each soul.

29   Do not thou be greedy in each eating, and pour thee (or thyself) not out upon each meat (or meal).

30   For in (too) many meats (or too much food) shall be sickness, and greediness shall nigh unto choler.

31   Many men died for (or from) gluttony; but he that is abstinent, shall increase or add (to his) life.

WISDOM OF SOLOMON   CHAPTER 13

1   Forsooth all men be vain, *that is, void of truth,* in which the knowing (or knowledge) of God is not; and of these things that be seen (to be) good, they might not understand him, that is, and they perceiving the works knew not, who was the worker or the craftsman;

2   but they guessed (to be) the gods (and) governors of the world, either the fire, either the wind, either the air made swift, either the compass of the stars, either full much water, either the

sun and moon;

3   and if they delighted in the fairness (or the beauty) of those things, and guessed *them* (to be) gods, know they, how much the Lord of those things is fairer (or more beautiful) than them; for why the engenderer or the begetter of fairness made all these things.

4   Or if they wondered on the virtue and works of those things, understand they of those things, that he that made these things, is stronger than those or them;

5   for by the greatness or the muchliness of the fairness (or the beauty) and of the creatures the Creator of these might be seen knowingly, *either might be known by his works.*

6   But nevertheless yet in these men is less complaint; for they err, in hap seeking God, and willing (or desiring) to find (him).

7   For when they live in his works, they seek, and hold for a sooth (or a truth), that those things be good, that be seen.

8   Again soothly it oweth (or ought) not to be forgiven to these men.

9   For if they might know so much, that they might guess (at) the world, how found they not lightlier (or easier) the Lord thereof?

10   forsooth they be unhappy and cursed, and the hope of them is among the dead, that called gods the works of the hands of men, gold, and silver, the finding of craft, and the likenesses of beasts, or an unprofitable stone, the work of an old hand.

11   Or if any craftsman, a carpenter, heweth down of the woods a straight tree, and eraseth or pareth away perfectly or taughtly all the rind thereof, and useth his craft diligently, and maketh a vessel full profitable into conversation of life;

12   soothly he useth the reliefs (or the remnants) of this work to the making ready of (his) meat (or for cooking his food);

13   and the residue of these things, which he maketh to no work or that to none use, a crooked tree, and full of knots, he engraveth

diligently by his voidness, *that is, made of (or by) him by his engraving,* and by the knowing (or knowledge) of his craft he figureth it, and likeneth it to the image of a man,

14 either maketh it like to some of beasts, and anointeth (it) with red colour, and maketh the colour thereof ruddy with painture, and anointeth or daubing, or painting each spot which is in it,

15 and maketh to (or for) it a worthy dwelling place, and setteth it in the wall, and he fasteneth it with iron,

16 lest peradventure it fall down; and he purveyeth for it, and knoweth, that it may not (or cannot) help itself; for it is an image (or an idol), and help is needful thereto.

17 And he maketh a vow, and inquireth of (or about) his chattel or substance, and of (or about) his sons, and of (or about) weddings; he is not ashamed to speak with him, that is without a soul;

18 and soothly for health he beseecheth a thing unmighty or feeble, and for life he prayeth (to) a thing without life or (to) the dead, and he calleth an unprofitable thing into (or for) help. And for (a good) journey he asketh of (or from) that thing, that may not go (or cannot move);

19 and of (or about) getting or purchasing and of (or about) working, and of (or about) the befalling or the chance of all things he asketh of him or it, which is unprofitable in all things. Δ

DAY 26

PSALM 113

1   *Alleluia*. Servants, praise ye the Lord; praise ye the name of the Lord.

2   The name of the Lord be blessed; from this time now, and till into the world (or forever).

3   From the rising of the sun till to the going down (of the same); the name of the Lord *is* worthy to be praised.

4   The Lord *is* high above all folks (or all the nations); and his glory *is* above the heavens.

5   Who *is* as our Lord God, that dwelleth in high things (or places);

6   and beholdeth meek things (both) in heaven and in earth?

7   Raising (up) a needy man from the earth; and enhancing a poor man from drit (or lifting up the poor out of the dirt).

8   (So) that he set him with princes; (yea), with the princes of his people.

9   Which maketh a barren woman dwell in the house; (yea, to become) a glad mother of sons.

PSALM 114

1   *Alleluia*. In the going out of Israel from Egypt; of the house of Jacob from the heathen people (with strange voice);

2   Judah was made the hallowing of him; Israel the power of him.

3   The (Red) Sea saw (it), and fled (away); the Jordan (River) was turned aback.

4   Mountains full out joyed (or rejoiced) as rams; and little hills as the lambs of sheep.

5   Thou (Red) Sea, what was to thee, for thou fleddest (away);

and thou, Jordan (River), for thou were turned aback?

6   (O) mountains, ye made full out joy (or rejoiced) as rams; and (ye) little hills, as the lambs of sheep.

7   The earth was moved from the face (or shaken by the presence) of the Lord; from the face of God of Jacob.

8   Which (or Who) turned a stone into a pond (or a pool) of waters; and an hard rock into wells of waters (or a spring of water).

PSALM 115

1   *Alleluia.* Lord, not to us, Lord, not to us; but give thou glory to thy name. Of thy mercy, and of thy truth;

2   lest any time heathen men say, Where is the God of them?

3   Forsooth our God in heaven; did all things, whichever he would (or whatever he desireth).

4   The simulacra (or The idols) of heathen men *be* (*made of*) silver and gold; the works of men's hands.

5   They have mouths, and shall not speak; they have eyes, and shall not see.

6   They have ears, and shall not hear; they have nostrils, and shall not smell.

7   They have hands, and shall not grope; they have feet, and shall not go; they shall not cry in their throat.

8   (Let) they that make those *simulacra* be made like them; and all that trust in them.

9   The house of Israel hoped (or trusted) in the Lord; he is the helper of them, and the defender of them.

10   The house of Aaron hoped (or trusted) in the Lord; he is the helper of them, and the defender of them.

11   They that dread (or fear, or revere) the Lord, hoped (or trusted) in the Lord; he is the helper of them, and the defender of them.

12   The Lord was mindful of (or remembered) us; and blessed us. He blessed the house of Israel; he blessed the house of Aaron.

13   He blessed all men that dread the Lord; both little and greater.

14   (May) the Lord add, *either increase,* on you; on you, and on your sons.

15   Blessed be ye of (or by) the Lord; that made heaven and earth.

16   The heaven of heaven/s *is* to the Lord; but he gave the earth to the sons of men.

17   Lord, not the dead shall praise thee (or the dead shall not praise thee); neither all men that go down into hell.

18   But we that live, bless the Lord; from this time now, and till into the world (or forever).

PSALM 116

1   *Alleluia.* I loved *the Lord*; for the Lord shall hear the voice of my prayer.

2   For he bowed down his ear to me; and I shall inwardly call (to) him in (all) my days.

3   The sorrows of death encompassed me; and the perils of hell (or Sheol) found me. I found tribulation and sorrow;

4   and I called inwardly the name of the Lord. Thou, Lord, deliver my soul, (or Saying, O Lord, save me!);

5   the Lord *is* merciful, and rightwise; and our God doeth mercy.

6   And the Lord keepeth (safe) little children; I was meeked (or brought low), and (or but) he delivered me.

7   My soul, return thou (again) into thy rest; for the Lord hath done well (or been good) to thee.

8   For he hath delivered my soul from death; (he stopped) mine eyes from weepings, and my feet from falling down (or stumbling).

9   I shall please the Lord; in the country of them that live (or in

the land of the living).

10   I believed, for which thing I spake; forsooth I was made low full much.

11   I said in my passing (or in my panic, or fear); Each man *is* a liar.

12   What shall I yield to the Lord; for all things which he hath yielded to me?

13   I shall take the cup of health (or salvation); and I shall inwardly call the name of the Lord.

14   I shall yield (or pay) my vows to the Lord before all his people;

15   the death of (any of the) saints of the Lord (or of God's people) *is* precious in his sight.

16   O! Lord, for I *am* thy servant; I *am* thy servant, and the son of thine handmaid (or thy servantess). Thou hast broken my bonds,

17   to thee I shall offer a sacrifice of praising; and I shall inwardly call the name of the Lord.

18   I shall yield (or pay) my vows to the Lord, in the sight of all his people;

19   in the foreyards (or the courtyards) of the house of the Lord, in the midst of thee, (O) Jerusalem.

PSALM 117

1   *Alleluia.* All heathen men, praise ye the Lord; all the peoples, praise ye him.

2   For his mercy is confirmed on us (or his love is firm toward us); and the truth of the Lord dwelleth without end.

PSALM 118

1   *Alleluia.* Acknowledge ye (or Give thanks) to the Lord, for he is good; for his mercy *is* without end (or forever).

2   Israel say now, for he is good; for his mercy (or his love) *is* without end.

3   The house of Aaron say now; for his mercy (or his love) *is* without end.

4   They that dread (or fear, or revere) the Lord, say now; for his mercy (or love) *is* without end.

5   (Out) of tribulation I inwardly called the Lord; and the Lord heard me in largeness (or answered, and set me free).

6   The Lord *is* an helper to me; I shall not dread (or fear) what man shall do to me.

7   The Lord *is* an helper to me; and I shall despise mine enemies.

8   It is better to trust in the Lord; than for to trust in man.

9   It is better for to hope (or trust) in the Lord; than to hope in princes.

10   All the folks (or the nations) encompassed me; and in the name of the Lord *it befelled*, for I am avenged on them.

11   They compassing encompassed me; and in the name of the Lord, for I am (or but I was) avenged (up)on them.

12   They encompassed me as bees, and they burnt out as a fire among the thorns; and in the name of the Lord, for I am (or but I was) avenged (up)on them.

13   I was hurled, and turned upside-down, (so) that I should fall down; and (or but) the Lord took (or helped) me up.

14   The Lord *is* my strength, and my praising; and he is made to me into health (or he is my salvation).

15   The voice of full out joying and of health (or victory); *be* in the tabernacles (or the tents) of rightwise men. The right hand of the Lord hath done virtue (or hath done mightily),

16   the right hand of the Lord enhanced me (or lifted me up); the right hand of the Lord hath done virtue (or hath done mightily).

17   I shall not die, but I shall live; and I shall tell (out) the works

of the Lord.

18   The Lord chastising hath chastised me; and he gave not me to death.

19   Open ye to me the gates of rightwiseness, and I shall enter by them, and I shall acknowledge to (or praise) the Lord;

20   this gate *is* of the Lord, and rightwise men shall enter by it.

21   I shall acknowledge to (or praise) thee, for thou heardest me; and art made to me into health (or salvation).

22   The stone which the builders reproved; this is made into the head of the corner (or the chief cornerstone).

23   This thing is made of (or from) the Lord; and it is wonderful before our eyes.

24   This is the day which the Lord made; make we full out joy (or rejoice), and be we glad therein.

25   O! Lord, make thou me safe (or save me), O! Lord, make thou well (for us) prosperity;

26   blessed *is he* that cometh in the name of the Lord. We blessed you of (or from) the house of the Lord;

27   God *is* Lord, and he hath given light to us. Ordain ye a solemn day in thick *peoples* (or bind the sacrifice with cords); unto the horns of the altar.

28   Thou art my God, and I shall acknowledge to (or praise) thee; thou art my God, and I shall enhance (or exalt) thee. I shall acknowledge to thee, for thou heardest me; and thou art made to me into health (or salvation).

29   Acknowledge ye to (or praise) the Lord, for he is good; for his mercy *is* without end.

PROVERBS CHAPTER 26

1   As snow in summer, and rain in harvest; so glory is unseemly

to a fool.

2   For as a bird flying over to high things, and *as* a sparrow going into uncertain; so cursing brought forth without reasonable cause shall come over into some man.

3   Beating be to an horse, and a bridle to an ass; and a rod to the back of unprudent men.

4   Answer thou not to a fool after his folly, lest thou be made like him.

5   Answer thou (to) a fool after his folly, lest he seem to (or thinketh) himself to be wise.

6   (As) an halting man in feet, and drinking wickedness, *that is, drink harmful to himself,* (is) he that sendeth words by a fond or a foolish messenger.

7   As an halting man hath fair legs in vain; so a parable is unseemly in the mouth of fools.

8   As he that sendeth a stone into the broad place of the sling; so he that giveth honour to an unwise man.

9   As if a thorn groweth in the hand of a drunken man; so *is* a parable in the mouth of fools.

10   Doom (or Judgement) determineth causes; and he that putteth silence to a fool, assuageth wraths.

11   As a dog that turneth again to his spewing or a hound to his vomit; so *is* an unprudent man, that rehearseth his folly.

12   Thou hast seen a man seem wise to himself; an unknowing man shall have hope more than he.

13   A slow man saith, A lion is in (or on) the way, a lioness is in (or on) the footpaths.

14   As a door is turned in his (or on its) hinges; so a slow man in his bed.

15   A slow man hideth his hands under his armpit; and he travaileth (or laboureth), if he turneth them up to his mouth.

16   A slow man seemeth wiser to himself, than seven men speaking sentences.

17   As he that taketh a dog by the ears; so he that passeth, and *is* unpatient, and is meddled or mingled (or mixed in) with the chiding of another man.

18   As he is guilty, that sendeth spears and arrows into death,

19   so a man that annoyeth (or harmeth) guilefully his friend, and when he is taken, he shall say, (all) I did (was) playing.

20   When trees fail, the fire shall be quenched; and when a privy backbiter is withdrawn, strives rest.

21   As dead coals at quick coals, and trees at the fire; so a wrathful man (that) raiseth chidings (or strives).

22   The words of a privy backbiter *be* as simple; and they come unto the innerest or innermost things of the heart.

23   As if thou wouldest adorn a vessel of earth (or of clay) with the dross of silver, so *be* swelling lips fellowshipped with a full wicked heart.

24   An enemy is understood by his lips, when he treateth guiles (or treacheries) in *his* heart.

25   When he maketh low his voice, believe thou not to him; for seven wickednesses be in his heart.

26   The malice of him that covereth hatred guilefully (or deceitfully), shall be showed in a council.

27   He that delveth a ditch, shall fall into it; and if a man walloweth (or rolleth) a stone, it shall turn again (on)to him.

28   A false tongue loveth not the truth; and a slippery mouth worketh fallings.

ECCLESIASTICUS CHAPTER 38

1   Honour thou a leech (or a physician), for need; for why the

Highest hath made or formed him.

2   For why all medicine is of (or from) God; and he shall take of (or receive from) the king a gift (or honour).

3   The knowing of a leech shall enhance his head (or The knowledge of a physician shall exalt or lift up his head); and he shall be praised in the sight of (or before) great men.

4   The Highest hath made or formed (out) of the earth medicine; and a prudent man shall not loathe it.

5   Whether bitter water was not made sweet of (or by) a tree? The virtue (or power) of those things *came by experience* to the knowing (or knowledge) of men;

6   and the Highest gave knowing (or knowledge) to men, for to be honoured in his marvels (or for his marvellous works).

7   A man healing or curing in (or with) these things, shall assuage sorrow,

8   and an ointment-maker shall make pigments of sweetness, and shall make anointings of (or for) health; and his works shall not be ended. For why the peace of God *is* upon the face of the earth.

9   My son, despise not thyself in thy sickness; but pray thou (to) the Lord, and he shall heal or cure thee.

10   Turn thou away from sin, and address (or direct) thine hands, and cleanse thine heart from all sin.

11   Give thou sweetness, and the mind (or a memorial) of clean or tried flour of wheat, and make thou a fat offering;

12   and give thou place to a leech (or to a physician). For the Lord made him, and depart he not or go he not away from thee; for his works be needful to thee.

13   For why a time is (or shall be), when thou shalt fall into the hands of them.

14   Forsooth they shall beseech the Lord, that he address (or direct) the work of them, and (give) health for their living (or a long life).

15   He that trespasseth in the sight of (or before) him, that made
him, shall fall into the hands of the leech (or the physician).

16   Son, bring thou forth tears on (or over, or for) a dead man,
and thou as suffering hard things begin to weep; and by or after
doom (or according to custom), cover thou the body of him, and
despise thou not his burying.

17   But for backbiting, bear thou bitterly the mourning of him (for)
one day; and be thou comforted for sorrow or take comfort for
heaviness. And make thou mourning after his merit or deserving
(for) one day, or two, for backbiting.

18   For why death hasteneth of (or from) sorrow, and covereth
virtue (or strength); and the sorrow of heart boweth the head.

19   Sorrow dwelleth in leading away; and the chattel or the
substance of a needy man *is* after his heart.

20   Give thou not thine heart in sorrow, but put it away from
thee; and have thou mind on (or remember) the last things,

21   and do not thou forget. For why no returning is *from death to
this present life*, and thou shalt nothing profit to this *dead man* or
to this thou shalt nothing profit; and thou shalt harm worst thyself.

22   Be thou mindful of my doom (or Remember my judgement);
for also thine shall be thus, to me yesterday, and to thee today.

23   In the rest of a dead man, make thou his mind (or his memory)
to have rest; and comfort thou him, in the going out of his spirit.

24   Write thou wisdom in the time of voidness; and he that is
made less in (doing) deeds, shall perceive wisdom; for he shall be
filled with wisdom.

25   He that holdeth the plow, and he that hath glory in a goad,
driveth oxen with a prick, and he liveth in (or by) the works of
them; and his telling *is* in the sons of bulls.

26   He shall give his heart to turn furrows; and his waking *shall
be* about the fatness of the kine (or the cattle).

27   So each carpenter, and principal workman, that passeth the night as the day; that engraveth images engraved or the which engraved engraved brooches, and the busyness of him diverseth or varieth the painture (or the painting); he shall give his heart into the likeness of the painture, and by his waking (or his watch) he performeth the work.

28   So a smith sitting beside the anfelt (or the anvil), and beholding the work of iron, the heat of the fire burneth his fleshes; and he striveth in the heat of the furnace. The voice (or sound) of a hammer maketh new his ear; and his eye *is* against (or towards) the likeness of a vessel. He shall give his heart into the performing of the works; and by his waking he shall adorn unperfection, *that is, matter (or material) which he bringeth to perfection of form.*

29   So a potter sitting at his work, turning a wheel with his feet, which is put evermore in busyness for his work; and all his working is unnumberable.

30   In his arm he shall form the clay; and before his feet he shall bow (down) his virtue (or his strength). He shall give his heart to end perfectly something; and by his waking he shall cleanse the furnace.

31   All these men hoped (or trusted) in their hands; and each man is wise in his craft.

32   A city is not builded without all these men. And (or But) they shall not dwell in, neither go in;

33   and they shall not skip over into the church. They shall not sit on the seat of a judge; and they shall not understand the testament of doom (or the sentence of judgement), neither they shall make open teaching and doom; and they shall not be found in parables (or where parables be spoken).

34   But they shall confirm the creature (or the nature) of the world, and their prayer (or desire) *is* (in) the working of (their) craft.

DAY 26

WISDOM OF SOLOMON CHAPTER 14

1   Again another thinking to sail, and beginning to make journey through fierce waves, inwardly calleth (upon) a tree (or a piece of wood) more frail than the tree (or piece of wood) that beareth him.

2   For why covetousness to get *money* or winning found (or was the reason to create) that *idol*; and a craftsman made it by his wisdom.

3   But thou, Father, governest by purveyance, for thou gavest a way in the sea, and a most steadfast path among the waves;

4   showing that thou art mighty to make whole of or to heal all things, yea, (even) if a man goeth to the sea without a ship;

5   but that the works of thy wisdom should not be void, for this thing men betake their lives, yea, to a little tree, and they pass (over) the sea, and be delivered (or saved) by a ship.

6   But at or from the beginning, when proud giants perished, the hope of the world fled to a ship, and sent again seed of birth to the world, which was governed by thine hand.

7   For why blessed is the tree (or the wood), by which rightfulness or rightwiseness was made or done.

8   But the idol which is made by hands is cursed, both it, and he that made it, for soothly he wrought great trespass; soothly that *idol*, when it was frail, was named God (or a god).

9   Forsooth in like manner the wicked man and his wickedness be hateful to God.

10   For why that that is made shall suffer torments, with him that made *it*.

11   For this thing and to the idols of nations shall not be a beholding or a reward; for the creatures of God be made into hatred, and into temptation to the soul of men, and into a trap or a mouse-catch,

to the feet of unwise men.

12   For the beginning of fornication, *that is, idolatry, which is ghostly (or spiritual) fornication*, is the seeking out of idols, and the finding of those *idols* is the corruption of life.

13   Forsooth they were not at or from the beginning, nor shall be into without end.

14   For why the voidness of men found (or brought) these *idols* into the world; and therefore the end of them is (or shall be) found short(ly) (or soon).

15   For why the father making sorrow with bitter mourning, made soon to him an image of the son *that was* ravished (or taken away); and began to worship (or to honour) him now as a god, that was dead then as a man; and he ordained holy things or temples and sacrifices among his servants.

16   Afterward in time coming betwixt, when the wicked custom was strong, this error was kept as a law, and images were worshipped by the lordship (or under the commands) of tyrants.

17   The figure of them was brought from afar, which the men might not honour in open, for they were far (off); and they made an open image of the king, whom they would honour; that by their busyness they should worship him as present, that was absent.

18   Forsooth the noble or the great diligence of a craftsman brought in also them, that knew not, to the worshipping of these *things* or these *kings*.

19   For he willing (or desiring) more to please the *king*, that took him, *that is, chose him to make an image to (or of) the king*, travailed (or laboured) perfectly by his craft, to make a likeness into better, *that is, in making the king (appear) fairer*.

20   Soothly the multitude of men, deceived by the fairness of the work, guessed or esteemed him now a god, that was honoured as a man before *that* time.

21   And this was the deceit or the deceiving of man's life; for why men serving greatly, either to affection, either to kings, putted to stones and trees the uncommunicable name (or the name that cannot be communicated, or spoken).

22   And it sufficed not, that they erred about the knowing of God; but also they living in the great battle of unknowing (or in the great war of ignorance), call so many and so great evils peace.

23   For either they slaying their sons in sacrifice, or making dark sacrifices, either having watches full of madness,

24   keep now neither clean life, neither clean weddings or spousals; but also one man slayeth another man by (or for) envy, or (by) doing adultery maketh sorry (or sorroweth) *his neighbor.*

25   And all things be meddled or mingled (or mixed) together, blood, manslaughter, theft, and feigning, corruption, unfaithfulness, disturbing (or troubling), and forswearing,

26   noise or strife, forgetting of goods of (or of the good things from) the Lord, defouling of souls, changing of birth (or gender), unsteadfastness of weddings or the unstableness of bridals, the unordaining of lechery and of unchastity or uncleanness.

27   For why the worshipping of cursed idols is the cause, and the beginning, and the end, of all evil.

28   For why either they wax mad, while they be glad; or certainly they prophesy false things, or they live unjustly, or they forswear soon.

29   For the while they trust in idols, that be without a soul, they swear evil (or falsely), and hope not, that they shall be annoyed (or harmed).

30   Therefore ever either shall come to them worthily; for they deemed evil of God, and gave attention to idols, and they swore unjustly in (or by) an idol, and they despised rightwiseness.

31   For why an oath is not virtue, but the pain of sinners goeth forth evermore, into the breaking of just or rightwise things. ∆

DAY 27

PSALM 119

1   *Alleluia. Aleph.* Blessed *be* men without wem (or blemish) in (or on) the way; that go in the law of the Lord.

2   Blessed *be they*, that seek his witnessings (or his testimonies); and seek him in (or with) all the heart.

3   For they that work wickedness; went not in his ways.

4   Thou hast commanded; that thy behests be kept greatly (or diligently).

5   I would (or I desire) that my ways were addressed (or directed); to keep thy justifyings (or so that I obey thy statutes).

6   Then I shall not be shamed; when I shall behold perfectly in(to) all thy behests (or thy commandments).

7   I shall acknowledge to (or praise) thee in the addressing (or the directing) of *mine* heart; in that that I learned the dooms (or the judgements) of thy rightwiseness.

8   I shall keep thy justifyings; forsake thou not me on each side.

9   *Beth.* In what thing amendeth a young waxing (or growing) man his way? in keeping (or obeying) thy words.

10   In (or With) all mine heart I sought thee; put thou me not away from thy behests (or thy commands, or commandments).

11   In mine heart I hid thy speeches; (so) that I do not sin against thee.

12   Lord, thou art blessed; teach thou me thy justifyings (or thy statutes).

13   In my lips I have pronounced; all the dooms of (or the judgements or laws from) thy mouth.

14   I delighted in the way of thy witnessings (or thy testimonies); (as much) as in all riches.

15   I shall be exercised, *either busily occupied*, in thy behests (or thy commandments, or precepts); and I shall behold (or study) thy ways.

16   I shall bethink in thy justifyings (or upon thy statutes); I shall not forget thy words.

17   *Gimel.* Yield to thy servant; quicken thou (or revive) me, and I shall keep (or obey) thy words.

18   Lighten thou (or Open) mine eyes; and I shall behold the marvels of thy law.

19   I am a comeling in (or a newcomer on) the earth; hide thou not thy behests (or thy commands) from me.

20   My soul coveted to desire thy justifyings; in (or at) all times.

21   Thou blamedest the proud; they be cursed, that bow away from thy behests (or thy commandments).

22   Do thou away from me shame and despising; for I sought thy witnessings (or thy testimonies).

23   For why princes sat, and spake against me; but thy servant was exercised in thy justifyings (or thy statutes).

24   For why and thy witnessings (or thy teachings) is my thinking (or study); and my counsel is thy justifyings.

25   *Daleth.* My soul cleaved to the pavement (or My body lieth in the dust); quicken thou (or revive) me by thy word.

26   I told out my ways (or all that I had done), and thou heardest me; teach thou me thy justifyings (or thy statutes).

27   Learn thou (or Teach) me the way of thy justifyings (or thy precepts); and I shall be exercised in (or study) thy marvels.

28   My soul napped for (or because of) harm; confirm thou me in thy words.

29   Remove thou from me (or Keep me away from) the way of wickedness; and in thy law have thou mercy on me.

30   I chose the way of truth; I forgat not thy dooms (or thy

judgements).

31   Lord, I cleaved to thy witnessings (or thy testimonies); do not thou shame me.

32   I ran the way of thy commandments; when thou alargedest mine heart.

33   *He.* Lord, set thou to me a law, the way of thy justifyings (or thy statutes); and I shall seek it evermore.

34   Give thou understanding to me, and I shall seek thy law; and I shall keep it in (or with) all mine heart.

35   Lead me forth in (or on) the path of thy behests (or thy commands, or commandments); for I would it (or I delight in them, or that is what I desire).

36   Bow down mine heart into thy witnessings (or thy testimonies); and not into avarice.

37   Turn thou away mine eyes, (so) that they see not vanity (or what is empty and futile); quicken thou (or revive) me in thy way.

38   Ordain thy speech (or thy word) to thy servant; (who is) in thy dread (or fear, or who hath reverence for thee).

39   Cut away my shame, which I supposed; for thy dooms (or thy judgements) *be* merry.

40   Lo! I coveted thy commandments; quicken thou me in thine equity (or revive me with thy fairness).

41   *Vau.* And, Lord, (let) thy mercy (or thy love) come upon me; thine health (or thy salvation) *come* by thy speech.

42   And I shall answer a word to men saying shame to me; for I hoped in (or put my trust in) thy words.

43   And take thou not away from my mouth the word of truth utterly; for I hoped above in thy dooms (or I put my hope in thy judgements or decrees).

44   And I shall keep (or obey) thy law evermore; into the world, and into the world of world (or forever and ever).

45 And I went (or walked) in largeness; for I sought (out) thy commandments.

46 And I spake of thy witnessings (or thy testimonies, or teachings) in the sight of kings; and I was not a/shamed.

47 And I bethought in thy behests (or thy commandments); which I loved.

48 And I raised mine hands to thy commandments, which I loved; and I shall be exercised in thy justifyings.

49 *Zain.* Lord, have thou mind on (or remember) thy word to thy servant; in which *word* thou hast given hope to me.

50 This comforted me in my lowness; for thy word quickened me.

51 Proud men did wickedly (to me) by all things; but I bowed (or turned) not away from thy law.

52 Lord, I was mindful of thy dooms from the world (or I will always remember thy judgements); and I was comforted.

53 Failing (or Anger) held me; for (or because of) sinners forsaking thy law.

54 Thy justifyings (or Thy statutes) were delightable to me to be sung; in the place of (or here on) my pilgrimage.

55 Lord, I had mind of (or remembered) thy name by night; and I kept thy law.

56 This thing was made (true) to me; for I sought (or obeyed) thy justifyings (or thy precepts).

57 *Cheth.* Lord, my part (or my portion); I said to (thee that I will) keep thy law.

58 I besought thy face in (or with) all mine heart; have thou mercy on me by thy speech.

59 I bethought (on) my ways; and I turned my feet into thy witnessings (or thy testimonies).

60 I am ready, and I am not troubled; to keep (or to obey) thy commandments.

61   The cords of sinners have embraced me; and I have not forgotten thy law.

62   At midnight, I rose to acknowledge to (or to praise) thee; on the dooms of thy justifyings (or for all thy just judgements).

63   I am a partner of all that dread (or fear, or revere) thee; and keep (or obey) thy behests (or thy commands).

64   Lord, the earth is full of thy mercy (or thy love); teach thou me thy justifyings (or thy statutes).

65   *Teth.* Lord, thou hast done goodness with thy servant; by thy word.

66   Teach thou me goodness, and lore, *either chastising*, and knowing (or knowledge); for I believed to (or trust in) thy behests.

67   Before that I was made meek, I trespassed; therefore I kept thy speech (or but now I obey thy words).

68   Thou art good; and in thy goodness teach thou me thy justifyings.

69   The wickedness of them that be proud, is multiplied upon me; but in (or with) all mine heart I shall seek thy behests.

70   The heart of them is crudded (or curdled), *either made hard*, as milk; but I bethought (on) thy law.

71   It is good to (or for) me, that thou hast made me meek (or brought low); (so) that I learn thy justifyings (or thy statutes).

72   The law (out) of thy mouth is better to me; than thousands of gold and silver.

73   *Jod.* Thine hands made me, and formed me; give thou understanding to me, (so) that I (can) learn thy behests.

74   They that dread (or fear, or revere) thee shall see me, and they shall be glad; for I hoped more on (or trust in) thy words.

75   Lord, I knew, that thy dooms *be* equity (or that thy judgements *be* just); and in thy truth thou hast made me meek.

76   Thy mercy be made, that it comfort me; by thy speech to thy

servant.

77   (Let) thy merciful doings come to me, and (then) I shall live;
for thy law is my thinking (or my delight).

78   (Let) they that be proud be shamed, for unjustly they did
wickedness against me; but I shall be exercised in thy behests (or I
shall think about thy commands or precepts).

79   (Let) they that dread (or fear, or revere) thee be turned to me;
and they that know thy witnessings (or thy testimonies, or teachings).

80   Mine heart be made unwemmed (or unblemished) in thy
justifyings; (so) that I be not shamed.

81   *Caph.* My soul failed into thine health (or fainteth while
waiting for thy salvation); and I hoped more in thy word.

82   Mine eyes failed into thy speech; saying, When shalt thou
comfort me?

83   For I am made as a bouget (or a bottle) in frost; (yet) I have not
forgotten thy justifyings (or thy statutes).

84   How many be the days of thy servant; when thou shalt make
doom of them that pursue me (or till thou bring judgement upon
those who persecute me)?

85   Wicked men told to me janglings (or quarrelling); but (they
be) not as thy law (or they be contrary to thy Law).

86   All thy commandments *be* truth; wicked men have pursued
(or persecuted) me, help thou me.

87   Almost they ended me in (or here on) the earth; but I forsook
not thy commandments.

88   By thy mercy quicken thou (or revive) me; and I shall keep
the witnessings (or the testimonies) of (or from) thy mouth.

89   *Lamed.* Lord, thy word dwelleth in heaven; without end.

90   Thy truth *dwelleth* in generation, and into generation (or for
all generations); thou hast founded the earth, and it dwelleth (or
remaineth).

91 The day lasteth continually by thy ordinances; for all things serve to thee.

92 But for thy law was my thinking; then peradventure I had perished in my lowness (or in my time of trouble).

93 Without end I shall not forget thy justifyings; for in (or by) them thou hast quickened (or revived) me.

94 I am thine, make thou me safe (or save me); for I have sought thy justifyings (or thy precepts).

95 Sinners abode me, for to lose (or to destroy) me; I understood thy witnessings (or thy testimonies).

96 I saw the end of all end; thy commandment *is* full large (or forever).

97 *Mem.* Lord, how loved I thy law; all day (long) it is my thinking.

98 Above (or Over all) mine enemies thou madest me prudent by thy commandment; for it is to (or with) me without end.

99 I understood over all men teaching me; for thy witnessings is my thinking.

100 I understood above (or better than) old men; for I sought (out) thy commandments.

101 I forbade my feet from all evil way; (so) that I keep (or obey) thy words.

102 I bowed not from thy dooms (or thy judgements); for thou hast set (or taught) the law to me.

103 Thy speeches be full sweet to my cheeks; above honey to my mouth.

104 I understood (because) of thy behests (or thy commands, or precepts); therefore I hated all the ways of wickedness.

105 *Nun.* Thy word *is* a lantern to my feet; and a light to my paths.

106 I swore, and purposed steadfastly; to keep the dooms (or the

judgements) of thy rightfulness or rightwiseness.

107 I am made low by all things; Lord, quicken thou (or revive) me by thy word.

108 Lord, make thou well pleasing (or accept) the willful things of my mouth; and teach thou me thy dooms.

109 My soul *is* evermore in mine hands; and I forgat not thy law.

110 Sinners setted a snare to me; and I erred not from thy commandments.

111 I purchased thy witnessings by heritage without end (or Thy testimonies be my inheritance forever); for they be the full out joying of mine heart.

112 I bowed mine heart to do thy justifyings without end; for (that itself is my) reward.

113 *Samech.* I hated wicked men; and I loved thy law.

114 Thou art mine helper, and mine up-taker; and I hoped more in thy word.

115 Ye wicked men, bow (or go) away from me; and (then) I shall seek (or obey) the commandments of my God.

116 Up-take thou me (or Lift me up) by thy word, and I shall live; and shame thou not me for mine abiding (or do not let me be shamed for trusting *in thee*).

117 Help thou me, and I shall be safe; and I shall bethink evermore in thy justifyings (or about thy statutes).

118 Thou hast forsaken all men going away from thy dooms (or thy judgements); for the thought of them *is* unjust (or improper).

119 I areckoned all the sinners of the earth (to be) breakers of the law; therefore I loved thy witnessings (or thy testimonies).

120 Nail thou my flesh with thy dread; for I dreaded of thy dooms (or I feared thy judgements).

121 *Ain.* I did doom and rightwiseness; betake thou not me to them that falsely challenge (or oppress) me.

122   Take up thy servant into goodness; they that be proud challenge not me.

123   Mine eyes failed into thine health (or waiting for thy salvation); and into the speech of thy rightwiseness (or and for thy righteous words).

124   Do thou with thy servant after thy mercy (or according to thy love); and teach thou me thy justifyings (or thy statutes).

125   I am thy servant; give thou understanding to me, (so) that I (can) know thy witnessings (or thy teachings).

126   Lord, *it is* time to do (or to act); they have destroyed thy law.

127   Therefore I loved thy commandments; more than gold and topaz.

128   Therefore I was addressed to (or directed by) all thy behests (or thy commandments); I hated all wicked way.

129   *Pe.* Lord, thy witnessings (or thy testimonies) *be* wonderful; therefore my soul sought them.

130   Declaring of thy words lighteneth; and *it* giveth understanding to meek men (or even to the simple, *or untaught*).

131   I opened my mouth, and drew the spirit (or my breath, *yea, I panted*); for I desired thy commandments.

132   Behold thou (up)on me, and have mercy on me; by the doom of them (or for those) that love thy name.

133   Address (or Direct) thou my goings by thy speech; that all unrightfulness have not lordship on (or rule over) me.

134   Again-buy thou (or Redeem) me from the false challenges (or oppression) of men; (so) that I (can) keep (or obey) thy behests (or thy commands, or commandments).

135   Lighten thy face upon thy servant; and teach thou me thy justifyings (or thy statutes).

136   Mine eyes led forth the outgoings of waters; for they kept not thy law.

137 *Tzaddi.* Lord, thou art just; and thy doom (or thy judgement) is rightful.

138 Thou hast commanded rightfulness or rightwiseness, thy witnessings (or thy testimonies); and thy truth greatly *to be kept* (or *obeyed*).

139 My fervent love made me to be melted, *either languished*; for mine enemies forgat (or disobeyed) thy words.

140 Thy speech is set afire (or tried by fire); and thy servant loved it.

141 I am young, and despised; (but) I forgat not thy justifyings (or thy precepts).

142 Lord, thy rightwiseness *is* rightwiseness without end; and thy law *is* truth.

143 Tribulation and anguish have found me; thy behests (or thy commandments) is my thinking.

144 Thy witnessings *is* equity (or just) without end (or forever); give thou understanding to me, and I shall live.

145 *Koph.* I cried in (or with) all mine heart, Lord, hear thou me; I shall seek thy justifyings (or shall follow thy statutes).

146 I cried to thee, make thou me safe (or save me); (so) that I keep (or can obey) thy commandments.

147 I before came in ripeness, and I cried; I hoped above on thy words.

148 Mine eyes before came to thee full early; (so) that I should bethink (on) thy speeches (or about thy words).

149 Lord, hear thou my voice by (or in) thy mercy; and quicken thou me by thy doom (or thy judgement).

150 They that pursue me nighed to wickedness; forsooth they be made far from thy law.

151 Lord, thou art nigh; and all thy ways (or thy commands) *be* truth.

152 In the beginning (or Long ago) I knew of thy witnessings; for

thou hast founded them (to last) without end.

153   *Resh.* See thou my meekness (or my troubles), and deliver thou me; for I forgat not thy law.

154   Deem thou my doom (or Decide my judgement), and again-buy thou me; quicken me for thy speech (or according to thy word).

155   Health (or Salvation) *is* far from sinners; for they sought not thy justifyings (or do not seek out thy statutes).

156   Lord, thy mercies *be* many; quicken thou me by thy doom (or revive me according to thy judgement, or decree).

157   *They be* many that pursue (or persecute) me, and do tribulation to me; I bowed not away from thy witnessings (or thy testimonies).

158   I saw breakers of the law, and I was melted, *either languished*; for they kept not thy speeches, (or I was greatly distressed; for they did not obey thy words, *or thy commands*).

159   Lord, see thou, for I loved thy commandments; quicken thou me in thy mercy (or according to thy love).

160   The beginning of thy word *is* truth; all the dooms of thy rightwiseness *be* without end (or all thy righteous judgements *be* forever).

161   *Schin.* Princes pursued (or persecuted) me without cause; and my heart dreaded (or was in awe) of thy words.

162   I shall be glad on thy speeches (or rejoice in thy words); as he that findeth many spoils (or much prey).

163   I hated and loathed wickedness; forsooth I loved thy law.

164   I said praisings to thee seven times in the day; on the dooms of thy rightfulness (or for thy righteous judgements).

165   Much peace *is* to them that love thy law; and no cause of (or reason for) stumbling is to them.

166   Lord, I abode thine health (or I wait for thy salvation); and I loved thy behests (or thy commandments).

167   My soul kept thy witnessings (or obeyed thy testimonies); and loved them greatly.

168   I kept (or obey) thy commandments, and thy witnessings; for all my ways *be* in thy sight (or before thee)

169   *Tau.* Lord, my beseeching come nigh in thy sight; by thy speech (or thy words) give thou understanding to me.

170   (Let) mine asking enter into thy sight (or come before thee); by thy speech deliver thou me.

171   My lips shall tell out an hymn (praising thee); when (or for) thou hast taught me thy justifyings (or thy statutes).

172   My tongue shall pronounce thy speech (or tell out thy words); for why all thy commandments *be* equity (or just).

173   Thine hand be made, (so) that it save me; for I have chosen thy behests (or thy commandments, or thy precepts).

174   Lord, I coveted thine health (or thy salvation); and thy law is my thinking.

175   My soul shall live, and *it* shall praise thee; and thy dooms (or thy judgements) shall help me.

176   I erred as a sheep that perished (or was lost); Lord, seek thy servant, for I forgat not thy commandments.

PROVERBS CHAPTER 27

1   Have thou not glory of the morrow (or Do not boast about tomorrow), that knowest not what thing the day coming shall bring forth.

2   Another man, and not thy (own) mouth praise thee; a stranger, and not thy lips.

3   A stone is heavy, and gravel is chargeous (or burdensome); but the wrath of a fool is heavier than ever either.

4   Wrath hath no mercy, and strong vengeance breaking out

hath no mercy; and who may suffer the fierceness of a spirit stirred?

5   Better is open reproving or amending, than hid love.

6   Better be the wounds of him that loveth, than the guileful (or deceitful) kisses of him that hateth.

7   A man filled shall despise an honeycomb; but an hungry man shall take, yea, bitter thing for sweet.

8   As a bird passing over from his nest, so is a man that forsaketh his place.

9   The heart delighteth in ointment, and diverse odours; and a soul is made sweet by the good counsels of a friend.

10   Forsake thou not thy friend, and the friend of thy father; and enter thou not into the house of thy brother, in the day of thy torment. Better is a neighbour nigh, than a brother afar.

11   My son, study thou about wisdom, and make thou glad mine heart; (so) that thou mayest answer a word to a despiser.

12   A fell (or A prudent) man seeing evil was hid; little men of wit (or men of little wit, or understanding) passing forth suffered harms.

13   Take thou away his cloth (or his cloak), that promised for a stranger; and take thou away a wed (or a pledge) from him for an alien (or a foreign, or an unknown) man.

14   He that blesseth his neighbour with a great voice; and riseth by night, shall be like him that curseth (him).

15   Roofs dropping (or dripping) in the day of cold, and a woman full of chiding, be likened together.

16   He that withholdeth her, (is) as if he holdeth the wind; and voideth the oil (out) of his right hand.

17   Iron is whetted by iron; and a man whetteth the face (or the countenance) of his friend.

18   He that keepeth a fig tree (safe), shall eat the fruits thereof; and he that is a keeper of his lord, shall be glorified.

19   As the cheers (or the faces) of men beholding (themselves)

shine in waters; so the hearts of men be open to prudent men.

20   Hell and perdition shall not be filled; so and the eyes of men be not able to be (ful)filled.

21   As silver is proved in a welling place, and gold *is proved* in a furnace; so a man is proved by the mouth of his praisers.

22   Though thou poundedest a fool in a mortar, as with a pestle smiting above dried barley, his folly shall not be done away from him.

23   Know thou diligently the cheer (or the face) of thy beast; and behold thou thy flocks.

24   For thou shalt not have power continually; but a crown shall be given to thee in generation and into generation (or for all generations).

25   The meadows be opened, and green herbs appeared; and hay is gathered from the hills.

26   Lambs be to (or for) thy clothing; and kids *be* to (or for) the price of the field.

27   The milk of goats suffice to thee for thy meats (or thy food); into the necessary things of thine house, and to lifelode of (or for livelihood for) thine handmaidens.

WISDOM OF SOLOMON   CHAPTER 15

1   Forsooth thou, our God, *art* sweet, and true, and patient, and disposeth all things in mercy (or love).

2   For if we sin, we be thine, and know thy greatness; and if we sin not, we know, that we be accounted at thee or (that) with thee we be counted.

3   For why to know thee, is perfect rightwiseness; and to know thy rightwiseness, and virtue, is the root of undeadliness (or immortality).

4   Forsooth the thinking out of evil craft of men brought not us into error, neither the shadow of painting travail (or labour) without fruit, an image graven (or a carved idol) by (or with) diverse colours;

5   whose beholding or sight giveth covetousness to an unwise man, and he loveth the likeness of a dead image without a soul.

6   The lovers of evils be worthy (of) the death, that have hope in such things; and they that make them, and they that love (them), and they that worship (them) *be worthy (of) the death.*

7   But also a potter, thrusting (or squeezing) the nesh (or soft) earth, by great travail (or labour) maketh each vessel to (or for) our uses; and (out) of the same clay he maketh vessels that be clean to use (or be for clean uses), and in like manner those that be contrary to these; forsooth what use is of these vessels, the potter is the judge.

8   And (then) he that was made of earth a little before, maketh a god of the same clay with vain travail (or empty and futile labour); and the potter, asked *to yield* the debt of the soul which he had, leadeth himself after a little time (back) *to the earth*, from whence he was taken.

9   But he hath care, not for he shall travail (or labour), neither for his life is short, but he striveth with goldsmiths and silversmiths; but also he pursueth or followeth workers of brass, and setteth before glory; for he maketh superfluous or over-void things.

10   For the heart of him is ashes, and superfluous earth is his hope, and his life is viler or fouler than clay.

11   For he knew not *God*, that made him, and that inspired a soul (in)to him; and he loveth those things which he hath wrought; and *he knew not God*, that blew into him a spirit of life.

12   But they guessed fleshly delighting or a playing place to be our life, and the conversation of life *to be* made to (or for) winning,

either covetousness, and that it behooveth to get on each side, yea, of (or by) evil.

13   Forsooth this man that maketh frail vessels, and graven images (or carved idols) of the matter (or material) of earth, knoweth that he trespasseth above all men.

14   Forsooth, *Lord*, all the unwise men and cursed be proud over the measure of their soul, and *be* enemies of thy people, and upbraid it;

15   for they guessed all the idols of the nations *to be* gods, that have neither sight of eyes to see, neither nostrils to perceive a spirit, *either wind* (*or breath*), neither ears to hear, neither fingers of hands to touch, but also their feet *be* slow to go.

16   For why a man made them, **and he that borrowed a spirit**, made them; for why no man may make a god like himself.

17   For since he is deadly (or mortal), with wicked hands he maketh a dead *idol*; for he is better than these *gods*, which he worshippeth; for soothly he lived, when he was deadly (or mortal), but they *lived* never.

18   But also most wretched men worship beasts; for why unreason-able *beasts*, comparisoned to these men, be worse than they.

19   But neither by sight any man may of (or can) these beasts behold good things; forsooth they have driven away or (have) fled the praising of God, and his blessing. Δ

DAY 28

PSALM 120

1   *The song of degrees.* When I was set in tribulation (or beset with troubles), I cried to the Lord; and he heard me.

2   Lord, deliver thou my soul from wicked lips; and from a guileful (or deceitful) tongue.

3   What shall be given to thee, either what shall be laid to thee; to a guileful tongue (or O deceitful tongue)?

4   Sharp arrows of (or from) the mighty; with coals that make desolate.

5   Alas to (or for) me! for my dwelling in an alien (or foreign) land is made (too) long, I dwelled with men dwelling in Kedar;

6   my soul was (too) much (time) a comeling (or a newcomer). I was peaceable with them that hated peace;

7   when I spake to them, they impugned, *either against-said*, me without cause.

PSALM 121

1   *The song of degrees.* I raised (up) mine eyes to the hills; from whence help shall come to me.

2   Mine help *is* of (or from) the Lord; that made heaven and earth.

3   *The Lord* give not thy foot into moving (or slipping); neither he (shall) nap, that keepeth thee (safe).

4   Lo! he shall not nap, neither sleep; that keepeth Israel (safe).

5   The Lord keepeth thee (safe); the Lord is thy protection above thy right hand.

6   The sun shall not burn thee by day; neither the moon by night.

7   The Lord keep thee from all evil; (yea), the Lord keep (safe)

thy soul.

8   The Lord keep (safe) thy going in and thy going out; from this time now and into the world (or forever).

PSALM 122

1   *The song of degrees (or for steps of ascending) of David.* I am glad in (or for) these things, that be said to me; We shall go into the house of the Lord.

2   Our feet were standing; in thy halls or foreyards (or gates), thou Jerusalem.

3   Jerusalem, which is builded as a city; whose partaking is into itself (or whose people be united).

4   For the lineages (or the tribes), the lineages of the Lord, ascended thither, the witnessing of Israel; to acknowledge to (or to praise) the name of the Lord.

5   For they sat there on seats in doom (or on the thrones for judgement); the seats on (or the thrones in) the house of David.

6   Pray ye those things, that be to (or for) the peace of Jerusalem; and (may) abundance be to them that love thee.

7   (May) peace be made in thy strength; and abundance in thy towers.

8   For (the sake of) my brethren and my neighbours; I spake peace of (or for) thee.

9   For the (sake of the) house of our Lord God; I sought good things to (or for) thee.

PSALM 123

1   *The song of degrees.* To thee I have raised (up) mine eyes; that dwellest in the heavens (or who livest in heaven).

2   Lo! as the eyes of servants *be* in (or *look* to) the hands of their lords. As the eyes of the handmaid *be* in (or *look* to) the hands of her lady; so our eyes *be* (or *look*) to our Lord God, till he have mercy on us.

3   Lord, have thou mercy on us, have thou mercy on us; for we be much filled with despising (or be greatly despised).

4   For our soul is much filled; *we be* shame to them that be abundant *with riches*, and despising to proud men.

PSALM 124

1   *The song of degrees of David.* (Let) Israel say now, No but for the Lord was in us (or If the Lord was not with us, or for us);

2   no but for the Lord was in us (or if the Lord was not with us, or for us). (Then) when men rose up against us;

3   in hap they had swallowed us quick (or alive). When the strong vengeance of them was wroth against us;

4   in hap water had swallowed us up. Our soul passed through a stream;

5   in hap our soul had passed through a water unsufferable (or the insufferable waters had gone over our heads).

6   Blessed be the Lord; that gave not us into the taking (or) the catching of (or by) the teeth of them.

7   Our soul, as a sparrow, is delivered; from the snare of hunters. The snare is all-broken; and we be delivered.

8   Our help *is* in the name of the Lord; that made heaven and earth.

PSALM 125

1   *The song of degrees.* They that trust in the Lord *be* as the hill of

Zion; he shall not be moved without end, that dwelleth in Jerusalem.

2   The hills *be* in the compass of it, and the Lord *is* in the compass of his people; from this time now, and into the world (or forever).

3   For the Lord shall not leave the rod of sinners on the part (or over the land) of rightwise men; (so) that the rightwise men hold not forth their hands to wickedness.

4   Lord, do thou well (or good) to good men; and to the rightful in heart.

5   But the Lord shall lead them that bow into obligations (or turn to crooked ways), with them that work wickedness; peace *be* upon Israel.

PSALM 126

1   *The song of degrees.* When the Lord turned the captivity of Zion (or restored prosperity to Zion); we were made as comforted (or like in a dream).

2   Then our mouth was filled with joy; and our tongue with full out joying. Then they shall say among the heathen men; The Lord magnified to do with them (or hath done great things for them).

3   The Lord magnified to do with us (or did great things for us); we be made glad.

4   Lord, turn thou (again) our captivity; as a stream in the south.

5   They that sow in tears; shall reap in full out joying.

6   They going, went, and wept; sending (out) their seeds. But they coming, shall come with full out joying; bearing their handfuls (or carrying their harvest).

PSALM 127

1   *The song of degrees of Solomon.* No but the Lord build the

house; they that built it have travailed (or laboured) in vain. No but the Lord keepeth (or guardeth) the city; he waketh in vain that keepeth (or guardeth) it.

2   It is vain to you (or How useless it is for you) to rise before the light; rise ye after ye have set (and then stay up late), (all so) that (ye can) eat the bread of sorrow. When he shall give sleep to his loved;

3   lo! the heritage (or the inheritance) of the Lord *is* sons, the meed (or the reward) *is* the fruit of womb.

4   As arrows *be* in the hand of the mighty; so the sons of them that be shaken out (or so be the sons that a man hath when he is young).

5   Blessed *is* the man, that hath full-filled his desire of them (or filled his quiver full of them); he shall not be ashamed, when he shall speak to his enemies in the gate (or in court).

PSALM 128

1   *The song of degrees.* Blessed *be* all men, that dread (or fear, or revere) the Lord; that go in his ways.

2   For thou shalt eat the travails (or the fruits) of thine hands; thou art blessed, and it shall be well to (or with) thee.

3   Thy wife *shall be* as a plenteous vine; in (or by) the sides of thine house. Thy sons as the new springs of olive trees; in the compass of thy board (or thy table).

4   Lo! so a man shall be blessed; that dreadeth (or feareth, or revereth) the Lord.

5   (May) the Lord bless thee from Zion; and see thou the goods (or the good things) of Jerusalem in all the days of thy life.

6   And see thou the sons of thy sons; *see thou* (that) peace (be) upon Israel.

PSALM 129

1   *The song of degrees.* (Let) Israel say now; Oft they have fought against me from my youth.

2   Oft they have fought against me from my youth; and soothly they might not to me (or could never overcome me).

3   Sinners forged on my back; they made long (and deep) their wickedness.

4   The Lord is rightwise, (he) shall beat (together) the nolls of the sinners;

5   all that hate Zion be they shamed, and turned (or driven) aback.

6   Be they made as the hay of (or on) the housetops; that dried up, before that it (could) be drawn (or pulled) up.

7   Of which hay he that shall reap, shall not fill his hand; and he that shall gather handfuls, *shall not fill* his bosom.

8   And (so) they that passed forth (or by) said not, The blessing of the Lord *be* upon you; we blessed you in the name of the Lord.

PSALM 130

1   *The song of degrees (or ascending).* Lord, I cried to thee from the depths;

2   Lord, hear thou my voice. Thine ears be made attentive into the voice of my beseeching (or Please listen to the words of my plea).

3   Lord, if thou keepest (a record of our) wickednesses; Lord, who shall (be able to) sustain, *or abide*? (or survive? or who will not be condemned?)

4   For mercy is at (or with) thee, (and I stand in awe of thee);

5   and, Lord, for thy law I abode (or waited for) thee. My soul sustained in (or because of) his word;

6   my soul hoped in the Lord. From the morrowtide keeping till to the night;

7   Israel hope in the Lord. For why mercy *is* at (or with) the Lord; and plenteous redemption *is* at (or with) him.

8   And he shall again-buy (or redeem the people of) Israel; from all the wickednesses thereof.

PSALM 131

1   *The song of degrees to David.* Lord, mine heart is not enhanced (or exalted); neither mine eyes be raised (up). Neither I went in (or with) great things; neither in (or after) marvels above me.

2   If I feeled not meekly; but I enhanced (or raised up) my soul. As a child weaned upon his mother; so yielding *be* in my soul.

3   Israel, hope (or trust) in the Lord; from this time now and into the world.

PROVERBS CHAPTER 28

1   A wicked man fleeth, when no man pursueth; but a rightwise man as a lion trusting shall be without fearedfulness.

2   For the sins of the land *there be* many princes of it; and for the wisdom of a man, and for the knowing of these things that be said, the life of the duke (or the leader) shall be the longer.

3   A poor man falsely challenging poor men, is like a great rain, wherein hunger is made ready.

4   They that forsake the law, praise the wicked man; they that keep *the law*, be kindled, *or stirred up*, against him.

5   Wicked men think not *on* doom (or *about* judgement); but

they that seek the Lord, perceive all things.

6   Better is a poor man going in his simpleness (or honesty), than a rich man in his shrewd (or depraved, or wicked) ways.

7   He that keepeth the law, is a wise son; but he that feedeth gluttons, shameth his father.

8   He that gathereth together riches by usuries, and free(ly) (made) increases, gathereth them together against poor men.

9   His prayer shall be made cursed, that boweth (or turneth) away his ear, (so) that he hear not the law.

10   He that deceiveth just men in (or with) an evil way, shall fall in his perishing; and just men shall wield his goods.

11   A rich man seemeth wise to himself; but a poor man (and) prudent shall search him (out, or see right through him).

12   In the enhancing (or raising up) of rightwise men is much glory; when wicked men reign, fallings of men be.

13   He that hideth his great trespasses, shall not be made rightful; but he that acknowledgeth and forsaketh them, shall get mercy.

14   Blessed *is* the man, which is ever dreadful (or fearful, or reverent); but he that is of hard heart, shall fall into evil.

15   A roaring lion, and an hungry bear, is a wicked prince on (or over) a poor people.

16   A duke needy of prudence shall oppress many men by false challenge; but the days of him that hateth avarice shall be made long.

17   No man sustain a man that falsely challengeth the blood of a man, (even) if he fleeth unto the pit.

18   He that goeth simply (or honestly) shall be safe; (but) he that goeth by wayward ways, shall fall down once, *without rising again.*

19   He that worketh his land, shall be filled with loaves; he that pursueth or followeth idleness, shall be filled with neediness.

20   A faithful man shall be praised much; but he that hasteneth to

be made rich, shall not be innocent.

21   He that knoweth a face in doom (or showeth favouritism when judging), doeth not well; this man forsaketh the truth, yea, for a morsel of bread.

22   A man that hasteneth to be made rich, and hath envy to other men, knoweth not that neediness shall come upon him.

23   He that reproveth a man, shall find grace afterward with him, (or He who rebuketh someone, shall find favour afterward with him); more than he that deceiveth by flatterings of the tongue.

24   He that withdraweth anything from his father and from his mother, and saith that this is no sin, is partner of a man-queller (or a murderer).

25   He that avaunteth himself, and alargeth, raiseth up strives; but he that hopeth (or trusteth) in the Lord, shall be saved.

26   He that trusteth in his (own) heart, is a fool; but he that goeth wisely, shall be praised.

27   He that giveth to a poor man, shall not be needy; he that despiseth *a poor man* beseeching, shall suffer neediness.

28   When unpious men rise, men shall be hid; and when they have perished, the rightwise shall be multiplied.

ECCLESIASTICUS   CHAPTER 39

1   And they give their soul, and they ask together or together seeking in the law of the Highest, (or But he that giveth his soul, seeking in the law of the Highest). A wise man shall seek out the wisdom of all the old men; and he shall give attention in (or to) the prophets.

2   He shall keep the tellings of the named men; and he shall enter altogether into the hard sentences or the slynesses of parables.

3   He shall seek out the privy (or the secret) things of proverbs;

and he shall be conversant in the hid things of parables.

4   He shall minister in the midst of great men; and he shall appear in the sight of the chief judge. He shall pass into the land of alien folks (or foreign nations); for he shall assay goods, and evils in all *things*.

5   He shall give his heart to wake early to the Lord that made him; and he shall beseech in the sight of the Highest. He shall open his mouth in prayer; and he shall beseech for his trespasses.

6   For if the great Lord will (or desire to), he shall fill him with the spirit of understanding. And he shall send the words of his wisdom, as rains; and in prayer he shall acknowledge to (or praise) the Lord.

7   And he, *that is, the Lord*, shall address (or direct) his counsel, and teaching; and shall counsel in his hid things.

8   He shall make open the wisdom of his teaching; and he shall have glory in the law of the testament of the Lord.

9   Many men shall praise his wisdom; and it shall not be done away till into the world (or forever). The memory of him shall not go away; and his name shall be sought from generation into generation.

10   The folks (or The nations) shall tell out his wisdom; and the church shall tell out his praising.

11   If his name dwelleth, he shall leave more than a thousand; and if he resteth, it shall profit to him. (If he resteth, or die, he shall leave a greater name than a thousand others; and if he dwelleth, or live, he shall increase it.)

12   Yet I shall take counsel to tell out, for I am full-filled as with madness; and *mine inner spirit* saith in voice,

13   Ye fruits of God, hear me, and make ye fruit, as roses planted on (or by) the rivers of the waters.

14   Have ye odour of sweetness, as the Lebanon *hath*. Bring forth

flowers, as a lily; give ye odour, and make ye boughs into grace. And praise ye together a song; and bless ye the Lord in (or for) his works.

15   Give ye great honour to his name, and acknowledge ye to (or praise) him in (or with) the voice of your lips, in songs of lips, and in (or on) harps; and thus ye shall say in acknowledging (or praising),

16   All the works of the Lord be full good.

17   Forsooth water as an heap *of stones* stood at his word; and as receptacles of waters in the word of his mouth.

18   For why peaceableness is made in his commandment; and no default or lessening is in the health of him (or his salvation), *that is, in the saving made by him.*

19   The works of each flesh or all flesh *be* before him; and nothing is hid from his eyes.

20   He beholdeth from the world unto the world (or forever); and nothing is wonderful or marvellous in his sight.

21   It is not to say, What is this thing, either, What is that thing? for why all things shall be sought in their time.

22   The blessing of him shall flow as a flood (or a river);

23   and as the great flood filled greatly the earth, so his wrath shall inherit in folks (or so the nations shall inherit his wrath), that sought not him.

24   As he turned waters into drynesses or into drought, and the earth was dried (up), and his ways were addressed (or directed) to the ways of them; so offensions (or offenses, or stumbling blocks) in his wrath *be addressed* (*or directed*) to sinners.

25   Good things were made at the beginning to (or for) good men; so good things and evil *be made* to (or for) the worst men.

26   The beginning of needful or necessary things to (or for) the life of men, (be) water, fire, and iron, and salt, and milk, and bread of clean or tried flour of wheat, and honey, and a cluster of grapes, and oil, and clothing.

27   All these things shall turn to holy men into goods (or good things); so and to unfaithful or unpious men and to sinners into evils.

28   Spirits be that be made or formed to (or for) vengeance; and in their madness they confirmed their torments. And in the time of ending they shall pour out virtue; and they shall confound (or confuse) the strong vengeance of him that made them.

29   Fire, hail, hunger, and death; all these things be made or be formed to (or for) vengeance;

30   the teeth of beasts, and scorpions, and serpents, and a sword punishing wicked men into destroying.

31   In the commandments of him, they shall eat, and they shall be made ready on the earth in need; and in their times they shall not pass (over) one word.

32   Therefore from the beginning I was confirmed (or certain); and I counselled, and thought, and left (it all) written (down).

33   All the works of the Lord *be* good; and each work shall serve in his (or its) hour.

34   It is not to say, This is (more) worse than that; for why all things shall be approved in their time.

35   And now in all the heart and mouth praise ye together, and bless ye the name of the Lord.

ECCLESIASTICUS CHAPTER 40

1   Great occupation is made to all men, and an heavy yoke upon the sons of Adam, from the day of the going out of the womb of their mother, unto the day of burying into the mother of all men, *that is, into the earth.*

2   The thoughts of them, and the dreads (or the fears) of the heart, the findings of abiding, and the day of ending;

3   from him that sitteth before on a glorious seat (or a throne of glory), unto a man made low into earth and ashes;

4   from him that useth jacinth (or hyacinth) or blue silk, and beareth a crown, unto him that is covered with raw linen cloth (or a linen cloak),

5   madness (or anger), envy, noise, doubting, and dread (or fear) of death, wrathfulness dwelling continually, and strife; and in the time of resting or repast in the bed, the sleep of night changeth his knowing (or his knowledge).

6   Forsooth a little *is* as nought (or nothing) in rest; beholding *is* of him in sleep as in the day. He is disturbed (or troubled) in the sight of his heart, as he that escaped in the day of battle.

7   He rose up in the day of his health (or his deliverance), and dreading not at any dread (or having no fear),

8   with all flesh, from man unto beast, and sevenfold (more), *that is, grievous punishment, shall come* upon the sinners.

9   At these things, death, blood, striving or strife, and sword, oppressings, hunger, and sorrow, and beatings;

10   all these things be made upon wicked men, and the great flood was made for them.

11   For why all the things that be of the earth, shall return into the earth; and all (the things that be of) the waters shall return into the sea.

12   All gift, *given for the destroying of rightfulness*, and wickedness, *done for gift*, shall be done away; and faith shall stand into the world (or forever).

13   The riches or The substances of unjust men shall be made dry or dried (up) as a flood; and shall sound as a great thunder in the rain.

14   *An unjust man* shall be glad in opening his hands; so trespassers or law-breakers shall fail in the end.

15   The sons of the sons of wicked or unpious men shall not

multiply branches; and (they be like) unclean roots sown on the top of a stone.

16 Greenness beside each water; and at the brink of the flood (or on the bank of the river), it shall be drawn out by the root before all the hay.

17 Grace as a paradise (or a garden) in blessings; and mercy dwelleth into the world (or forever).

18 The life of a workman sufficient to himself shall be made sweet; and thou shalt find treasure in it.

19 The building of a city shall confirm a name; and a woman without wem or undefouled shall be reckoned above or over this, *for why her steadfastness shall stand without end.*

20 Wine and music make glad the heart; and (or but) the love of wisdom *gladdeth* above or over ever either.

21 Pipes and a psaltery (or a lyre) make sweet melody; and (or but) a sweet tongue (is) above or over ever either.

22 An eye shall desire grace and fairness (or beauty); and green sowings above or over these green tilthes.

23 A friend and a meat-fellow (or a dining companion) coming together in time; and (or but) a woman with a man (is) above or over ever either.

24 Brethren into help in the time of tribulation *comfort much*; and (or but) mercy shall deliver more than or over them.

25 Gold and silver, and setting of feet (or can make thee stand firm); and (or but) counsel well-pleasing *is* above or over ever either.

26 Riches and virtues enhance (or raise up) the heart; and (or but) the dread (or the fear) of (or reverence for) the Lord is more than this. Making less is not in the dread of the Lord; and in that *drcad* it is not to seek help.

27 The dread (or fear) of the Lord *is* as a paradise (or a garden) of blessing; and *the blessings of God* covered him above all glory.

28   Son, in the time of thy life, be thou not needy, *that is, in the time of (thy) present life, granted to thee to work well, be thou not idle*; for it is better to die, then to be needy, *that is, it is better to die bodily, then to be idle, by which a man dieth ghostly (or spiritually)*.

29   A man beholding into another man's board (or depending upon another man's table), his life is not in the thought of lifelode (or about livelihood); for he sustaineth his life with other men's meats (or foods). Forsooth a chastised or disciplined man and learned or taught, shall keep himself.

30   Neediness shall be made in the mouth of an unprudent, *or a slow and idle*, man; and (or but) fire shall burn in his womb.

PRAYER OF MANASSEH

1   Lord God Almighty of our (fore)fathers, Abraham, Isaac, and Jacob, and of their rightwise seed,

2   which (or who) madest heaven and earth, with all the adorning of them,

3   which hast marked the sea by the word of thy commandment, which hast enclosed altogether the depth or the deepness, of the waters, and hast marked *them* to (or hast sealed them by, or with) thy fearedful and praiseable name,

4   which all men dread, and tremble of the cheer of thy virtue, (whom all men fear, and tremble in the presence of or before thy power,)

5   and the wrath of thy threatening upon the sinners is unsufferable, *either may not be sustained*.

6   Soothly the mercy of thy promise is full great and unsearchable, *either may not be comprehended by man's wit (or cannot be comprehended by one's understanding)*;

7   for thou art the Lord most high over all the earth; *thou art* patient or long-abiding, and much merciful, and doing penance or repenting, upon the malices of men. Truly, Lord, by thy goodness thou hast promised penance of forgiveness of sins, *that is, forgiving of sins for the repenting of men;*

8   and thou, *Lord, that art* God of just or rightwise men, hast not set penance to just or rightwise men, (as) to Abraham, Isaac, and Jacob, (yea), to them that sinned not against thee, (but thou hast set penance unto me that am a sinner). (and thou, *Lord, who art* God of the righteous, hast not appointed repentance for the righteous, for Abraham, Isaac, and Jacob, yea, for those who sinned not against thee, but thou hast appointed repentance unto me, who is a sinner.)

9   For I have sinned more than the number is of the gravel (or the sand) of the sea;

10   my wickednesses be multiplied. I am bowed (down) with much bonds (or with many bands) of iron, and no breathing is to (or for) me; for I have stirred thy wrathfulness, and I have done evil before thee, and I have set (up) abominations, and I have multiplied offensions (or offences).

11   And now, I bow the knees of mine heart, and beseech goodness of (or from) thee, Lord.

12   I have sinned, Lord; I have sinned, and I acknowledge my wickedness.

13   I ask, and I pray thee, Lord; forgive thou to me, forgive thou to me; lose (or destroy) thou me not altogether with my wickednesses, neither reserve thou evils to me without end (or forever).

14   For, Lord, by thy great mercy thou shalt save me (who is) unworthy, and I shall praise thee ever(more) in all the days of my life; for all the virtue, *that is, all those orders of angels*, of heavens praiseth thee (or for all the powers of the heavens praise thee), and to thee is glory into worlds of worlds (or forever and ever). Amen. Δ

DAY 29

PSALM 132

1   *The song of degrees.* Lord, have thou mind on (or remember) David; and of all his mildness (or meekness amid tribulations).

2   As he swore to the Lord; he made a vow to the God of Jacob.

3   I shall not enter into the tabernacle of mine house; I shall not go up into the bed of my resting.

4   I shall not give sleep to mine eyes; and (or) napping to mine eyelids.

5   And rest to my temples, till I find a place to (or for) the Lord; a tabernacle to (or for) the God of Jacob.

6   Lo! we heard that *the ark of the testament* (is) in Ephratah; we found it in the fields of the wood.

7   We shall enter into the tabernacle of him; we shall worship in the place, where his feet stood.

8   Lord, rise thou into thy rest; thou, and the ark of thine hallowing.

9   Thy priests be clothed with rightwiseness; and thy saints make full out joy (or God's people rejoice).

10   For (the sake of) David, thy servant; turn thou not away the face of thy christ (or turn not away thy face from thine anointed *king*).

11   The Lord swore (in) truth to David, and he shall not make him (or he did not say) in vain; Of the fruit of thy womb I shall put upon thy seat (or I shall put the fruit of thy loins upon thy throne).

12   If thy sons shall keep my testament (or covenant); and my witnessings (or testimonies), these which I shall teach them. And the sons of them till into the world (or forever); they shall sit upon thy seat (or thy throne).

13   For the Lord chose Zion; he chose it into a dwelling to (or for) himself.

14   This is my rest into the world of world (or shall be my resting place forever and ever); I shall dwell here, for I chose it.

15   I blessing shall bless the widow of it (or Zion's widows); I shall fulfill with loaves the poor men of it.

16   I shall clothe with health (or salvation) the priests thereof; and the holy men thereof shall make full out joy in full out rejoicing.

17   Thither I shall bring forth the horn of David; I have made ready a lantern to my christ (or for my anointed *king*).

18   I shall clothe his enemies with shame; but mine hallowing shall flower out upon him (or but a shining crown shall be upon his head).

PSALM 133

1   *The song of degrees.* Lo! how good and how merry (or pleasant) *it is*; that brethren (shall) dwell together.

2   As ointment in (or on) the head; that goeth down into (or onto) the beard, into (or onto) the beard of Aaron. That goeth down into (or onto) the collar of his cloth (or cloak);

3   as the dew of Hermon, that goeth down into (or onto) the hills of Zion. For there the Lord sent blessing; and life till into the world, *that is, without end.*

PSALM 134

1   *The song of degrees.* Lo! now bless ye the Lord; all the servants of the Lord. Ye that stand in the house of the Lord; in the halls or forcyards (or courtyards) of the house of our God.

2   In nights raise your hands into holy things (or in the holy place); and bless ye the Lord.

3   The Lord bless thee from Zion; the which *Lord* made heaven

and earth.

PSALM 135

1   *Alleluia.* Praise ye the name of the Lord; ye servants of the Lord, praise ye (him).

2   Ye that stand in the house of the Lord; in the halls or foreyards (or courtyards) of the house of our God.

3   Praise ye the Lord, for the Lord is good; sing ye to his name, for it is sweet (or pleasant to do so).

4   For the Lord chose Jacob to (or for) himself; and Israel into possession to himself (or as his special possession).

5   For I have known, that the Lord is great; and our God (is) before all gods.

6   The Lord made all things, whatever things he would (or desired), in heaven and in (or on) the earth; in the sea, and in all the depths of the waters.

7   He led out clouds from the farthest part of the earth; and made lightnings into rain. Which bringeth forth winds from his treasuries;

8   which killed the first begotten things of Egypt, from man unto beast.

9   He sent out signs and great wonders, in(to) the middle of thee, thou Egypt; into (or against) Pharaoh, and into (or against) all his servants.

10   Which smote many folks (or nations); and killed strong kings.

11   Sihon, the king of Amorites, and Og, the king of Bashan; and all the realms (or kingdoms) of Canaan.

12   And he gave the land of them heritage (or as an inheritance); *to be* heritage to (or an inheritance for) Israel, his people.

13   Lord, thy name *is* without end (or everlasting); Lord, thy

memorial *be* in generation and into generation (or thou shalt be remembered by all generations).

14 For the Lord shall deem (or judge) his people; and he shall be prayed in (or have compassion on) his servants.

15 The simulacra (or idols) of heathen men *be* silver and gold; the works of the hands of men.

16 Those *images* (*or idols*) have a mouth, and shall not speak; they have eyes, and shall not see.

17 They have ears, and shall not hear; for there is no spirit (or breath) in the mouth of them.

18 (Let) they that make those things, be made like them; and all that trust in them.

19 The house of Israel, bless ye the Lord; the house of Aaron, bless ye the Lord.

20 The house of Levi, bless ye the Lord; ye that dread (or fear, or revere) the Lord, bless ye the Lord.

21 Blessed be the Lord of (or from) Zion; (he) that dwelleth in Jerusalem.

PSALM 136

1 *Alleluia.* Acknowledge ye (or give thanks) to the Lord, for he is good; for his mercy *is* without end.

2 Acknowledge ye (or give thanks) to the God of gods.

3 Acknowledge ye (or give thanks) to the Lord of lords.

4 Which (or Who) alone maketh great marvels.

5 Which made the heavens by understanding (or by his wisdom).

6 Which made steadfast the earth (or Who made the earth firm) upon the waters.

7 Which made the great lights.

8 The sun into the power of the day.

9   The moon and the stars into (or to have) power of (or over) the night.

10   Which smote Egypt with the first engendered things (or Who struck down the first-born) of them.

11   Which led out Israel from the midst of them.

12   (Yea), in (or with) a mighty hand, and in (or with) an high arm.

13   Which parted the Red Sea or the Reed Sea into partings (or in two).

14   And led out Israel through the midst thereof.

15   And he cast adown Pharaoh and his power, or virtue, in the Red Sea.

16   Which led over his people through the desert (or wilderness).

17   Which smote great kings.

18   And killed strong kings.

19   Sihon, the king of Amorites.

20   And Og, the king of Bashan.

21   And he gave the land of them *to be* (or for) an heritage (or an inheritance).

22   (Yea), a heritage to (or an inheritance for) Israel, his servant.

23   For in our lowness (or our defeat) he had mind on (or remembered) us.

24   And he again-bought (or redeemed, or rescued) us from our enemies.

25   Which giveth meat to each flesh. (Who giveth food to all his creatures.)

26   Acknowledge ye (or give thanks) to the God of heaven. Acknowledge ye to the Lord of lords; for his mercy *is* without end.

PSALM 137

1   On the floods (or By the rivers) of Babylon, there we sat, and

wept; while we bethought on (or about) Zion.

2   In sallows in the midst thereof; we hanged up our organs. (On the willows nearby; we hung up our harps.)

3   For they that led us prisoners; asked us there (for) the words of songs. And they that led away us *said*; Sing ye to us an hymn of the songs of Zion.

4   (But) how shall we sing a song of the Lord; in an alien (or a foreign or unknown) land?

5   If I forget thee, Jerusalem; (may) my right hand be given to forgetting.

6   (And may) my tongue cleave to my cheeks; if I bethink not on thee. If I purposed (or thought) not of thee, Jerusalem; in the beginning of my gladness (or as my greatest joy).

7   Lord, have thou mind on (or remember) the sons of Edom; for the day of Jerusalem. Which say, Extinguish ye, extinguish ye; till to the foundament of it.

8   Thou wretched daughter of Babylon; he *is* blessed, that yieldeth to thee thy yielding, which thou yieldest to us.

9   He *is* blessed, that shall (take) hold (of); and hurtle down his (or thy) little children at the stone.

PSALM 138

1   *The psalm of David*. Lord, I shall acknowledge to (or praise) thee in (or with) all mine heart; for thou heardest the words of my mouth. My God, I shall sing to thee in the sight of the angels;

2   I shall worship to(ward) thine holy temple, and I shall acknowledge to (or praise) thy name. On thy mercy (or For thy love) and thy truth; for thou hast magnified thine holy name above all things.

3   In (or On) whatever day I shall inwardly call thee, hear thou

me; thou shalt multiply virtue (or strength) in my soul.

4   Lord, all the kings of the earth acknowledge to (or shall praise) thee; for they heard all the words of thy mouth.

5   And sing they in (or of) the ways of the Lord; for the glory of the Lord is great.

6   For the Lord *is* high (above), and beholdeth meek things; and knoweth afar high things (or knoweth the proud from afar).

7   (Yea), if I shall go in the midst of tribulation, thou shalt quicken me; and thou stretchedest forth thine hand on (or against) the wrath of mine enemies, and thy right hand made me safe (or saved me).

8   The Lord shall yield for me, Lord, thy mercy *is* without end (or thy love *is* everlasting); despise thou not the works of thine hands.

PROVERBS   CHAPTER 29

1   Sudden perishing shall come upon that man, that with hard noll, *that is,* (*with*) *an obstinate soul,* despiseth a blamer (or a rebuker); and health shall not follow him.

2   The commonality shall be glad in the multiplying of rightwise men; when wicked men have taken (or received) the princehood, the people shall wail.

3   A man that loveth wisdom, maketh glad his father; but he that nourisheth a strumpet, shall lose his chattel or substance.

4   A just king raiseth up the land; an avaricious man shall destroy it.

5   A man that speaketh by flattering and feigned words to his friend, spreadeth abroad a net to his steps.

6   A snare shall wrap a wicked man doing sin; and the rightwise shall praise, and make joy.

7   The rightwise knoweth the cause of poor men; and an

unpious man knoweth not knowing (it).

8   Men full of pestilence destroy a city; but wise men turn away strong vengeance.

9   If a wise man striveth with a fool, whether he be wroth, or laugh, he shall not find rest.

10   Men-quellers or men of bloods hate a simple (or honest) man; but just men seek his soul (or care about him).

11   A fool bringeth forth all his spirit; a wise man delayeth, and reserveth into the time (to) coming afterward.

12   A prince that heareth willfully (or willingly) the words of leasing (or lies), shall have all *his* servants unfaithful.

13   A poor man and a lender met themselves; the Lord is the lightener of ever either (or giveth light or sight to both).

14   If a king deemeth (or judgeth) poor men in truth, his throne shall be made steadfast without end.

15   A rod and chastising shall give wisdom; but a child, that is left to his *own* will, shameth his mother.

16   Great trespasses shall be multiplied in the multiplying of wicked men; and rightwise men shall see the fallings of them.

17   Teach thy son, and he shall comfort thee; and he shall give delights to thy soul.

18   When prophecy faileth, the people shall be destroyed; but he that keepeth the law, is blessed.

19   A servant may not (or cannot) be taught (only) by words; for he understandeth that that thou sayest, and (or but) he despiseth to answer.

20   Thou hast seen a man swift to speak; folly shall be hoped more than his amending or correction.

21   He that nourisheth his servant delicately from childhood, shall find him a rebel afterward.

22   A wrathful man stirreth chidings or strives; and he that is light

to have indignation, shall be more inclined to sins.

23 Lowness followeth a proud man; and glory shall up-take a meek (or humble) man of spirit.

24 He that taketh part with a thief, hateth his soul; he heareth a man charging greatly, or the adjurer, and showeth (or but speaketh) not.

25 He that dreadeth (or feareth) a man, shall fall soon; he that hopeth (or trusteth) in the Lord, shall be raised up.

26 Many men seek the face of the prince; and the doom (or but the judgement) of all men shall go forth of (or from) the Lord.

27 Rightwise men have an abomination of (or for) a wicked man; and wicked men have an abomination of (or for) them, that be in a rightful way.

ECCLESIASTICUS CHAPTER 41

1 O! death, thy mind is full bitter to an unjust man, and having peace in his riches; to a restful or quiet man, and whose ways be addressed (or directed) in all things, *that is, hath prosperity in all temporal things*, and yet mighty to take meat (or to receive food).

2 O! death, thy doom (or thy judgement) is good to (or for) a needy man, and which is made less in strengths, and faileth for age, and to whom is care of all things, and unbelieveful, that loseth (or destroyeth) wisdom.

3 Do not thou dread the doom (or fear the judgement) of death, *that is, set thou thee in such a state, (so) that the doom of death be good to (or for) thee*; have thou mind (or remember) what things were before thee, and what things shall come upon (or after) thee; this doom *is* of (or from) the Lord to (or for) each man.

4 And those things that shall come upon (or after) thee in the good pleasance (or through the good pleasure) of the Highest;

whether ten years, either an hundred, either a thousand. For why none accusing (or excusing) of life is in hell (or in the grave), *that is, no man may excuse him(self) there, in alleging the goodness of (his) life.*

5   The sons of abominations be the sons of sinners; and they that dwell beside the houses of wicked men.

6   The heritage (or inheritance) of the sons of sinners shall perish; and the continuance of shame or reproof with the seed of them.

7   The sons (will) (com)plain of a wicked father; for they be in shame or reproof for him.

8   Woe to you, ye wicked men, that have forsaken the law of the Highest.

9   And if ye be born, ye shall be born in cursedness; and if ye be dead, your part shall be in cursedness.

10   All things that be of the earth, shall return into the earth; so wicked men *shall turn* from cursing into perdition.

11   The mourning of men *is* in (or for) the body of them; but the name of wicked men shall be done away.

12   Have thou busyness of (or for) a good name; for why this shall dwell more with thee, than a thousand treasures great and precious.

13   The number of days *is the term* of a good life; but a good name shall dwell without end.

14   Sons, keep ye teaching in peace; for why wisdom hid, and treasure unseen, what profit is in ever either?

15   Better is a man that hideth his folly, than a man that hideth his wisdom.

16   Nevertheless return ye again in these things that come forth of (or from) or go out of my mouth. For it is not good to keep all unreverence, and not all things please all men in faith.

17   Be ye ashamed of fornication, before father, and before mother; and of a leasing (or of a lie), before a justice, and before a

mighty man;

18   and of trespass, before a prince, and before a judge; and of wickedness, before a synagogue, and a people; and of unrightfulness or unrightwiseness, before a fellow, and a friend;

19   and of theft, in the place wherein thou dwellest; of the truth and the testament of God; of sitting down at the meat in (or for the meal of) loaves; and of the blemishing or darkening of the gift (or of giving), and (of) taking;

20   of stillness, before them that greet or saluting (thee); of the beholding of a lecherous woman; and of the turning away of the cheer (or the face) of a cousin.

21   Turn thou not away thy face from thy neighbour; and *be thou ware* of taking away a part, and not restoring (it). Behold thou not the woman of another man;

22   and ensearch thou not (or go looking for) her handmaid, neither stand thou at her bed. Be thou ware of friends, of the words of upbraiding or reproof; and when thou hast given, upbraid thou not.

23   Double thou not a word of hearing, (and) of the showing of an hid word;

24   and thou shalt be verily (or truly) without shame or confusion, and thou shalt find grace in the sight of (or before) all men.

ECCLESIASTICUS   CHAPTER 42

1   Be thou not ashamed for all these things; and take or accept (or favour) thou not a person, (so) that thou do trespass.

2   *Be thou ware* of the law and testament (or covenant) of the Highest, of doom (or judgement) to justify a wicked man or the unpious;

3   of the word of fellows, and of way-goers, and of the giving of

the heritage (or inheritance) of friends;

4   of the evenness of balance, and of weights, of the getting of many things, and of few things;

5   of the corruption of buying, and of merchants, and of much chastising or much discipline of sons; and of a worst servant, to make the side to bleed.

6   A sealing, *either closing*, is good upon a wicked woman. Where be many hands, close thou (up);

7   and whatever thing thou shalt betake (or receive), number thou, and weigh thou; forsooth describe thou, *either write* (*down*), each gift, and taking (or receiving in).

8   *Abstain thou* from the teaching of an unwitty (or unwise) man, and a fool, and of elder men that be deemed of (or by the) young men; and thou shalt be learned in all things, and thou shalt be commendable or approvable (or approved) in the sight of all men.

9   An hid daughter of a father is waking or watch(ing) and busy-ness of (or for) him; she shall take away sleep; lest peradventure she be made an adulteress in her young waxing (or growing) age, and lest she dwelling with the husband, be made hateful;

10   lest anytime she be defouled in her virginity or be polluted in her maidenhood, and be found with child in the keeping of her father; lest peradventure she dwelling with the husband, do trespass, either certainly be made barren.

11   Ordain thou a keeping or a ward upon a lecherous daughter, lest any time she make thee to come into shame or reproof to (or with) thine enemies, of (or for) backbiting in the city, and of (or for) casting out of the people; and she make thee ashamed in the multitude of people.

12   Do not thou take heed to each man (or each person) in the fairness (or beauty), *that is, in delighting in the beholding of his* (*or their*) *fairness*; and do not thou dwell in the midst of women.

13   For why a moth cometh forth of (or from) clothes, and the wickedness of a man *cometh forth* of (or from) a woman.

14   For why the wickedness of a man is better, *that is, less evil*, than a woman doing well, and a woman shaming into shame (or reproach).[1]

15   Therefore be thou mindful of (or remember) the works of the Lord; and I shall tell (out) the works of the Lord, which I saw, in the words of the Lord.

16   The sun lightening or shining through beheld by all things; and the work thereof is full of the glory of the Lord.

17   Whether the Lord made not holy men to tell out all his marvels, which the Lord Almighty steadfast in his glory shall confirm?

18   He shall ensearch the depth, and the heart of men; and he shall think in (or on) the fellness or the sly wit, *or guile*, of them. For the Lord knew all knowing (or knowledge), and beheld into the signs of the world;

19   telling out those things that be passed, and those things that shall come; showing the steps of hid things.

20   And no thought passeth him (by), and no word hideth itself from him.

21   He made fair the great works of his wisdom, which is before the world, and till into the world (or forever); neither anything is increased or added, neither is decreased or lessened, and he hath no need to (or for) the counsel of any man.

22   All his works be fully desirable, and to behold, as a sparkle (or like a spark) which is (so small and yet still seen).

23   All these things live, and dwell into the world (or forever); and all things obey to him in all need (or for any and all uses).

24   All things *be* double, one against one; and he made not

---

[1] Unhelpful, small, petty, uninspired, unnecessary commentary NOT from God. (T.P.N.)

anything to fail.

25 He shall confirm the goods of each or of everything; and who shall be filled, seeing his glory?

PRAYER OF MORDECAI

1 Lord God, King Almighty, all things be set in thy lordship, *either power*, and there is none, that may against-stand or withstand thy will; if thou deemest for to save Israel, we shall be delivered anon (or at once).

2 Thou madest heaven and the earth, and whatever thing or and all thing that is contained in the compass of heaven.

3 Thou *art* Lord of all things, and there is none that against-standeth thy majesty.

4 Thou knowest all things, and knowest, that not for pride and spite, *neither* for any covetousness of *vain* glory I did this thing, that I worshipped not or honoured not Haman the most proud *man*;

5 for I was ready willfully (or willingly) to kiss, yea, the steps of his feet for the health (or the deliverance) of Israel,

6 but I dreaded, lest I should bear over to (any) man, the honour of (or for) my God, and lest I should worship any man except my God.

7 And now, Lord King, God of Abraham, have thou mercy on thy people, for our enemies will lose us (or they desire to destroy us), and do away thine heritage (or thy inheritance);

8 despise not thy part (or portion), which thou again-boughtest (or redeemedest) from Egypt (or broughtest out of Egypt).

9 Hear thou my prayer, and be thou merciful to the lot, and the part of thine heritage; and turn thou our mourning into joy, (so) that we living praise thy name, Lord; and close thou not the mouths of men praising thee. (Amen.)

PRAYER OF ESTHER

1   My Lord, which alone art our King, help me a woman left
alone, and of whom none other helper is except thee;

2   my peril is in my hands.

3   I have heard of (or from) my father, that thou, *Lord*, hast taken
away Israel from all the folks (or nations), and our fathers from all
their greater men before, (so) that thou shouldest wield an
everlasting heritage (or inheritance); and thou hast done to them,
as thou hast spoken, *or (hast) promised (them)*.

4   We have sinned in thy sight (or before thee), and therefore
thou hast betaken us into the hands of our enemies;

5   for we worshipped the gods of them. Lord, thou art rightwise;

6   and now it sufficeth not to them, that they oppress us with
hardest servage (or with the harshest servitude), but they reckon
the strength of their hands to the power of (their) idols,

7   and *therefore* they will change thy behests (or thy commands),
and do away thine heritage (or inheritance), and close the mouths
of men praising thee, and quench the glory of thy temple and of
thine altar,

8   and they will open the mouths of heathen men, and praise the
strength of (their) idols, and preach a fleshly king without end.

9   Lord, give thou not thy king's rod (or thy sceptre) to them, that
be nought (or nothing), lest they laugh at our falling; but turn thou
the counsel of them upon themselves, and destroy thou him, that
began to be cruel against us.

10   Lord, have thou mind (or remember), and show thee to us in
the time of our tribulation; and, Lord, King of gods, and *King* of all
power, give thou trust to me;

11   give thou a word well addressed (or well-directed) or a

seemly word, in my mouth in the sight of the lion *Ahasuerus*, and turn over his heart into the hatred of our enemy, (so) that both he perish, and other men that consented to him.

12   But deliver us in (or with) thine hand, and help me, having none other help but thee,

13   Lord, that hast the knowing (or the knowledge) of all things; and Lord, thou knowest that I hate the glory of wicked men, and that I loathe the bed of uncircumcised men, and of all the heathen.

14   *Lord*, thou knowest my frailty and my need, that I hold abominable or loathe the sign of my pride and of my glory, which is upon mine head in the days of my showing, and that I loathe it as the cloth of a woman having unclean blood, or in the flux of blood, and I bear (it) not, *or use it*, in the days of my stillness or silence,

15   and that I ate not in the board of Haman (or at Haman's table), neither the feast of the king pleased me, and I drank not the wine of sacrifices (or the drink offerings),

16   and that thine handmaid was never glad (or happy), since I was translated (or brought) hither unto the present day, but (or except) in thee, Lord God of Abraham.

17   A! (or O) strong God above all, hear thou the voice of them, that have none other hope *than thee*, and deliver thou us from the hands of wicked men, and deliver thou me from my dread. (Amen.) ∆

DAY 30

PSALM 139

1   *To victory, the psalm of David.* Lord, thou hast proved (or assayed or tested) me, and hast known me;

2   thou hast known my sitting (down), and my rising again. Thou hast understood my thoughts from afar;

3   thou hast inquired (into) my path and my cord (or resting places). And thou hast before-seen all my ways;

4   for no word is in (or on) my tongue. Lo! Lord, thou hast known all things,

5   the new things and old; thou hast formed me, and hast set thine hand upon me.

6   Thy knowing (or knowledge) is made wonderful of (or to) me; it is comforted (or so strong), and I shall not be able to (comprehend) it.

7   Whither shall I go from thy spirit; and whither shall I flee from thy face?

8   If I shall ascend or go up into heaven, thou art there; if I shall go down into hell, thou art present.

9   If I shall take my feathers (or my flight) full early; and shall dwell in the last parts (or the farthest coast) of the sea.

10   And soothly thither thine hand shall lead me forth; and thy right hand shall hold me (or shall keep me safe).

11   And I said, In hap the darknesses shall defoul (or cover) me; and the night *is* my lightening in my delights.

12   For why darknesses shall not be made dark from thee, and the night shall be (as) lightened as the day; as the darknesses thereof, so and the light thereof.

13   For thou haddest in possession my reins; thou tookest me up

from (or madest me in) the womb of my mother.

14   I shall acknowledge to (or praise) thee, for thou art magnified dreadfully (or fearfully, or awesomely); thy works *be* wonderful, and my soul shall know (that) full much (or truly).

15   My bones, which thou madest in private (or in secret), is not hid from (or a mystery to) thee; and my substance (formed) in the lower parts of the earth.

16   Thine eyes saw mine unperfect thing, and all men shall be written in thy book; days shall be formed, and no man *is* in them, (or but when those days were formed, no man *was* there).

17   Forsooth, God, thy friends (or thy thoughts) be made honourable full much to me; the princehood of them is comforted full much.

18   I shall number them, and they shall be multiplied above the gravel (or the sand); I rose up, and yet I am (still) with thee.

19   For thou, God, shalt slay the sinners; ye men-quellers, bow away from me.

20   For they say in thought (or out loud); Take they their cities in vanity (or We shall take thy name in vain).

21   Lord, whether I hated not them that hated thee; and I failed, *that is, mourned greatly,* (or am greatly grieved) on (or by those who be) thine enemies?

22   By perfect hatred I hated them; they were made enemies to me (too).

23   God, prove thou me, and know thou mine heart; ask thou me, and know thou my paths (or my thoughts).

24   And see thou, if (any) way of wickedness is in me; and (then) lead thou me forth in the everlasting way.

PSALM 140

1   *To victory, the psalm of David.* Lord, deliver thou me from an

evil man; deliver thou me from a wicked man.

2   Which (or who) thought wickednesses in the heart; all day they ordained battles.

3   They sharpened their tongues as (the fangs of) serpents; the venom of snakes *is* under (or upon) the lips of them.

4   Lord, keep thou me (safe) from the hand (or the power) of the sinner; and deliver thou me from wicked men. Which (or Who) thought to deceive my goings;

5   proud men hid a snare to (or for) me. And they laid forth cords into a snare; they setted a trap to (or for) me beside the way.

6   I said to the Lord, Thou art my God; Lord, hear thou the voice of my beseeching (or the words of my plea).

7   Lord, Lord, the virtue of mine health (or my strong salvation); thou madest a shadow on (or over) mine head in the day of battle.

8   Lord, betake thou not me from my desire (un)to the (desires of) the sinners; they thought against me, forsake thou not me, lest peradventure they be enhanced (or gain an advantage over me).

9   The head of the compass of them; the travail of their lips shall cover them.

10   Coals shall fall upon them, thou shalt cast them down into fire; in(to) wretchednesses (where) they shall not (be able to) stand (or shall never be able to escape).

11   A man *that is* a great jangler shall not be (well)-dressed (or directed) in earth (or successful in the world); evils shall take an unjust or unrightwise man in(to) perishing.

12   I have known, that the Lord shall make doom of (or judgement for) a needy man or the helpless; and the vengeance of (or for) the poor.

13   Nevertheless the rightwise shall acknowledge to (or praise) thy name; and rightful men shall dwell with thy cheer (or in thy presence).

PSALM 141

1   *The psalm of David.* Lord, I cried to thee, hear thou me; give thou attention to my voice, when I shall cry to thee.

2   (Let) my prayer be addressed (or directed) as incense in thy sight; (let) the raising up of mine hands *be as* the eventide sacrifice.

3   Lord, set thou a keeping to (or a guard at) my mouth; and a door of standing about to my lips (or a sentry at the door of my lips).

4   Bow thou not down mine heart into words of malice; to excuse excusings in sin. With men working wickedness; and I shall not commune with the chosen men of them.

5   The rightwise man shall reprove me in mercy, and he shall blame me; but the oil of a sinner make not fat mine head. For why and yet my prayer *is* in the well pleasant things of them (or always against their evil deeds);

6   for the doomsmen of them joined to the stone were sopped up (or their judges or leaders shall be thrown down from the cliffs). Hear they my words, for they were mighty.

7   As fatness is broken out upon the earth; our bones be scattered nigh hell.

8   Lord, Lord, for mine eyes be to thee, I hoped (or trusted) in thee; take thou not away my soul (or do not let me die!).

9   Keep thou me from the snare which they ordained to (or for) me; and from the traps of them that work wickedness.

10   Sinners shall fall in the net thereof; I am alone till I (safely) pass (by).

PSALM 142

1   *The learning of David; his prayer, when he was in the den (or*

the cave). With my voice I cried to the Lord; with my voice I prayed heartily to the Lord.

2   I poured out my prayer in his sight; and I pronounced my tribulation before him (or I told him about all my troubles).

3   While my spirit faileth of (or within) me; and thou hast known my paths. In this way in which I went; proud men hid a snare to (or for) me.

4   I beheld to the right side, and I saw; and none there was that knew me. Flight perished from me; and none there is that seeketh (to help) my soul.

5   Lord, I cried to thee; I said, Thou art mine hope; my part in the land of livers (or in the land of the living).

6   Give thou attention to my beseeching; for I am made low full greatly. Deliver thou me from them that pursue me; for they be comforted on me (or be too strong for me).

7   Lead my soul out of keeping (or this prison) to acknowledge to thy name (or so that I can praise thy name); the rightwise abide (or gather around) me, till thou yield to (or reward) me.

PSALM 143

1   *The psalm of David.* Lord, hear thou my prayer, with ears perceive thou (or listen to) my beseeching; in thy truth hear thou me, and in thy rightwiseness.

2   And enter thou not into doom with (or do not judge) thy servant; for each man living shall not be made just or justified in thy sight (or before thee).

3   For the enemy pursued my soul; he made low my life in the earth. He hath set (or put) me in dark places, as the (long) dead of the world,

4   and my spirit was anguished upon me; mine heart was

troubled in me.

5   I was mindful of the old days, I bethought in (or on) all thy works; I bethought in (or about) the deeds of thine hands.

6   I held forth mine hands to thee; my soul (was) as earth (or dry ground) without water to (or thirsting for) thee.

7   Lord, hear thou me swiftly; my spirit failed (or fainted). Turn thou not away thy face from me; and (or) I shall be like them that go down into the pit.

8   Make thou early thy mercy heard to me; for I hoped (or trusted) in thee. Make thou known to me the way in which I shall go; for I raised (up) my soul to thee.

9   Deliver thou (or save) me from mine enemies; Lord, I fled to thee;

10   teach thou me to do thy will, for thou art my God. Thy good spirit shall lead me forth into a rightful land;

11   Lord, for thy name('s) (sake) thou shalt quicken me in thine equity (or fairness). Thou shalt lead my soul out of tribulation;

12   and in thy mercy (or love for me) thou shalt scatter mine enemies. And thou shalt lose (or destroy) all them, that trouble my soul; for I am thy servant.

PSALM 144

1   *A psalm of David.* Blessed *be* my Lord God, that teacheth mine hands to (or for) war; and my fingers to (or for) battle.

2   My mercy, and my refuge; my taker up, and my deliverer. My defender, and I hoped (or trusted) in him; and thou makest subject my people under me.

3   Lord, what is a man, for thou hast made (thyself) known to him; either the son of man, for thou areckonest (or esteemest) him of some value?

4　　A man is made like vanity (or but a puff of air); his days pass as a shadow.

5　　Lord, bow down thine heavens, and come thou down; touch thou the hills, and they shall make smoke.

6　　Light thou shining (or Send out thy lightning), and thou shalt scatter them (or thine enemies); send thou out thine arrows, and thou shalt trouble them.

7　　Send out thine hand from on high, ravish (or take) me out (of here), and deliver thou me from many waters; and from the hand of alien (or foreign) sons.

8　　The mouth of whom spake vanity (or emptiness and lies); and the right hand of them *is* the right hand of wickedness.

9　　God, I shall sing to thee a new song; I shall say a psalm to thee in psaltery (or with a lyre) of ten strings.

10　　Which givest health (or Who givest salvation) to kings, which again-boughtest (or who redeemest) David, thy servant; from the wicked sword ravish thou out me (or deliver me).

11　　And deliver thou me from the hand of alien sons; the mouth of which spake vanity (or emptiness and lies), and the right hand of them *is* the right hand of wickedness.

12　　Whose sons *be* as new plantings in their youth. The daughters of them *be* arrayed; adorned about as the likeness of a temple (or a palace).

13　　The cellars of them *be* full; bringing out from this *vessel* into that or from one *vessel* into another. The sheep of them *be* with lambs, plenteous in their goings out (or innumerable);

14　　their kine (or their cattle) *be* fat. There is no falling of their wall, neither passing over (of it); neither cry *is* in the streets of them.

15　　They said, The people *is* blessed, that hath these things; blessed *is* the people, whose Lord is the God of them.

DAY 30

PROVERBS CHAPTER 30

1   The words of him that gathereth, of the son spewing. The prophecy which a man spake, with whom God was, and which *man* was comforted by God dwelling with him, and said,

2   I am the most foolish of men; and the wisdom of men is not with me.

3   I learned not wisdom; and I knew not the knowing (or knowledge) of holy men.

4   Who ascended or went up into heaven, and came down (again)? Who held together the spirit (or the wind) in his hands? who bound together waters as in a cloth (or a cloak)? Who raised (up) all the ends of the earth? What is the name of him? and what is the name of his son, if thou knowest?

5   Each word of God *is* a shield set afire, to all that hope (or trust) in him.

6   Add thou not anything to the words of him, and thou be reproved, and be found a liar.

7   I prayed (for) thee two things; deny not thou *them* to me, before that I die.

8   Make thou far from me vanity (or emptiness and futility) and words of leasing (or lies); give thou not to me begging and riches; *but* give thou only necessaries to my lifelode (or livelihood);

9   lest peradventure I be full-filled, and be drawn to deny, and say, Who is the Lord? and lest I be compelled by neediness, and steal, and forswear the name of my God.

10   Accuse thou not a servant to his lord, lest peradventure he curse thee, and thou fall down.

11   (There is) a generation that curseth his father, and that blesseth not his mother.

12   (There is) a generation that seemeth clean to itself, and nevertheless is not washed from his (or its) filths.

13   (There is) a generation whose eyes be high, and the eyelids thereof be raised up into high things.

14   (There is) a generation that hath swords for teeth, and eateth with his (or its) cheek teeth; (so) that it eat the helpless or the needy men of the earth, and the poor men from (or of) men.

15   The water leach hath two daughters, saying, Bring (me), bring (me). Three things be unable to be (ful)filled, and the fourth, that saith never, It sufficeth;

16   hell; and the mouth of the womb; and the earth that is never filled with water; but fire (that) saith never, It sufficeth.

17   (Let) the crows of the streams peck out that eye, that scorneth the father, and that despiseth the child-bearing of his mother; and (let) the young of an eagle eat that eye.

18   Three things be hard to me, and utterly I know not the fourth thing;

19   the way of an eagle in the heavens; the way of a serpent on a stone; the way of a ship in the middle of the sea; and the way of a man in (his) young waxing (or growing) age.

20   Such is the way of a woman adulteress, which eateth, and wipeth her mouth, and saith, I wrought not evil.

21   The earth is moved by three things, and *by* the fourth thing, which it may not sustain;

22   by a servant, when he reigneth; by a fool, when he is filled with meat (or with food);

23   by an hateful woman, when she is taken in matrimony; and by an handmaid, when she is the heir of her lady.

24   Four things be the least things of the earth, and they be wiser than wise men;

25   ants, a feeble people, that make ready meat (or food) in

harvest to (or for) themselves;

26   a hare (or rock badgers), a people unmighty, that setteth his (or its) bed in a stone (or on the rocks);

27   a locust, (that) hath no king, and (yet) all goeth out by companies;

28   a lizard, (that) endeavoureth with (its) hands, and dwelleth in the houses of kings.

29   Three things there be, that go well, and the fourth thing, that goeth richly, *or wealsomely* (*or prosperously*).

30   A lion, strongest of beasts, shall not dread (or fear), at the meeting of any man;

31   a cock, girded up to the loins; and a ram, (and a king), and none there is that shall against-stand him.

32   He that appeareth a fool, after that he is raised up on high; for if he had understood, he had put (his) hand on his mouth.

33   Forsooth he that thrusteth strongly teats (or nipples), to draw out milk, thrusteth out butter; and he that smiteth greatly, draweth out blood; and he that stirreth wraths, bringeth forth discords.

ECCLESIASTICUS   CHAPTER 43

1   The firmament of the highness or the height is the fairness thereof; the fairness of heaven in the sight of glory.

2   The sun in beholding, telling in going out, *is* a wonderful vessel, the work of the high *God* or the (Most) High.

3   In the time of midday it burneth the earth; and who shall be able to suffer (or to endure) in the sight of his (or its) heat?

4   Keeping a furnace in the works of heat; the sun burning the hills in three manners, sending out beams of fire or blasting out fiery beams, and shining again with his (or its) beams, blindeth the eyes.

5   The Lord *is* great, that made it; and in (or by) the words of him it hastened (its) journey or hied the way.

6   And the moon in all *men* or all things in his (or its) time *is* a showing of time, and a sign of the world.

7   A sign of the feast day or holy day *is taken* of (or from) the moon; the light which is made little in the end.

8   The month is increasing by (or according to) the name thereof, wonderfully into the ending. A vessel of castles or tents (or of the hosts) in high things, shining gloriously in the firmament of heaven.

9   The fairness of heaven *is* the glory of stars; the Lord on high lighteneth the world.

10   In (or At) the words of the Holy (One), those (or they) shall stand at the doom (or the judgement); and they shall not fail in their wakings or their watches.

11   See thou the *rain*bow, and bless thou him that made it; it is full fair in his (or its) shining.

12   It went about heaven in the compass or the circuit of his (or its) glory; the hands of the high *God* or the (Most) High opened it.

13   By his commandment he hastened the snow; and he hasteneth to send out the lightnings of his doom (or judgement).

14   Therefore the treasures were opened, and the clouds fled out as bees or flew away birds.

15   In his greatness he setted or put the clouds; and the stones of hail were broken.

16   The hills shall be moved in (or at) his sight (or before him); and the south wind shall blow in (or at) his will.

17   The voice of his thunder beateth the earth; the tempest of the north, and the gathering together of the wind. And as a bird putting down to sit sprinkleth (or scattereth) the snow, and the coming down of that *snow is* as a locust drowning down.

18   The eye shall wonder or marvel on (or at) the fairness of the

whiteness thereof; and an heart dreadeth or the heart quaketh on the rain thereof.

19   He shall pour out frost as salt upon the earth; and while *the wind* bloweth, it shall be made as the tops of a briar or the bramble bush.

20   The cold northern wind blew, and the crystal of the water froze together; it resteth on all the gathering together of waters, and it clotheth itself with waters, as with an habergeon (or a breastplate).

21   And it shall devour the hills, and it shall burn the desert; and it shall quench the green things as fire.

22   The medicine of all things *is* in the hastening of a cloud; a dew, meeting *the heat* coming of (or after the) burning, shall make it low.

23   The wind was still or held his (or its) peace in (or by) the word *of God*; by his thought he made peaceable the depth of the waters; and the Lord Jesus, *that is, God, which is the Saviour of all men and women*, planted it.

24   They that sail in (or on) the sea, tell out the perils of it; and we hearing with our ears, shall wonder.

25   There *be* full clear works, and wonderful or marvellous, diverse kinds of beasts, and of all little beasts, and the creatures (or the creation) of wonderful fishes.

26   The end of the way is confirmed for (or by) him; and all things be made in (or by) the word of him.

27   We say many things, and (yet) we fail in words; forsooth he is the (full) ending of words.

28   To what thing shall we be mighty, that have (or who hath) glory in all things? for he *is* all-mighty above or over all his works.

29   The Lord *is* fearedful, and full great; and his power *is* wonderful.

30   Glorify ye the Lord as much as ever ye may (or as ye can), yet he shall be mightier; and his great doing *is* wonderful or marvellous.

Ye blessing the Lord, enhance (or exalt) him as much as ye may (or as ye can); for he is more than all praising. Ye enhancing (or exalting) him shall be filled with virtue (or power); travail ye not *to know God perfectly in this life*, for ye shall not take (or shall not receive it) perfectly, *that is, for it is unpossible.*

31   Who saw him, and shall tell (it) out? and who shall magnify him, as he is from the beginning?

32   Many things greater than these be hid *from us*; for we have seen (only a) few things of his works.

33   Forsooth the Lord made all things; and he gave wisdom to men doing faithfully or piously.

PRAYER OF AZARIAH

1   Blessed art thou, Lord God of our Fathers, and worthy to be praised, and thy name *is* glorious into worlds (or forever);

2   for thou art rightful in all the things which thou didest to us, and all thy works *be* true; and thy ways *be* rightful or right, and thy dooms (or thy judgements) *be* true.

3   For thou hast done true dooms (or judgements), by (or according to) all the things which thou broughtest in upon us, and upon Jerusalem, the holy city of our fathers; for in truth and in doom (or judgement), thou broughtest in all these things for our sins.

4   For we sinned, and did wickedly, going away from thee,

5   and we trespassed in all things, and we heard not (or did not listen), neither kept thy commandments, neither we did as thou commandedest to us, (so) that it should be well to (or with) us.

6   Therefore thou didest by thy very doom (or in thy true judgement) all the things which thou broughtest in upon us, and all the things which thou didest to us;

7   and thou hast betaken us in(to) the hands of (our) enemies,

wicked men, and the worst trespassers, and to the unjust king, and the worst over all the earth.

8   And now we may not (or we cannot) open the mouth; we be made a shame and a reproof to thy servants, and to them that worship thee.

9   We beseech (thee), give thou not us *to (our) enemies* without end, for thy name, and destroy thou not thy testament (or thy covenant),

10   and take thou not away thy mercy from us, for Abraham, thy darling or thy dearworthy, and Isaac, thy servant, and Israel, *or Jacob*, thine holy (one);

11   to which thou spakest, promising that thou shouldest multiply their seed as the stars of the heavens, and as the gravel or the sand which is in (or on) the brink of the sea.

12   For why, Lord, we be made little, more than all the folks or heathen men, and we be low in all the earth today, for our sins.

13   And in this time there is no prince, and (or) duke, and (or) prophet, neither burnt sacrifice, neither sacrifice, neither offering, neither incense, neither place of first fruits before thee, (so) that we may (or we can) find thy mercy;

14   but be we received in (or with a) contrite soul, and in (or with a) spirit of meekness (or humility).

15   As in the burnt sacrifice of rams, and of bulls, and as in thousands of fat lambs, so our sacrifice be made today in thy sight, that it please thee; for no shame is to them that trust in thee.

16   And now we pursue (or follow) thee in (or with) all the heart, and we dread (or fear, or revere) thee, and we seek thy face.

17   Shame thou not us, but do with us by (or according to) thy mildness, and by (or according to) the multitude of thy mercy.

18   And deliver thou us in thy marvels, and give thou glory to thy name, Lord; and (let) all men be ashamed, that show evils to thy

servants;

19   be they shamed in all thy might (or in all their power), and (let) the strength of them be all-broken;

20   and they shall know, that thou art the Lord God alone, and glorious on (or over) the roundness of the lands or of the earth. (Amen). Δ

DAY 31

PSALM 145

1   *The psalm of David.* My God, (and my) King, I shall enhance (or exalt) thee; and I shall bless thy name into the world (or forever), and into the world of world (or forever and ever).

2   By all days I shall bless thee; and I shall praise thy name into the world, and into the world of the world.

3   The Lord *is* great, and worthy to be praised full much; and none end there is of his greatness.

4   Generation and generation shall praise thy works; and they shall pronounce, *either tell afar,* thy power.

5   They shall speak of the magnificence of the glory of thine holiness; and they shall tell (of all) thy marvels.

6   And they shall say (or tell) of the strength of thy fearedful things; and they shall tell of thy greatness.

7   They shall bring forth the mind (or the remembrance) of the abundance of thy sweetness (or goodness); and they shall tell with full out joying of thy rightwiseness.

8   The Lord *is* a merciful doer (or giver of mercy) and merciful in will (or compassionate); patient, and much merciful.

9   The Lord *is* sweet in all things (or good to all); and his merciful doings *be* above (or over or upon) all his works.

10   Lord, all thy works (or creatures) acknowledge to (or shall praise) thee; and thy saints (shall) bless thee.

11   They shall say (or tell) of the glory of thy realm or kingdom; and they shall speak of thy power.

12   (So) that they make thy power known to the sons of men; and the glory of the magnificence of thy realm.

13   Thy realm *is* the realm of all worlds (or forever); and thy

lordship (or rule) *is* in all generation and into generation (or for all generations). The Lord *is* faithful in all his words; and holy in all his works.

14   The Lord lifteth up all that fall down; and raiseth up all men hurtled down.

15   Lord, the eyes of all *beasts* hope in (or trust) thee; and thou givest the meat (or food) of them in covenable (or at an opportune) time.

16   Thou openest thine hand; and thou fulfillest each beast with blessing.

17   The Lord *is* just or rightwise in all his ways; and holy in all his works.

18   The Lord is nigh to all that inwardly call him; to all that inwardly call him in truth (or with sincerity).

19   He shall do the will of them (or fulfill the desires of those), that dread him; and he shall hear the beseeching of them, and he shall make them safe (or shall save them).

20   The Lord keepeth (safe) all men loving him; and he shall destroy all the sinners.

21   My mouth shall speak the praising (or declare the praises) of the Lord; and each man bless his holy name into the world (or forever), and into the world of world (or forever and ever).

PSALM 146

1   *Alleluia.* My soul, praise thou the Lord;

2   I shall praise the Lord in (or all) my life; I shall sing to my God as long as I shall be.

3   Do not ye trust in princes; neither in the sons of men, in whom is no health (or help or deliverance).

4   The spirit (or breath) of him, (your prince), shall go out, and

he shall turn again into his earth (or shall return to the dust); in that day all the thoughts of them shall perish.

5   He *is* blessed, of whom the God of Jacob is his helper; his hope *is* in his Lord God,

6   that made heaven, and earth; the sea, and all things that be in them. Which keepeth truth into the world (or Who keepeth faith forever),

7   *he* maketh doom to them (or justice for them) that suffer wrong; *he* giveth meat to them (or food for them) that be hungry. The Lord unbindeth fettered men;

8   the Lord lighteneth blind men. The Lord raiseth (up) men hurtled down; the Lord loveth just or rightwise men.

9   The Lord keepeth comelings (or newcomers safe); he shall take up (or uphold) a motherless child, and a widow; and he shall destroy the ways of sinners.

10   The Lord shall reign into the worlds (or forever); Zion, thy God shall reign in generation and into generation.

PSALM 147

1   *Alleluia.* Praise ye the Lord, for the psalm is good; (let our) praising be merry, and fair (or beautiful or pleasing) to our God.

2   The Lord shall build up Jerusalem; and he shall gather together the scatterings (or dispersed people) of Israel.

3   The which *Lord* maketh whole men contrite in heart; and bindeth together the sorrows (or wounds) of them.

4   Which numbereth the multitude of stars; and calleth names to all of them.

5   Our Lord *is* great, and his virtue (or power) *is* great; and of his wisdom there is no number (or measure).

6   The Lord taketh (or raiseth) up mild (or humble) men; forsooth

he maketh low the sinners (down) till to the earth (or unto the ground).

7   Before sing ye to the Lord in acknowledging (or with thanksgiving); say ye psalm to our God in (or with) an harp.

8   Which covereth heaven with clouds; and maketh ready rain to the earth. Which bringeth forth hay in the hills; and herbs (or plants) to the service of men.

9   Which giveth meat (or food) to their work beasts; and to the birds (or younglings) of crows calling him.

10   He shall not have will (or take delight) in the strength of an horse; neither it shall be well pleasant (or well pleasing) to him in the legs of a man.

11   It is well pleasant (or well pleasing) to the Lord on men that dread him; and in them that hope in his mercy (or trust in his love).

12   Jerusalem, praise thou the Lord; Zion, praise thou thy God.

13   For he hath comforted (or strengthened) the locks of thy gates; he hath blessed thy sons (with)in thee.

14   Which hath set (or Who hath put) thy coasts at peace; and filleth thee with the fatness (or finest) of wheat.

15   Which sendeth out his speech to the earth; his word runneth swiftly.

16   Which giveth snow as wool; he spreadeth abroad a cloud as ashes.

17   He sendeth (out) his crystal (or ice) as morsels; who shall be able to suffer before the face of his coldness (or to survive his cold)?

18   He shall send out his word, and shall melt them; his spirit (or his breath) shall blow, and the waters shall flow.

19   Which telleth his word to Jacob; and his rightfulnesses and dooms (or his statutes and laws) to Israel.

20   He did not so to each nation (or for any other nation); and he showed not his dooms (or his laws or decrees) to them.

PSALM 148

1 *Alleluia.* Ye of heavens, praise the Lord; praise ye him in high things (or high places).

2 All his angels, praise ye him; all his virtues (or hosts), praise ye him.

3 Sun and moon, praise ye him; all stars and light (or all the stars of light, or all the shining stars), praise ye him.

4 Heavens of heavens (or the highest Heaven), praise ye him; and the waters that be above the heavens,

5 praise they the name of the Lord. For he said, and things were made; he commanded, and (all) things were made of nought (or out of nothing).

6 He ordained those things into the world (or forever), and into the world of world (or forever and ever); he setted or put (forth) a commandment, and it shall not pass (away).

7 Ye of the earth, praise the Lord; dragons, and all the depths of waters (or all the creatures and the depths).

8 Fire, hail, snow, ice, spirits (or the winds) of tempests; that do his word.

9 Mountains, and all little hills; trees bearing fruit, and all cedars.

10 Wild beasts, and all tame beasts; serpents, and feathered birds.

11 The kings of the earth, and all the peoples; the princes, and all the judges of the earth.

12 Young men, and virgins, old men with the younger (ones),

13 praise the name of the Lord; for the name of him alone is enhanced (or only his name should be exalted). His acknowledging *be* on (or His glory and majesty *be* over) heaven and the

earth;

14   and he hath enhanced (or hath exalted) the horn (or the strength) of his people. An hymn *be* to all his saints; to the children of Israel, to a people nighing to him (or close to him).

PSALM 149

1   *Alleluia.* Sing ye to the Lord a new song; (let) his praising *be* in the church of saints (or in the congregation of his people).

2   (Let) Israel be glad in him that made him (or them); and the daughters of Zion make full out joy in their King.

3   Praise they his name in a quire (or with a dance); say they a psalm to him in (or with) a tympan, and a psaltery (or a lyre).

4   For the Lord is well pleased in (or with) his people; and he hath raised mild men into health (or hath given salvation to the humble).

5   The saints (or God's people) shall make full out joy in glory; they shall be glad in their beds (or shall sing joyfully all night long).

6   The full out joyings of God in the throat of them (or Let there be praising for God on their lips or in their mouths); and swords sharp on both sides in the hands of them.

7   To do vengeance in nations; and blamings in (or to punish the) peoples.

8   To bind (up) the kings of them in stocks; and the noble men of them in iron manacles.

9   (So) that they make in them the doom written (or the judgement written for them); this is the glory to all his saints.

PSALM 150

1   *Alleluia.* Praise ye the Lord in his saints (or in his sanctuary);

praise ye him in the firmament of his virtue (or of his power or in his mighty heavens).

2   Praise ye him in his virtues (or for his mighty works); praise ye him by the multitude (or for the abundance) of his greatness.

3   Praise ye him in (or with) the sound of a trump; praise ye him in a psaltery (or with a lyre) and a harp.

4   Praise ye him in a tympan and quire (or with drums and dancing); praise ye him in (or with) strings and an organ.

5   Praise ye him in cymbals sounding well (or good-sounding), praise ye him in (or with) cymbals of jubilation;

6   each spirit (or every creature that hath breath), praise the Lord. Amen.

PROVERBS CHAPTER 31

1   The words of Lemuel, the king; the vision by which his mother taught him.

2   What, my darling? what, the darling of my womb? what, the darling of my desires?

3   Give thou not thy chattel or substance to women, and thy riches to do away kings.

4   A! Lemuel, do not thou give wine to kings; for no private there is, where drunkenness reigneth.

5   Lest peradventure they drink, and forget dooms (or the law), and change (or pervert) the cause of the sons of a poor man.

6   Give ye cider to them that mourn, and wine to them that be of bitter soul.

7   Drink they, and forget they of their neediness; and think they no more on their sorrow.

8   Open thy mouth for a dumb (or mute) man, and open thy mouth for the causes of all the sons that pass forth (by thee).

9   Deem thou that that is just or rightwise, and deem thou a needy man and a poor man.

10   Who shall find a strong woman? the price of her *is* far, and from the last ends (or *is* far above precious).

11   The heart of her husband trusteth in her; and he shall not have need to (or for) robberies (to be able to satisfy her).

12   She shall yield to him good, and not evil, in all the days of her life.

13   She sought wool and flax; and wrought (or worked) by the counsel of her hands.

14   She is made as the ship of a merchant, that beareth his bread from afar.

15   And she rose by night, and gave lifelode to her menials (or livelihood to her servants), and meats (or food) to her handmaidens.

16   She beheld a field, and bought it; of the fruit of her hands she planted a vinery (or a vineyard).

17   She girded her loins with strength, and made strong her arm.

18   She tasted, and saw, that her merchandise was good; her lantern shall not be quenched in the night.

19   She put her hands to the wharve, and her fingers took to the spindle.

20   She opened her hand to the needy man, and stretched forth her hands to a poor man.

21   She shall not dread (or fear) for her house from the colds of snow; for all her menials be clothed with double *clothes.*

22   She made to her a ray-cloth; bis, *either white silk,* and purple *is* the cloth of her (or her cloak).

23   Her husband *is* noble in the gates, when he sitteth with the senators of the earth (or the elders of the land).

24   She made linen cloth, and sold *it*; and gave a girdle to a merchant.

25 Strength and fairness *is* the clothing of her; and she shall laugh in the last day.

26 She opened her mouth to wisdom; and the law of mercy *is* on her tongue.

27 She beheld the paths of her house; and she ate not bread idly.

28 Her sons rose up, and preached her most blessed; her husband *rose* (up), and praised her.

29 Many daughters have gathered riches; (but) thou passedest all.

30 Fairness is deceivable grace, and vain, (or Beauty is deceptive and empty); (but) that woman, that dreadeth the Lord, she shall be praised.

31 Give ye to her of the fruit of her hands; and let her works bring praise to her in the gates.

ECCLESIASTICUS CHAPTER 51

1 Lord King, I shall acknowledge to (or thank) thee; and I shall altogether praise thee, my Saviour. I shall acknowledge to (or praise) thy name,

2 for thou art made an helper and defender to me; and thou hast delivered my body from perdition, from the snare of a wicked tongue, and from the lips of them that work a leasing (or lies); and in the sight of them that stand nigh, thou art made an helper to me.

3 And thou hast delivered me, by (or according to) the multitude of mercy of thy name, from roarers made ready to (or for my) meat; from the hands of them that sought my soul, and from many tribulations that encompassed me;

4 from the over-laying of flames that encompassed me, and (or but) in the midst of the fire I was not burnt;

5 from the depth of the womb of hell, and from a tongue defouled (or defiled), and from a word of leasing (or from lying

words);

6   from a wicked king, and from an unrightwise tongue. Unto the death, my soul shall praise thee, Lord; and my life was nighing into hell (or the grave) beneath.

7   They encompassed me on each side, and none was that helped (me); I was beholding into (or looking for) the help of men, and none was.

8   Lord, I had mind on (or remembered) thy mercy, and on thy working altogether, that be from the world (or forever); for thou deliverest them that abide thee, and thou deliverest them from the hands of heathen men.

9   Thou enhancedest (or liftedest up) my dwelling (here) on the earth; and I besought (him) for (or because of) death flowing down.

10   I called for help from the Lord, the Father of my Lord, that he forsake not me in the day of my tribulation, and *forsake not me* without help, in the time of them that be proud.

11   I shall praise thy name continually, and I shall praise it altogether in acknowledging or in confession; and *I know that* my prayer is heard.

12   And (or For) thou hast delivered me from perdition, and thou hast delivered me from the wicked time. Therefore I shall acknowledge (or thank) thee, and I shall say praising to thee; and I shall bless the name of the Lord.

13   When yet I was younger, before that I erred (or I wandered, or before I travelled abroad), I sought wisdom openly in my prayer.

14   Before the time *of old age*, I asked for it, and unto the last things or breath, I shall inquire for it. or I shall greatly seek it;

15   and it shall flower as a grape ripe before others. Mine heart was glad therein, or in it, my foot went a rightful way; from my youth I sought it.

16   I bowed down a little mine ear, and I took (or I received) it. I

found much wisdom in myself,

17   and I profited much therein, or in it. I shall give glory to him, that giveth wisdom to me.

18   For why I took counsel to do it; I loved fervently or greatly (that which is) good, and I shall not be shamed or ashamed.

19   My soul wrestled altogether therein, or in it; and I was confirmed in doing it. I stretched forth mine hands on high; and my soul wailed in the wisdom of him, and he enlightened mine unknowings (or my ignorances).

20   I addressed (or directed) my soul to it; and I found it in knowing (or in knowledge). I welded with them my heart from the beginning (or I have joined my heart with it from the beginning); for this thing I shall not be forsaken.

21   My soul was disturbed (or troubled) in seeking it; therefore I shall wield a good possession.

22   For why the Lord gave to me a tongue for my meed (or my reward); and with it I shall praise him.

23   Ye untaught men, cometh nigh to me; and gather ye you into the house of teaching.

24   What (or Why) yet ye tarry? and what say ye in these things? your souls thirst greatly.

25   I opened my mouth, and I spake, Buy ye wisdom for yourselves without silver,

26   and make your neck subject to the yoke of it, and your soul receive teaching or discipline; for why it is in the next (moment) to find it.

27   See ye with your eyes, that I travailed (or laboured) only a little, and then I found much rest for me.

28   Take ye teaching for much number of silver, and wield ye (or get) plenteous or much gold in it.

29   Your soul be glad (or rejoice) in the mercy of him; and ye

shall not be shamed or ashamed in the praising of him.

30   Work ye your work before the time; and he shall give to you your meed (or reward) in his (good) time.

SONG OF THE THREE

1   Lord God of our fathers, blessed art thou, and worthy to be praised, and glorious, and above enhanced or raised into worlds (or exalted forever);

2   and blessed *is* the name of thy glory, which *name* is holy, and worthy to be praised, and above enhanced or raised into all worlds (or exalted forever).

3   Blessed art thou in the holy temple of thy glory, and above praiseable, and glorious into worlds (or forever).

4   Blessed art thou on the throne of thy realm, and above praiseable, and above enhanced or raised into worlds (or exalted forever).

5   Blessed art thou, that beholdest the depths or the deepnesses of the waters, and sittest upon cherubim, and praiseable, and above enhanced or raised into worlds (or exalted forever).

6   Blessed art thou in the firmament of heaven, and praiseable, and glorious into worlds (or forever).

7   All the works of the Lord, bless ye the Lord; praise ye, and above enhance or raise ye him into worlds (or exalt Him forever).

8   Angels of the Lord, bless ye the Lord; praise ye, and above enhance or raise ye him into worlds (or exalt Him forever).

9   Heavens, bless ye the Lord; praise ye, and above enhance or raise ye him into worlds (or exalt Him forever).

10   All the waters that be above the heavens, bless ye the Lord; praise ye, and above enhance or raise ye him into worlds (or exalt Him forever).

11   All the virtues (or hosts, or powers) of the Lord, bless ye the Lord; praise ye, and above enhance or raise ye him into worlds (or exalt Him forever).

12   Sun and the moon, bless ye the Lord; praise ye, and above enhance or raise ye him into worlds (or exalt Him forever).

13   Stars of the heavens, bless ye the Lord; praise ye, and above enhance or raise ye him into worlds (or exalt Him forever).

14   Rain and dew, bless ye the Lord; praise ye, and above enhance or raise ye him into worlds (or exalt Him forever).

15   Each spirit of God (or Each and every wind), bless ye the Lord; praise ye, and above enhance or raise ye him into worlds (or exalt Him forever).

16   Fire and heat, bless ye the Lord; praise ye, and above enhance or raise ye him into worlds (or exalt Him forever).

17   Cold and summer, bless ye the Lord; praise ye, and above enhance or raise ye him into worlds (or exalt Him forever).

18   Dews and white frost, bless ye the Lord; praise ye, and above enhance or raise ye him into worlds (or exalt Him forever).

19   Black or binding frost and cold, bless ye the Lord; praise ye, and above enhance or raise ye him into worlds (or exalt Him forever).

20   Ices and snows, bless ye the Lord; praise ye, and above enhance or raise ye him into worlds (or exalt Him forever).

21   Nights and days, bless ye the Lord; praise ye, and above enhance or raise ye him into worlds (or exalt Him forever).

22   Light and darkness, bless ye the Lord; praise ye, and above enhance or raise ye him into worlds (or exalt Him forever).

23   Lightnings and clouds, bless ye the Lord; praise ye, and above enhance or raise ye him into worlds (or exalt Him forever).

24   The earth, bless ye the Lord; praise ye, and above enhance or raise ye him into worlds (or exalt Him forever).

25   Mountains and little hills, bless ye the Lord; praise ye, and above enhance or raise ye him into worlds (or exalt Him forever).

26   All burgeoning (or growing) things in the earth, bless ye the Lord; praise ye, and above enhance or raise ye him into worlds (or exalt Him forever).

27   Wells (or Springs), bless ye the Lord; praise ye, and above enhance or raise ye him into worlds (or exalt Him forever).

28   Seas and floods (or rivers), bless ye the Lord; praise ye, and above enhance or raise ye him into worlds (or exalt Him forever).

29   Whales, and all things that be moved (or that move) in the waters, bless ye the Lord; praise ye, and above enhance or raise ye him into worlds (or exalt Him forever).

30   All birds of the air, bless ye the Lord; praise ye, and above enhance or raise ye him into worlds (or exalt Him forever).

31   All wild beasts and tame beasts, bless ye the Lord; praise ye, and above enhance or raise ye him into worlds (or exalt Him forever).

32   Sons and daughters of men, bless ye the Lord; praise ye, and above enhance or raise ye him into worlds (or exalt Him forever).

33   Israel, bless ye the Lord; praise ye, and above enhance or raise ye him into worlds (or exalt Him forever).

34   Priests of the Lord, bless ye the Lord; praise ye, and above enhance or raise ye him into worlds (or exalt Him forever).

35   Servants of the Lord, bless ye the Lord; praise ye, and above enhance or raise ye him into worlds (or exalt Him forever).

36   Spirits and souls of the rightwise, bless ye the Lord; praise ye, and above enhance or raise ye him into worlds (or exalt Him forever).

37   Holy men and women, and meek (or humble) of heart, bless ye the Lord; praise ye, and above enhance or raise ye him into worlds (or exalt Him forever).

38   Hananiah, Azariah, and Mishael, bless ye the Lord; praise ye, and above enhance or raise ye him into worlds (or exalt Him forever). The which *Lord* delivered us from hell (or the grave), and saved us from the hand of death, and delivered us from the midst of the burning flame, and delivered us from the midst of the fire.

39   Acknowledge ye to (or Praise) the Lord, for he is good; for his mercy *is* into the worlds (or forever).

40   All religious men and women, bless ye the Lord, God of gods; praise ye, and acknowledge to (or thank) him, for his mercy *is* into all worlds (or forever and ever). (Amen.) Δ

About the Editor

Terry Noble attended the University of British Columbia (BA'75) and the Vancouver School of Theology. His articles have appeared in numerous magazines and newspapers. He has edited the following books: **The Sculpture of Elek Imredy** (1993), **Wycliffe's New Testament** (2001, 2011), **Wycliffe's Old Testament** (2001, 2010), **Wycliffe's Bible** (2012, 2015), **Wycliffe's Apocrypha** (2014), **Wycliffe's Bible with Modern Spelling** (2017), **Wycliffe's Bible with Apocrypha** (2018), which is also available in individual smaller paperback/larger print books consisting of **Wycliffe's Pentateuch**, **Wycliffe's Gospels and Acts**, **Wycliffe's Words of Wisdom**, and **Wycliffe's Bible Readers 1-4** (all published in 2018). His interests in photography and travel have taken him to the 7 continents. Terry and Quynh live in Vancouver, Canada.

Made in the USA
San Bernardino, CA
09 December 2019

61123672R00257